CONTEMPORARY DIGITAL FORENSIC INVESTIGATIONS OF CLOUD AND MOBILE APPLICATIONS

CONTEMPORARY DIGITAL FORENSIC INVESTIGATIONS OF CLOUD AND MOBILE APPLICATIONS

Edited by

KIM-KWANG RAYMOND CHOO
University of Texas at San Antonio, San Antonio, TX, United States
University of South Australia, Adelaide, SA, Australia

ALI DEHGHANTANHA
University of Salford, Salford, United Kingdom

ELSEVIER

AMSTERDAM • BOSTON • HEIDELBERG • LONDON
NEW YORK • OXFORD • PARIS • SAN DIEGO
SAN FRANCISCO • SINGAPORE • SYDNEY • TOKYO

SYNGRESS.

Syngress is an Imprint of Elsevier

Syngress is an imprint of Elsevier
50 Hampshire Street, 5th Floor, Cambridge, MA 02139, United States

Notices
Knowledge and best practice in this field are constantly changing. As new research and experience broaden our
understanding, changes in research methods, professional practices, or medical treatment may become necessary.

Practitioners and researchers must always rely on their own experience and knowledge in evaluating and using
any information, methods, compounds, or experiments described herein. In using such information or methods
they should be mindful of their own safety and the safety of others, including parties for whom they have a
professional responsibility.

To the fullest extent of the law, neither the Publisher nor the authors, contributors, or editors, assume any liability
for any injury and/or damage to persons or property as a matter of products liability, negligence or otherwise, or
from any use or operation of any methods, products, instructions, or ideas contained in the material herein.

Library of Congress Cataloging-in-Publication Data
A catalog record for this book is available from the Library of Congress

British Library Cataloguing-in-Publication Data
A catalogue record for this book is available from the British Library

ISBN: 978-0-12-805303-4

For information on all Syngress publications
visit our website at https://www.elsevier.com/

Working together
to grow libraries in
developing countries

www.elsevier.com • www.bookaid.org

Publisher: Sara Tenney
Acquisition Editor: Elizabeth Brown
Editorial Project Manager: Anna Valutkevich
Production Project Manager: Priya Kumaraguruparan
Cover Designer: Mark Rogers

Typeset by SPi Global, India

Contents

Contributors   ix
About the Editors   xi

1. Contemporary Digital Forensics Investigations of Cloud and Mobile Applications

K.-K.R. CHOO, A. DEHGHANTANHA

References   3

2. Forensics Analysis of Android Mobile VoIP Apps

T. DARGAHI, A. DEHGHANTANHA, M. CONTI

1   Introduction   7
2   Related Work   8
3   Experimental Setup   10
4   Results and Discussion   14
5   Conclusion and Future Work   17
References   17

3. Investigating America Online Instant Messaging Application: Data Remnants on Windows 8.1 Client Machine

T.Y. YANG, A. DEHGHANTANHA, K.-K.R. CHOO, Z. MUDA

1   Introduction   21
2   Related Work   22
3   Research Methodology   23
4   AIM Forensics   26
5   Conclusion and Future Work   34
References   36

4. Forensic Investigation of Social Media and Instant Messaging Services in Firefox OS: Facebook, Twitter, Google+, Telegram, OpenWapp, and Line as Case Studies

M.N. YUSOFF, A. DEHGHANTANHA, R. MAHMOD

1   Introduction   41
2   Methodology   43
3   Experiment Setup   45
4   Discussion and Analysis   51
5   Conclusion   60
References   60

5. Network Traffic Forensics on Firefox Mobile OS: Facebook, Twitter, and Telegram as Case Studies

M.N. YUSOFF, A. DEHGHANTANHA, R. MAHMOD

1   Introduction   63
2   Experiment Setup   65
3   Discussion and Analysis   70
4   Conclusion and Future Works   76
References   77

6. Mobile Phone Forensics: An Investigative Framework Based on User Impulsivity and Secure Collaboration Errors

M. PETRAITYTE, A. DEHGHANTANHA, G. EPIPHANIOU

1   Introduction   79
2   Review of Related Work   80
3   Experiment Design   82
4   Results and Discussion   83
5   Forensics Investigation Guideline   84
6   Limitations   86
7   Conclusion and Further Research   87
References   88

7. Performance of Android Forensics Data Recovery Tools

B.C. OGAZI-ONYEMAECHI, A. DEHGHANTANHA, K.-K.R. CHOO

1   Introduction   91
2   Related Work   92

3 Experiment Setup 94
4 Results and Discussions 96
5 Conclusion and Future Works 107
References 108

8. Honeypots for Employee Information Security Awareness and Education Training: A Conceptual EASY Training Model

L. CHRISTOPHER, K.-K.R. CHOO, A. DEHGHANTANHA

1 Introduction 111
2 Experiment Setup 112
3 Findings: Dionaea 114
4 Findings: Kippo 117
5 A Conceptual EASY Training Model 120
6 Conclusion and Future Work 127
Acknowledgments 128
References 128

9. Implications of Emerging Technologies to Incident Handling and Digital Forensic Strategies: A Routine Activity Theory

N.H. AB RAHMAN, G.C. KESSLER, K.-K.R. CHOO

1 Introduction 131
2 Background and Related Work 132
3 Methodology 134
4 Cyber Threat Landscape From a Rat Perspective 136
5 Discussion 141
6 Conclusion and Future Work 143
Appendix 1 Questionnaire Items 143
References 145

10. Forensic Readiness: A Case Study on Digital CCTV Systems Antiforensics

A. ARIFFIN, K.-K.R. CHOO, Z. YUNOS

1 Introduction 147
2 Our Proposed Antiforensics Framework for Digital CCTV Systems 148
3 Case Studies 151
4 Conclusion 161
References 162

11. Forensic Visualization: Survey and Future Research Directions

C. TASSONE, B. MARTINI, K.-K.R. CHOO

1 Introduction 163
2 Digital Forensics 164
3 Visualization is Key 169
4 Forensic Visualization Selection Criteria 175
5 Conclusion and Future Research 180
References 181

12. Investigating Storage as a Service Cloud Platform: pCloud as a Case Study

T. DARGAHI, A. DEHGHANTANHA, M. CONTI

1 Introduction 185
2 Research Methodology 188
3 Analysis and Findings 191
4 Network Traffic 200
5 Conclusion 200
References 202

13. Cloud Storage Forensics: Analysis of Data Remnants on SpiderOak, JustCloud, and pCloud

S.H. MOHTASEBI, A. DEHGHANTANHA, K.-K.R. CHOO

1 Introduction 205
2 Research Methodology 208
3 Findings: SpiderOak 213
4 Findings: JustCloud 221
5 Finding: pCloud 234
6 Conclusion and Future Work 244
References 244

14. Residual Cloud Forensics: CloudMe and 360Yunpan as Case Studies

A. DEHGHANTANHA, T. DARGAHI

1 Introduction 247
2 Research Methodology 248
3 Results and Discussion 254
4 Reporting and Presentation 278
5 Conclusion 278
References 282

15. An Android Cloud Storage Apps Forensic Taxonomy

M. AMINE CHELIHI, A. ELUTILO, I. AHMED,
C. PAPADOPOULOS, A. DEHGHANTANHA

1 Introduction   285
2 Experiment Setup   286
3 Discussion   288
4 Results   289
5 Conclusion and Future Works   293
Appendix 1 List of Application Versions   293
Appendix 2 Dataset List (EDRM)   294
Appendix 3 Retrieved Artifacts   296
Appendix 4 Network Traffic   298
References   304

Index   307

Contributors

N.H. Ab Rahman   University of South Australia, Adelaide, SA, Australia; Universiti Tun Hussein Onn Malaysia, Johor, Malaysia

I. Ahmed   University of Salford, Salford, United Kingdom

M. Amine Chelihi   University of Salford, Salford, United Kingdom

A. Ariffin   CyberSecurity Malaysia, Mines Resort City, Malaysia

K.-K.R. Choo   University of Texas at San Antonio, San Antonio, TX, United States; University of South Australia, Adelaide, SA, Australia

L. Christopher   The Honeynet Project, Singapore Chapter, Singapore

M. Conti   University of Padua, Padua, Italy

T. Dargahi   Islamic Azad University, Tehran, Iran

A. Dehghantanha   University of Salford, Salford, United Kingdom

A. Elutilo   University of Salford, Salford, United Kingdom

G. Epiphaniou   University of Bedfordshire, Luton, United Kingdom

G.C. Kessler   Embry-Riddle Aeronautical University, Daytona Beach, FL, United States; Edith Cowan University, Joondalup, WA, Australia

R. Mahmod   Universiti Putra Malaysia, Serdang, Malaysia

B. Martini   University of South Australia, Adelaide, SA, Australia

S.H. Mohtasebi   Shabakeh Gostar Ltd. Co., Tehran, Iran

Z. Muda   Universiti Putra Malaysia, Serdang, Malaysia

B.C. Ogazi-Onyemaechi   University of Salford, Salford, United Kingdom

C. Papadopoulos   University of Salford, Salford, United Kingdom

M. Petraityte   University of Salford, Salford, United Kingdom

C. Tassone   University of South Australia, Adelaide, SA, Australia

T.Y. Yang   Universiti Putra Malaysia, Serdang, Malaysia

Z. Yunos   CyberSecurity Malaysia, Mines Resort City, Malaysia

M.N. Yusoff   University Science Malaysia, George Town, Malaysia

About the Editors

Kim-Kwang Raymond Choo currently holds the cloud technology endowed professorship at The University of Texas at San Antonio, and is an associate professor at the University of South Australia, and a guest professor at China University of Geosciences. He has been an invited speaker for a number of events, such as the 2011 UNODC-ITU Asia-Pacific Regional Workshop on Fighting Cybercrime, the Korean (Government) Institute of Criminology (2013), the UNAFEI and UAE Government conference in 2014, and the World Internet Conference (Wuzhen Summit) in 2014, jointly organized by the Cyberspace Administration of China and the People's Government of Zhejiang Province. He has also been a keynote/plenary speaker at conferences such as SERENE-RISC Spring 2016 Workshop, IEEE International Conference on Data Science and Data Intensive Systems (DSDIS, 2015) and those organised by Infocomm Development Authority of Singapore, A*Star, Nanyang Technological University and Singapore Management University (2015), Cloud Security Alliance New Zealand (2015), CSO Australia and Trend Micro (2015), Anti-Phishing Working Group (2014), National Taiwan University of Science and Technology (2014), Asia Pacific University of Technology & Innovation (Malaysia; 2014), Nanyang Technological University (Singapore; 2011), and National Chiayi University (Taiwan; 2010); and an Invited Expert at UNAFEI Criminal Justice Training in 2015, at INTERPOL Cyber Research Agenda Workshop 2015, and at Taiwan Ministry of Justice Investigation Bureau's 2015 International Symposium on Regional Security and Transnational Crimes. He was named 1 of 10 emerging leaders in the innovation category of The Weekend Australian Magazine/Microsoft's Next 100 series in 2009, and is the recipient of various awards including ESORICS 2015 Best Research Paper Award, winning team in Germany's University of Erlangen-Nuremberg (FAU) Digital Forensics Research Challenge 2015, Highly Commended Award from Australia New Zealand Policing Advisory Agency in 2014, Fulbright Scholarship in 2009, British Computer Society's Wilkes Award in 2008, and 2008 Australia Day Achievement Medallion. He is a Fellow of the Australian Computer Society, and a senior member of the IEEE.

Ali Dehghantanha is serving as a Mari-Curie International Incoming Research Fellow in cyber forensics at University of Salford, Manchester, United Kingdom. He has served for several years in a variety of industrial and academic positions with leading players in cyber-security and digital forensics. He has a long history of working in different areas of computer security as a security researcher, malware analyzer, penetration tester, security consultant, and forensic analyst. He regularly travels the globe on speaking, teaching, and consulting engagements and assist clients in securing their information assets. He is imminently qualified in the field of cyber-security; he holds PhD in Security in Computing and a number of professional qualifications namely GREM, CCFP, CISSP, CISM ISMS L.A., CEH, CHFI, ECSA, and ECIH and he is the founder of annual "International Conference in Cyber-Security, Cyber Warfare and Digital Forensics (CyberSec)."

Contemporary Digital Forensics Investigations of Cloud and Mobile Applications

K.-K.R. Choo*,†, A. Dehghantanha‡

*University of Texas at San Antonio, San Antonio, TX, United States †University of South Australia, Adelaide, SA, Australia ‡University of Salford, Salford, United Kingdom

The US government defined cyberspace as "the interdependent network of information technology infrastructures that includes the Internet, telecommunications networks, computer systems, embedded processors, and controllers in critical industries" [1]. The increasing number and role of cyber elements in both civil and military infrastructures and applications have attracted the attention of cybercriminals (including state-sponsored actors) [2]. As observed by Choo, Smith, and McCusker, there are a number of attack vectors, ranging from syntactic—exploiting technical vulnerabilities (e.g., use of malware [3])—to semantic—exploiting social vulnerabilities to blended approaches compromising both social and technical exploitations [4].

Cybercrime can be loosely defined as an unlawful activity involving computers, as the subject, object, or tools of a crime [5]. Increasingly popularity has also resulted in the importance of digital forensics (also known as cyber forensics, computer forensics and network forensics) [6,7]. While there are a number of definitions for digital forensics, it can be broadly defined to be the identification, collection, preservation, analysis, and reporting of digital evidences [8]. While conducting a forensic investigation, it is important to ensure that one is familiar with the local and relevant laws and regulations for handling digital evidence [9–11], data privacy regulation [12–16], and the relevant technical guidelines (e.g., guidelines for computer forensics [8,17–19], Internet forensics [20], and mobile forensics [10,21–25]), as well as maintaining up-to-date technical proficiency in investigating a broad range of attacks [26], malware [3,27–29], and popular consumer technologies such as cloud [11,20,30] and internet of things [31,32].

Any new consumer technology created and deployed will at some point come under scrutiny in the course of an investigation, criminal or civil. Cloud computing, for example, has seen massive growth in recent years. Although cloud computing are often being credited for enabling promising and cost-competitive solutions, it is subject to potential abuse. Identification, collection, preservation, and analysis of evidence in a cloud environment can be "cloudy" [33,34], as data of interest are likely stored in a cloud server outside the jurisdiction of the investigators. Mobile devices are, however, a potential evidential source as such devices are commonly used to access cloud services. Thus, it is not surprising that cloud and mobile forensics are emerging as popular forensic research focuses [2,35,36].

The first (and one of the most widely cited) cloud forensic framework(s) was proposed by Martini and Choo [20,37], which was derived from the McKemmish investigation framework [38] and the NIST mobile forensics guideline [39]. This framework had been used in a number of cloud forensic studies investigating ownCloud [20], Amazon EC2 [40], XtreemFS [41], SkyDrive [42], Dropbox [43], Google Drive [44–47], SugarSync [48], MEGA [49], hubiC [50], and Ubuntu One [51]. Chung et al. [52] proposed another methodology for cloud forensics and utilized it to investigate Amazon S3, Google Docs, and Evernote. Other studies have demonstrated that it is possible to partially retrieve residual evidences of cloud platforms such as synchronizing history and synchronized files from unstructured datasets [53]. Developing tools and techniques to acquire evidence from different cloud platforms [54–57] analyzing the effectiveness of data acquisition functions of existing cloud forensics tools [58,59] are also topics of ongoing research interest. A number of researchers have also pointed out potential complications in preserving cloud data remnants [45,60].

Cloud computing is not the only consumer technology of forensic importance [20,43,44,49–51,55,61–66]. Instant messaging mobile applications such as American Online Messenger [67–69], MSN Messenger [67,70], Yahoo Messenger [71,72], Facebook Messenger [19,73], Skype [74–76] and even Trillian [77], and Pidgin [78] have been the subject of forensic examinations. In addition to mobile (and cloud) app forensics, a number of researchers have also focused on mobile device forensics, such as Blackberry [79,80], Nokia [81,82], and Samsung [83].

Suffice it to say that the need for digital forensics is unlikely to fade away in the foreseeable future, and in fact with the increasing digitalization of our society, the importance of digital forensics will be more important than ever.

This book seeks to provide both digital forensic practitioners and researchers an up-to-date and advanced knowledge in collecting, preserving, and analyzing digital evidence from different cloud services such as platform as a service, infrastructure as a service, and storage as a service.

The structure of the remaining of this book is as follows.

Chapter 2: Forensics Analysis of Skype, Viber, and WhatsApp on Android Platform
Chapter 3: Investigating America Online Instant Messaging Application: Data Remnants on Windows 8.1 Client Machine
Chapter 4: Forensic Investigation of Social Media and Instant Messaging Services in Firefox OS: Facebook, Twitter, Google+, Telegram, OpenWapp, and Line as Case Studies
Chapter 5: Network Traffic Forensics on Firefox Mobile OS: Facebook, Twitter, and Telegram as Case Studies
Chapter 6: Mobile Phone Forensics: An Investigative Framework Based on User Impulsivity and Secure Collaboration Errors
Chapter 7: Performance of Android Forensics Data Recovery Tools

Chapter 8: Honeypots for Employee Information, Security Awareness, and Education Training: A Conceptual EASY Training Model
Chapter 9: Implications of Emerging Technologies to Incident Handling and Digital Forensic Strategies: A Routine Activity Theory
Chapter 10: Forensic Readiness: A Case Study on Digital CCTV Systems Anti-Forensics
Chapter 11: Forensic Visualization: Survey and Future Research Directions
Chapter 12: Investigating Storage as a Service Cloud Platform: pCloud as a Case Study
Chapter 13: Cloud Storage Forensics: Analysis of Data Remnants on SpiderOak, JustCloud, and pCloud
Chapter 14: Residual Cloud Forensics: CloudMe and 360Yunpan as Case Studies
Chapter 15: An Android Cloud Storage Apps Forensic Taxonomy

References

[1] M. Ganji, A. Dehghantanha, N. Izuraudzir, M. Damshenas, Cyber warfare trends and future, Adv. Inf. Sci. Serv. Sci. 5 (2013) 1–10.

[2] K.-K.R. Choo, Organised crime groups in cyberspace: a typology, Trends Organ. Crime 11 (3) (2008) 270–295.

[3] M. Damshenas, A. Dehghantanha, R. Mahmoud, A survey on malware propagation, analysis and detection, Int. J. Cyber-Security Digit. Forensics 2 (4) (2013) 10–29.

[4] K.-K.R. Choo, R. McCusker, R.G. Smith, Future Directions in Technology-Enabled Crime: 2007–09, Australian Institute of Criminology, 2007, http://www.aic.gov.au/media_library/publications/rpp/78/rpp078.pdf.

[5] R. Mercuri, Criminal defense challenges in computer forensics, in: 1st Int. Conf. Digit. Forensics Cyber Crime, ICDF2C 2009, vol. 31 LNICST, 2010, pp. 132–138.

[6] K.-K.R. Choo, The cyber threat landscape: challenges and future research directions, Comput. Secur. 30 (8) (2011) 719–731.

[7] M.K. Rogers, K.C. Seigfried-Spellar (Eds.) Digital Forensics and Cyber Crime, 4th International Conference, ICDF2C 2012, Lafayette, IN, USA, October 25–26, 2012.

[8] G.C. Kessler, Advancing the science of digital forensics, Computer (Long. Beach. Calif.) 45 (12) (2012) 25–27.

[9] B. Martini, Q. Do, K.-K.R. Choo, Conceptual evidence collection and analysis methodology for Android devices, in: R. Ko, K.-K.R. Choo (Eds.), Cloud Secur. Ecosyst., Syngress, Cambridge, MA, 2015, pp. 285–307, http://dx.doi.org/10.1016/B978-0-12-801595-7.00014-8.

[10] A. Aminnezhad, A. Dehghantanha, M.T. Abdullah, M. Damshenas, Cloud forensics issues and opportunities, Int. J. Inf. Process. Manag. 4 (4) (2013) 76–85.

[11] K.-K.R. Choo, R.G. Smith, Criminal exploitation of online systems by organised crime groups, Asian J. Criminol. 3 (1) (2007) 37–59.

[12] F. Daryabar, A. Dehghantanha, N.I. Udzir, N. Fazlida, A survey on privacy impacts of digital investigation, J. Next Gener. Inf. Technol. 4 (8) (2013) 57–68.

[13] V. Ho, A. Dehghantanha, K. Shanmugam, A guideline to enforce data protection and privacy digital laws in Malaysia, in: 2010 Second International Conference on Computer Research and Development, 2010, pp. 3–6.

[14] A. Aminnezhad, M.T.A. Ali Dehghantanha, A survey on privacy issues in digital forensics, Int. J. Cyber-Security Digit. Forensics 1 (4) (2012) 311–323.

[15] A. Dehghantanha, K. Franke, Privacy-respecting digital investigation, in: 2014 Twelfth Annual International Conference on Privacy, Security and Trust, 2014, pp. 129–138.

[16] K.-K.R. Choo, R. Sarre, Balancing privacy with legitimate surveillance and lawful data access, IEEE Cloud Comput. 2 (4) (2015) 8–13.

[17] D. Bennett, The challenges facing computer forensics investigators in obtaining information from mobile devices for use in criminal investigations, Inf. Secur. J. A Glob. Perspect. 21 (3) (2012) 159–168.

[18] W. Wang, Steal This Computer Book 4.0: What They Won't Tell You About the Internet, fourth ed., No Starch Press, San Francisco, CA, 2006.

[19] T.Y. Yang, A. Dehghantanha, K.-K.R. Choo, Z. Muda, Windows instant messaging app forensics: Facebook and Skype as case studies, PLoS ONE 11 (3) (2016) e0150300.

[20] D. Quick, B. Martini, K.-K.R. Choo, Cloud Storage Forensics, Elsevier, 2013.

[21] Q. Do, B. Martini, K.-K.R. Choo, A forensically sound adversary model for mobile devices, PLoS ONE 10 (9) (2015) e0138449.

[22] E.R. Mumba, H.S. Venter, Mobile forensics using the harmonised digital forensic investigation process, in: 2014 Information Security for South Africa, 2014, pp. 1–10.

[23] J. Lessard, G. Kessler, Android Forensics: Simplifying Cell Phone Examinations, ECU Publications Pre. 2011, 2010.

[24] F. Norouzizadeh Dezfouli, A. Dehghantanha, B. Eterovic-Soric, K.-K.R. Choo, Investigating Social Networking applications on smartphones detecting Facebook, Twitter, LinkedIn and Google+ artefacts on Android and iOS platforms, Aust. J. Forensic Sci. 46 (4) (2016) 469–488.

[25] M. Yusoff, R. Mahmod, A. Dehghantanha, M. Abdullah, Advances of mobile forensic procedures in Firefox OS, Int. J. Cyber-Security Digit. Forensics (IJCSDF) 3 (4) (2014). Society of Digital Information and Wireless Communications (SDIWC).

[26] G. Kessler, D. Browning, Bluetooth Hacking: A Case Study, ECU Publications Pre. 2011, 2009.

[27] M. Damshenas, A. Dehghantanha, K.K.R. Choo, R. Mahmud, M0Droid: an Android behavioral-based malware detection model, J. Inf. Priv. Secur 11 (3) (2015) 141–157.

[28] S. Kondakci, A concise cost analysis of Internet malware, Comput. Secur. 28 (7) (2009) 648–659.

[29] K. Shaerpour, A. Dehghantanha, R. Mahmod, Trends in Android malware detection, J. Digit. Forensic Secur. Law 8 (3) (2013) 21–40.

[30] Q. Do, B. Martini, K.K.R. Choo, A cloud-focused mobile forensics methodology, IEEE Cloud Comput. 2 (4) (2015) 60–65.

[31] E. Oriwoh, D. Jazani, G. Epiphaniou, P. Sant, Internet of things forensics: challenges and approaches, in: Proceedings of the 9th IEEE International Conference on Collaborative Computing: Networking, Applications and Worksharing, 2013, pp. 608–615.

[32] M. O'Neill, The internet of things: do more devices mean more risks? Comput. Fraud Secur. 2014 (1) (2014) 16–17.

[33] F. Daryabar, A. Dehghantanha, A review on impacts of cloud computing and digital forensics, Int. J. Cyber-Security Digit. Forensics (IJCSDF) 3 (4) (2014) 183–199. Society of Digital Information and Wireless Communications (SDIWC).

[34] S.B.S. Farid Daryabar, A. Dehghantanha, N. Izura Udzir, N.F. Mohd Sani, A survey about impacts of cloud computing on digital forensics, Int. J. Cyber-Security Digit. Forensics 2 (2) (2013) 77–94.

[35] N.H. Ab Rahman, K.-K.R. Choo, A survey of information security incident handling in the cloud, Comput. Secur. 49 (2015) 45–69.

[36] O. Osanaiye, H. Cai, K.-K.R. Choo, A. Dehghantanha, Z. Xu, M. Dlodlo, Ensemble-based multi-filter feature selection method for DDoS detection in cloud computing, EURASIP J. Wirel. Commun. Netw. (1) (2016) 130.

[37] B. Martini, K.-K.R. Choo, An integrated conceptual digital forensic framework for cloud computing, Digit. Investig. 9 (2) (2012) 71–80.

[38] R. McKemmish, What is forensic computing? Australian Institute of Criminology, Canberra, 1999.

[39] R. Ayers, W. Jansen, S. Brothers, Guidelines on mobile device forensics (NIST Special Publication 800-101 Revision 1), 1 (2014) 85.

[40] C. Bagh, Amazon EC2 helps researcher to crack WiFi password in 20 minutes, 2011.

[41] B. Martini, K.-K.R. Choo, Distributed filesystem forensics: XtreemFS as a case study, Digit. Investig. 11 (4) (2014) 295–313.

[42] D. Quick, K.-K.R. Choo, Digital droplets: Microsoft SkyDrive forensic data remnants, Futur. Gener. Comput. Syst. 29 (6) (2013) 1378–1394.

[43] F. Daryabar, A. Dehghantanha, B. Eterovic-Soric, K.-K.R. Choo, Forensic investigation of OneDrive, Box, GoogleDrive and Dropbox applications on Android and iOS devices, Aust. J. Forensic Sci. (2016) 1–28, http://dx.doi.org/10.1080/00450618.2015.1110620.

[44] D. Quick, K.-K.R. Choo, Google drive: forensic analysis of data remnants, J. Netw. Comput. Appl. 40 (2014) 179–193.

[45] D. Quick, K.-K.R. Choo, Forensic collection of cloud storage data: does the act of collection result in changes to the data or its metadata? Digit. Investig. 10 (3) (2013) 266–277.

[46] C. Federici, Cloud data imager: a unified answer to remote acquisition of cloud storage areas, Digit. Investig. 11 (1) (2014) 30–42.

[47] N.H. Ab Rahman, N.D.W. Cahyani, K.-K.R. Choo, Cloud incident handling and forensic-by-design: cloud storage as a case study, Concurr. Comput. Pract (2016), http://dx.doi.org/10.1002/cpe.3868/.

[48] M. Shariati, A. Dehghantanha, K.-K.R. Choo, SugarSync forensic analysis, Aust. J. Forensic Sci. 48 (1) (2015) 95–117.

[49] F. Daryabar, A. Dehghantanha, K.-K.R. Choo, Cloud storage forensics: MEGA as a case study, Aust. J. Forensic Sci. (2016) 1–14, http://dx.doi.org/10.1080/00450618.2016.1153714.

[50] B. Blakeley, C. Cooney, A. Dehghantanha, R. Aspin, Cloud Storage Forensic: hubiC as a case-study, in: 2015 IEEE 7th International Conference on Cloud Computing Technology and Science (CloudCom), 2015, pp. 536–541.

[51] M. Shariati, A. Dehghantanha, B. Martini, K.-K.R. Choo, Chapter 19—Ubuntu One investigation: detecting evidences on client machines, in: R.K.-K.R. Choo (Ed.), The Cloud Security Ecosystem, Syngress, Boston, 2015, pp. 429–446.

[52] H. Chung, J. Park, S. Lee, C. Kang, Digital forensic investigation of cloud storage services, Digit. Investig. 9 (2) (2012) 81–95.

[53] D. Quick, K.-K.R. Choo, Digital droplets: Microsoft SkyDrive forensic data remnants, Futur. Gener. Comput. Syst. 29 (6) (2013) 1378–1394.

[54] D. Quick, K.-K.R. Choo, Big forensic data reduction: digital forensic images and electronic evidence, Clust. Comput. 19 (2) (2016) 723–740.

[55] M. Scanlon, J. Farina, N.A. Le Khac, T. Kechadi, Leveraging Decentralization to Extend the Digital Evidence Acquisition Window: Case Study on BitTorrent Sync, 2014. arXiv:1409.8486 [cs].

[56] J. Dykstra, A.T. Sherman, Understanding issues in cloud forensics: two hypothetical case studies, in: Proceedings of the 2011 ADSFL Conference on Digital Forensics, Security, and Law, 2011, pp. 45–54.

[57] T. Gebhardt, H.P. Reiser, Network forensics for cloud computing, in: J. Dowling, F. Taïani (Eds.), Distributed applications and interoperable systems, no. 7891, Springer, Berlin, Heidelberg, 2013, pp. 29–42.

[58] J. Dykstra, A.T. Sherman, Acquiring forensic evidence from infrastructure-as-a-service cloud computing: Exploring and evaluating tools, trust, and techniques, Digit. Investig. 9 (2012) S90–S98.

[59] N. Thethi, A. Keane, Digital forensics investigations in the cloud, in: Proc. Int'l Advance Computing Conf. (IACC 14), 2014, pp. 1475–1480.

[60] J. Dykstra, A.T. Sherman, Design and implementation of FROST: digital forensic tools for the OpenStack cloud computing platform, Digit. Investig. 10 (2013) S87–S95.

[61] D. Quick, K.-K.R. Choo, Dropbox analysis: data remnants on user machines, Digit. Investig. 10 (1) (2013) 3–18.

[62] S. Mehreen, B. Aslam, Windows 8 cloud storage analysis: Dropbox forensics, in: 2015 12th International Bhurban Conference on Applied Sciences and Technology (IBCAST), 2015, pp. 312–317.

[63] B. Martini, Q. Do, K.-K.R. Choo, Chapter 15—mobile cloud forensics: an analysis of seven popular Android apps, The Cloud Security Ecosystem, 2015, pp. 309–345.

[64] G. Grispos, W.B. Glisson, T. Storer, Chapter 16—Recovering residual forensic data from smartphone interactions with cloud storage providers, Cloud Secur. Ecosyst., 2015, pp. 347–382.

[65] G. Grispos, W.B. Glisson, T. Storer, Using smartphones as a proxy for forensic evidence contained in cloud storage services, in: 2013 46th Hawaii International Conference on System Sciences, 2013, pp. 4910–4919.

[66] M. Shariati, A. Dehghantanha, K.-K.R. Choo, SugarSync forensic analysis, Aust. J. Forensic Sci. 48 (1) (2016) 95–117.

[67] M. Dickson, An examination into MSN Messenger 7.5 contact identification, Digit. Investig. 3 (2) (2006) 79–83.

[68] J. Reust, Case study: AOL instant messenger trace evidence, Digit. Investig. 3 (4) (2006) 238–243.

[69] M. Kiley, S. Dankner, M. Rogers, Forensic analysis of volatile instant messaging, in: I. Ray, S. Shenoi (Eds.), Advances in Digital Forensics IV, no. 285, Springer, US, 2008.

[70] W.S. van Dongen, Forensic artefacts left by Windows Live Messenger 8.0, Digit. Investig. 4 (2) (2007) 73–87.

[71] M. Dickson, An examination into Yahoo Messenger 7.0 contact identification, Digit. Investig. 3 (3) (2006) 159–165.

[72] M. Levendoski, T. Datar, M. Rogers, Yahoo! Messenger forensics on Windows vista and Windows 7, in: P. Gladyshev, M.K. Rogers (Eds.), Digital Forensics and Cyber Crime, no. 88, Springer, Berlin Heidelberg, 2012, pp. 172–179.

[73] N. Al Mutawa, I. Al Awadhi, I. Baggili, A. Marrington, Forensic artifacts of Facebook's instant messaging service, in: 2011 International Conference for Internet Technology and Secured Transactions ICITST, 2011, pp. 771–776.

[74] T.Y. Yang, A. Dehghantanha, K.R. Choo, Z. Muda, Windows instant messaging app forensics: Facebook and Skype as case studies, PLoS ONE (2016).

[75] M. Simon, J. Slay, Recovery of Skype application activity data from physical memory, in: ARES'10 International Conference on Availability, Reliability, and Security, 2010, 2010, pp. 283–288.

[76] J. McQuaid, Skype Forensics: Analyzing Call and Chat Data From Computers and Mobile, Magnet Forensics, 2012.

[77] M. Dickson, An examination into Trillian basic 3.x contact identification, Digit. Investig. 4 (1) (2007) 36–45.

[78] W.S. van Dongen, Forensic artefacts left by Pidgin Messenger 2.0, Digit. Investig. 4 (3–4) (2007) 138–145.

[79] M. Al Marzougy, I. Baggili, A. Marrington, BlackBerry playbook backup forensic analysis, Lect. Notes Inst. Comput. Sci. Soc. Informatics Telecommun. Eng.—Digit. Forensics Cyber Crime 114 (2013) 239–252.

[80] N. Al Mutawa, I. Baggili, A. Marrington, Forensic analysis of social networking applications on mobile devices, Digit. Investig. 9 (Suppl.) (2012) S24–S33.

[81] S. Mohtasebi, H.G.B. Ali Dehghantanha, Smartphone forensics: a case study with Nokia E5-00 Mobile Phone, Int. J. Digit. Inf. Wirel. Commun. 1 (3) (2011) 651–655.

[82] N.D.W. Cahyani, B. Martini, K.-K.R. Choo, A.M.N. Al-Azhar, Forensic data acquisition from cloud-of-things devices: windows Smartphones as a case study, Concurr. Comput. Pract. (2016).

[83] S. Parvez, A. Dehghantanha, H.G. Broujerdi, Framework of digital forensics for the Samsung Star Series phone, in: 2011 3rd International Conference on Electronics Computer Technology, vol. 2, 2011, pp. 264–267.

2

Forensics Analysis of Android Mobile VoIP Apps

T. Dargahi*, A. Dehghantanha†, M. Conti‡

Islamic Azad University, Tehran, Iran †University of Salford, Salford, United Kingdom ‡University of Padua, Padua, Italy

1 INTRODUCTION

In recent years, we have witnessed a rapid increase in the use of Voice over Internet Protocol (VoIP) services as an online communication method on mobile devices. This is not surprising due to the increasing proliferation of smartphones: it has been predicted that by 2019 the number of smartphone users will be more than 2.6 billion [1]. These days people use their smartphone devices not only for making voice calls and exchanging SMS, but also for obtaining several services that are offered due to the ubiquitous access to Internet, such as mobile banking, and location-based services. Meantime, the use of VoIP applications, which could be delivered easily through mobile VoIP applications (mVoIP apps), would enable people to interact, share information, and become socialized at a very low cost compared to most of the traditional communication techniques. However, such applications could also be exploited by criminals or be targeted by cybercriminals (e.g., with malware infection to steal financial data) [2, 3]. For these reasons, mobile devices (including smartphones) attracted a lot of attention from the security research community [4], in particular from the perspective of malware [5–12], security enforcement [13–16], and authentication mechanisms [17–19].

Smartphones are a common source of evidence in both criminal investigations and civil litigations [20–25]. However, the constant evolution and nature (e.g., closed source operating system and diverse range of proprietary hardware) of mobile devices and mobile apps complicates forensic investigations [26]. Among the existing smartphone operating systems in the market, *Android* dominated the market with more than 80% of the total market share in 2015 Q2 [27, 28]. Therefore Android popularity attracted several researchers to focus on investigating several different security aspects of Android, ranging from user identification [29, 30], feasibility of encryption methods on Android [31], cloud storage apps forensics [32], and social networking apps forensics [3]. Due to the increasing use of mVoIP apps for malicious activities on different platforms including Android, forensic investigation of such apps needs an extensive coverage [33, 34], and therefore in this chapter, we provide an investigative study of the three popular VoIP apps for Android on Google Play (see Table 1), namely: *Viber* [35], *Skype* [36], and *WhatsApp* [37]. The features of these VoIP apps are summarized in Table 2. In particular, we aim to answer the following question: "What artifacts of forensic value can be recovered from the use of Viber, Skype, and WhatsApp Android apps?"

TABLE 1   Number of Installations for Each Application [35–37]

Application	Number of Google Play Downloads and Installations as of March 2016
Viber	100,000,000–500,000,000
Skype	500,000,000–1,000,000,000
WhatsApp	1,000,000,000–5,000,000,000

TABLE 2   Features of mVoIP Applications

Features	Viber	Skype	WhatsApp
Text-chat	✓	✓	✓
Send and receive image	✓	✓	✓
Send and receive video	✓	✓	✓
Send and receive audio	✓	✓	✓
Incoming and outgoing calls	✓	✓	✓
Group call		✓	
Group chat	✓	✓	✓
V-card and contact sharing			✓

2 RELATED WORK

These days, several trusted and untrusted providers launch various categories of applications for mobile devices. This has led to the ever increasing trend in using mobile devices in order to benefit from the services offered by these applications. This tendency motivated the forensic community to concentrate on forensic investigation of the mobile devices. In this regard Dezfoli et al. [26] perused the future trends in digital investigation and determined that mobile phone forensics is receiving more and more attention by the community and is one of the fastest growing fields. In [38], the authors provided a comprehensive discussion on the nature of digital evidence on mobile devices, along with a complete guide on forensic techniques to handle, preserve, extract, and analyze evidence from mobile devices. Moreover, they presented examples of commercial forensic tools that can be used to obtain data from mobile phones, such as Access Data Forensic Toolkit (FTK), Cellebrite Physical, XACT, along with the case example of the adopted Digital Forensic Framework (DDF) plug-in. In the same line of study, Mohtasebi and Dehghantanha [39] presented a unified framework for investigating different types of smartphone devices. Parvez et al. [40] proposed a forensics framework for investigating Samsung phones. Several researchers have proposed various frameworks for the investigation of Nokia mobile devices and Firefox OS [25, 41].

A comparison of forensic evidence recovery techniques for a Windows Mobile smartphone demonstrates that there are different techniques to acquire and decode information of potential forensic interest from a Windows Mobile smartphone [42]. Furthermore, forensic examination of the Windows Mobile device database (the `pim.vol`) file confirmed that `pim.vol` contains information related to contacts, call history, speed-dial settings, appointments, and tasks [43]. Moreover, in [44], the authors provided a number of possible methods of acquiring and examining data on Windows Mobile devices, as well as the locations of potentially useful data, such as text messages, multimedia, email, Web browsing artifacts, and Registry entries. They also used *MobileSpy* monitoring software as a case example to highlight the importance of forensic analysis. They showed that the existence of such a malicious monitoring software on a Windows phone could be detectable on the device being investigated by forensics analyst. In another recent study, Yang et al. [45] carried out an investigative study on two popular Windows instant messaging apps, i.e., Facebook and Skype. The authors showed that several artifacts are recoverable, such as contact lists, conversations, and transferred files.

A research project published at the DFRWS 2010 Annual Conference discussed technical issues that are in place when capturing Android physical memory [46]. A critical review of 7 years of mobile device forensics [47] demonstrated that there are several research studies in the area of Android device forensics in the literature. However, very few of them support the varying levels of Android memory investigation. Lessard and Kessler [48] showed that it is possible to acquire a logical image of Android-based smartphones, such as Samsung Galaxy, using either a logical method or a physical method. The logical acquisition technique consists of obtaining a binary image of the device's memory, which requires root access to the device. More so, Vidas et al. [49] discussed an acquisition methodology based on overwriting the "Recovery" partition on the Android device's SD card with specialized forensic acquisition software. Likewise, Canlar et al. [21] proposed *LiveSD Forensics*, which is an on-device live data acquisition approach for Windows Mobile devices. They proposed a method to obtain artifacts from both the Random-Access Memory (RAM) and the Electronically Erasable Programmable Read Only Memory (EEPROM). In [50], the authors proposed a methodology for the collection and analysis of evidential data on Android devices, which used the principles of Martini and Choo's cloud forensics framework [51]. The steps within this methodology are as follows: the collection of the physical image of the device partitions with the aid of a live OS bootloader, and the examination of app files in private and external storage, app databases, and accounts data for all apps of interest, on the android device. Using this methodology, in [52], the authors carried out an analysis of seven popular Android apps within three categories: storage (Dropbox, OneDrive, Box and ownCloud), note-taking (Evernote and OneNote), and password syncing (Universal Password Manager, UPM). Such analysis proves the validity of their proposed methodology.

In order to facilitate the forensic investigation of mobile devices that are rapidly changing in their structure, Do et al. [53] proposed a forensically sound adversary model. Azfar et al. [54] considered this adversary model as a template to map a potential adversary's capabilities and constraints, in order to evaluate the usefulness of such a model by carrying out a forensic analysis of five popular Android social apps (Twitter, POF Dating, Snapchat, Fling, and Pinterest). They showed that useful artifacts are recoverable using this model, including databases, user account information, contact lists, images, and profile pictures. They could also discover timestamps for notifications and tweets, as well as a Facebook authentication token string used by the apps.

There is also a vast interest of digital investigators in studying the instant messaging artifacts in the stream of research in this area of digital forensics. The first claimed work to carry out a forensic analysis of Skype on the Android platform [55] investigated both the NAND and RAM flash memories in different scenarios. Their obtained results showed that chat and call patterns can be found in both of NAND and RAM flash memories of mobile devices, regardless of whether the Skype account has been signed out, signed in, or even after deleting the call history. In [34, 56], the authors showed that, while conducting recoveries of digital evidences relating to VoIP applications in computer systems, the Skype information is recoverable from the physical memory. Moreover, [57] presents another forensic analysis of several instant messaging applications including Skype and WhatsApp focusing on encryption algorithms used by these applications. Similar work has also been conducted by forensically analyzing WhatsApp on Android platforms [58, 59]. In the same line of study, a forensic analysis of four popular social networking applications (Facebook, Twitter, LinkedIn, and Google+) have been carried out which showed that artifacts useful as evidence in a potential criminal investigation are recoverable from smartphone devices using such applications [3]. Moreover, Yang et al. suggested an approach for forensics investigation of instant messaging applications on Windows 8.1 and applied it to detecting remnants of Facebook Instant Messaging and Skype application. Another important research direction that has always been a concern for digital investigators in investigation of instant messaging applications is *privacy* [60–62]. Ntantogian et al. [63] evaluated 13 Android mobile applications focusing on privacy. They tried to recover artifacts that provide information relating to authentication credentials. They showed that the users' credentials are recoverable in the majority of the applications. Moreover, they determined specific patterns for the location of such credentials within a memory dump. In another research study [64], Farden et al. explored the privacy of user data with regards to mobile apps usage by evaluating the privacy risks that are inherent when using popular *mobile dating Apps*. They showed that in almost half of the investigated applications, the chat messages are recoverable, and in some cases details of other nearby users could also be extracted. Likewise, Azfar et al. [65] provided a forensic taxonomy of Android mHealth apps, by examining 40 popular Android mHealth apps. Their findings could potentially help facilitate forensic analysis of those particular mobile health applications.

In this paper we thoroughly analyze forensics remnants of three popular instant messaging applications, namely Viber, Skype, and WhatsApp on Android platform to provide a guideline for forensics practitioners in conducting similar investigations. Compared to previous studies, this research is delving into forensically valuable evidences in the context of Android platform and provides a comparative study of different VoIP applications remnants. Moreover, it is furthering forensics attention to lesser studied Viber and WhatsApp applications forensics.

3 EXPERIMENTAL SETUP

Our investigative methodology is based on the digital forensic framework proposed by Martini and Choo [51]. In this study, we first identified the potential evidence sources and set up the experimental environment (Section 3.1). Thereafter, we carry out logical acquisition in order to collect evidential data (Section 3.2). Finally, by analyzing the collected data, we investigate possible remnant artifacts (Section 3.3). We further demonstrated and discussed the experimental results in Section 4, and presented the conclusions drawn from our investigation in Section 5; both of which exemplify the third and fourth steps of the framework methodology [51], i.e., "Examination and Analysis" and "Reporting and Presentation," in which the results of the forensic study should be analyzed and presented appropriately.

Since without rooting the smartphone device, we would not be able to access that without a rooting the smartphone device, we would not be able to access some of the stored files (we will explain in Section 3.2), we utilized a rooted Android phone, i.e., Samsung Galaxy S3 GT-i9300, in order to conduct our experiments. We set up and configured necessary workstations and tools (including both software and hardware), as listed in Table 3. Moreover, Table 4 reports the authentication methods required for our considered mVoIP applications and their details.

Our examination and analysis process consist of three phases, which we explain in the following.

TABLE 3   Adopted Forensic Tools

Tool	Version	Details
Android platform phone	Samsung S3 GT-i9300, Firmware version 3.0.31	Mobile device used for this study
mVoIP applications	Viber 4.3.3	Applications that are investigated
	Skype 4.9.0.45564	
	WhatsApp 2.11.238	
AccessData FTK Imager	V 3.1.4.6	Used to explore the acquired logical image (internal memory) of the phone
SQLite database browser	2.0bl	Visual tool that is used to explore the database extracted from each application after identifying the folders using AccessData FTK Imager
Internet evidence finder timeline	IEF v6.3	Provides a view of each artifact on a visual timeline without any need to convert artifacts like timestamps
Root-Kit	Frameware CF-Auto-Root-m0 m0xx-gti9300	Frameware is used to root the device
Odin3	V 3.07	Enables uploading of the root-kit frameware to the Android device
Epoch & Unix timestamp converter		Used to convert the timestamp found in hex format

3.1 Phase I: Setup Phase—First Iteration

The first phase of our study is to identify and preserve the source of evidence, which is the first iteration. In this phase, we downloaded three mVoIP applications from the Google Play Store and installed them on a Samsung Galaxy S3 GT-i9300 smartphone. For WhatsApp and Viber applications, an active mobile SIM is required to activate the application, while Skype

TABLE 4   Application Details and Authentication Methods on the Supported Android 4.3 Platform

mVoIP Applications	Size (MB)	Version	Authentication Method
Viber	20	4.3.3	Mobile phone number (e.g., +1 xxxxxx)
Skype	15	4.9.0.45564	Username and password
WhatsApp	15	2.11.238	Mobile phone number (e.g., +1 xxxxxx)

TABLE 5   Performed Activities Using the mVoIP Applications

Features	Viber	Skype	WhatsApp
Text-chat	✓	✓	✓
Send image	✓	✓	✓
Receive image	✓	✓	✓
Send video	✓	✓	✓
Receive video	✓	✓	✓
Send audio	✓	✓	✓
Receive audio	✓	✓	✓

could be activated by the username and password of the registered account (see Table 4). For each application, we performed several activities, as described in Table 5, continuously for 1 month before the logical acquisition.

3.2 Phase II: Logical Acquisition

The smartphone device that we used for the experiments, i.e., Samsung Galaxy S3 GT-i9300 Firmware version 3.0.31, was originally not rooted. However, without a root access on the phone, many data files would be inaccessible. Therefore, we used the Odin3 (version 3.07) tool [66] to root the device by uploading the rook-kit frameware (`CF-Auto-Root-m0-m0xx-gti9300`) to the device. The installed root-kit gives the user root access, i.e., the user has the privilege control over the OS, which allows the user to attain privileged control within the Android's subsystem, and bypass the limitation placed on the device by the manufacturer. The root access grants the user the privilege to access a certain protected directory that holds some of the artifacts needed for this experiment (e.g., `[root]/data/directories`). The needed directory is then backed up and later accessed with the use of other tools mentioned earlier (see Table 3). The procedure that we adopted in our data acquisition is forensically sound according to [49]; however, there are other methods to acquire a logical image on Android devices without having to root the device. After rooting the phone, the bit-by-bit physical acquisition of `dd` image is acquired using the following SSH command: `'sshroot@(Device IP Address) dd if=/dev/block/mmcblk0p12 | of=(Location on your computer)`. The "mmcblk0p12" (which might be different in several devices) is the internal memory block of the Android device, which is 16GB and so, it takes hours to be fully acquired.

This phase of the experiments leads to acquisition of the logical image of the Android device, which is considered to be the most crucial phase in mobile forensics investigation process, as the generated hash values play a vital role when presenting the case in court of law [67].

3.3 Phase III: Identification and Analysis—Second Iteration

This third phase of the experiment includes identification of folders and files on the logical image acquired in the previous phase. Examination and analysis of the files in order to check the existence of artifacts such as timestamps, location, GPS coordination, contact info, text-chat, SMS, file location, and any significant data that could be relevant to the research area. We conducted forensic examinations manually, with the aid of the tools listed in Table 3. After acquiring the logical image, as described in Phase II, we used "AccessData FTK Imager" to analyze the acquired dd image which resulted in the creation of the directory default path. This allows us to access all the files in each directory, and therefore navigating to each one of the files. Fig. 1 shows the three folders of our three under investigation applications, Viber,

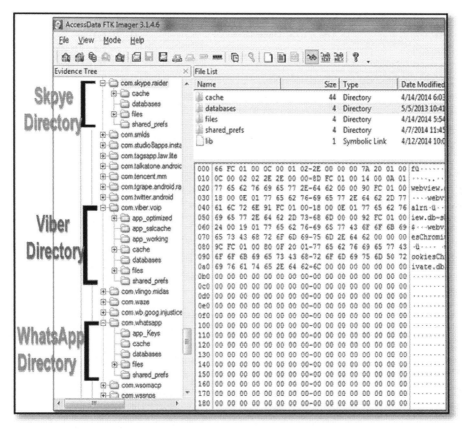

FIG. 1 Folder directory of all the applications in the devices.

Skype, and WhatsApp Messenger. After identifying these folders, in the next step, we need to carry out a deep inspection on each application's database to know whether we can find any potential evidentiary artifact.

4 RESULTS AND DISCUSSION

This section describes the potential artifacts found in each mVoIP application's directory. Furthermore, we discuss the evidentiary values of the artifacts found for each of the mVoIP applications.

4.1 Viber Artifacts

This section describes the Viber artifacts found in both manual forensic analysis and using IEF tool. We found two unique database directories after examining dd image with the FTK imager for Viber application, which are:

- [*root*]/data/com.viber.voip/databases/viber_ data.db
- [*root*]/data/com.viber.voip/databases/viber_ messages.db

The Viber application has two databases: viber_ data.db, which contains the same information as wa.db in WhatsApp; and viber_ messages.db, which has the same information as msgstore.db in WhatsApp application. Once again, using a rooted device enabled us to access the database information in plaintext format. The viber_ data.db file contains data related to the outgoing calls, Viber contact names and numbers. In this experiment, we considered no blocked numbers; however, in case of having some blocked numbers, they would be recoverable as well. All these potential artifacts have evidentiary value relevant to a forensic investigation. On the other hand, the viber_ messages.db file stores geographical location information, contacts, and all the sent or received messages in a chat database. Through performing a forensic examination on this database, one would be able to determine the message exchange and also the actual source and destination of each exchanged message. With the aid of the IEF forensic tool, it is possible to determine whether a particular message was either sent or received by a particular sender or recipient. These artifacts are useful in helping a forensic investigator to determine if a particular suspect is worth taking to court.

4.2 Skype Artifacts

In order to examine the Skype application, after obtaining the dd image in the same way as Viber and WhatsApp, we used the IEF tool. We discovered that, Skype stores information in an SQLite database called main.db, and the file directory is: [root]/data/com.skype. raider/files/SkypeID/main.db, in which the "SkypeID" indicates a particular user account. The database contains information about a user's account such as messages, calls, group chat, voicemails, contacts, SMS messages, and file transfers. We analyzed the main.db with the SQLite viewer. The timestamp was in Unix epoch time but later converted using the converting tool. Recoverable artifacts from the Skype contact lists include the Skype name, full name, birthday, gender, country, mobile number, email address, and registered date timestamp. Text-chat artifacts include the text message, message type, status, chat ID, and recipient ID. The call related artifacts that could be recovered are: the local user details, remote user details, call duration, and whether the call was incoming or outgoing. The artifacts related to file transfer that we could recover are: timestamp, file size (bytes), and status. Voicemail related artifacts include: the caller's ID, voicemail size, and status. Finally, IP location related artifacts included the userID, IP address, and timestamp.

Most people actually believe that by physically deleting or clearing chat histories, the Skype logs will be deleted, and the data associated with a particular account cannot be recovered. In mobile devices, evidential data that contains such recoverable artifacts can prove fruitful and provide a rich source of evidence for investigating crimes related to Skype. The artifacts showing an incoming and an outgoing call have timestamps that are also captured along with the call duration. With such evidence, a suspect cannot deny initiating or engaging in such a call. This would give forensic examiners a stronger convincing power in the court of law when handling a case. Moreover, it is possible to recover full contact details of the Skype owner, i.e., full name, date of birth, phone number (if any), date of Skype creation, and email; this makes it easy for the suspect in question to be tracked down. The IP address reflects the "externally visible" IP address of the device where Skype is running, i.e., the IP address of the outermost NAT gateway connecting the device to the Internet. The IP address plays a significant role in terms of determining the geographical location of parties involved in the crime. This artifact can be useful for attribution as it indicates the IP address that the device used to connect to the Internet. This may help tie a subject to a particular IP address and activity originating from that address. Having found artifacts like name, email, mobile number, date of birth, gender, and country, it would be easy for a forensic investigator to further carry out the investigation based on what has been found and also to geographically point to where the relevant subjects reside.

4.3 WhatsApp Artifacts

In this section, we describe the WhatsApp Messenger artifacts that we found in this investigation. In fact, by examining the dd image with the FTK imager tool, we found out three unique directories: two of them are databases, while one is a directory path.

- [*root*]/data/com.whatsapp/files/Avatars/60xxxx@s.whatsapp.net
- [*root*]/data/com.whatsapp/databases/wa.db
- [*root*]/data/com.whatsapp/databases/msgstore.db

We could find the avatar icon of each contact in the WhatsApp application, along with user related MD5 and SHA1 hashes, which have evidentiary value, since they can be directly linked to a particular WhatsApp account, and hence can be used to identify the user who is using this account. Alongside the avatar pictures, the name and phone number of the user are also valuable to forensic specialists.

Since we used a rooted device in the experiments, the database appeared in plain text format. We discovered that the records and logs of all the activities carried out by the user that are listed in Table 5 are stored in two different database files: wa.db and msgstore.db. The wa.db file contains all the information relating to the contacts including the contact names, contact phone numbers, and WhatsApp status. These artifacts can be of great value to actually track down suspects, for example, a certain WhatsApp status update may betray information relating to a criminal activity. Having these kinds of artifacts, a digital forensic specialist would be able to potentially relate the status to an actual incident and back up their case accordingly. On the other hand, the `msgstore.db` contains artifacts with timestamps relating to sent and received text-chat messages, images, videos, and audios. By analyzing the same database using IEF tool, we could obtain the source and the destination of each message in order to detect the actual sender and receiver of each message.

We summarized the results acquired from our investigation in Table 6. Both WhatsApp Messenger and Viber share almost the same potential evidentiary artifacts, however in WhatsApp Messenger, there is neither call duration, nor GPS coordination. Skype leaves more interesting artifacts, such as both local and private IP addresses which are capable of facilitating further investigation on a particular case.

So far only a few research studies have explored and addressed the forensic recovery and analysis of activities carried out on social network and instant messaging applications on smartphones. These studies provide limited information in terms of logical acquisition and artifacts recovery. On the contrary, our study explored the forensic acquisition, examination, and analysis of the logical image of a smartphone. Our experiment consisted of: (1) installation of three top-rated mVoIP applications, (2) carrying out the usual user activities on each of these applications, followed by the acquisition of the logical image using a forensically sound approach, and (3) performing a manual forensic analysis on each of the installed mVoIP applications. When carrying out such a digital forensic examination, however, there could be some potential obstacles that could make accurate data recovery difficult. For example, there are many varieties of lock screen apps, app lock, SMS, and picture locks; some of which encrypt the data stored on the mobile device, and also lock the device interface [68]. This could be an issue for a digital forensic specialist when examining such a device.

TABLE 6   Summary of Potential Found Evidentiary Artifacts

Potential Evidentiary Artifacts	mVoIP Application		
	Viber	Skype	WhatsApp
Messages	✓	✓	✓
Contact details	✓	✓	✓
Phone number	✓	✓	✓
Voicemail		✓	
Email		✓	
Images, videos, audios	✓	✓	✓
Location information	✓	✓	

5 CONCLUSION AND FUTURE WORK

In this chapter, we carried out a forensic analysis of the most popular mVoIP applications, i.e., Viber, Skype, and WhatsApp Messenger when running on an Android smartphone. Artifacts listed in Table 6 can provide vital evidence that can open up a case or offer a wealth of information for further investigation when dealing with crime related to mobile devices and mobile applications.

This study successfully applies a methodology adapted from an existing digital forensics framework, which uses various techniques from the existing literature, in order to perform a forensic analysis of Viber, Skype, and WhatsApp Messenger applications on an Android platform. We showed that potential evidentiary artifacts can be found on Android devices, which have forensic value to be presented in the court of law by a forensic investigator when handling a case related to cyber terrorism or cybercrime conspiracies. A possible future research direction could be a comprehensive research on different mobile operating system platforms, considering another mVoIP apps. This would provide vital information for digital forensic specialists.

References

[1] Number of smartphone users worldwide from 2014 to 2019, 2016. http://www.statista.com/statistics/330695/number-of-smartphone-users-worldwide/ (accessed 11.03.16).

[2] M.I. Husain, R. Sridhar, iForensics: forensic analysis of instant messaging on smart phones, in: Digital Forensics and Cyber Crime, Springer, New York, 2009, pp. 9–18.

[3] F. Norouzizadeh Dezfouli, A. Dehghantanha, B. Eterovic-Soric, K.-K.R. Choo, Investigating Social Networking applications on smartphones detecting Facebook, Twitter, LinkedIn and Google+ artefacts on Android and iOS platforms, Aust. J. Forensic Sci. 48 (4) (2016) 469–488, http://dx.doi.org/10.1080/00450618.2015.1066854.

[4] A. Dehghantanha, N.I. Udzir, R. Mahmod, Towards data centric mobile security, in: Proceedings of the 7th International Conference on Information Assurance and Security (IAS'11), IEEE, 2011, pp. 62–67.

[5] P. Faruki, A. Bharmal, V. Laxmi, V. Ganmoor, M.S. Gaur, M. Conti, M. Rajarajan, Android security: a survey of issues, malware penetration, and defenses, IEEE Commun. Surv. Tutorials 17 (2) (2015) 998–1022.

[6] J. Gajrani, J. Sarswat, M. Tripathi, V. Laxmi, M. Gaur, M. Conti, A robust dynamic analysis system preventing SandBox detection by Android malware, in: Proceedings of the 8th International Conference on Security of Information and Networks (SIN'15), ACM, 2015, pp. 290–295.

[7] P. Faruki, A. Bharmal, V. Laxmi, M.S. Gaur, M. Conti, M. Rajarajan, Evaluation of Android anti-malware techniques against dalvik bytecode obfuscation, in: Proceedings of the 13th International Conference on Trust, Security and Privacy in Computing and Communications (TrustCom'14), IEEE, 2014, pp. 414–421.

[8] P. Faruki, V. Kumar, B. Ammar, M. Gaur, V. Laxmi, M. Conti, Platform neutral sandbox for analyzing malware and resource hogger apps, in: Proceedings of the International Conference on Security and Privacy in Communication Networks (SecureComm'14), Springer, 2014, pp. 556–560.

[9] V.F. Taylor, R. Spolaor, M. Conti, I. Martinovic, AppScanner: automatic fingerprinting of smartphone apps from encrypted network traffic, in: Proceedings of the 1st IEEE European Symposium on Security and Privacy (EuroSP'16), IEEE, 2016.

[10] K. Shaerpour, A. Dehghantanha, R. Mahmod, Trends in Android malware detection, J. Digit. Forensics Sec. Law 8 (3) (2013) 21.

[11] M. Damshenas, A. Dehghantanha, R. Mahmoud, A survey on malware propagation, analysis, and detection, Int. J. Cyber-Sec. Digit. Forensics 2 (4) (2013) 10–29.

[12] M. Damshenas, A. Dehghantanha, K.-K.R. Choo, R. Mahmud, M0droid: An Android behavioral-based malware detection model, J. Inf. Privacy Sec. 11 (3) (2015) 141–157.

[13] Y. Zhauniarovich, G. Russello, M. Conti, B. Crispo, E. Fernandes, MOSES: supporting and enforcing security profiles on smartphones, IEEE Trans. Depend. Secure Comput. 11 (3) (2014) 211–223.

[14] M. Conti, N. Dragoni, S. Gottardo, MITHYS: Mind the hand you shake-protecting mobile devices from ssl usage vulnerabilities, in: Security and Trust Management, Springer, 2013, pp. 65–81.

[15] M. Conti, B. Crispo, E. Fernandes, Y. Zhauniarovich, Crêpe: a system for enforcing fine-grained context-related policies on Android, IEEE Trans. Inf. Forensics Sec. 7 (5) (2012) 1426–1438.

[16] T. Dargahi, M. Ambrosin, M. Conti, N. Asokan, ABAKA: a novel attribute-based k-anonymous collaborative solution for LBSs, Comput. Commun. 85 (2016) 1–13.

[17] C. Giuffrida, K. Majdanik, M. Conti, H. Bos, I sensed it was you: authenticating mobile users with sensor-enhanced keystroke dynamics, in: Proceedings of the 11th Conference on Detection of Intrusions and Malware, and Vulnerability Assessment (DIMVA'14), Springer, 2014, pp. 92–111.

[18] M. Conti, I. Zachia-Zlatea, B. Crispo, Mind how you answer me!: transparently authenticating the user of a smartphone when answering or placing a call, in: Proceedings of the 6th ACM Symposium on Information, Computer and Communications Security (SIGSAC ASIACCS'11), ACM, 2011, pp. 249–259.

[19] V.-D. Stanciu, R. Spolaor, M. Conti, C. Giuffrida, On the effectiveness of sensor-enhanced keystroke dynamics against statistical attacks, in: Proceedings of the 6th ACM Conference on Data and Application Security and Privacy (SIGSAC CODASPY'16), ACM, 2016.

[20] H.-C. Chu, S.-W. Yang, S.-J. Wang, J.H. Park, The partial digital evidence disclosure in respect to the instant messaging embedded in Viber application regarding an Android smart phone, in: Information Technology Convergence, Secure and Trust Computing, and Data Management, Springer, 2012, pp. 171–178.

[21] E.S. Canlar, M. Conti, B. Crispo, R. Di Pietro, Windows mobile LiveSD forensics, J. Netw. Comput. Appl. 36 (2) (2013) 677–684.

[22] M.N. Yusoff, R. Mahmod, A. Dehghantanha, M.T. Abdullah, An approach for forensic investigation in Firefox OS, in: Proceedings of the 3rd International Conference on Cyber Security, Cyber Warfare and Digital Forensic (CyberSec'14), IEEE, 2014, pp. 22–26.

[23] M.N. Yusoff, R. Mahmod, M.T. Abdullah, A. Dehghantanha, Mobile forensic data acquisition in Firefox OS, in: Proceedings of the 3rd International Conference on Cyber Security, Cyber Warfare and Digital Forensic (CyberSec'14), IEEE, 2014, pp. 27–31.

[24] M. Damshenas, A. Dehghantanha, R. Mahmoud, A survey on digital forensics trends, Int. J. Cyber-Sec. Digit. Forensics 3 (4) (2014) 209–235.

[25] M.N. Yusoff, R. Mahmod, M.T. Abdullah, A. Dehghantanha, Performance measurement for mobile forensic data acquisition in Firefox OS, Int. J. Cyber-Sec. Digit. Forensics 3 (3) (2014) 130–140.

[26] F.N. Dezfoli, A. Dehghantanha, R. Mahmoud, N.F.B.M. Sani, F. Daryabar, Digital forensic trends and future, Int. J. Cyber-Sec. Digit. Forensics 2 (2) (2013) 48–76.

[27] IDC, Smartphone OS Market Share, 2015 Q2, 2015. http://www.idc.com/prodserv/smartphone-os-market-share.jsp (accessed 11.03.16).

[28] Gartner, Gartner Says Emerging Markets Drove Worldwide Smartphone Sales to 15.5 Percent Growth in Third Quarter of 2015, 2011. http://www.gartner.com/newsroom/id/3169417 (accessed 11.03.16).

[29] M. Conti, L.V. Mancini, R. Spolaor, N.V. Verde, Analyzing android encrypted network traffic to identify user actions, IEEE Trans. Inf. Forensics Sec. 11 (1) (2016) 114–125.

[30] M. Conti, L.V. Mancini, R. Spolaor, N.V. Verde, Can't you hear me knocking: identification of user actions on Android apps via traffic analysis, in: Proceedings of the 5th ACM Conference on Data and Application Security and Privacy (CODASPY'15), ACM, 2015, pp. 297–304.

[31] M. Ambrosin, M. Conti, T. Dargahi, On the feasibility of attribute-based encryption on smartphone devices, in: Proceedings of the 2015 Workshop on IoT Challenges in Mobile and Industrial Systems (IoT-Sys'15), ACM, 2015, pp. 49–54.

[32] F. Daryabar, A. Dehghantanha, B. Eterovic-Soric, K.-K.R. Choo, Forensic investigation of OneDrive, Box, GoogleDrive and Dropbox applications on Android and iOS devices, Aust. J. Forensic Sci. (2016) 1–28, http://dx.doi.org/10.1080/00450618.2015.1110620.

[33] M. Ibrahim, M.T. Abdullah, A. Dehghantanha, VoIP evidence model: a new forensic method for investigating VoIP malicious attacks, in: Proceedings of the 2012 International Conference on Cyber Security, Cyber Warfare and Digital Forensic (CyberSec), IEEE, 2012, pp. 201–206.

[34] M. Ibrahim, A. Dehghantanha, Modelling based approach for reconstructing evidence of VoIP malicious attacks, Int. J. Cyber-Sec. Digit. Forensics 3 (4) (2014) 183–199.

[35] Viber Android Apps on Google Play [online], https://play.google.com/store/apps/details?id=com.viber.voip&hl=en (accessed 11.03.16).

[36] Skype—Free IM & video calls Android Apps on Google Play [online], https://play.google.com/store/apps/details?id=com.skype.raider&hl=en (accessed 11.03.16).

[37] WhatsApp Messenger Android Apps on Google Play [online], https://play.google.com/store/apps/details?id=com.whatsapp&hl=en (accessed 11.03.16).

[38] E. Casey, B. Turnbull, Digital evidence on mobile devices, In: E. Casey (Ed.), Digital Evidence and Computer Crime. Forensic Science, Computers, and the Internet, third ed., Academic Press, Waltham, MA, USA, 2011.

[39] S.H. Mohtasebi, A. Dehghantanha, Towards a unified forensic investigation framework of smartphones, Int. J. Comput. Theory Eng. 5 (2) (2013) 351.

[40] S. Parvez, A. Dehghantanha, H.G. Broujerdi, Framework of digital forensics for the Samsung Star Series phone, in: Proceedings of the 3rd International Conference on Electronics Computer Technology (ICECT'11), 2, IEEE, 2011, pp. 264–267.

[41] S. Mohtasebi, A. Dehghantanha, H.G. Broujerdi, Smartphone forensics: a case study with Nokia E5-00 mobile phone, Int. J. Digit. Inf. Wirel. Commun. 1 (3) (2011) 651–655.

[42] G. Grispos, T. Storer, W.B. Glisson, A comparison of forensic evidence recovery techniques for a windows mobile smart phone, Digit. Investig. 8 (1) (2011) 23–36.

[43] M. Kaart, C. Klaver, R.B. van Baar, Forensic access to Windows mobile pim.vol and other Embedded Database (EDB) volumes, Digit. Investig. 9 (3) (2013) 170–192.

[44] E. Casey, M. Bann, J. Doyle, Introduction to windows mobile forensics, Digit. Investig. 6 (3) (2010) 136–146.

[45] T.Y. Yang, A. Dehghantanha, K.-K.R. Choo, Z. Muda, Windows instant messaging app forensics: Facebook and Skype as case studies, PLoS ONE 11 (3) (2016) e0150300.

[46] V.L.L. Thing, K.-Y. Ng, E.-C. Chang, Live memory forensics of mobile phones, Digit. Investig. 7 (2010) S74–S82.

[47] K. Barmpatsalou, D. Damopoulos, G. Kambourakis, V. Katos, A critical review of 7 years of Mobile Device Forensics, Digit. Investig. 10 (4) (2013) 323–349.

[48] J. Lessard, G. Kessler, Android forensics: simplifying cell phone examinations, Small Scale Digit. Device Forensics J. 4 (1) (2010) 1–12.

[49] T. Vidas, C. Zhang, N. Christin, Toward a general collection methodology for Android devices, Digit. Investig. 8 (2011) S14–S24.

[50] B. Martini, Q. Do, K.-K.R. Choo, Conceptual evidence collection and analysis methodology for Android devices, in: R. Ko, K.-K.R. Choo (Eds.), Cloud Secur. Ecosyst., Syngress, Cambridge, MA, 2015, pp. 285–307. http://dx.doi.org/10.1016/B978-0-12-801595-7.00014-8.

[51] B. Martini, K.-K.R. Choo, An integrated conceptual digital forensic framework for cloud computing, Digit. Investig. 9 (2) (2012) 71–80.

[52] B. Martini, Q. Do, K.-K.R. Choo, Mobile cloud forensics: an analysis of seven popular Android apps, in: R. Ko, K.-K.R. Choo (Eds.), Cloud Secur. Ecosyst., Syngress, Cambridge, MA, 2015, pp. 285–307. http://dx.doi.org/10.1016/B978-0-12-801595-7.00015-X.

[53] Q. Do, B. Martini, K.-K.R. Choo, A forensically sound adversary model for mobile devices, PLoS ONE 10 (9) (2015) e0138449.

[54] A. Azfar, K.-K.R. Choo, L. Liu, An Android social app forensics adversary model, in: Proceedings of the 49th Annual Hawaii International Conference on System Sciences (HICSS'16), IEEE, 2016, 5597–5606.

[55] M.I. Al-Saleh, Y.A. Forihat, Skype forensics in Android devices, Int. J. Comput. Appl. 78 (7) (2013).

[56] M. Simon, J. Slay, Recovery of skype application activity data from physical memory, in: Proceedings of the International Conference on Availability, Reliability, and Security (ARES'10), IEEE, 2010, pp. 283–288.

[57] N.B. Al Barghuthi, H. Said, Social networks IM forensics: encryption analysis, J. Commun. 8 (11) (2013) 708–715.

[58] A. Mahajan, M.S. Dahiya, H.P. Sanghvi, Forensic analysis of instant messenger applications on Android devices, 2013. arXiv preprint arXiv:1304.4915.

[59] C. Anglano, Forensic analysis of WhatsApp messenger on android smartphones. Digital Invest. J. 11 (3) (2014) 201–213, http://dx.doi.org/10.1016/j.diin.2014.04.003.

[60] A. Dehghantanha, K. Franke, Privacy-respecting digital investigation, in: Proceedings of the 12th Annual International Conference on Privacy, Security and Trust (PST'14), IEEE, 2014, pp. 129–138.

[61] F. Daryabar, A. Dehghantanha, N.I. Udzir, N.F.B. Mohd Sani, S.B. Shamsuddin, F. Norouzizadeh, A survey about impacts of cloud computing on digital forensics, Int. J. Cyber-Sec. Digit. Forensics 2 (2) (2013) 77–94.

[62] A. Aminnezhad, A. Dehghantanha, M.T. Abdullah, A survey on privacy issues in digital forensics, Int. J. Cyber-Sec. Digit. Forensics 1 (4) (2012) 311–323.

[63] C. Ntantogian, D. Apostolopoulos, G. Marinakis, C. Xenakis, Evaluating the privacy of Android mobile applications under forensic analysis, Comput. Sec. 42 (2014) 66–76.

[64] J. Farnden, B. Martini, K.-K.R. Choo, Privacy risks in mobile dating apps, in: Proceedings of the 21st Americas Conference on Information Systems, (AMCIS 2015), (2015), http://aisel.aisnet.org/cgi/viewcontent. cgi?article=1427&context=amcis2015

[65] A. Azfar, K.-K.R. Choo, L. Liu, Forensic taxonomy of popular Android mHealth apps, in: Proceedings of the 21st Americas Conference on Information Systems, (AMCIS 2015), (2015), http://aisel.aisnet.org/cgi/viewcontent.cgi?article=1217&context=amcis2015.

[66] Samsung Odin [online], http://odindownload.com/.

[67] K. Kumar, S. Sofat, S.K. Jain, N. Aggarwal, Significance of hash value generation in digital forensic: a case study, Int. J. Eng. Res. Dev. 2 (5) (2012).

[68] A. Skillen, D. Barrera, P.C. van Oorschot, Deadbolt: locking down android disk encryption, in: Proceedings of the 3rd ACM Workshop on Security and Privacy in Smartphones & Mobile Devices, ACM, 2013, pp. 3–14.

Investigating America Online Instant Messaging Application: Data Remnants on Windows 8.1 Client Machine

T.Y. Yang*, A. Dehghantanha†, K.-K.R. Choo‡,§, Z. Muda*

*Universiti Putra Malaysia, Serdang, Malaysia †University of Salford, Salford, United Kingdom
‡University of Texas at San Antonio, San Antonio, TX, United States §University of South Australia, Adelaide, SA, Australia

1 INTRODUCTION

Instant messaging (IM) is popular on both traditional computing devices (e.g., personal computers and laptops) and smart mobile devices (e.g., Android devices and iOS devices), as it allows users to exchange information with their peers in real time using text messaging, voice and video messaging, and file sharing (e.g., pictures and videos). The number of worldwide IM accounts in 2015 is reportedly over 3.2 billion and is expected to increase to more than 3.8 billion by the end of 2019 [1].

Similar to other popular consumer technologies, IM services have been exploited to commit frauds and scams [2–5], disseminate malware [6–10], groom children online with the purpose of sexual exploitation [11–14], and to commit other criminal activities [15–18]. The chat logs may provide information of evidential value to forensic practitioners [19,20], which can often be used to reconstruct events or reveal information such as a suspect's physical location, true identity, transactional information, incriminating conversations, and victim's information (e.g., email addresses and bank account numbers) [21].

Due to the increased user privacy requirements [22–24] and demands for data security, it is increasingly challenging to collect evidential data from IM service providers—similar to the trend of users storing data in a cloud platform [25,26]. The data are often protected using proprietary protocols and strong encryption, compounding the challenge to collect meaningful information from external networks [27]. Even if the artifacts could be identified, collecting data from a multitenancy cloud environment may breach the data privacy policies of the IM service providers [28,29]. These challenges are compounded by cross-jurisdictional investigations, which may prohibit cross-border transfer of information [21,30].

Depending on the IM app in use, the end user device is often a potential source for the recovery of IM artifacts [20,31–49]. Such terrestrial artifacts can be useful in establishing whether a suspect has a direct connection to a crime [50]. While a practitioner should be cognizant of techniques of digital forensics, it is just as important to maintain an up-to-date understanding of the potential artifacts that could be forensically recovered from different types of IM products.

In this chapter we seek to identify the potential terrestrial artifacts that may remain after the use of the popular America Online Instant Messenger desktop application (AIM) version 7.5.14.8 (AIM 7) on a Windows 8.1 client machine. Similar to the approaches of Quick and Choo [51–53], we seek to answer the following questions in this research

1. What data remains on a Windows 8.1 device and their locations on a hard drive after a user has used AIM 7?
2. What data remains in random access memory (RAM) after a user has used AIM 7 on a Windows 8.1 device?
3. What data can be seen in network traffic?

Findings from this research will contribute to the forensic community's understanding of the types of terrestrial artifacts that are likely to remain after the use of IM applications on devices running Windows 8.1.

The structure of this chapter is as follows. Section 2 describes background and related work. Section 3 outlines the research methodology, including the framework and experiment environment and setup. In Sections 4 and 5, we present our findings from Windows 8.1, and conclude the paper as well as outline future research areas.

2 RELATED WORK

Dickson [34] investigated AIM 5.5 on a Windows XP machine and detected records of the contact lists and transferred files from registry, user settings, and other application-specific files on the hard disk. By searching for the suspect's screen name, Dickson [34] was able to reconstruct portion of the conversation texts from the unstructured datasets such as memory dumps, slack space, free space, and swap files in plain text and Hyper Text Markup Language (HTML), even without the chat logging. Reust [44] concluded that the artifacts may not be of evidential value without timestamp information.

Kiley et al. [54] approached evidence extraction of AIM Express (web application) and only recovered artifacts of the contact lists and conversations from the memory dump and hard disk's free space. However, the keyword search is only limited to unique phrases predefined in the experimental setup ("bananas," "weirdtheme," "this is a space," etc.). A study of such may not be useful for evidence acquisition without prior knowledge of the incriminating conversations. Gladyshev and Almansoori [55] proposed a method for acquiring known AIM conversation fragments from the memory dumps of Apple Mac computers. The researchers identified that the conversation fragments could be generally classified into four different formats, all of which held corresponding screen names, conversation texts, and timestamp information.

Yasin et al. [56] examined the AIM protocol (and other IM protocols) for Digsby IM aggregator application and determined that the RC4 decryption key (for the Digsby password) is the SHA-1 hash of the concatenated system product identification (ID), install date, and Digsby client ID. In the subsequent studies, Yasin and Abulaish [57,58] examined the artifacts from memory dumps, swap files, and slack space and were able to recover complete conversation sessions from the unstructured datasets. Husain et al. [59] focused on logical acquisition of the AIM (version 2.0.2.4) artifacts for iOS and managed to retrieve forensically relevant information (i.e., records of conversations, user accounts, plain text password, and buddy list) from the iTunes backup of a nonjailbroken iPhone 3GS in Apple Property List (PLIST) format.

To the best of our knowledge, there is no published forensic research that studies the newer AIM client application on computer desktops running newer OS (i.e., Windows 8 or later)—a gap that this paper aims to contribute towards.

3 RESEARCH METHODOLOGY

The examination procedure of this research was derived from the four-stage digital forensic framework of McKemmish [60], which are identification of digital evidence, preservation of digital evidence, analysis, and presentation. The purpose is to enable acquisition of realistic data similar to that found in real world investigations. This paper mainly focuses on the analysis stage, although we also briefly discuss the evidence source identification, preservation, and presentation to demonstrate how this research can be applied in practice.

The first step of the experiment involved the creation of four (4) fictional accounts to play the role of suspects and victims in this research (see Table 1). The IM accounts were assigned with a unique "display icon" and username which was used within the respective IM apps and Windows operating system. This eased identification of the user roles. Next was to create the test environments for the suspects and the victims, which consisted two control base VMware Workstations (VMs) version 9.0.0 build 812388 running Windows 8.1 Professional (Service Pack 1, 64 bit, build 9600). As explained by Quick and Choo [51–53], using physical hardware to undertake setup, erasing, copying, and reinstalling would have been an onerous exercise. Moreover, a virtual machine allows room for error by enabling the test environment to be reverted to a restore point should the results be unfavorable. The workstations were configured with the minimal space (2GB of physical memory and 20GB hard drive space) in order to reduce the time required to analyze the considerable amounts of snapshots in the latter stage.

TABLE 1 User Details for IM Experiments

Username	Email	Role
Suspect	UC3F1211FC@gmail.com	Suspect
Victim	UC3F1211FC2@gmail.com	Victim 1
VictimTwo	victimtwo@aol.com	Victim 2
VictimThree	victimthree@aol.com	Victim 3

In the third step we conducted a predefined set of activities to simulate various real world scenarios of using the apps on each workstation/test environment. The base assumptions are that the practitioner encounters a live system running Microsoft Windows 8.1 in a typical home environment. Similar to the approaches of Quick and Choo [51–53], the 3111th email message of the University of California (UC) Berkeley Enron email dataset (downloaded from http://bailando.sims.berkeley.edu/enron_email.html on Sep. 24, 2014) was used to create the sample files and saved as SuspectToVictim.rtf, SuspectToVictim.txt, SuspectToVictim.docx, SuspectToVictim.jpg, SuspectToVictim.zip, SuspectToVictim.jpg (printscreen), VictimToSuspect.rtf, VictimToSuspect.txt, VictimToSuspect.docx, VictimToSuspect.jpg (printscreen), VictimToSuspect.zip, and VictimToSuspect.jpg to simulate the transferring and receiving of files of different formats using the IM apps. As the filenames suggest, the "SuspectToVictim" (and "VictimToSuspect") files were placed on the suspect's workstation (and victims' workstations respectively) and subsequently transferred to the victims' workstations (and suspect's workstation respectively). The Enron dataset was also used to create four additional files, namely SUCCESS.dat, REJECTED.dat, ABORTED.dat, and BLOCKED.dat to examine the artifacts in relation to successful (accepted), rejected, aborted, and blocked file transfers.

The experiments were predominantly undertaken in a NATed (where NAT stands for Network Address Translation) network environment and without firewall outbound restriction to represent a typical IM situation. Wireshark was deployed on the host machine to capture the network traffic from the suspect's workstation for each scenario. After each experiment was carried out, we saved a copy of the network capture file in .PCAP format, and acquired a bit-stream (dd) image of the virtual memory (.VMEM) file prior to shutdown. We then took a snapshot of each workstation after being shutdown and made a forensic copy of the virtual disk (.VMDK) file in Encase Evidence (E01) format. This resulted in the creation of ten snapshots (one for each environment) as highlighted in Table 2 and Figs. 1 and 2. The decision to instantiate the physical memory dumps and hard disks with the virtual disk and memory files was to prevent the datasets from being adulterated with the use of memory/image acquisition tools [51–53].

The final step of this research was to analyze the datasets using a range of forensically recognized tools (as highlighted in Table 3) and present the findings. Both indexed and non-indexed, as well as Unicode and non-Unicode, string searches were included as part of the evidence searches. The experiments were repeated at least thrice (at different dates) to ensure consistency of findings.

TABLE 2   Details of VM Snapshots Created for AIM 7 Investigations on Window 8.1

Snapshot	Description
1.0 Base-Snapshot	A control base snapshot was made to create the control media to determine changes from each IM scenario
A1.1 Install-Snapshot	Using a duplicate copy of the control base snapshot (1.0), we downloaded and subsequently installed the AIM client software version 7.5.14.8 from https://www.aim.com/download#windows
A1.1.1 Login-Snapshot	A snapshot was created of the install snapshot (A1.1) to analyze the process of logging into AIM 7 on a Windows 8.1 machine. The options "Remember Me," "Remember My Password," and "Automatically Sign Me In" were checked as is the case by default

TABLE 2 Details of VM Snapshots Created for AIM 7 Investigations on Window 8.1—cont'd

Snapshot	Description
A1.1.2 Buddy List-Snapshot	A second snapshot was made of the install snapshot (A1.1) to examine the process of adding contacts and saving the Buddy List on a Windows 8.1 machine. Using the suspect's account, we added the victim accounts "VictimTwo," "uf3f1211fc2@gmail. com," and "VictimThree" to three separate groups, namely "Buddies," "family," and "Group 1" (custom group), respectively. We then assigned a friendly name (i.e., "Phantom Friend 1," "Victim," and "Phantom Buddy 1," respectively) for each of the victim accounts. Finally, we saved the Buddy List as "savedbuddylist.blt" on the desktop of the suspect's workstation
A1.1.3 Conversations/ File transfers-Snapshot	A third copy of the install snapshot (A1.1) was made to undertake mock conversations and file transfers between two chat participants using the default settings (without IM logging)
A1.1.4 IM Logs-Snapshot	A fourth copy of the install snapshot (A1.1) was made to examine the conversation and file transfer artifacts of the IM logging, which was explicitly enabled prior to carrying out the experiment
A1.1.4.1 Uninstall-Snapshot	A snapshot was created of the IM Logs snapshot (A1.1.4) to examine the artifacts left behind after uninstalling AIM 7 on a Windows 8.1 client machine. Uninstallation was undertaken using the "Uninstall AIM" executable file
A1.1.5 Chat room-Snapshot	A fifth snapshot was created of the install snapshot (A1.1) to examine the group conversation artifacts of AIM 7. The suspect's account was used to create a chat room namely "devi" and subsequently add all the victims into the chat room for group conversations
A1.1.6 Buddy Icon-Snapshot	Another snapshot was made of the install snapshot (A1.1) to examine the user image ("buddy icon" in the context of AIM) artifacts of AIM 7
A1.1.7 What is Happening-Snapshot	A final snapshot was made of the install snapshot (A1.1) to examine the process of creating personal message ("what is happening" message in the context of AIM) in AIM 7

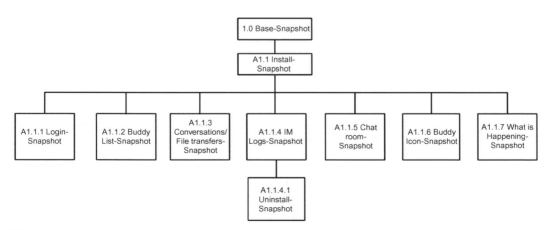

FIG. 1 VM snapshots created for AIM experiments.

TABLE 3   Tools Used for IM Analysis on Windows 8.1

Tool	Usage
FTK Imager Version 3.2.0.0	To create forensic images for the .VMDK files
Autopsy 3.1.1	To parse the file system, produce directory listings, as well as extracting or analyzing stored files, browsing history, "NTUSER.dat" registry files (using the RegRipper plugin), "pagefile.sys" Windows swap file, and unallocated spaces located within the forensics images of VMDK files
HxD Version 1.7.7.0	To conduct keyword searches in the unstructured datasets
Volatility 2.4	To analyze the running processes (using the "pslist" function), network statistics (using the "netscan" function), and detecting the location of a string (using the "yarascan" function) recorded in the physical memory dumps
Photorec 7.0	To data carve the unstructured datasets
SQLite Browser Version 3.4.0	To view the contents of SQLite database files
Wireshark Version 1.10.1	To analyze the network traffics
Network Miner Version 1.6.1	To analyze and data carve the network files
Who is command	To determine the registration information of the IP addresses
Nirsoft Web Browser Passview 1.19.1	To recover the credential details stored within web browsers
Nirsoft cache viewer, ChromeCacheView 1.56, MozillaCacheView 1.62, IECacheView 1.53	To analyze the web browsing cache
BrowsingHistoryView v.1.60	To analyze the web browsing history
Thumbcacheviewer Version 1.0.2.7	To examine the Windows thumbnail cache
Windows Event Viewer Version 1.0	To view the Windows event logs
Windows File Analyser 2.6.0.0	To analyze the Windows prefetch and link files
NTFS Log Tracker V1.2	To parse and analyze the $LogFile, $MFT, and $UsnJrnl New Technology File System (NTFS) files

4 AIM FORENSICS

AIM is a free messaging application first launched in May 1997 and the Windows version was released on May 31, 2012 [61]. The users are required to sign up for an account (nominally a "screen name" in the context of AIM) in order to use the service. AIM reportedly uses a proprietary communication protocol called the Open System for Communication in Realtime (OSCAR), which has been the subject of various reverse-engineering attempts [62].

AIM keeps track of the contacts in the Buddy List (the term "Buddy" is an AIM term for contact), which can be saved as a text file and exported in .BLT format. Although there are default groups for buddies, family, and co-workers, custom groups can be added. There is also a special "Recent Buddies" group that holds the screen names with whom the user recently contacted [63]. The Buddy List also holds user-specific preferences for the contacts (or screen names added), such as nicknames (friendly names in the context of AIM), display of IMs, notification sounds, and other relevant settings [63].

In this section, we present results of our investigation of artifacts left behind after the use of AIM version 7.5.14.8 on a Windows 8.1 client machine, such as usernames, passwords, profile pictures, contact lists, away messages, personal messages, text of conversations, transferred files, and the associated the timestamps.

4.1 Installation of the AIM 7 Client Application

Analysis of the directory listing determined that the installation and application folders can be located at *%Program Files%\AIM* and *%AppData%\Local\AIM*, respectively. We also located link files (shortcuts) for the loader file (*%Program Files (x86)%\AIM\aim.exe*) at *%Desktop%\AIM.lnk* and *%AppData%\Roaming\Microsoft\Internet Explorer\Quick Launch\AIM.lnk*, which held timestamp records that reflected the install (creation) and last accessed times.

Examinations of the prefetch files (stored in *%SystemRoot%\Prefetch*) revealed five prefetch files associated with the AIM client application, namely "AIM.EXE.pf," "AIMINST.EXE.pf," "AIMLAN~1.EXE.pf," "SETUP.EXE.pf," and "INSTALL_AIM.EXE.pf." The prefetch files provided additional information such as the number of times the application has been loaded, last run time, and other associated timestamps. Analysis of the thumbnail cache in *%AppData%\Local\Microsoft\Windows\Explorer* located thumbnail images for the loader file, installer, and client application's logo, which may be indicative of recent AIM usage.

Looking through the registry entries, it was observed that the installation can be ascertained from the presence of the *HKEY_LOCAL_MACHINE\SOFTWARE\Wow6432Node\America Online* and *HKEY_LOCAL_MACHINE\SOFTWARE\Wow6432Node\AOL* registry hives, but it appears that only the installation metadata i.e., directory paths for the loader, diagnostic, and shortcut files can be recovered from the registry. Similar to any other Windows applications, when the AIM client was configured to run automatically whenever the Windows starting, we were able to locate the last run time for the client application in *Software\Microsoft\Windows\CurrentVersion\Run*. Fig. 2 illustrates that the entry could be differentiated by its verb.[1]

```
user_run v.20130425
(NTUSER.DAT) [Autostart] Get autostart key contents from NTUSER.DAT hive

Software\Microsoft\Windows\CurrentVersion\Run
LastWrite Time Sun Jan 18 15:54:10 2015 (UTC)
  Aim: "C:\Program Files (x86)\AIM\aim.exe" /d locale=en-US
```

FIG. 2   Last run time recorded in the "Run" registry key.

Analysis of the *Software\Microsoft\Windows\CurrentVersion\Explorer\ComDlg32* registry revealed the last accessed time for the loader file in the "CIDSizeMRU," "OpenSavePidlMRU," and "LastVisitedPidlMRU" registry subkeys (see Fig. 3), where MRU is the abbreviation for Most-Recently-Used. The findings suggested that the AIM client was recently used, had been opened or saved within a Windows shell dialog box, and was used to open the files documented in the "OpenSaveMRU" subkey, respectively [32]. Additionally, we also located references to the directory paths and last access times for the loader and link files in

---

[1]A verb is a text string used by the Windows Shell to define the command on the shortcut menu of a file [64].

Software\Microsoft\CurrentVersion\Explorer\UserAssist, indicating that the AIM client was opened frequently on the machine under investigation [65].

```
comdlg32 v.20121008

Software\Microsoft\Windows\CurrentVersion\Explorer\ComDlg32
LastWrite Time Sun Jan 18 16:03:39 2015 (UTC)
CIDSizeMRU
LastWrite: Sun Jan 18 16:03:39 2015
Note: All value names are listed in MRUListEx order.

    aim.exe

LastVisitedPidlMRU
LastWrite: Sun Jan 18 16:03:39 2015
Note: All value names are listed in MRUListEx order.

    aim.exe - My Computer\Unknown Type (0x2e)
```

FIG. 3   Last accessed time recorded in the "ComDlg32" registry key.

Examination of the running processes using the "pslist" function of Volatility revealed the process identifier (PID), parent process identifiers, as well as process initiation and termination times from the memory dump; an excerpt is shown in Fig. 4. The PID can prove useful for correlating data associated with the client application during further analysis (i.e., using the "Yarascan" function of Volatility).

Offset(V)	Name	PID	PPID	Thds	Hnds	Sess	Wow64	Start	Exit
0xfffffe00000486900	explorer.exe	2988	2960	51	0	1	0	2015-01-19 03:48:22 UTC+0000	
0xfffffe00000657900	aim.exe	2704	2988	0		1	0	2015-01-19 03:48:46 UTC+0000	2015-01-19 04:06:37 UTC+0000

FIG. 4   An excerpt of the "pslist" output for the AIM client.

4.2 Logins

By default, in AIM 7 "Remember Me," "Remember My Password," and "Automatically Sign Me In" options are enabled. The "Remember My Password" option stores the login credentials using Blowfish encryption (along with base 64 encoding) in the aimx.bin file located in the application folder. From a digital forensics perspective, this option can be beneficial to provide investigator's access to the suspect's online AIM account from the computer or forensic image under investigation without needing the user password. Moreover, the option can also provide a practitioner the opportunity to recover the credential details using AIM Password Decryptor [66]. Alternatively, it was observed that the user's screen name/login email can be located in cache files such as *%AppData%\Local\Microsoft\Windows\INetCache\ IE\<Cache ID>\AIM_UAC_v2.htm* and *%AppData%\Roaming\acccore\caches\users\<User's Screen Name>\buddyicon\bartIDs_devformat_01*.

An inspection of the network log (*%AppData%\Local\AIM\Logs\network_log_#.txt*) located references to the host's external IP addresses, prefixed by "host address" i.e., "00:26.29 Connection 039456E8: host address 152.163.9.73." Pairing the corresponding IP addresses/ screen name with the relevant timestamps will allow a practitioner to correlate any external data that might have been obtained from an ISP or other external provider. Analysis of the memory dump was able to recover copies of the login password in Unicode string format, but no obvious pattern could be located to enable future searches.

When the logins occurred, it was observed that the host first established a session with Cyberlink Internet Services AG (i.e., IP address 62.12.173.139 on port 443) for key authentication and then to the America Online (AOL) server (i.e., IP address 64.12.104.89), but we were unable to identify the purpose of the latter due to lack of information from the URL as well as encrypted traffic. The next IP addresses accessed were 205.188.87.7 and 205.188.98.4 (in our research) on port 80 to retrieve the certification revocation lists from the AOL servers. Afterwards, the host accessed the login server (i.e., IP address 207.200.74.12 on port 443 with URL referencing "my.screenname.aol.com") for login authentication. A search for the user's screen name returned multiple matches in the HTTP "referer" request header for the Atwola advertisement cookie tracking server (i.e., IP addresses 64.12.96.217 and 207.200.74.71) in the form of "http://www.aim.com/redirects/inclient/AIM_UAC_v2.adp?locale=en-US& magic=93321503&width=180&height=150&sn=<Screen name>," indicating that the user's screen name can be potentially recovered from the network captures using the link identified. Table 4 lists the network information observed in our research.

TABLE 4 Network Information Observed for the AIM Client

Registered Owner	IP Address(es)	URL(s) Observed
Cyberlink Internet Services AG	62.12.173.139	Kdc-aim.egslb.aol.com, Kdc.uas.aol.com
AOL. Inc.	64.12.104.89	bos-m016a-new-rdr2.blue.aol.com
AOL. Inc.	149.174.110.118	www.aol.com
AOL. Inc.	205.188.14.120	ars.oscar.aol.com (Windows)
AOL. Inc.	205.188.87.7	crl.egslb.aol.com, crl.aol.com
AOL. Inc.	205.188.88.125	abapi.abweb.aol.com
AOL. Inc.	205.188.98.4	ocsp.egslb.aol.com, ocsp.web.aol.com
AOL. Inc.	207.200.74.66	www.aim.com
	199.7.52.72	ocsp.verisign.net, ocsp.verisign.com
AOL. Inc.	207.200.74.12	my.screenname.aol.com.aol.akadns.net, my.screenname.aol.com
AOL. Inc.	64.12.96.217, 207.200.74.71	at.atwola.com

Reconstructing the network captures using Netminer, we only recovered certificates that were used to authenticate the HTTPS sites, HTML documents from the HTTP sites, as well as JavaScript and XML files for the advertisement cookies. Although most of the network traffics were encrypted and the credential details were not recovered, the IP addresses and URLs highlighted as part of our research may assist a practitioner in scoping and timelining the AIM activities undertaken by a suspect in future investigations. Alternatively, it was determined that the network information can be partly recovered from the memory dump using the "netscan" function of Volatility, which includes the associated PID, process creation time (if any), and socket states.

4.3 Buddy Lists

Examinations of the directory listings only located the manually saved Buddy List, which could be easily differentiated by the extension .BLT. An inspection of the Buddy List saved in our experiment observed that the user's screen name was prefixed by "screenName" in the "User" tag. The "Buddy" tag held details associated with the groups, each group name formed an opening and closing subtag (curly bracket) in the "list" subtag. Within the group name subtags there were additional subtags that held the nicknames (friendly names in the context of AIM) and personal notes for the screen names added to the groups. However, it is noteworthy that the saving of group names as well as nicknames and personal notes for the contacts' screen names is subject to user-settings for the Buddy List.

A search for the suspect and the victim's screen names and group names such as "Co-Workers," "Family," and "Recent Buddies" recovered copies of the saved Buddy List from the memory dump in plain text. It was also identified that the saved Buddy List can be differentiated from the header "43 6F 6E 66 69 67 20 7B" in hexadecimal or "Config.{" in American Standard Code for Information Interchange (ASCII) format, but there was no common structure to determine the footer, and hence data carving is not possible for the saved Buddy List. In the circumstance when the Buddy List was not manually saved, we could recover clear text copies of the screen names displayed in the Buddy List window (of the client application) from the memory dump and swap file. Fig. 5 illustrates that a practitioner can potentially locate the screen names with whom a suspect had recently communicated following the group name "Recent Buddies" in the unstructured datasets.

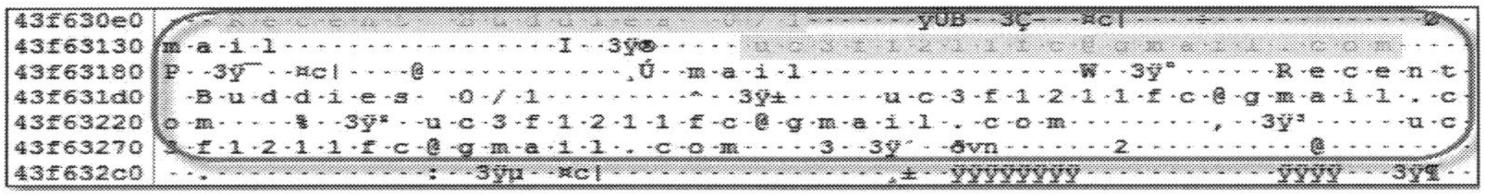

FIG. 5   Remnants of recent buddy list recovered from RAM in plain text.

4.4 Conversations and Transferred Files

The downloaded files were saved in *%Desktop%* by default. Each of which was given an alternate data stream (ADS) ZoneTransfer marker (ZoneID) with reading "ZoneID=3," indicating that the files were downloaded from Internet zone [67]. This suggests that a practitioner can potentially identify files associated with the download from files with ADS ZoneID=3 on the desktop. Inspection of the timestamps of the downloaded files revealed that the creation and accessed times were the times when the files were successfully downloaded on the recipient's machine, and the modified time of the receiving files on the recipient's machine remained unchanged from the original modified time of the files on the sender's machine. The last written time was retained from the original last written time recorded on the sender's machine.

When the transferred and downloaded files were opened, we located shortcuts for the transferred and downloaded in the recent documents directory (located at *%AppData%\Roaming\Microsoft\Windows\Recent*). The shortcuts can provide a potential alternative method for timelining the last modified, accessed, and creation times associated with the transferred or downloaded files. The findings also indicate records of the last accessed times can for the viewed files in the *Software\Microsoft*Windows*CurrentVersion\Explorer*

RecentDocs (henceforth "RecentDocs") registry key. Analysis of the thumbcache files (located in *%AppData%\Local\Microsoft\Windows\Explorer*) recovered thumbnail images for the transferred and downloaded PDF and image files, suggesting that thumbnail cache is a source for possible data associated with AIM use.

When the IM logging was not enabled, we only managed to recover artifacts of the conversations from unstructured datasets such as memory dump and swap file. The artifacts contained incoming and outgoing fragments of conversations texts, screen names of the user and the correspondent(s), away messages, filenames for the transferred/downloaded files, as well as the associated timestamp information in plain text and HTML; Fig. 6 shows an example of the plain text remnants in Unicode string format. A search for the texts (from the remnants) using the "Yarascan" function of Volatility determined that most of the artifacts were attributed to "aim.exe" in the memory dump, indicating the texts were remnants from the AIM client application. The suspect's screen name can be a useful keyword for future searches. Our findings also revealed that filenames for the successful transferred files can be found prefixed by the terms "Cool FileXfer"[2] as well as "transfer complete" in the unstructured datasets; we hypothesize that the former was remnants from the payloads of the file transfer threads. Once the filenames are identified for the transferred/downloaded files, the practitioner can correlate filenames with the directory listing, $LogFile, $MFT, $UsnJrnl, or other sources of relevance to identify file paths.

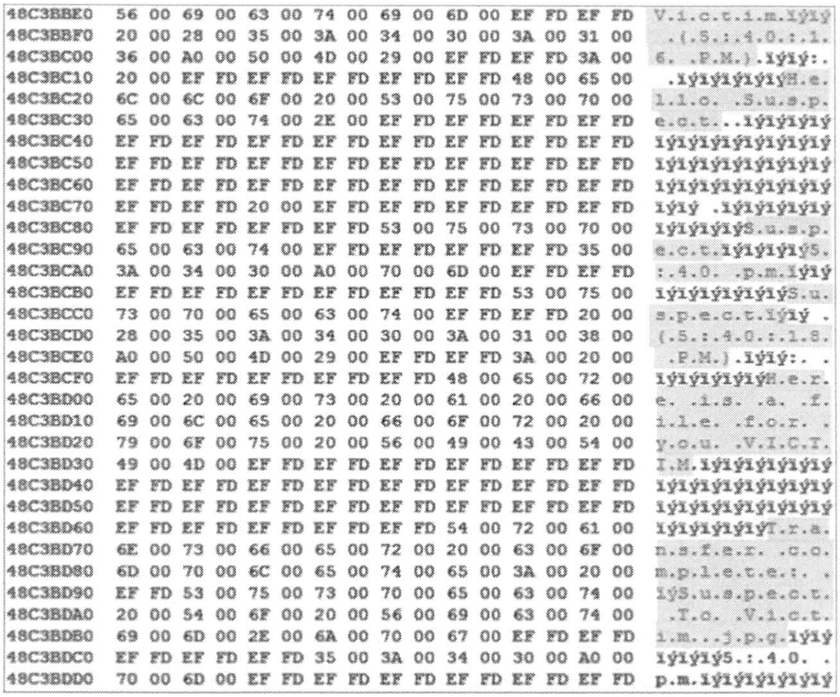

```
48C3BBE0  56 00 69 00 63 00 74 00 69 00 6D 00 EF FD EF FD  V.i.c.t.i.m.ïýïý
48C3BBF0  20 00 28 00 35 00 3A 00 34 00 30 00 3A 00 31 00   .(.5.:.4.0.:.1.
48C3BC00  36 00 A0 00 50 00 4D 00 29 00 EF FD EF FD 3A 00  6. .P.M.).ïýïý:.
48C3BC10  20 00 EF FD EF FD EF FD EF FD EF FD 48 00 65 00   .ïýïýïýïýïýH.e.
48C3BC20  6C 00 6C 00 6F 00 20 00 53 00 75 00 73 00 70 00  l.l.o. .S.u.s.p.
48C3BC30  65 00 63 00 74 00 2E 00 EF FD EF FD EF FD EF FD  e.c.t...ïýïýïýïý
48C3BC40  EF FD EF FD EF FD EF FD EF FD EF FD EF FD EF FD  ïýïýïýïýïýïýïýïý
48C3BC50  EF FD EF FD EF FD EF FD EF FD EF FD EF FD EF FD  ïýïýïýïýïýïýïýïý
48C3BC60  EF FD EF FD EF FD EF FD EF FD EF FD EF FD EF FD  ïýïýïýïýïýïýïýïý
48C3BC70  EF FD EF FD 20 00 EF FD EF FD EF FD EF FD EF FD  ïýïý .ïýïýïýïýïý
48C3BC80  EF FD EF FD EF FD EF FD 53 00 75 00 73 00 70 00  ïýïýïýïýS.u.s.p.
48C3BC90  65 00 63 00 74 00 EF FD EF FD EF FD EF FD 35 00  e.c.t.ïýïýïýïý5.
48C3BCA0  3A 00 34 00 30 00 A0 00 70 00 6D 00 EF FD EF FD  :.4.0. .p.m.ïýïý
48C3BCB0  EF FD EF FD EF FD EF FD EF FD EF FD 53 00 75 00  ïýïýïýïýïýïýS.u.
48C3BCC0  73 00 70 00 65 00 63 00 74 00 EF FD EF FD 20 00  s.p.e.c.t.ïýïý .
48C3BCD0  28 00 35 00 3A 00 34 00 30 00 3A 00 31 00 38 00  (.5.:.4.0.:.1.8.
48C3BCE0  A0 00 50 00 4D 00 29 00 EF FD EF FD 3A 00 20 00   .P.M.).ïýïý:. .
48C3BCF0  EF FD EF FD EF FD EF FD EF FD 48 00 65 00 72 00  ïýïýïýïýïýH.e.r.
48C3BD00  65 00 20 00 69 00 73 00 20 00 61 00 20 00 66 00  e. .i.s. .a. .f.
48C3BD10  69 00 6C 00 65 00 20 00 66 00 6F 00 72 00 20 00  i.l.e. .f.o.r. .
48C3BD20  79 00 6F 00 75 00 20 00 56 00 49 00 43 00 54 00  y.o.u. .V.I.C.T.
48C3BD30  49 00 4D 00 EF FD EF FD EF FD EF FD EF FD EF FD  I.M.ïýïýïýïýïýïý
48C3BD40  EF FD EF FD EF FD EF FD EF FD EF FD EF FD EF FD  ïýïýïýïýïýïýïýïý
48C3BD50  EF FD EF FD EF FD EF FD EF FD EF FD EF FD EF FD  ïýïýïýïýïýïýïýïý
48C3BD60  EF FD EF FD EF FD EF FD EF FD 54 00 72 00 61 00  ïýïýïýïýïýT.r.a.
48C3BD70  6E 00 73 00 66 00 65 00 72 00 20 00 63 00 6F 00  n.s.f.e.r. .c.o.
48C3BD80  6D 00 70 00 6C 00 65 00 74 00 65 00 3A 00 20 00  m.p.l.e.t.e.:. .
48C3BD90  EF FD 53 00 75 00 73 00 70 00 65 00 63 00 74 00  ïýS.u.s.p.e.c.t.
48C3BDA0  20 00 54 00 6F 00 20 00 56 00 69 00 63 00 74 00   .T.o. .V.i.c.t.
48C3BDB0  69 00 6D 00 2E 00 6A 00 70 00 67 00 EF FD EF FD  i.m...j.p.g.ïýïý
48C3BDC0  EF FD EF FD EF FD 35 00 3A 00 34 00 30 00 A0 00  ïýïýïý5.:.4.0. .
48C3BDD0  70 00 6D 00 EF FD EF FD EF FD EF FD EF FD EF FD  p.m.ïýïýïýïýïýïý
```

FIG. 6 Remnants of AIM conversations recovered from suspect's RAM in plain text.

[2]"Cool FileXfer" is the identification string for the OSCAR File Transfer 3 (OFT3) Header [62].

Undertaking data carving of the memory dump recovered copies of the transferred and downloaded files intact, with the exception of the .DAT files as there were no common header and footer information to determine the file structure. Alternatively, it was observed that contents of the transferred and downloaded files can be manually recovered from the memory dump in plain text. The artifacts can be useful in the circumstance when data carving is not applicable i.e., due to missing header and footer information. In a real world circumstance, the contents can be identified using a number of methods including directly from the user, hints from the incriminating IM conversations, or via the filename references recorded in the registry, directory listings, memory dump, and other unstructured datasets.

Analysis of the network traffic observed that the conversations were established with 64.12.104.* (see Table 4) on port 443. When the file transfers occurred, it was observed that the host established a direct TCP connection with the correspondents, and hence the IP addresses could be detected. In the case when direct communication was prohibited [62], the sessions were engaged with the proxy server i.e., IP address 205.188.14.120 in our research. OFT3 was seen as the carrying protocol for the both types (direct and proxied) of transfers, from which we managed to recover filenames for the transferred files, prefixed by 89-byte NULL Dummy block [62] in the respective headers. It was also observed that transfers that were completed could be differentiated from the header "type" (7th to 8th byte) given the value of "0x0204," indicating that the recipients had received the files successfully [62]; an example is shown in Fig. 7. The identification string "Cool FileXfer" can be a suitable keyword for future searches.

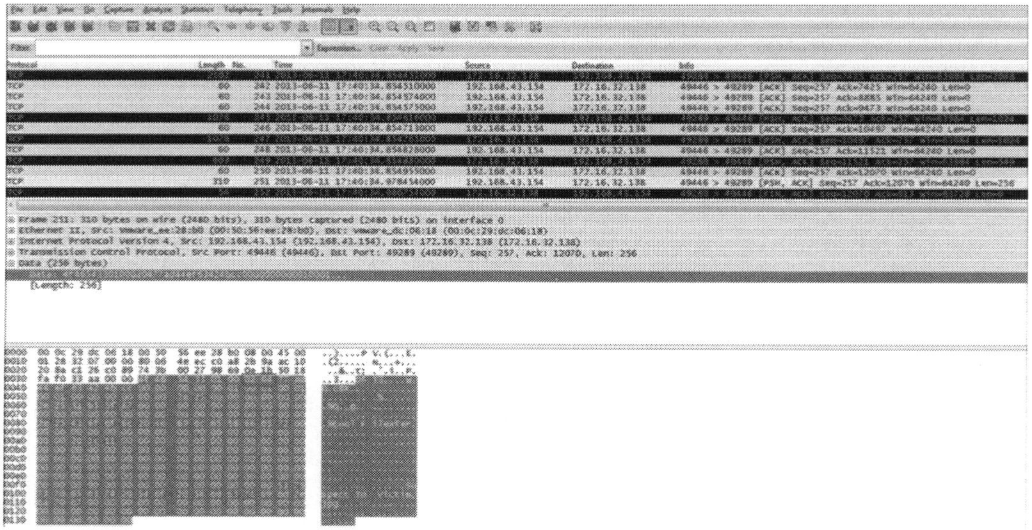

FIG. 7   OFT3 file transfer Header for successful file transfer.

4.5 IM Logs

The IM logs were saved at *%Documents%\AIMLogger\[User's screen name]\IM Logs\ [Correspondent's Screen Name].html* by default. As the filename suggests, the AIM client application created a new log for each screen name with whom the user had communicated. Analysis of the IM logs determined that incoming and outgoing text of conversations, away status, and the corresponding timestamp information can be recovered from the IM logs, but not for the away messages, file transfer statuses, and filenames for the transferred/downloaded files. Alternatively, it was determined that portion of the IM logs can be located in *%ProgramData%\Microsoft\Search\Data\Applications\Windows\Windows.edb* and *%ProgramData%\Microsoft\Search\Data\Applications\Windows\edb#####.log* (when a log file is nearing 1MB, a new log file, numbered sequentially, will be created) using the phrase "IM history with buddy." The Windows.edb file is a database of the Windows Search service, which provides search results, property caching, and content indexing for files, emails and other relevant data stored in the file system [68].

Examinations of the unstructured datasets (i.e., memory dump, swap file, and unallocated space) identified that the IM Logs can be potentially carved using the header and footer value of "3C 3F 78 6D 6C 20 76 65 72 73 69 6F 6E 3D 22… 3C 2F 62 6F 64 79 3E 0D 0A 3C 2F 68 74 6D 6C 3E," but the findings may be subject to software updates. A search for the suspect's screen name and phrase "IM history with buddy" produced matches to the IM logs in the unstructured datasets in plain text and HTML, indicating that copies of the IM logs can be extracted from unstructured datasets via keyword search. An inspection of the HTML coding indicated the corresponding screen names, conversation texts, timestamps, and other conversation information as detailed in Fig. 8; the values "LOCAL" and "REMOTE" in the "class" attribute reflect incoming and outgoing conversations respectively.

```
<tr><td class='time'>[DAY,MONTH,NUMBER OF DAY,YEAR]</td></tr>..<tr><td class='[LOCAL OR REMOTE]'>[IM SCREEN
NAME];[(TIME IN HOUR:MINUTE:SECOND;AM OR PM])</td><td class='msg' width='[WIDTH]'><FONT face='[FONT TYPE]'
size='[SIZE]' color='[COLOR CODE]'>[MESSAGE CONTENT]</FONT></td></tr>
```

FIG. 8   Excerpt of HTML coding for the IM log.

4.6 Buddy Icons

A "buddy icon" is an AIM term for user image. Artifacts of the user images (for the user and the correspondents) were only located in the thumbcache folder as well as unstructured datasets (i.e., memory dump, swap file, and unallocated space) in JPEG format, but there were no common structures to enable future identification of the user images. However, it was determined that a practitioner can retrieve the currently used image for a screen name from the Application Programming Interface (API) link http://api.oscar.aol.com/expressions/get?f=native&type=buddyIcon&t=[Screen Name].

4.7 "What is Happening" Messages

A "What is Happening" message is an AIM term for personal message. This feature can be exploited in social engineering (i.e., scam) where a criminal broadcasts hoaxes or links to malware or phishing to lure potential victims. In our research, it was observed that artifacts of the personal messages could only be located in the memory dump, with no associated string that would enable future searches. However, it was identified that a practitioner may potentially retrieve the recently updated personal messages in relation to a screen name alongside the timestamp information from the Lifestream[3] profile via the link http://lifestream.aol.com/ [Screen Name].

4.8 Uninstallation of AIM Client Software

During uninstallation, an AIM user may choose to remove the application data and IM logs from the client device completely; both options were selected in our research. An analysis of the directory listing determined that only *%AppData%\Local\AIM* and *%AppData%\Local\ AOL\AOLDiag* remained after uninstallation, but the folders were empty. The uninstallation process also created two uninstaller files ("A~NSISu_" and "B~NSISu_") in *%AppData%\ Local\Temp* as well a prefetch file (UNINST.EXE.pf), and the last accessed/run timestamp of which could indicate the uninstall time.

While inspecting the registry files, it was observed that only *HKCU\Software\America Online*, *HKLM\SOFTWARE\Wow6432Node\America Online*, and *HKLM\SOFTWARE\ Wow6432Node\AOL* were retained, but the entries were removed. Other remnants (from memory dump, swap files, unallocated space, thumbcache, "RecentDocs," "UserAssist," "Run," and "ComDIg32" registry keys, etc.) were unaffected by the uninstallation, but results may not be definitive.

5 CONCLUSION AND FUTURE WORK

In this research, we discussed forensic analysis of artifacts left by AIM 7 on Windows 8.1 desktop client. In general, our results concluded the opposite from the previous studies [34–36,44] based on registry, application data, contact, and log files. One of the major changes is that the registry no longer holds caches of recent conversations and login credentials, suggesting that registry is no longer a source of potential data for AIM 7. Although there were no common structures to enable identification of the user images and personal messages on the desktop client, our findings indicate that a practitioner may potentially retrieve the latest user image and recently updated personal messages from the server using the corresponding links identified in our research. As with any other Windows client applications and OS versions, our examination of the system files such as shortcuts, event logs, thumbcache, $LogFile, $MFT, $UsnJrnl, as well as registry keys, i.e., "RecentDocs," "UserAssist," "Run," and "ComDig32" revealed that additional timestamp and file path information can be recovered to support evidence found on the target system.

In the absence of the user manual saved buddy list and IM logs, it appears that artifacts of the contact lists (buddy lists) and conversations can only be recovered from memory dump in an unstructured form, although portion of the HTML coding can be recovered in some cases. This seems to agree with the findings of Dickson [34–36] and Reust [44]. The fact that there was no clear text password in the memory dump should perhaps not be unsurprising

---

[3]Lifestream is an integrated feature in AIM Express, AIM 7 and AIM for Mac that keeps track of updates made by the user and the correspondents on AIM, Facebook, Twitter, and other social networking or IM platforms [69].

because the credential information is securely encrypted in the aimx.bin file [66]. With the use of known file structures, we determined that it is possible to recover copies of the IM logs and transferred files from the memory dump intact, assuming that the data is not overwritten. Nevertheless, a practitioner must keep in mind that memory changes frequently according to users' activities and will be wiped as soon as the system is shut down. Our experiments also suggested that a practitioner can potentially recover portion of the conversations and transferred files from the swap files and unallocated space, which are potentially resulted from remnants of the inactive memory pages swapped to the hard disk. Hence, a practitioner should not underestimate the importance of analyzing physical memory dump, swap file, and unallocated space when undertaking forensic investigation in relation to the newer AIM client application.

Although most of the network traffics were encrypted and the credential information was not recovered, we contend that the IP addresses and URLs highlighted as part of our research may assist a practitioner in scoping the actions undertaken by a suspect on AIM, ensuring that relevant follow-up actions can be undertaken in a timely manner. Table 5 summarizes the key artifacts located as part of our research. As the remnants were recovered with minimal space configuration in our research, we believe there will be a greater chance of remnants on a typically larger system.

TABLE 5   Summary of Findings

Source of Evidence	Details
Registry branches of forensic interest	• *HKEY_LOCAL_MACHINE\SOFTWARE\Wow6432Node\America Online* • *HKEY_LOCAL_MACHINE\SOFTWARE\Wow6432Node\AOL* • Software\Microsoft\CurrentVersion\Explorer\UserAssist • Software\Microsoft\Windows\CurrentVersion\Run • Software\Microsoft\Windows\CurrentVersion\Explorer\ComDlg32 • Software\Microsoft\Windows\CurrentVersion\Explorer\RecentDocs
Files/folders of forensic interest	• *%AppData%\Local\aimx.bin* • *%AppData%\Local\AIM\Settings\[User's Screen Name]\settings.xml* • *%AppData%\Local\Microsoft\Windows\INetCache\IE\<Cache id>\AIM_UAC_v2.htm* • *%AppData%\Roaming\acccore\caches\users\<User's Screen Name>\buddyicon\ bartIDs_devformat_01* • .BLT buddy list file • *%Documents%\AIMLogger\[User's screen name]\IM Logs\[Correspondent's Screen Name].html* • *%ProgramData%\Microsoft\Search\Data\Applications\Windows\Windows* • *%ProgramData%\Microsoft\Search\Data\Applications\Windows\edb#####.log*
URLs of forensic interest	• http://api.oscar.aol.com/expressions/get?f=native&type=buddyIcon&t=[Screen Name] • http://lifestream.aol.com/[Screen Name]
Prefetch files	• AIM.EXE.pf • AIMINST.EXE.pf • AIMLAN~1.EXE.pf • SETUP.EXE.pf • INSTALL_AIM.EXE.pf

Continued

TABLE 5 Summary of Findings—cont'd

Source of Evidence	Details
Link files	• The link file could be discerned from "AIM.lnk" • Located link files for the transferred or downloaded files in %\AppData\Roaming\Microsoft\Windows\Recent\
Thumbcache files	• Icon images used by the client application • Thumbnail images for the transferred or downloaded PDF and image files • User images of the user and the contacts
Memory dumps, swap files, and unallocated space	• Copies of the files of forensic interest as well as transferred or downloaded files unencrypted • Filename and path references for the files of forensic interest and transferred or downloaded files • Unstructured screen names and conversation texts, which included the timestamp information • Copies of the Buddy List appeared in the Buddy List windows • The process name could be discerned from "aim.exe" in the memory dump
Network traffics	• OFT3 header containing filenames for downloaded/transferred files and the transfer statuses • Host and servers' IP addresses • Host and correspondents' IP addresses when file transfers occurred • Associated timestamps • Web documents and image files from the HTTP sites

Taken together, these findings echo the trend of users storing their data in the cloud. Unsurprisingly, AIM 7 uses encrypted channels to allow users to communicate securely and privately. However, this complicates forensic investigations. On Oct. 16, 2014, for example, the Federal Bureau of Investigation's director remarked that "going dark" (i.e., law enforcement not being able to access evidential data due to technological measures in place to protect the security and privacy of technology users) *will have very serious consequences for law enforcement and national security agencies at all levels [as] Sophisticated criminals will come to count on these means of evading detection* [70].

To keep pace with technological advances, future work would include investigating the newer versions and AIM for other platforms to have an up-to-date forensic understanding of the artifacts that can be used to inform investigations.

References

[1] Radicati Team, The Radicati Group, Inc. "Radicati Press Release" The Radicati Group Releases "Instant Messaging Statistics Report, 2015–2019", 2015.
[2] City of London Police. Online dating fraud up by 33% last [WWW Document]. URL https://www.cityoflondon.police.uk/advice-and-support/fraud-and-economic-crime/nfib/nfib-news/Pages/online-dating-fraud.aspx, 2015 (accessed 29.05.15).
[3] J. Farnden, B. Martini, K.-K.R. Choo, Privacy risks in mobile dating apps, in: Proceedings of the 21st Americas Conference on Information Systems, (AMCIS 2015), (2015), http://aisel.aisnet.org/cgi/viewcontent.cgi?article=1427&context=amcis2015.

[4] S.L. Meyers, Special Report, Part 1: "Diploma mill" scams continue to plague Milwaukee's adult students. Milwaukee Neighborhood News Service, 2014.

[5] N. Timoney, Consumer contact: job advertising fraud. WABI TV5. URL http://wabi.tv/2014/05/12/consumer-contact-job-advertising-fraud/ (accessed 12.18.15).

[6] M. Damshenas, A. Dehghantanha, R. Mahmoud, A survey on malware propagation, analysis, and detection, Int. J. Cyber-Sec. Digit. Forensics 2 (2013) 10–29.

[7] F. Daryabar, A. Dehghantanha, H.G. Broujerdi, Investigation of malware defence and detection techniques, Int. J. Digit. Inf. Wireless Commun. 1 (2011) 645–650.

[8] F. Daryabar, A. Dehghantanha, N.I. Udzir, N.F. Mohd Sani, S. Shamsuddin, F. Norouzizadeh, Analysis of known and unknown malware bypassing techniques, Int. J. Inf. Process. Manage. 4 (2013) 50–59.

[9] Help Net Security, Instant messaging Trojan spreads through the UK [WWW Document], http://www.net-security.org/malware_news.php?id=2773, 2014 (accessed 19.12.15).

[10] S. Mohtasebi, A. Dehghantanha, A mitigation approach to the privacy and malware threats of social network services, in: V. Snasel, J. Platos, E. El-Qawasmeh (Eds.), Digital Information Processing and Communications, Communications in Computer and Information Science, Springer, Berlin Heidelberg, 2011, pp. 448–459.

[11] T. Barnes, Margate paedophile jailed for five years [WWW Document], Thanet Gazette, http://www.thanetgazette.co.uk/Margate-paedophile-jailed-years/story-20922860-detail/story.html, 2014 (accessed 24.05.15).

[12] M. Godfrey, Pedophiles coercing kids using phone app [WWW Document]. URL http://news.smh.com.au/breaking-news-national/pedophiles-coercing-kids-using-phone-app-20130327-2gu3a.html, 2014 (accessed 24.05.15).

[13] N. McCallum, Pedophile posed as Bieber to lure victims [WWW Document], http://www.9news.com.au/world/2013/09/17/10/30/pedophile-posed-as-bieber-to-lure-victims, 2013 (accessed 24.05.15).

[14] The Federation Bureau of Investigation (FBI), Jacksonville man sentenced in child pornography case [WWW Document], FBI, https://www.fbi.gov/charlotte/press-releases/2015/jacksonville-man-sentenced-in-child-pornography-case, 2015 (accessed 18.12.15).

[15] F. Daryabar, A. Dehghantanha, N.I. Udzir, N.F. Mohd Sani, S. Shamsuddin, F. Norouzizadeh, A survey on privacy impacts of digital investigation, J. Next Gener. Inf. Technol. 4 (2013) 57–68.

[16] F.N. Dezfoli, A. Dehghantanha, R. Mahmoud, N.F.B.M. Sani, F. Daryabar, Digital forensic trends and future, Int. J. Cyber-Sec. Digit. Forensics 2 (2013) 48–76.

[17] M. Ganji, A. Dehghantanha, N.I. Udzir, M. Damshenas, Cyber warfare trends and future, Adv. Inf. Sci. Serv. Sci. 5 (2013) 1–10.

[18] S. Mohtasebi, A. Dehghantanha, Defusing the hazards of social network services, Int. J. Digit. Inf. Wireless Commun. 1 (2011) 504–515.

[19] D. Ali, Mining the Social Web: Data Mining Facebook, Twitter, LinkedIn, Google+, Github, and More. J. Inf. Priv. Secur. 11 (2015) 137–138, http://dx.doi.org/10.1080/15536548.2015.1046287.

[20] F. Norouzi, A. Dehghantanha, B. Eterovic-Soric, K.-K.R. Choo, Investigating Social Networking applications on smartphones detecting Facebook, Twitter, LinkedIn, and Google+ artifacts on Android and iOS platforms, Aust. J. Forensic Sci. 48 (4) (2015) 469–488.

[21] National Criminal Justice Reference Service (NCJRS), Investigative uses of technology: devices, tools, and techniques [WWW Document], https://www.ncjrs.gov/App/Publications/Abstract.aspx?id=262206, 2007 (accessed 06.12.14).

[22] A. Aminnezhad, A. Dehghantanha, M.T. Abdullah, A survey on privacy issues in digital forensics, Int. J. Cyber-Sec. Digit. Forensics 1 (2012) 311–323.

[23] A. Azfar, K.-K.R. Choo, L. Liu, Android mobile VoIP apps: a survey and examination of their security and privacy. Electron. Commer. Res. 16 (1) (2016) 73–111, http://dx.doi.org/10.1007/s10660-015-9208-1.

[24] N.B.A. Barghuthi, H. Said, Social networks IM forensics: encryption analysis. J. Commun. 8 (2013) 708–715, http://dx.doi.org/10.12720/jcm.8.11.708-715.

[25] M. Shariati, A. Dehghantanha, B. Martini, K.-K.R. Choo, Chapter 19—Ubuntu one investigation: detecting evidences on client machines, in: R. Ko, K.-K.R. Choo (Eds.), The Cloud Security Ecosystem, Syngress, Cambridge, MA, 2015, pp. 429–446.

[26] M. Shariati, A. Dehghantanha, K.-K.R. Choo, SugarSync forensic analysis. Aust. J. Forensic Sci. (2015) 1–23, http://dx.doi.org/10.1080/00450618.2015.1021379.

[27] M. Damshenas, A. Dehghantanha, R. Mahmoud, A survey on digital forensics trends, Int. J. Cyber-Sec. Digit. Forensics 3 (2014) 209–235.

[28] A. Dehghantanha, K. Franke, Privacy-respecting digital investigation. in: 2014 Twelfth Annual International Conference on Privacy, Security and Trust (PST), 2014, pp. 129–138, http://dx.doi.org/10.1109/PST.2014.6890932.

[29] European Union Agency for Network and Information Security (ENISA), Procure secure: a guide to monitoring of security service levels in cloud contracts—ENISA [WWW Document], https://www.enisa.europa.eu/activities/Resilience-and-CIIP/cloud-computing/procure-secure-a-guide-to-monitoring-of-security-service-levels-in-cloud-contracts, 2012 (accessed 12.10.15).

[30] M. Damshenas, A. Dehghantanha, R. Mahmoud, S. bin Shamsuddin, Forensics investigation challenges in cloud computing environments. in: 2012 International Conference on Cyber Security, Cyber Warfare and Digital Forensic (CyberSec), 2012, pp. 190–194, http://dx.doi.org/10.1109/CyberSec.2012.6246092.

[31] A. Azfar, K.-K.R. Choo, L. Liu, Forensic taxonomy of popular Android mHealth apps, in: Proceedings of the 21st Americas Conference on Information Systems, (AMCIS 2015), (2015), http://aisel.aisnet.org/cgi/viewcontent.cgi?article=1217&context=amcis2015.

[32] H. Carvey, Instant messaging investigations on a live Windows XP system. Digit. Investig. 1 (2004) 256–260, http://dx.doi.org/10.1016/j.diin.2004.10.003.

[33] M. Damshenas, A. Dehghantanha, K.-K.R. Choo, R. Mahmud, M0Droid: an android behavioral-based malware detection model. J. Inf. Priv. Secur. 11 (2015) 141–157, http://dx.doi.org/10.1080/15536548.2015.1073510.

[34] M. Dickson, An examination into AOL Instant Messenger 5.5 contact identification. Digit. Investig. 3 (2006) 227–237, http://dx.doi.org/10.1016/j.diin.2006.10.004.

[35] M. Dickson, An examination into MSN Messenger 7.5 contact identification. Digit. Investig. 3 (2006) 79–83, http://dx.doi.org/10.1016/j.diin.2006.04.002.

[36] M. Dickson, An examination into Yahoo Messenger 7.0 contact identification. Digit. Investig. 3 (2006) 159–165, http://dx.doi.org/10.1016/j.diin.2006.08.009.

[37] M. Dickson, An examination into Trillian basic 3.x contact identification. Digit. Investig. 4 (2007) 36–45, http://dx.doi.org/10.1016/j.diin.2007.01.003.

[38] Q. Do, B. Martini, K.-K.R. Choo, A forensically sound adversary model for mobile devices. PLoS ONE 10 (2015) e0138449. http://dx.doi.org/10.1371/journal.pone.0138449.

[39] M. Ibrahim, M.T. Abdullah, A. Dehghantanha, Modelling based approach for reconstructing evidence of VoIP malicious attacks, Int. J. Cyber-Sec. Digit. Forensics 1 (2012) 324–340.

[40] F. Immanuel, B. Martini, K.-K.R. Choo, Android cache taxonomy and forensic process. in: 2015 IEEE Trustcom/BigDataSE/ISPA, 2015, pp. 1094–1101, http://dx.doi.org/10.1109/Trustcom.2015.488.

[41] M.D. Leom, C.J. D'Orazio, G. Deegan, K.-K.R. Choo, Forensic collection and analysis of thumbnails in android. in: 2015 IEEE Trustcom/BigDataSE/ISPA, 2015, pp. 1059–1066, http://dx.doi.org/10.1109/Trustcom.2015.483.

[42] S. Mohtasebi, A. Dehghantanha, H.G. Broujerdi, Smartphone forensics: a case study with Nokia E5-00 mobile phone, Int. J. Digit. Inf. Wireless Commun. 1 (2011) 651–655.

[43] S. Parvez, A. Dehghantanha, H.G. Broujerdi, Framework of digital forensics for the Samsung Star Series phone. in: 2011 3rd International Conference on Electronics Computer Technology (ICECT), 2011, pp. 264–267, http://dx.doi.org/10.1109/ICECTECH.2011.5941698.

[44] J. Reust, Case study: AOL instant messenger trace evidence. Digit. Investig. 3 (2006) 238–243, http://dx.doi.org/10.1016/j.diin.2006.10.009.

[45] J. Talebi, A. Dehghantanha, R. Mahmoud, Introducing and analysis of the Windows 8 event log for forensic purposes, in: U. Garain, F. Shafait (Eds.), Computational Forensics, Lecture Notes in Computer Science, Springer International Publishing, Cham, Switzerland, 2015, pp. 145–162.

[46] W.S. Van Dongen, Forensic artefacts left by Pidgin Messenger 2.0. Digit. Investig. 4 (2007) 138–145, http://dx.doi.org/10.1016/j.diin.2008.01.002.

[47] W.S. Van Dongen, Forensic artefacts left by Windows Live Messenger 8.0. Digit. Investig. 4 (2007) 73–87, http://dx.doi.org/10.1016/j.diin.2007.06.019.

[48] M.N. Yusoff, M. Ramlan, A. Dehghantanha, M.T. Abdullah, Advances of mobile forensic procedures in Firefox OS. Int. J. Cyber-Sec. Digit. Forensics 3 (2014) 183–199, http://dx.doi.org/10.17781/P001338.

[49] M.N. Yusoff, R. Mahmod, M.T. Abdullah, A. Dehghantanha, Performance measurement for mobile forensic data acquisition in Firefox OS. Int. J. Cyber-Sec. Digit. Forensics 3 (2014) 130–140, http://dx.doi.org/10.17781/P001333.

[50] S.H. Mohtasebi, A. Dehghantanha, Towards a unified forensic investigation framework of smartphones. Int. J. Comput. Theory Eng. 5 (2) (2013) 351–355, http://dx.doi.org/10.7763/IJCTE.2013.V5.708.

[51] D. Quick, K.-K.R. Choo, Digital droplets: Microsoft SkyDrive forensic data remnants. Futur. Gener. Comput. Syst. 29 (2013) 1378–1394, http://dx.doi.org/10.1016/j.future.2013.02.001.

[52] D. Quick, K.-K.R. Choo, Dropbox analysis: data remnants on user machines. Digit. Investig. 10 (2013) 3–18, http://dx.doi.org/10.1016/j.diin.2013.02.003.

[53] D. Quick, K.-K.R. Choo, Google drive: forensic analysis of data remnants. J. Netw. Comput. Appl. 40 (2014) 179–193, http://dx.doi.org/10.1016/j.jnca.2013.09.016.

[54] M. Kiley, S. Dankner, M. Rogers, Forensic analysis of volatile instant messaging, in: I. Ray, S. Shenoi (Eds.), Advances in Digital Forensics IV, IFIP—The International Federation for Information Processing, Springer, New York, 2008, pp. 129–138.

[55] P. Gladyshev, A. Almansoori, Reliable acquisition of RAM dumps from Intel-based Apple Mac computers over Firewire, in: I. Baggili (Ed.), Digital Forensics and Cyber Crime, Lecture Notes of the Institute for Computer Sciences, Social Informatics and Telecommunications Engineering, Springer, Berlin Heidelberg, 2010, pp. 55–64.

[56] M. Yasin, M. Abulaish, M.N.N. Elmogy, Forensic analysis of Digsby log data to trace suspected user activities, in: J.H. (James) Park, J. Kim, D. Zou, Y.S. Lee (Eds.), Information Technology Convergence, Secure and Trust Computing, and Data Management, Lecture Notes in Electrical Engineering, Springer, Netherlands, 2012, pp. 119–126.

[57] M. Yasin, M. Abulaish, DigLA—a Digsby log analysis tool to identify forensic artifacts. Digit. Investig. 9 (2013) 222–234, http://dx.doi.org/10.1016/j.diin.2012.11.003.

[58] M. Yasin, F. Kausar, E. Aleisa, J. Kim, Correlating messages from multiple IM networks to identify digital forensic artifacts. Electron. Commer. Res. 14 (2014) 369–387, http://dx.doi.org/10.1007/s10660-014-9145-4.

[59] M.I. Husain, I. Baggili, R. Sridhar, A simple cost-effective framework for iPhone forensic analysis, in: I. Baggili (Ed.), Digital Forensics and Cyber Crime, Lecture Notes of the Institute for Computer Sciences, Social Informatics and Telecommunications Engineering, Springer, Berlin Heidelberg, 2011, pp. 27–37.

[60] R. McKemmish, What is Forensic Computing? Australian Institute of Criminology, Canberra, 1999.

[61] Old Apps, Old and new version of AOL instant messenger download. [WWW Document], http://www.oldapps.com/aim.php, n.d. (accessed 18.12.15).

[62] Carnegie Mellon University (CMU), On sending files via OSCAR Google Summer of Code 2005 Gaim project [WWW Document], http://www.cs.cmu.edu/~jhclark/aim/On%20Sending%20Files%20via%20OSCAR.odt, 2006 (accessed 05.04.15).

[63] America Online Inc (AOL), How do I manage my Buddy List/IM settings in the AOL software? [WWW Document], https://help.aol.com/articles/how-do-I-manage-my-buddy-listim-settings-in-the-aol-software, 2015 (accessed 21.12.15).

[64] Microsoft Inc., Verbs and file associations (Windows) [WWW Document], https://msdn.microsoft.com/en-us/library/windows/desktop/cc144175(v=vs.85).aspx, 2015 (accessed 24.05.15).

[65] Nirsoft, UserAssistView—decrypt and displays the list of all UserAssist items in the registry [WWW Document], http://www.nirsoft.net/utils/userassist_view.html, 2015 (accessed 24.05.15).

[66] N. Talekar, SecurityXploded Blog—New Software—AIM Password Decryptor, 2011.

[67] Microsoft Inc., About URL security zones (Windows) [WWW Document], https://msdn.microsoft.com/en-us/library/ms537183.aspx#internet, 2015 (accessed 24.05.15).

[68] J. Metz, Windows Search forensics | ForensicFocus.com [WWW Document], Forensic Focus, http://www.forensicfocus.com/windows-search-forensics, n.d. (accessed 06.01.16).

[69] America Online Inc (AOL), What is Lifestream? [WWW Document], https://help.aol.com/, https://help.aol.com/articles/what-is-lifestream, 2014 (accessed 09.01.16).

[70] The Federation Bureau of Investigation (FBI), Going dark: are technology, privacy, and public safety on a collision course? [WWW Document], FBI, https://www.fbi.gov/news/speeches/going-dark-are-technology-privacy-and-public-safety-on-a-collision-course, 2014 (accessed 18.12.15).

4

Forensic Investigation of Social Media and Instant Messaging Services in Firefox OS: Facebook, Twitter, Google+, Telegram, OpenWapp, and Line as Case Studies

M.N. Yusoff*, A. Dehghantanha†, R. Mahmod‡

*University Science Malaysia, George Town, Malaysia †University of Salford, Salford, United Kingdom ‡Universiti Putra Malaysia, Serdang, Malaysia

1 INTRODUCTION

The exponential growth of social media and instant messaging applications has facilitated development of many serious cybercrime and malicious activities [1]. Cybercriminals are constantly changing their strategies to target rapidly growing social media and instant messaging users. The misuse of social media and instant messaging in mobile devices may allow cybercriminals to utilize these services for malicious purposes [2] such as spreading malicious codes, and obtaining and disseminating confidential information. Many social media and instant messaging providers have extended their services to mobile platforms, [3] which worsen the situation as users are in danger of losing even more private information [4]. Copyright infringement, cyber stalking, cyber bullying, slander spreading, and sexual harassment are becoming serious threats to social media and instant messaging mobile users [5]. Therefore it is common to be confronted with different types of mobile devices during variety of forensics investigation cases [6]. Mobile devices are now an important source of forensic remnants relevant to users' social media and instant messaging activities [7]. However, difference between mobile devices mandate forensics investigators to develop customized methods and techniques for the investigation of different phones [8].

With the emergence of smartphones, almost all parts of phones such as internal storage, flash memory, and internal volatile memory contain valuable evidence [9]. Chen extracted SMS, phone book, call recording, scheduling, and documents from Windows Mobile OS via Bluetooth, Infrared, and USB using Microsoft ActiveSync [10]. The acquired data were extracted from the mobile phone internal storage, SIM card, as well as removable memory. Irwin and Hunt have successfully mapped internal and external memory of Windows Mobile ver.5 running on IPAQ Pocket PC over wireless connections using their own developed forensic tools [11]. Pooters has developed a forensic tool called the Symbian Memory Imaging Tool (SMIT) to create bit-by-bit copies of the internal flash memory of Symbian OS phones such as the Nokia E65, E70, and N78 models [12]. Lessard and Kessler [13] have acquired a bit-by-bit logical image of a HTC Hero memory using UNIX dd command and analyzed the resulted images using AccessData Forensic Toolkit (FTK) Imager v2.5.1 [14]. Gómez-Miralles and Arnedo-Moreno have utilized a Jailbroken iPad's camera connection kit to acquire an image of the device via USB connection [15]. Iqbal has enhanced the Gómez-Miralles and Arnedo-Moreno method by developing a method to acquire iOS memory images without jailbreaking the device [16]. Sylve has presented a methodology and toolset for acquisition of volatile physical memory of Android devices by creating a new kernel module for dumping the memory [17].

Beyond evidence acquisition, many researchers have shown big interest in investigating social media and instant messaging services on different mobile platforms. Husain and Sridhar have analyzed AIM, Yahoo! Messenger, and Google Talk instant messaging applications in Apple iOS to detect potential application of these instant messaging services, particularly in cyber bullying and cyber stalking [18]. They have managed to detect username, password, buddy list, last login time, and conversation contents together with timestamp. Jung has analyzed eight social media applications in Apple iOS namely Cyworld, Me2Day, Daum Yozm, Twitter, Facebook, NateOn UC., KakaoTalk, and MyPeople [19] and managed to retrieve user info, friend list, message, contact and media information of each application. Tso has observed the diversification of the backup files for Facebook, WhatsApp Messenger, Skype, Windows Live Messenger, and Viber in Apple iOS [20]. Anglano has analyzed WhatsApp Messenger application remnants on an Android smartphone and reconstructed the list of contacts and the chronology of communicated messages [21]. Karpisek has successfully decrypted the network traffic of WhatsApp Messenger and managed to obtain forensic artifacts related to call features and visualized messages that have been exchanged between users [22]. Walnycky has examined 20 popular instant messaging applications on an Android platform and has reconstructed some or the entire message content of 16 applications [23]. Said has conducted a comparative study of Facebook and Twitter remnants on Apple iOS, Windows Mobile, and RIM BlackBerry [24] and extracted Facebook and Twitter remnants of Apple iOS and Facebook. Mutawa has compared evidence of Facebook, Twitter, and MySpace in three different operating systems namely Apple iOS, Google Android, and RIM BlackBerry and could not recover any artifact from Blackberry while iPhones and Android contained many valuable artifacts [25]. Iqbal et al. [26] has compared artifacts of Samsung's ChatON application between a Samsung Galaxy Note running Android 4.1 and an Apple iPhone running with iOS 6 and managed to detect all sent and received messages with timestamp and location of the sent files on both platforms. Dezfouli investigated Facebook, Twitter, LinkedIn, and Google+ on Android and Apple iOS platforms and managed to recover many artifacts including username, contact information, location, friend list, social media post, messages, comments, and IP addresses of selected social media applications on both platforms [3]. Table 1 summarizes the literature on social media and instant messaging investigation forensics.

TABLE 1 Summary of Social Media and Instant Messaging Investigation on Multiple Mobile Platforms

Researcher(s)	Application(s)	Platform(s)
Husain and Sridhar [18]	AIM, Yahoo! Messenger, Google Talk	Apple iOS
Jung et al. [19]	Cyworld, Me2Day, Daum Yozm, Twitter, Facebook, NateOn UC., KakaoTalk, MyPeople	Apple iOS
Tso et al. [20]	Facebook, WhatsApp Messenger, Skype, Windows Live Messenger, Viber	Apple iOS
Anglano [21]	WhatsApp Messenger	Google Android
Karpisek et al. [22]	WhatsApp Messenger	Google Android
Walnycky et al. [23]	WhatsApp Messenger, Viber, Instagram, Okcupid, ooVoo, Tango, Kik, Nimbuzz, eetMe, MessageMe, TextMe, Grindr, HeyWire, Hike, textPlus, Facebook Messenger, Tinder, Wickr, Snapchat, Blackberry Messenger	Google Android
Said et al. [24]	Facebook, Twitter	Apple iOS, Windows mobile, RIM BlackBerry
Al Mutawa et al. [25]	Facebook, Twitter, MySpace	Apple iOS, Google Android, RIM Blackberry
Iqbal et al. [26]	Samsung's ChatON	Apple iOS, Google Android
Dezfouli et al. [3]	Facebook, Twitter, LinkedIn, Google+	Apple iOS, Google Android

As can be seen from Table 1, there was no previous work investigating remnants of Facebook, Twitter, Google+, Telegram, OpenWapp, and Line applications on Firefox OS (FxOS) which is the gap targeted in this paper. In this chapter we present investigation of a Geeksphone, model name Peak [27] running FxOS 1.1.1 as the main subject of the investigation. Two binary images were taken from the phone internal storage and internal memory and then valuable forensics remnants were examined. We have mainly focused on the evidential remnants of user activities with Facebook, Twitter, Google+, Telegram, OpenWapp, and Line applications.

The rest of this chapter is organized as follows. In Section 2 we explain the methodology used in our research and in Section 3 we outline the setup for our experiment. In Section 4 we present our research findings and conclude our research in Section 5.

2 METHODOLOGY

This research has performed an investigation on Mozilla FxOS running on a phone released by Geeksphone, called Peak [27]. Released in Apr. 2013, this phone is equipped with FxOS version 1.1.1. Table 2 shows the full specification of Geeksphone Peak.

TABLE 2   Geeksphone Peak Full Specification

Hardware	Detail
Processor	1.2 GHz Qualcomm Snapdragon S4 8225 processor (ARMv7)
Memory	512 MB Ram
Storage	- Internal 4 GB - Micro SD up to 16 GB
Battery	- 1800 mAh — micro-USB charging
Data inputs	Capacitive multitouch IPS display
Display	540×960 px (qHD) capacitive touchscreen, 4.3″
Sensor	- Ambient light sensor - Proximity sensor - Accelerometer
Camera	8 MP (Rear), 2 MP (Front)
Connectivity	- WLAN IEEE 802.11 a/b/g/n - Bluetooth 2.1 +EDR - micro-USB 2.0 - GPS - mini-SIM card - FM receiver
Compatible network	- GSM 850/900/1800/1900 - HSPA (Tri-band) - HSPA/UMTS 850/1900/2100
Dimension	- Width: 133.6 mm (5.26 in) - Height: 66 mm (2.6 in) - Thickness: 8.9 mm (0.35 in)

As illustrated in Fig. 1, initially the device settings were wiped and restored to the default factory settings. The acquisition process was then executed to acquire FxOS phone image (.ffp) and memory image (.ffm). The first two binary images were then marked as a base image and their MD5 hash values were preserved. Next the investigator installed social media or instant messaging applications to the phone via Mozilla Market Place. The investigator simulated the actual use of the application by running communication activities such as posting, sending private message, received reply, upload picture, mentioning, following, and many more social media and instant messaging activities. Each of detail steps, credentials, and communication activities were documented properly in a forensically sound manner. Finally a second acquisition process was performed to identify and investigate what artifacts are likely to remain, what type of credential can be extracted, and what data remnants could be recovered. Both images were named according to the type of application installed and its MD5 hash values were taken. This step meant for comparison to the earlier data acquisition to see if there were any differences with the other MD5 hash values.

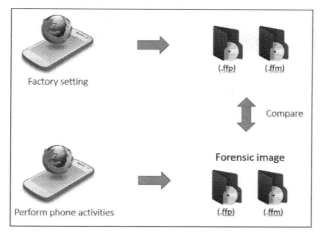

FIG. 1 Method to create forensic evidences.

Our method to create forensic evidence in Fig. 1 was performed by using Facebook, Twitter, Telegram, OpenWapp, and Line applications. We also repeated this method using Facebook, Twitter, Google+, and Telegram mobile web in order to compare both FxOS applications artifacts and mobile web activities artifacts. However, comparison was not possible for OpenWapp and Line application artifacts because both applications were not offered in mobile web platforms. It is vital to include the mobile web activities in this investigation because FxOS application were designed based on web application. Therefore this research was attempting to prove that the investigation result of web-centric OS are totally different with other mobile OS investigation.

3 EXPERIMENT SETUP

The research experiment was divided into five stages; (1) preparing the host machine for acquisition process and analysis work; (2) acquisition of phone image and memory image; (3) installing the phone with targeted application; (4) executed the activities and documenting all steps taken; and (5) comparing base image with activities images.

3.1 Preparing the Host Machine for Acquisition Process and Analysis Work

The evidence was acquired using Ubuntu 14.04 LTS and then analyzed in Windows 8.1 machine. The need to use a separated operating system is due to the fact that memory acquisition will only work on the Linux environment; whereas most of the analysis tools were design under a Windows operating system. To successfully capture the phone image using Ubuntu, the host machine needs to be running under Android Debug Bridge (ADB) [28–31]. The following command was used to configure ADB package in Ubuntu:

```
# sudo apt-get install android-tools-adb
```

As for the volatile memory acquisition, we configured Linux Memory Extractor (LiME) [17] using the following command:

```
# sudo apt-get install lime-forensics-dkms
```

AccessData Forensic Toolkit (FTK) version 3.1.2 [14] and HxD Hex Editor 1.7.7.0 [32] were installed in Windows machine to analyze captured forensic images and QtADB 0.81 Android Manager [33] was used to browse the system files in the Geeksphone Peak.

3.2 Acquisition of Phone Image and Memory Image

Two types of binary images, meant to be used as forensic evidence in our case studies, were extracted. The first binary image was extracted from the FxOS phone internal memory using dd command. The FxOS phone was first connected to the host machine and then an ADB connection was started before we proceeded to execute the dd command. We have used the following command to start the ADB connection between the phone and the host machine.

```
# adb shell
```

Once the connection was established, we performed the following dd command to copy bit-by-bit of the phone's internal memory into an SD card and we named it as FxOS phone memory (.ffp):

```
# dd if=/dev/block/mmcblk0 of=/mnt/emmc/base.ffp bs=2048
```

The whole binary image of the FxOS internal memory was then copied from the SD card into the host machine and we named it as base.ffp. We used block size 2 MB during the dd command execution as per suggested in previous studies [29].

The next step was the extraction of the second binary image from the FxOS phone's volatile memory using LiME. LiME was design as such to allow the acquisition of volatile memory from Linux-based devices and originally tested using Android phones [17]. ADB was then used to load LiME; the method of volatile memory acquisition at this step is similar to the dd command. We used the following command in ADB to load LiME from phone SD card:

```
# adb push lime.ko /mnt/emmc/lime.ko
```

After LiME was loaded, we ran insmod to copy live bit-by-bit of volatile memory into the SD card. For volatile memory, we named it as FxOS memory (.ffm)

```
# insmod /mnt/emmc/lime.ko "path=/mnt/emmc/base.ffm format=lime"
```

Both internal phone images (.ffp) and memory images (.ffm) were directed to the SD card. After the acquisition process was completed, we killed the ADB connection, and then mounted the SD card to copy both images. We set the same name for both images and only the extension and file size are left as the differences. The steps were repeated for every action in our experiment.

3.3 Installing the Phone With Targeted Application

The objective of this experiment is to investigate both the social media network and instant messaging platform in FxOS. Due to the limited number of applications offered in Mozilla Market Place, we have only managed to investigate five applications and four mobile webs as shows in Table 3.

TABLE 3   Selected Applications and Mobile Web

Group	Application	Mobile Web
Social media	1. Facebook 2. Twitter	1. Facebook 2. Twitter 3. Google+
Instant messaging	1. Telegram 2. OpenWapp 3. Line	1. Telegram

The investigations were performed on both application and the mobile web. The purpose of investigating both applications and mobile web were to list out the differences and similarities between FxOS applications with its mobile web.

3.4 Executing the Activities and Documenting All Steps Taken

Our investigation in this experiment started the moment we installed the applications in the phone. We also created a few dummy accounts for the experiments. All detail steps, credentials, and communication activities were properly documented. In order to facilitate the use of credential during our experiment, we created all social media accounts using the same email address and password which are "mohd.najwadi@gmail.com" and "najwadi87," respectively. In general, all social media and instant messaging applications will have one extra step; which is the installation of the application. On the contrary, for the mobile web, we can just browse directly from the site. Table 4 shows all of the steps and activities taken for the social media experiment.

TABLE 4   Detail Steps for Social Media Experiment

Social Media	Steps and Action	Image Filename
Facebook application	Installing Facebook application	Facebook-Install
	Login Facebook account (ID: Root Wadi) - Email: mohd.najwadi@gmail.com - Password: najwadi87	Facebook-Login
	Facebook activities - Post status: posting with love - PM Mohd Najwadi: hi. Test send msg - Received reply: received with thanks	Facebook-Post
Facebook Web	Login Facebook thru web www.facebook.com - Email: mohd.najwadi@gmail.com - Password: najwadi87	Facebook-Browse
	Facebook Activities - Post: posting from web - PM Mohd Najwadi: test again - Received reply: received second time	Facebook-xtvt

Continued

TABLE 4   Detail Steps for Social Media Experiment—cont'd

Social Media	Steps and Action	Image Filename
Twitter application	Installing Twitter Application	Twitter-Install
	Login Twitter account (ID: @wadieq) - Email: mohd.najwadi@gmail.com - Password: najwadi87	Twitter-Login
	Twitter Activities - Tweet: my first tweet - Mention: @wadieq test mention - Favorites: @wadieq Taman tepi rumah	Twitter-Tweet
Twitter Web	Login Twitter thru web www.twitter.com - Email: mohd.najwadi@gmail.com - Password: najwadi87	Twitter-Browse
	Twitter Activities - Tweet: my second tweet - Reply: @wadieq Reply comment - Unfollow @MunirRashid	Twitter-xtvt
Google+ Web	Login Google+ thru web plus.google.com - Email: mohd.najwadi@gmail.com - Password: najwadi87	Google-Login
	Google+ Activities - Follow people: tomska, british motogp - create circle: firefox plus - post: google plus firefox - comment: komen sendiri	Google-xtvt

There were 12 time acquisition processes performed for each internal phone image and memory image altogether; and the files were named according to the steps taken as shown in Table 4. We also tested both the applications and mobile web for Facebook and Twitter, whereas for Google+, we were only able to test the web because there was no application supported for Google+ in Mozilla Market Place at the time of the experiment. The phones were restored back to their factory setting only after we began a new application or mobile web experiment. For social media investigation, we restored the phones five times, the number of experiment conducted. After the completion of the social media investigation, we then proceeded with the instant messaging step. Instant messaging accounts were tied to different mobile numbers. In this experiment we registered the instant messaging account using mobile number "+60162444415" and we performed the communication with the mobile number "+60125999159." Table 5 shows all the steps and activities taken for the instant messaging experiment.

In the instant messaging experiment, we performed the acquisition processes 11 times for each internal phone image and memory image. The files were also named according to the step taken as shown in Table 5. The experiments were performed using OpenWapp and Line applications, and both Telegram application and mobile web. OpenWapp is the third party application for WhatsApp in FxOS because WhatsApp was not officially offered in Mozilla Market Place. Both WhatsApp and Line does not offer mobile web support. During our investigation, we restored the phone to their factory setting four times, the number of experiment conducted.

TABLE 5   Detail Steps for Instant Messaging Experiment

Instant Messaging	Steps and Action	Image Filename
Telegram application	Installing Telegram applications	Telegram-Install
	Register Telegram account - select Malaysia +60162444415 - generating telegram code: 99246 - received SMS from +93450009276	Telegram-Register
	Telegram activities - Sent to +60125999159: hi - Received from +60125999159: hello - Received from +60125999159: InstaSize_2015_4_36453.jpg - Save picture—asking for access picture > - Received from +60125999159: 200507000.pdf - Save file: asking for access memory card >	Telegram-Chat
Telegram Web	Login Telegram thru web web.telegram.org - select Malaysia +60162444415 - generating telegram code 34303 - received SMS from +93450009276	Telegram-Browse
	Telegram activities - Sent to +60125999159: hi from web - Received from +60125999159: hi back - Received from +60125999159: IMG_20150508_200905.jpg - Save picture: failed - Sent to +60125999159: thanks for the picture	Telegram-Webxtvt
OpenWapp	Installing OpenWapp application	OpenWapp-Install
	Register WhatsApp - select Malaysia +60162444415 - generating WhatsApp code 560-103 - received SMS from 63365	OpenWapp-Reg
	OpenWapp activities - Received from +60125999159: hello - Sent to +60125999159: testing openwapp from Firefox phone - Received from +60125999159: IMG_20150508_171904.jpg - Save picture: agxahpqv0gm3suwkv7glgnxz6ig4k_bh6jq_ bivja5q0.jpg	OpenWapp-Chat
Line application	Installing Line application	Line-Install
	Register Line account - select Malaysia +60162444415 - Reg code 1877 - Received SMS from +601117224258	Line-Reg
	Line activities - najwadi added syamsaziela as friend - najwadi sent msg: Hi syamsaziela (6.15PM) - syamsaziela replied: send to firefox phone (6.15PM) - syamsaziela sent: IMG_8933.jpg - najwadi received, saved (read 6.18PM): New folder name LINE—2015412_185355518.jpg	Line-xtvt

3.5 Comparing Base Images With Activities Images

Acquired forensic images were analyzed using AccessData Forensic Toolkit (FTK) version 3.1.2 and HxD Hex Editor 1.7.7.0. Our major analysis technique relied solely on the actions and execution to the phone during the experiment. The base images were then compared with the captured forensic images according to the detail steps and actions taken. MD5 hash values of all images were recorded as shown in Table 6.

TABLE 6   MD5 Hash Value for Acquired Images

Filename	Phone Image (.ffp)	Memory Image (.ffm)
Base	F080B51EDBCCA1DFB85023A96C86B95D	7D93024506D837EB85682AC6C2DAE7A9
Facebook-Install	94A4CCEB5333D5A8D7E8498E531DFCF7	24E0273A4CB7C852E20230E823675A50
Facebook-Login	755811F684ED0A987E07C2B27D047560	DA9A48B9F04F73415BE37E26F23B4612
Facebook-Post	51ABC84775AEA4326814707450D21D23	84EDE34F2059CE45CE55C195E6B4F116
Facebook-Browse	FCB0C5CFEEDC292185B340C809B63391	A040D89CBFBBD3F8A908F2E9F9ED4C3E
Facebook-xtvt	486719D871E0B71D198099E82C13D959	3C3F778E0FA59A93B4274265E4515967
Twitter-Install	BF63A51A105A6DDA94FC6A55D511FD76	E3178BA282723C70DBBB65DE9CBA2FFB
Twitter-Login	6B7F1035F1B2C4DECA3B793F3AF36CF5	987C447CC2B7651D283B53021121E93F
Twitter-Tweet	6A18EDCAD1A2AF26CA274067D1F27B34	516FB1B243A47AB1256B121321BF98E6
Twitter-Browse	57F6990C23DF171C32EF8BF81FF550A3	242247A35D866D8E9F642D171457EC52
Twitter-xtvt	4CE51367D17FD6FDE29EAC744E763A3B	872975E4C17319CCD44E0AF7E968CF33
Google-Login	C5B877501D82C2CA6998219FF3767FFD	E94A7D2141E3CF18A146AAA8BCB6D181
Google-xtvt	5BCBBD245F29662C7127B20B8341952B	CDD22BA569641831292E85C9C8F860E1
Telegram-Install	B15D74872C6E42244F859A73AD24C25B	079F5A0CBEDB4DD920B90A8CA26E3FCB
Telegram-Register	A46445F6DB4A79C6FFD354CED983DF0A	A43650BD2947C1CEF6AB1117C7F4070F
Telegram-chat	2424B5DE62DBE83F6BB8DAD19753A84D	55F5E5BD6B575113F3600F3A381F0D16
Telegram-Browse	B3DE5669770CEAAF61F602499513328D	3EB424F3D1D575F3E7A86A31948A83AB
Telegram-webxtvt	F261B40B276A572C93C3D34AD9738444	A0E12223ADD6BC1C7845B12527B1581C
OpenWapp-install	1BD68D8D6BD787AC41AC67E9CD1726AC	B4F80CF7E711D4FBD595673DB3DE84CB
OpenWapp-reg	EFE5DB509CEFFA005F4A60337AA3CF2F	BD6F684E93D53DE79E616088165A306E
OpenWapp-chat	56590158061E662FCAED3BC1A5C773ED	517D345BE8FBAD1FFFF45ED5CA7345F5
Line-Install	C5E85B3BA980E8DA7130DBB9556C6501	29908DE05F3B7DECEA3B17ADF1EDD946
Line-Reg	992818E14DD9684715EACB812CBB6FED	EF641273ABF57E76F4516803DEDE8216
Line-xtvt	D13BF7662CB491E73DB6ABF7E193F401	56C0CBE3B8DD306EBFFEDA68EEBDF5C3

MD5 hash values were taken and preserved. Any modification of the forensic images will be easily detected by looking at their hash value. In our experiment none of these forensic images shared the same hash values. This concluded that our forensic images were giving differences in value, modification, and evidence.

4 DISCUSSION AND ANALYSIS

In this section we have divided our analysis into two parts. The first analysis focused on the social media investigation, while the second part focused on the instant messaging investigation. For both analyses we started with the internal phone images (.ffp) and then proceeded with memory images (.ffm). The purpose of separating the two analyses was to differentiate between both analysis results. By doing these analyses separately, we discovered that certain information that was not recoverable in the phone images were able to be retrieved from memory images.

4.1 Social Media Investigation

In the social media experiment we were focusing the investigation for two social media applications and three social media mobile webs. We successfully separated the captured images based on major steps and details as shown in Table 3. There were several forensics worth of evidence that we were trying to recover and trace. First we explored the residual artifacts generated by the application and URL involved for the mobile web. Second we were trying find any ID name that was able to be captured after we logged in into social media. Third we searched for any credential involving username and password after the login process. Forth we traced back what activities had been captured in the images. Lastly we checked for the data remnant and leftover after complete uninstallation of the application.

4.1.1 Social Media Phone Image

Each of the phone images were opened using AccessData Forensic Toolkit (FTK) version 3.1.2 and HxD Hex Editor 1.7.7.0. The analyses were conducted manually by searching several keywords related to the previous experiment in a forensically sounds manner. The first binary search performed was the application keyword. This search executed once the selected application was successfully installed from Mozilla Market Place. Because our factory setting base image only comes with a preinstalled application and none of it was used in our investigation, we cannot find any keywords of selected social media from the base image. Fig. 2 shows Twitter keyword appear when we executed the first search.

The second search was performed to find a URL for social media mobile web. The mobile web is totally different with the application. We did not have to install it but only needed to browse using the preinstalled Firefox browser. Fig. 3 shows the Twitter URL was found in the images and the result also shows the visited date and time.

The third search was to find our profile name or user ID once we logged into the social media. A profile name is different than a username. A username was used to login into the social media while the profile name was the name displayed in our social media account. Fig. 4 shows our profile name together with the user ID and Facebook profile path that we managed to find.

```
23CD4320    63 6F 6E 6E 65 63 74 5F 6A 6F 69 6E 65 64 5F 74    connect_joined_t
23CD4330    77 69 74 74 65 72 5F 6F 6E 65 22 3A 22 59 6F 75    witter_one":"You
23CD4340    72 20 63 6F 6E 74 61 63 74 20 3C 73 70 61 6E 20    r contact <span
23CD4350    63 6C 61 73 73 3D 27 68 69 67 68 6C 69 67 68 74    class='highlight
23CD4360    27 3E 7B 7B 6E 61 6D 65 7D 7D 3C 2F 73 70 61 6E    '>{{name}}</span
23CD4370    3E 20 28 40 7B 7B 73 63 72 65 65 6E 5F 6E 61 6D    > (@{{screen_nam
23CD4380    65 7D 7D 29 20 69 73 20 6F 6E 20 54 77 69 74 74    e}}) is on Twitt
23CD4390    65 72 22 2C 22 63 6F 6E 6E 65 63 74 5F 72 65 74    er","connect_ret
23CD43A0    77 65 65 74 65 64 5F 62 79 5F 6D 61 6E 79 22 3A    weeted_by_many":
23CD43B0    22 3C 73 70 61 6E 20 63 6C 61 73 73 3D 27 68 69    "<span class='hi
23CD43C0    67 68 6C 69 67 68 74 27 3E 7B 7B 6E 61 6D 65 7D    ghlight'>{{name}
23CD43D0    7D 3C 2F 73 70 61 6E 3E 20 61 6E 64 20 3C 73 70    }</span> and <sp
23CD43E0    61 6E 20 63 6C 61 73 73 3D 27 68 69 67 68 6C 69    an class='highli
23CD43F0    67 68 74 27 3E 7B 7B 6E 75 6D 62 65 72 7D 7D 20    ght'>{{number}}
```

FIG. 2   Application keyword found after installation in phone image.

```
9D3573F0    00 00 00 00 00 00 00 00 00 00 00 00 00 00 00 00    ................
9D357400    00 01 00 13 00 00 00 00 00 00 00 01 55 4B DE 1C    ............UKÞ.
9D357410    55 4B DE 1D FF FF FF FF 00 00 00 00 00 00 00 25    UKÞ.ÿÿÿÿ........%
9D357420    00 00 15 9D 48 54 54 50 7E 31 30 31 38 7E 31 3A    ....HTTP~1018~1:
9D357430    68 74 74 70 73 3A 2F 2F 77 77 77 2E 74 77 69 74    https://www.twit
9D357440    74 65 72 2E 63 6F 6D 2F 00 72 65 71 75 65 73 74    ter.com/.request
9D357450    2D 6D 65 74 68 6F 64 00 47 45 54 00 72 65 73 70    -method.GET.resp
9D357460    6F 6E 73 65 2D 68 65 61 64 00 48 54 54 50 2F 31    onse-head.HTTP/1
9D357470    2E 31 20 33 30 31 20 4D 6F 76 65 64 20 50 65 72    .1 301 Moved Per
9D357480    6D 61 6E 65 6E 74 6C 79 0D 0A 43 6F 6E 74 65 6E    manently..Conten
9D357490    74 2D 4C 65 6E 67 74 68 3A 20 30 0D 0A 44 61 74    t-Length: 0..Dat
9D3574A0    65 3A 20 54 68 75 2C 20 30 37 20 4D 61 79 20 32    e: Thu, 07 May 2
9D3574B0    30 31 35 20 32 31 3A 31 35 3A 35 31 20 47 4D 54    015 21:15:51 GMT
9D3574C0    0D 0A 4C 6F 63 61 74 69 6F 6E 3A 20 68 74 74 70    ..Location: http
9D3574D0    73 3A 2F 2F 74 77 69 74 74 65 72 2E 63 6F 6D 2F    s://twitter.com/
```

FIG. 3   URL for social media mobile web found in phone image.

One of the most valuable pieces of information that we need to protect in social media are the account credentials. In the event that a person's account credentials fall into wrong hands, a stranger can definitely log into our account and pretend to be us. When that person commits any crime using our account, the prosecution will be charged under our name. The next search was to find the username and password that we used during our login process. The username rules were different between social media. Facebook and Google+ only accept email as username, while twitter can accept either email or a selected string. Fig. 5 shows how the Twitter username appeared in our search.

Activities and communication in social media have contributed to the massive amount of valuable information in forensic investigations. From the communication pattern, we might

```
61FBE340   30 61 62 34 32 39 62 30 66 32 62 37 66 34 39 39    0ab429b0f2b7f499
61FBE350   38 66 26 6F 65 3D 35 35 43 33 44 32 44 34 26 5F    8f&oe=55C3D2D4&_
61FBE360   5F 67 64 61 5F 5F 3D 31 34 33 38 39 36 34 32 35    _gda__=143896425
61FBE370   38 5F 37 38 38 66 66 32 65 66 36 35 39 63 36 65    8_788ff2ef659c6e
61FBE380   30 66 66 38 38 33 39 37 38 32 32 38 65 66 63 35    0ff883978228efc5
61FBE390   30 65 22 2C 22 74 65 78 74 22 3A 22 52 6F 6F 74    0e","text":"Root
61FBE3A0   20 57 61 64 69 22 2C 22 75 69 64 22 3A 31 30 30     Wadi","uid":100
61FBE3B0   30 30 35 36 37 36 36 30 38 37 30 35 2C 22 70 61    005676608705,"pa
61FBE3C0   74 68 73 22 3A 5B 5D 2C 22 62 6F 6F 74 73 74 72    ths":[],"bootstr
61FBE3D0   61 70 22 3A 31 7D 2C 7B 22 70 61 74 68 22 3A 22    ap":1},{"path":"
61FBE3E0   2F 70 72 6F 66 69 6C 65 2E 70 68 70 3F 69 64 3D    /profile.php?id=
61FBE3F0   37 31 32 31 36 39 30 34 33 22 2C 22 70 68 6F 74    712169043","phot
61FBE400   6F 22 3A 22 68 74 74 70 73 3A 2F 2F 66 62 63 64    o":"https://fbcd
61FBE410   6E 2D 70 72 6F 66 69 6C 65 2D 61 2E 61 6B 61 6D    n-profile-a.akam
```

FIG. 4   Facebook profile name appear in phone image.

```
23DCDC60   22 66 6F 6C 6C 6F 77 65 64 5F 62 79 22 3A 66 61    "followed_by":fa
23DCDC70   6C 73 65 7D 2C 22 74 6F 6B 65 6E 73 22 3A 5B 7B    lse},"tokens":[{
23DCDC80   22 74 6F 6B 65 6E 22 3A 22 6D 6F 68 64 22 7D 2C    "token":"mohd"},
23DCDC90   7B 22 74 6F 6B 65 6E 22 3A 22 6E 61 6A 77 61 64    {"token":"najwad
23DCDCA0   69 22 7D 2C 7B 22 74 6F 6B 65 6E 22 3A 22 77 61    i"},{"token":"wa
23DCDCB0   64 69 65 71 22 7D 2C 7B 22 74 6F 6B 65 6E 22 3A    dieq"},{"token":
23DCDCC0   22 40 77 61 64 69 65 71 22 7D 5D 2C 22 69 6E 6C    "@wadieq"}],"inl
23DCDCD0   69 6E 65 22 3A 66 61 6C 73 65 2C 22 66 6F 6C 6C    ine":false,"foll
23DCDCE0   6F 77 65 64 5F 62 79 22 3A 66 61 6C 73 65 7D 5D    owed_by":false}]
23DCDCF0   7D 7D 2C 22 74 6F 70 69 63 73 54 79 70 65 61 68    }},"topicsTypeah
23DCDD00   65 61 64 22 3A 7B 22 75 70 64 61 74 65 64 41 74    ead":{"updatedAt
23DCDD10   22 3A 31 34 33 31 30 33 33 36 32 38 32 33 39 2C    ":1431033628239,
23DCDD20   22 64 61 74 61 22 3A 7B 22 61 70 69 22 3A 22 74    "data":{"api":"t
23DCDD30   6F 70 69 63 73 54 79 70 65 61 68 65 61 64 22 2C    opicsTypeahead",
```

FIG. 5   Username in Twitter phone image.

be able to identify the occurrence of cyber bullying as well as cyber stalking. We also can also investigate if any sexual harassment had occurred. In the next search we were trying to find activities that can be recovered in our experiment. We purposely used a certain communication string in Malaysian language so that the search will not be redundant with common word like "hello" and "hi" in the images. Fig. 6 below shows the communication string that we use earlier in a Twitter experiment, appearing in the search result.

The search process was executed by using prepared detail steps with the phone images accordingly. If the information was able to be found and recovered, we marked it as right. After all searches had been executed and completed, the findings were recorded as shown in Table 7.

```
23E30660  33 36 36 31 36 34 38 33 31 34 33 32 37 30 34 22   366164831432704"
23E30670  2C 22 69 64 5F 73 74 72 22 3A 22 35 39 36 33 36   ,"id_str":"59636
23E30680  36 31 36 34 38 33 31 34 33 32 37 30 34 22 2C 22   6164831432704","
23E30690  74 65 78 74 22 3A 22 3C 64 69 76 20 63 6C 61 73   text":"<div clas
23E306A0  73 3D 5C 22 64 69 72 2D 6C 74 72 5C 22 20 64 69   s=\"dir-ltr\" di
23E306B0  72 3D 5C 22 6C 74 72 5C 22 3E 54 61 6D 61 6E 20   r=\"ltr\">Taman
23E306C0  74 65 70 69 20 72 75 6D 61 68 20 40 20 41 6C 65   tepi rumah @ Ale
23E306D0  78 61 6E 64 72 61 20 50 61 72 6B 2C 20 4D 61 6E   xandra Park, Man
23E306E0  63 68 65 73 74 65 72 20 3C 61 20 68 72 65 66 3D   chester <a href=
23E306F0  5C 22 68 74 74 70 73 3A 2F 2F 74 2E 63 6F 2F 69   \"https://t.co/i
23E30700  64 5A 75 34 32 56 70 6B 4B 5C 22 20 63 6C 61 73   dZu42VpkK\" clas
23E30710  73 3D 5C 22 74 77 69 74 74 65 72 2D 74 69 6D 65   s=\"twitter-time
23E30720  6C 69 6E 65 2D 6C 69 6E 6B 20 61 63 74 69 76 65   line-link active
23E30730  4C 69 6E 6B 20 64 69 72 2D 6C 74 72 5C 22 20 64   Link dir-ltr\" d
```

FIG. 6   Communication string that able to recover from phone image.

TABLE 7   Social Media Phone Image Finding Summary

Evidences	Facebook Application	Facebook Web	Twitter Application	Twitter Web	Google+ Web
Application keyword	✓	N/A	✓	N/A	N/A
Web URL	N/A	✓	N/A	✓	✓
Name after login	✓	✓	✓	✓	✗
Username after login	✗	✗	✓	✓	✗
Password after login	✗	✗	✗	✗	✗
Activities	✗	✗	✓	✓	✗
Uninstalled data remnant	✓	N/A	✓	N/A	N/A

In general, all application keywords appeared in the search once we successfully installed the application. These results show that there were changes in the application list once it was installed. The same search result happened to the web URL keywords. Once we visited the web, the keywords were stored in the browsing history, including date and time stamp. When we logged into the selected social media, all profile names were recorded in the phone except Google+ mobile web. As for social media username, only the Twitter application and Twitter mobile web were able to be retrieved. Not all social media allows for the retrieval of passwords. By the same token, the communications and activities only appear in the Twitter application and Twitter mobile web. No activities can be seen in Facebook and Google+. Data remnants were able to be retrieved from both Facebook and the Twitter application.

4.1.2 Social Media Phone and Memory Images

The analysis of the memory images were the same with the previous analysis. We performed the keyword search by using a prepared detail steps. The searches were repeated but confined to only the value that does not appear in our first search using phone images. Each of the memory images were also opened using AccessData FTK and HxD Hex Editor. For this analysis, we focused more on social media credentials and communication activities because most of this part was not recovered from the phone images analysis. Fig. 7 shows Facebook credentials that we used to login appearing in our first search attempt.

```
02178E30  00 00 00 00 82 FF FF FF 00 00 00 00 82 FF FF FF   ....‚ÿÿÿ....‚ÿÿ
02178E40  00 00 00 00 82 FF FF FF 00 00 00 00 87 FF FF FF   ....‚ÿÿÿ....‡ÿÿ
02178E50  58 03 1C 0C 80 36 16 0E 00 00 00 00 70 DE 1E 0E   X...€6......pÞ..
02178E60  06 00 00 00 37 00 00 00 B0 5F A5 0F 00 00 00 00   ....7...°_¥....
02178E70  6D 6F 68 64 2E 6E 61 6A 77 61 64 69 40 67 6D 61   mohd.najwadi@gma
02178E80  69 6C 2E 63 6F 6D 00 6D 6F 68 64 2E 6E 61 6A 77   il.com.mohd.najw
02178E90  61 64 69 40 67 6D 61 69 6C 2E 63 6F 6D 00 6E 61   adi@gmail.com.na
02178EA0  6A 77 61 64 69 38 39 FF 00 00 00 00 82 FF FF FF   jwadi89ÿ....‚ÿÿÿ
02178EB0  00 00 00 00 82 FF FF FF 00 00 00 00 82 FF FF FF   ....‚ÿÿÿ....‚ÿÿÿ
02178EC0  00 00 00 00 82 FF FF FF 00 00 00 00 82 FF FF FF   ....‚ÿÿÿ....‚ÿÿÿ
02178ED0  00 00 00 00 82 FF FF FF 00 00 00 00 87 FF FF FF   ....‚ÿÿÿ....‡ÿÿÿ
02178EE0  58 03 1C 0C 80 36 16 0E 00 00 00 00 DF 1E 0E   X...€6......ß..
02178EF0  0B 00 00 00 59 00 00 00 10 70 A5 0F 00 00 00 00   ....Y....p¥.....
02178F00  41 55 54 48 20 50 4C 41 49 4E 20 62 57 39 6F 5A   AUTH PLAIN bW9oZ
```

FIG. 7 Facebook credential found without encrypted in memory image.

The search was continued with other social media credentials and communication activities. The summary in Table 8 shows the result of what evidence can be retrieved from both phone images and memory images.

TABLE 8 Social Media Phone Images and Memory Images Finding Summary

Evidences	Facebook Application	Facebook Web	Twitter Application	Twitter Web	Google+ Web
Keyword after install	✓	N/A	✓	N/A	N/A
Web URL	N/A	✓	N/A	✓	✓
Name after login	✓	✓	✓	✓	✓
Username after login	✓	✓	✓	✓	✗
Password after login	✓	✓	✓	✓	✗
Activities	✗	✗	✓	✓	✗
Uninstalled data remnant	✓	N/A	✓	N/A	N/A

The finding of this analysis has shown that some credentials, especially the password, are unable to be seen in phone images, but we were able to retrieve them in memory images except for the Google+. As for the communication activities, we still did not find any keyword matching in Facebook and Google+. We then randomly checked with Facebook and Google+ memory images to find any communication occurrence other than what we recorded, but failed to find any. The result of the study was suggesting that the communication activities in Facebook and Google+ for FxOS were either encrypted or stored in their respective server only.

4.2 Instant Messaging Investigation

For instant messaging experiments and investigations, we have managed to acquire three instant messaging applications and one instant messaging mobile web activity. First we explored the residual artifacts generated by the application and URL involved for mobile web. Second we tried to find the user phone number used during registration. Third we tried to get the registration code and SMS or call verification received. Fourth we traced back what activities that has been captured in the images. Lastly we checked for data remnants after we completed the uninstallation the application.

4.2.1 Instant Messaging Phone Image

Like the previous experiment, each of the phone images was opened using AccessData Forensic Toolkit (FTK) version 3.1.2 and HxD Hex Editor 1.7.7.0. The analysis was also conducted by manually searching several keywords related to the previous experiment in a forensically sounds manner. The first binary search performed was the application keyword. This search was executed once the selected application successfully installed from Mozilla Market Place. Because our factory setting base image only comes with the preinstalled application and none of it was used in our investigation, we cannot find any keywords of selected instant messaging from the base image. Fig. 8 shows Telegram keywords appear when we executed the first search.

```
24101620   7C A2 35 C7 81 2D C0 FC 9F C6 21 41 1C 5F A9 0D   |¢5Ç.-ÀùÝÆ!A._©.
24101630   EB 4F BE B6 01 F2 7F 3C 3F 4F 32 14 01 B8 76 0E   ëO¾¶.ò.<?O2..,v.
24101640   4B 94 FD 03 87 CB 18 07 52 FF 71 3E 0F B7 28 F8   K"ý.‡Ë..Rÿq>.·(ø
24101650   84 56 73 20 22 7F C7 81 1F D8 4B C3 9C 7F 10 27   „Vs ".Ç..ØKÃœ..'
24101660   D8 D5 1B FC 0F AE 91 FF 00 50 4B 03 04 14 00 00   ØÕ.ü.®'ÿ.PK.....
24101670   00 08 00 29 8C 4D 46 ED 78 7C 96 43 04 00 00 7B   ...)ŒMFíx|–C...{
24101680   05 00 00 10 00 18 00 00 69 6D 67 2F 54 65 6C 65   ........img/Tele
24101690   72 61 6D 2E 70 6E 67 55 54 05 00 03 2E 0B DE 54   ram.pngUT.....ÞT
241016A0   75 78 0B 00 01 04 F6 01 00 00 04 14 00 00 00 EB   ux....ö........ë
241016B0   0C F0 73 E7 E5 92 E2 62 60 60 E0 F5 F4 70 09 02   .ðsçå'âb``àõôp..
241016C0   D2 F6 40 2C C0 C1 06 24 17 2E 5D 6E 03 A4 24 4B   Òö@,ÀÁ.$.]n.¤$K
241016D0   5C 23 4A 82 F3 D3 4A CA 13 8B 52 19 1C 53 F2 93   \#J‚óÓJÊ.‹R..Sò"
241016E0   52 15 3C 73 13 D3 53 83 52 13 53 2A 0B 4F A6 02   R.<s.ÓSƒR.S*.O¦.
241016F0   15 31 2B 65 86 44 94 44 F8 FA 58 25 E7 E7 EA 25   .1+e†D"DøúX%ççê%
```

FIG. 8   Application keyword found after installation in phone memory.

The second search was executed to find the URL for the instant messaging mobile web. In this experiment only Telegram was tested for the mobile web. The mobile web is totally different with the application. We did not have to install it, instead we only needed to browse using the preinstalled Firefox browser. Fig. 9 shows the Telegram URL was found in the images and the result also shows the visited date and time.

```
9CB253D0  00 00 00 00 00 00 00 00 00 00 00 00 00 00 00 00  ................
9CB253E0  00 00 00 00 00 00 00 00 00 00 00 00 00 00 00 00  ................
9CB253F0  00 00 00 00 00 00 00 00 00 00 00 00 00 00 00 00  ................
9CB25400  00 01 00 13 B1 00 00 35 00 00 00 03 55 4D 16 68  ....±..5....UM.h
9CB25410  55 4D 16 69 55 4D 1C 5C 00 00 02 7D 00 00 00 26  UM.iUM.\...}...&
9CB25420  00 00 10 90 48 54 54 50 7E 31 30 31 38 7E 31 3A  ....HTTP~1018~1:
9CB25430  68 74 74 70 73 3A 2F 2F 77 65 62 2E 74 65 6C 65  https://web.tele
9CB25440  67 72 61 6D 2E 6F 72 67 2F 00 72 65 71 75 65 73  gram.org/.reques
9CB25450  74 2D 6D 65 74 68 6F 64 00 47 45 54 00 72 65 73  t-method.GET.res
9CB25460  70 6F 6E 73 65 2D 68 65 61 64 00 48 54 54 50 2F  ponse-head.HTTP/
9CB25470  31 2E 31 20 32 30 30 20 4F 4B 0D 0A 53 65 72 76  1.1 200 OK..Serv
9CB25480  65 72 3A 20 6E 67 69 6E 78 2F 31 2E 36 2E 32 0D  er: nginx/1.6.2.
9CB25490  0A 44 61 74 65 3A 20 46 72 69 2C 20 30 38 20 4D  .Date: Fri, 08 M
9CB254A0  61 79 20 32 30 31 35 20 31 39 3A 32 38 3A 31 32  ay 2015 19:28:12
9CB254B0  20 47 4D 54 0D 0A 43 6F 6E 74 65 6E 74 2D 54 79  GMT..Content-Ty
```

FIG. 9   URL for instant messaging mobile Web found in phone image.

The third search was conducted to find the phone numbers used during registration. Most of our selected instant messaging services asked the phone number to be tied with account registration. Instant messaging services like Telegram and WhatsApp will display the phone number together with selected name when we send private message to other user, while Line will not display any number but only the selected name. The confirmation during registration was either a code from the SMS or a received call from the providers. Figs. 10 and 11 shows the phone number and registration code for WhatsApp services, respectively.

```
A59787E0  00 00 00 00 00 00 00 00 00 00 00 00 00 00 00 00  ................
A59787F0  00 00 00 00 00 00 00 00 00 00 00 00 00 00 00 00  ................
A5978800  7B 22 73 74 61 74 75 73 22 3A 22 6F 6B 22 2C 22  {"status":"ok","
A5978810  6C 6F 67 69 6E 22 3A 22 36 30 31 36 32 34 34 34  login":"60162444
A5978820  34 31 35 22 2C 22 70 77 22 3A 22 4E 43 69 30 66  415","pw":"NCi0f
A5978830  45 50 6F 51 43 69 37 59 55 50 65 63 53 64 30 63  EPoQCi7YUPecSd0c
A5978840  61 38 71 5A 51 41 3D 22 2C 22 74 79 70 65 22 3A  a8qZQA=","type":
A5978850  22 65 78 69 73 74 69 6E 67 22 2C 22 65 78 70 69  "existing","expi
A5978860  72 61 74 69 6F 6E 22 3A 31 34 36 32 36 30 37 39  ration":14626079
A5978870  39 36 2C 22 6B 69 6E 64 22 3A 22 66 72 65 65 22  96,"kind":"free"
A5978880  2C 22 70 72 69 63 65 22 3A 22 55 53 24 30 2E 39  ,"price":"US$0.9
A5978890  39 22 2C 22 63 6F 73 74 22 3A 22 30 2E 39 39 22  9","cost":"0.99"
A59788A0  2C 22 63 75 72 72 65 6E 63 79 22 3A 22 55 53 44  ,"currency":"USD
A59788B0  22 2C 22 70 72 69 63 65 5F 65 78 70 69 72 61 74  ","price_expirat
A59788C0  69 6F 6E 22 3A 31 34 33 33 37 39 38 31 39 31 7D  ion":1433798191}
```

FIG. 10   Phone number used during registration found in phone memory.

```
9CBC1420   00 00 10 3C 48 54 54 50 7E 31 30 32 31 7E 30 3A   ...<HTTP~1021~0:
9CBC1430   68 74 74 70 73 3A 2F 2F 76 2E 77 68 61 74 73 61   https://v.whatsa
9CBC1440   70 70 2E 6E 65 74 2F 76 32 2F 72 65 67 69 73 74   pp.net/v2/regist
9CBC1450   65 72 3F 63 63 3D 36 30 26 69 6E 3D 31 36 32 34   er?cc=60&in=1624
9CBC1460   34 34 34 31 35 26 63 6F 64 65 3D 35 36 30 31 30   44415&code=56010
9CBC1470   33 26 69 64 3D 25 42 44 25 41 45 25 32 31 25 46   3&id=%BD%AE%21%F
9CBC1480   39 25 44 31 25 45 41 25 36 44 25 36 32 25 35 38   9%D1%EA%6D%62%58
9CBC1490   25 46 35 25 45 41 25 34 42 25 38 31 25 36 33 25   %F5%EA%4B%81%63%
9CBC14A0   45 33 25 36 39 25 39 46 25 44 43 25 45 37 25 34   E3%69%9F%DC%E7%4
9CBC14B0   38 00 72 65 71 75 65 73 74 2D 6D 65 74 68 6F 64   8.request-method
9CBC14C0   00 47 45 54 00 72 65 73 70 6F 6E 73 65 2D 68 65   .GET.response-he
9CBC14D0   61 64 00 48 54 54 50 2F 31 2E 31 20 32 30 30 20   ad.HTTP/1.1 200
9CBC14E0   4F 4B 0D 0A 53 65 72 76 65 72 3A 20 59 61 77 73   OK..Server: Yaws
9CBC14F0   20 31 2E 39 38 0D 0A 44 61 74 65 3A 20 46 72 69   1.98..Date: Fri
9CBC1500   2C 20 30 38 20 4D 61 79 20 32 30 31 35 20 32 32   , 08 May 2015 22
```

FIG. 11   Registration code received during account confirmation found in phone memory.

The search process was executed by using prepared detailed steps with the phone images accordingly. If the information was able to be found and recovered, we marked it as right. After all searches has been executed and completed, the findings were recorded as shown in Table 9.

TABLE 9   Instant Messaging Phone Image Finding Summary

Evidences	Telegram Application	Telegram Web	OpenWapp Application	Line Application
Keyword after install	✓	N/A	✓	✓
Web URL	N/A	✓	N/A	N/A
Number after register	✗	✗	✓	✗
Registration code	✓	✓	✓	✓
SMS/Call verification	✓	✓	✓	✓
Activities	✗	✗	✗	✗
Uninstalled data remnant	✓	N/A	✓	✓

In general, all application keywords will appear in the search once we have successfully installed the application. These results show that there were changes in the application list once it was installed. The same search result happened to web URL keyword. Once we visited the web, the keywords were stored in the browsing history, including date and time stamp. We try to find the phone number we were using during registration but we only managed to find it in OpenWapp phone images. However, all registration codes, SMS as well as call verification, were managed to be found in all instant messaging phone images. On the contrary, no communication activities were managed to be traced in this analysis. Data remnants were able to be retrieved from both Facebook and Twitter application.

4.2.2 Instant Messaging Phone and Memory Images

An analysis of the memory images was the same as with the previous analysis. We also performed the keyword search using a prepared detailed steps. The search was repeated, but confined to the value that does not appear in our first search using phone images. Each of the memory images were also opened using AccessData Forensic Toolkit (FTK) version 3.1.2 and HxD Hex Editor 1.7.7.0. For this analysis, we focused more on registration number and instant messaging communication activities, because most of these parts were not recovered from the phone images analysis. Fig. 12 shows the OpenWapp communication string that we used during this experiment.

```
9CBC1690   76 4C 32 4E 6C 63 6E 52 70 5A 6D 6C 6A 59 58 52   vL2NlcnRpZmljjYXR
9CBC16A0   6C 63 79 35 6E 62 32 52 68 5A 47 52 35 4C 6D 4E   lcy5nb2RhZGR5LmN
9CBC16B0   76 62 53 39 79 5A 58 42 76 63 32 6C 30 62 33 4A   vbS9yZXBvc2l0b3J
9CBC16C0   35 4D 54 41 77 4C 67 59 44 56 51 51 44 45 79 64   5MTAwLgYDVQQDEyd
9CBC16D0   48 62 79 42 45 59 57 52 6B 65 53 42 54 5A 57 4E   HbyBEYWRkeSBTZWN
9CBC16E0   31 63 6D 55 67 51 32 56 79 64 47 6C 6D 61 57 4E   1cmUgQ2VydGlmaWN
9CBC16F0   68 64 54 65 73 74 69 6E 67 20 6F 70 65 6E 77 61   hdTesting openwa
9CBC1700   70 70 20 66 72 6F 6D 20 46 69 72 65 66 6F 78 20   pp from Firefox
9CBC1710   70 68 6F 6E 65 4D 6A 67 33 4D 42 34 58 44 54 45   phoneMjg3MB4XDTE
9CBC1720   30 4D 44 55 77 4D 54 49 77 4E 44 67 77 4E 56 6F   0MDUwMTIwNDgwNVo
9CBC1730   58 44 54 45 31 4D 54 49 7A 4D 54 45 77 4D 54 45   XDTE1MTIzMTEwMTE
9CBC1740   77 4D 6C 6F 77 50 44 45 68 4D 42 38 47 41 31 55   wMlowPDEhMB8GA1U
9CBC1750   45 43 78 4D 59 52 47 39 74 59 57 6C 75 49 45 4E   ECxMYRG9tYWluIEN
9CBC1760   76 62 6E 52 79 62 32 77 67 56 6D 46 73 61 57 52   vbnRyb2wgVmFsaWR
```

FIG. 12   OpenWapp communication string found in memory image.

The search was continued with other instant messaging communication activities and the phone number used in Telegram and Line. The summary in Table 10 shows the result of what evidence can be retrieved from both phone images and memory images.

TABLE 10   Instant Messaging Phone Images and Memory Images Finding Summary

Evidences	Telegram Application	Telegram Web	OpenWapp Application	Line Application
Keyword after install	✓	N/A	✓	✓
Web URL	N/A	✓	N/A	N/A
Number after register	✓	✓	✓	✓
Registration code	✓	✓	✓	✓
SMS/Call verification	✓	✓	✓	✓
Activities	✗	✗	✓	✗
Uninstalled data remnant	✓	N/A	✓	✓

The findings of this analysis has shown that all registration phone numbers that were not able to be seen in phone images were able to be traced in memory images. As for the communication activities, we have only managed to find the communication string in OpenWapp and still did not find any keywords matching in Telegram and Line. A random check of the Telegram and Line memory images was conducted to find any communication occurrence other than what we recorded, but it also failed to find any. The result of the studies suggest that the communication activities in Telegram and Line for FxOS were either encrypted or stored in their respective server only.

5 CONCLUSION

In this research, we have successfully acquired 24 forensic images, each from FxOS internal phone and volatile memory. The acquired images were then extracted based on the action performed as per documented in detailed steps, and were named accordingly. These images were then analyzed and the results were presented and tabled. The result of this research has indicated that most of valuable forensic information resides in volatile memory. The findings of this study also suggested that memory in the FxOS phone was not encrypted, hence it was readable with our forensic tools. Therefore we managed to recover and trace social media account credentials, especially on Facebook and Twitter services. On the contrary, all untraced information in phone images, such as profile names on Google+ and phone numbers used during registration for Telegram and Line, were traceable in memory images.

The other conclusion drawn from this research is that the FxOS applications behave the same way as their counterparts in mobile web. Therefore we managed to get the exact same forensic traces and evidences when we analyzed the same services, both in application and mobile web platforms. For example, Facebook, Twitter, and Telegram applications produce the same forensic trace with its mobile web. In short, these findings have significantly enhanced our understanding of the similarity of the FxOS application design, based on WebAPI, with its mobile web platforms. By using WebAPI, the FxOS application can be executed under very minimal memory requirements, just like opening the web browser.

On the other hand, the analysis of the acquired images has shown that application artifacts remained in the FxOS device after it has been uninstalled. The data remnant and leftovers from the application folders and browser history will be value added to the investigation and much more information has been successfully retrieved. Further, the findings from this research have also made several contributions to the current set of mobile forensic investigation standards. It is recommended that further research to be undertaken with more broad applications and mobile web platforms. More forensic investigation of the FxOS application would help us to establish a greater degree of accuracy in this study.

References

[1] S. Mohtasebi, A. Dehghantanha, Defusing the hazards of social network services, Int. J. Digit. Inf. Wirel. Commun. 1 (2011) 504–516.

[2] S. Mohtasebi, A. Dehghantanha, A mitigation approach to the privacy and malware threats of social network services, in: Digital Information Processing and Communications, Communications in Computer and Information Science, vol. 189, Springer, Berlin, Heidelberg, 2011, pp. 448–459, http://dx.doi.org/10.1007/978-3-642-22410-2_39.

[3] F.N. Dezfouli, A. Dehghantanha, B. Eterovic-Soric, K.-K.R. Choo, Investigating social networking applications on smartphones detecting Facebook, Twitter, LinkedIn and Google+ artefacts on Android and iOS platforms, Aust. J. Forensic Sci. 46(4) (2016) 469–488, http://dx.doi.org/10.1080/00450618.2015.1066854.

[4] M. Taylor, G. Hughes, J. Haggerty, D. Gresty, P. Almond, Digital evidence from mobile telephone applications, Comput. Law Secur. Rev. 28 (2012) 335–339, http://dx.doi.org/10.1016/j.clsr.2012.03.006.

[5] F.N. Dezfouli, A. Dehghantanha, R. Mahmod, N.F. Mohd Sani, S. Shamsuddin, A data-centric model for smartphone security, Int. J. Adv. Comput. Technol. 5 (2013) 9–17, http://dx.doi.org/10.4156/ijact.vol5.issue9.2.

[6] M. Damshenas, A. Dehghantanha, R. Mahmoud, A survey on digital forensics trends, Int. J. Cyber Secur. Digit. Forensic. 3 (2014) 1–26.

[7] S. Mohtasebi, A. Dehghantanha, Towards a unified forensic investigation framework of smartphones, Int. J. Comput. Theory Eng. 5 (2013) 351–355, http://dx.doi.org/10.7763/IJCTE.2013.V5.708.

[8] S. Mohtasebi, A. Dehghantanha, H.G. Broujerdi, Smartphone forensics: a case study with Nokia E5-00 mobile phone, Int. J. Digit. Inf. Wirel. Commun. 1 (2012) 651–655.

[9] T.Y. Yang, A. Dehghantanha, K.-K.R. Choo, Z. Muda, Windows instant messaging app forensics: Facebook and Skype as case studies, PLoS ONE 11 (2016), e0150300. http://dx.doi.org/10.1371/journal.pone.0150300.

[10] S. Chen, X. Hao, M. Luo, Research of mobile forensic software system based on Windows mobile, in: 2009 International Conference on Wireless Networks and Information Systems, IEEE, 2009, pp. 366–369. http://dx.doi.org/10.1109/WNIS.2009.32.

[11] D. Irwin, R. Hunt, Forensic information acquisition in mobile networks, in: 2009 IEEE Pacific Rim Conference on Communications, Computers and Signal Processing, IEEE, 2009, pp. 163–168. http://dx.doi.org/10.1109/PACRIM.2009.5291378.

[12] I. Pooters, Full user data acquisition from Symbian smart phones, Digit. Investig. 6 (2010) 125–135, http://dx.doi.org/10.1016/j.diin.2010.01.001.

[13] J. Lessard, G.C. Kessler, Android forensics: simplifying cell phone examinations, Small Scale Digit. Device Forensic J. 4 (2010) 1–12.

[14] Accessdata, Forensic Toolkit (FTK), 2007.

[15] L. Gómez-Miralles, J. Arnedo-Moreno, Versatile iPad forensic acquisition using the Apple Camera Connection Kit, Comput. Math. Appl. 63 (2012) 544–553, http://dx.doi.org/10.1016/j.camwa.2011.09.053.

[16] B. Iqbal, A. Iqbal, H.A. Obaidli, A novel method of iDevice (iPhone, iPad, iPod) forensics without jailbreaking, in: 2012 International Conference on Innovations in Information Technology (IIT), IEEE, 2012, pp. 238–243. http://dx.doi.org/10.1109/INNOVATIONS.2012.6207740.

[17] J. Sylve, A. Case, L. Marziale, G.G. Richard, Acquisition and analysis of volatile memory from android devices, Digit. Investig. 8 (2012) 175–184, http://dx.doi.org/10.1016/j.diin.2011.10.003.

[18] M.I. Husain, R. Sridhar, iForensics: forensic analysis of instant messaging on smart phones, in: S. Goel (Ed.), Digital Forensics and Cyber Crime, Lecture Notes of the Institute for Computer Sciences, Social Informatics and Telecommunications Engineering, vol. 31, Springer, Berlin, 2010, pp. 9–18. http://dx.doi.org/10.1007/978-3-642-11534-9_2.

[19] J. Jung, C. Jeong, K. Byun, S. Lee, Sensitive privacy data acquisition in the iPhone for digital forensic analysis, in: J.J. Park, J. Lopez, S.-S. Yeo, T. Shon, D. Taniar (Eds.), Secure and Trust Computing, Data Management and Applications, Communications in Computer and Information Science, vol. 186, Springer, Berlin, 2011, pp. 172–186. http://dx.doi.org/10.1007/978-3-642-22339-6_21.

[20] Y.-C. Tso, S.-J. Wang, C.-T. Huang, W.-J. Wang, iPhone social networking for evidence investigations using iTunes forensics, in: Proceedings of the 6th International Conference on Ubiquitous Information Management and Communication—ICUIMC'12, ACM Press, New York, NY, 2012, pp. 1. http://dx.doi.org/10.1145/2184751.2184827.

[21] C. Anglano, Forensic analysis of WhatsApp Messenger on Android smartphones, Digit. Investig. 11 (2014) 1–13, http://dx.doi.org/10.1016/j.diin.2014.04.003.

[22] F. Karpisek, I. Baggili, F. Breitinger, WhatsApp network forensics: decrypting and understanding the WhatsApp call signaling messages, Digit. Investig. 1–9 (2015), http://dx.doi.org/10.1016/j.diin.2015.09.002.

[23] D. Walnycky, I. Baggili, A. Marrington, J. Moore, F. Breitinger, Network and device forensic analysis of Android social-messaging applications, Digit. Investig. 14 (2015) S77–S84, http://dx.doi.org/10.1016/j.diin.2015.05.009.

[24] H. Said, A. Yousif, H. Humaid, IPhone forensics techniques and crime investigation, in: The 2011 International Conference and Workshop on Current Trends in Information Technology (CTIT 11), IEEE, 2011, pp. 120–125. http://dx.doi.org/10.1109/CTIT.2011.6107946.

[25] N. Al Mutawa, I. Baggili, A. Marrington, Forensic analysis of social networking applications on mobile devices, Digit. Investig. 9 (2012) S24–S33, http://dx.doi.org/10.1016/j.diin.2012.05.007.

[26] A. Iqbal, A. Marrington, I. Baggili, Forensic artifacts of the ChatON instant messaging application, in: International Workshop on Systematic Approaches to Digital Forensic Engineering, SADFE, 2014. http://dx.doi.org/10.1109/SADFE.2013.6911538.

[27] Geeksphone, Geeksphone Peak, http://www.geeksphone.com/other-devices-2/, 2013.

[28] M.N. Yusoff, R. Mahmod, M.T. Abdullah, A. Dehghantanha, Mobile forensic data acquisition in Firefox OS, in: The Third International Conference on Cyber Security, Cyber Warfare, and Digital Forensic (CyberSec2014), 2014, pp. 27–31.

[29] M.N. Yusoff, R. Mahmod, M.T. Abdullah, A. Dehghantanha, Performance measurement for mobile forensic data acquisition in Firefox OS, Int. J. Cyber Secur. Digit. Forensic. 3 (2014) 130–140.

[30] M.N. Yusoff, R. Mahmod, A. Dehghantanha, M.T. Abdullah, An approach for forensic investigation in Firefox OS, in: The Third International Conference on Cyber Security, Cyber Warfare, and Digital Forensic (CyberSec2014), IEEE, 2014, pp. 22–26.

[31] M.N. Yusoff, R. Mahmod, A. Dehghantanha, M.T. Abdullah, Advances of mobile forensic procedures in Firefox OS, Int. J. Cyber Secur. Digit. Forensic 3 (2014) 141–157.

[32] M. Hörz, HxD Hex Editor, 2009.

[33] QtADB, QtADB Android Manager, http://qtadb.wordpress.com, 2011.

5

Network Traffic Forensics on Firefox Mobile OS: Facebook, Twitter, and Telegram as Case Studies

M.N. Yusoff*, A. Dehghantanha†, R. Mahmod‡

*University Science Malaysia, George Town, Malaysia †University of Salford, Salford, United Kingdom ‡Universiti Putra Malaysia, Serdang, Malaysia

1 INTRODUCTION

The significant rise of social media networking, instant messaging platform, webmail, and other mobile web applications has spawned the idea to build mobile web-centric operating systems (OS) using different open web standards like HTML5, CSS3, and JavaScript. Due to that fact, Mozilla released the world's first mobile web-centric OS on Feb. 21, 2013. This mobile web-centric OS is based on the Firefox web browser rendering engine on top of a Linux kernel, called Firefox OS (FxOS) [1]. The emergence of a mobile web-centric OS has created new challenges, concentrations, and opportunities for digital investigators. In general, the growth of mobile devices may allow cybercriminals to utilize social media and instant messaging services for malicious purposes [2] such as spreading malicious codes and obtaining and disseminating confidential information. Furthermore, copyright infringement, cyber stalking, cyber bullying, slander spreading, and sexual harassment are becoming serious threats to mobile device users [3]. Therefore it is common to be confronted with different types of mobile devices during variety of forensics investigation cases [4].

Many previous studies were focused on the detection and analysis of network traffic artifacts for cyber forensics. Quick and Choo ran Dropbox cloud storage in virtual environment machine and all network activities were recorded [5]. Network Miner 1.0 [6] and Wireshark Portable 1.6.5 [7] were used to capture the network traffic in many circumstances and network traffic was seen on transmission control protocol (TCP) port 80 and 443 only. Quick and Choo also ran Microsoft SkyDrive in a virtual environment machine using the same method [8]. The results were tabled with more information such as IP start, IP finish, URL observed in network traffic, and registered owner. No usernames nor passwords were observed in the clear text network traffic. Quick and Choo continued the research and run Google Drive cloud storage as the case study [9]. The Google Drive account credential was observed but could not be seen in the network traffic, suggesting the data was encrypted. Martini and Choo observed network traffic from the virtual environment network adapter using ownCloud as a case study [10]. HTTP Basic authentications were captured and user's ownCloud credentials were successfully displayed. Farina produced an analysis of the sequence of network traffic and file I/O interactions in the torrent synchronization process [11]. Bittorrent client were used as the test subject.

Utilizing virtual machines for generating network traffic is very common in forensics research. Blakeley investigated cloud storage software using hubiC as a case study [12]. In the network analysis part it was observed that a redirect to HTTPS on port 8080 was returned when the initial request was made to https://www.hubic.com. This shows that there was no plaintext traffic accepted by the hubiC website. Shariati ran network analysis using SugarSync cloud storage [13]. The majority of communications were encrypted and no credentials nor contents of sample datasets were able to be recovered. Dezfouli investigated Facebook, Twitter, LinkedIn, and Google+ artifacts on Android and iOS. During the experiment, network activities were captured and the user's IP address, the domain name of connected social media sites, and corresponding session timestamps were able to be determined. Yang identified network artifacts of Facebook and Skype Windows Store application [14]. Yang was able to correlate the IP addresses with the timestamp information to determine when the application was started up and the duration of the application used during the experiment. Daryabar investigated OneDrive, Box, Google Drive, and Dropbox applications on Android and iOS devices [15]. In the network analysis part the connections were secured between the cloud client application and the server, thus no credentials were able to be seen. Daryabar also investigated the MEGA cloud client application on Android and iOS [16]. Daryabar identify network artifacts arising from user activities, such as login, uploading, downloading, deletion, and file sharing including timestamps. Table 1 reflects the literature summary of network analysis and monitoring captured through virtual environment network adapter.

TABLE 1   Summary of Network Analysis and Monitoring Captured Through Virtual Environment
Network Adapter

Researcher(s)	Application(s)	Application Type
Martini and Choo [10]	OwnCloud	Cloud storage
Quick and Choo [8]	Dropbox	Cloud storage
Quick and Choo [17]	Microsoft SkyDrive	Cloud storage
Quick and Choo [9]	Google Drive	Cloud storage
Farina et al. [11]	Bittorrent	Torrent client
Blakeley et al. [12]	hubiC	Cloud storage
Shariati et al. [13]	SugarSync	Cloud storage
Dezfouli et al. [3]	Facebook, Twitter, LinkdIn, Google+	Social media
Yang et al. [14]	Facebook, Skype	Social media, VoIP
Daryabar et al.[15,16]	OneDrive, Box, Google Drive, Dropbox	Cloud storage
Daryabar et al. [15,16]	MEGA	Cloud storage

As can be seen from Table 1, there was no previous study analyzing FxOS network traffic artifacts. FxOS is designed to allow mobile devices to communicate directly with HTML5 applications using JavaScript and newly introduced WebAPI. However, the use of JavaScript in HTML5 applications with solely no OS restriction might lead to security issues and further potential exploits and threats. FxOS is still not fully supported by most of the existing mobile forensic tools, which further stresses the urgency for further research development in this area [18].

In this chapter we were focused on the analysis of residual network traffic artifacts in FxOS. Two popular social networking applications (Facebook and Twitter) and one instant messaging application (Telegram) were investigated as case studies. In the earliest days investigators used to put the mobile phone in a special sandbox to monitor mobile GSM activities [19]. However, this method requires a lot of expensive devices and thus, the phone monitoring process became more complicated and very costly. The FxOS simulator is a virtualized version of the FxOS that provides full user experience and FxOS features. Therefore we have followed the method proposed by Quick and Choo and simulated FxOS in a virtual environment machine [17]. When we performed the communication activities using the FxOS simulator, we used the Network Analyzer to capture and monitor the network traffic.

The rest of this chapter is organized as follows. In Section 2 we explain the methodology used and outlined the setup for our experiment. In Section 3 we present our research findings and finally conclude our research in Section 4.

2 EXPERIMENT SETUP

Network analysis is a procedure for investigating the movement of data that travel across the targeted network. This procedure was performed by analyzing and carving the captured network artifacts. In general, the collection of network artifact for mobile devices is very difficult because of the limitation of mobile hardware and mobile OS itself. It is in contrast with conventional desktop OS, which we can easily capture the network files using various tools available. For that reason alone, we have adapted an approach for forensic collection of cloud artifacts [8,9,17] into our research methodology. Quick and Choo analyzed several cloud applications using virtual machines and captured and analyzed network traffic activities. In this chapter we run the FxOS simulator within VMware (VM) [20], configured with two popular social networking applications (Facebook and Twitter) and one instant messaging application (Telegram); which we will perform communication tasks in different scenarios. All the network activities are then captured and analyzed using network analysis tools.

The FxOS Simulator is an add-on simulator for the Firefox browser that enables users to run FxOS on any desktop computer. It comes with the Dashboard, a tool hosted by Firefox web browser that enables users to start and stop the simulator; install and uninstall the applications; and to debug FxOS applications. The Dashboard is also used to push applications to a real device and checks application manifests for any common problems. Three applications that are two popular social networking applications (Facebook and Twitter) and one instant messaging application (Telegram) installed in the VM disk and communications activities were performed to detect and investigate residential artifacts. Separated VM disks were then created for every action taken and all the network activities were captured and monitored. Fig. 1 illustrates our experiments setup.

Capture all
network activities
using Wireshark

Firefox OS simulator running
under virtual machine

Network packet

FIG. 1   FxOS network traffic analysis methodology.

As the network analyzer captures all VM network activities, including Windows 8.1 services, we filtered out nonrelevant network data using Wireshark 1.12.5. Werepeated our investigation using Ubuntu 14.04 LTS and the network packets in both environment were complementarities. This research experiment setup was divided into four stages: (1) preparing virtual machines with selected applications; (2) executing the activities and documenting all steps taken; (3) capturing the network activities; and (4) conducting network analysis.

2.1 Preparing Virtual Machines

In this experiment we run the FxOS simulator on Windows 8.1 and Ubuntu 14.04 LTS utilizing VM Player 10.0.1. Our experiments were mainly focused on applications that regularly stimulate user communications and applications usage. We configured two popular social networking applications (Facebook and Twitter) and one instant messaging application (Telegram) as our test subjects. Several tasks were performed in different sets of scenarios and all the network activities were captured using Wireshark 1.12.5 and Microsoft Network Monitor 3.4 [21]. For the analysis part we used the Network Miner 1.6.1 to carve related network artifacts. Table 2 shows all the software and applications that were used in our experiment.

TABLE 2   Software and Applications for FxOS Network Traffic Investigation

Software or Application	Purpose
Windows 8.1	Operating system
Ubuntu 14.04 LTS	Operating system
VMware Player 10.0.1	Provides virtual environment
Wireshark 1.12.5	Capturing and monitoring network activities
Microsoft Network Monitor 3.4	Monitoring network activities
Network Miner 1.6.1	Carving and identifying evidences from network packets
Facebook	Test application (social media)
Twitter	Test application (social media)
Telegram	Test application (instant messaging)

As shown in Fig. 2, a total of 11 VMs on 11 physical systems were created for Windows and Ubuntu, respectively. Each VM disk represents a scenario in our experiment. All VM disks were configured with Windows or Ubuntu installed on 20 GB virtual hard drive and equipped with 1 GB RAM.

In general, the VMs were grouped into four groups which are Base, Facebook, Twitter, and Telegram groups. The Base VM01 consists of standard OS setup. From this point the disk was copied and the Firefox browser, as well as the FxOS simulator, were installed in VM02. The following three VMs are copies of VM02 that were configured with applications of interest (Facebook (VM03), Twitter (VM06), and Telegram (VM09)) and named accordingly. The remaining VMs were created in accordance with scenario experiments out of the first VM disks of each group.

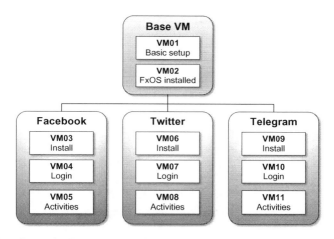

FIG. 2   Virtual machine hierarchy for network analysis investigation.

2.2 Executing Activities

Each step of the activities was documented for future reference and to support the soundness of investigation. Every scenario was performed with predefined communication activities as shown in Table 3.

To initiate logins, we created a dummy account with email and password of mohd.najwadi@gmail.com and "najwadi87," respectively. For instant messaging account, we registered the account using mobile number "+60162444415" communication with another mobile number "+60125999159."

2.3 Capturing Network Activities

The objective of this analysis was to identify the correct traffic path for several famous communication activities in mobile phone. From the packets, we need to identify what data can be seen in network traffic, what protocols were being used, who issued the certificates, and what credentials are able to be captured. In this experiment we run the FxOS simulator in the VM player. All network traffic from the FxOS simulator were captured once with Wireshark 1.12.5 and another time using Microsoft Network Monitor 3.4 as a backup capturing tool. In order to capture the network traffic from VM player, VM network adapter was set to NAT. Fig. 3 shows the network packets captured by Wireshark when we executed the communication activities using the FxOS simulator.

TABLE 3   Configuration of Virtual Machine With the Communication Activities

VM Disk	Scenario	Details
Base		
VM01	Base	Base configuration was installed with Windows 8.1 or Ubuntu 14.04 on 20 GB virtual hard drive and 1 GB Ram
VM02	Install Simulator	VM01 was copied. Firefox Browser and FxOS simulator was installed
Facebook		
VM03	Installation	VM02 was copied and Facebook application was installed
VM04	Login process	VM03 was copied and used to login with prepared social media account
VM05	Activities	VM04 was copied and performed posting, comment, like comment, reply comment, send message, add friend, and follow
Twitter		
VM06	Installation	VM02 was copied and Twitter application was installed
VM07	Login process	VM06 was copied and used to login with prepared social media account
VM08	Activities	VM07 was copied and performed tweet, reply tweet, favorite tweet, retweet, use hashtag, follow, and unfollow
Telegram		
VM09	Installation	VM02 was copied and Telegram application was installed
VM10	Registration	VM09 was copied and used to register telegram account
VM11	Activities	VM10 was copied and performed create contacts, send text, reply text, received picture, and share location

Apart from capturing the network activities, we have also saved the virtual memory by copying all virtual memory (.vmem) files generated by VMs. The virtual memory files were copied after performing all the activities prior to shutting down VMs. At the end of experiments we had three files of network packets (.pcap), virtual hard drive (.vmdk), and virtual memory (.vmem) for analysis. However, this paper only reports our analysis of .pcap

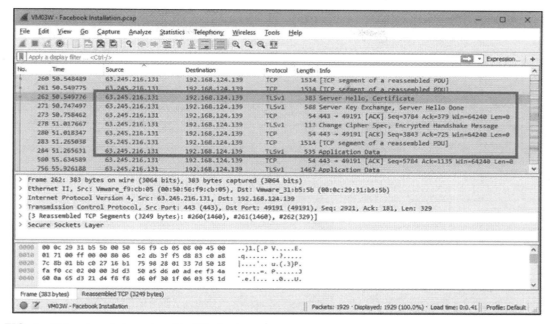

FIG. 3   Network packets captured by Wireshark.

network traffic files and interested readers may refer to authors previous publications reporting analysis of other files [18,22–24].

2.4 Conducting Network Analysis

Network traffic analysis is the process of capturing, reviewing, and analyzing network
traffic for the purpose of security, performance, and management. The process of analyzing
the network traffic can be performed manually or using automated techniques. In this paper
network packets were analyzed manually using Network Miner 1.6.1 to find the source and
destination IP address, communication port, owner of the IP, domain and subdomain, credential, images, certificate used, certificate validity, etc. The detected IP was then checked
with an IP address lookup website at http://www.ipchecking.com/, in an attempt to find the
owner, hostname, country origin, and reverse DNS.

We also monitored and analyzed the packets using Wireshark 1.12.5 and Microsoft
Network Monitor 3.4 to detect the timestamp, flow of handshakes for SSL encrypted traffic,
and to extract the certificate (in $\NetworkMiner_1-6-1\AssembledFiles folder according the
source IP subfolder). Fig. 4 shows an example of a certificate retrieved from communication
with Facebook.

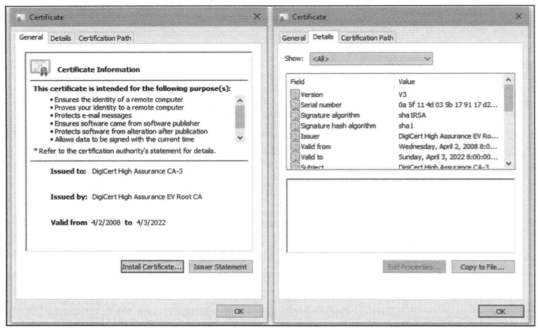

FIG. 4   Captured SSL certificate detail information.

3 DISCUSSION AND ANALYSIS

First our network analysis started by observing the network traffic during installation of FxOS simulator. This simulator was installed as an add-on in the Firefox browser. To install the simulator, we navigated to the Firefox add-on download page, and searched for the FxOS simulator. The moment we click the "+ Add to Firefox" button, the initial connection was established on "download.dynect.mozilla.net" with the observed IP of 63.245.217.39 over the port 80. This IP was registered to Mozilla and we also managed to capture all account credentials with the username of "_ga = GA1.2.389580134.1432816473" without any password required for the login process.

During the downloading process, we saw high traffic movement from "*.cdn.mozilla.net" with the observed IP of 68.232.34.191 over the port 443. The connections were encrypted and the certificate was issued by DigiCert High Assurance CA-3. In addition, we also detected network traffic from "aus4.mozilla.com" with the observed IP of 63.245.217.43, 63.245.217.138, and 63.245.217.219 over the port 80 but no data of forensic evidence worth was captured. Our next step was to observe and analyze the network movement for each of our selected applications.

3.1 Network Analysis of Facebook

Facebook is one of the most highly used social network applications across all mobile platforms. A forensic investigation of Facebook contained huge amounts of worthy forensic evidence. A network analysis for Facebook applications consisted of three stages starting from the application installation, credential login, and communication activities was performed using Facebook application in FxOS. VM disks were created for the installation, credential login, and communication activities stages for ease of organizing and monitoring purposes. When accessing the FxOS marketplace, the initial session was established on "marketplace. firefox.com" with the observed IP of 63.245.216.131 over the port 80. The network movements were also detected on port 443 simultaneously and its certificates were issued by DigiCert SHA2 Extended Validation Server CA and DigiCert High Assurance EV Root CA. In addition for this case, we also detected network traffic from the Google Internet Authority with the observed IP of 216.58.210.46. These services were encrypted, whereas their certificates were issued by Google Internet Authority G2, GeoTrust Global CA, and Equifax Secure Certificate Authority.

When browsing the application list in the marketplace, we again saw the network traffic from "*.cdn.mozilla.net" with the observed IP of 68.232.34.191 over the port 443, the same IP server when we downloaded the simulator. Once we found the Facebook application in the list, we clicked its icon and we then received the packet from "m.facebook.com" with the observed IP of 31.13.90.2 over the port 443. Twelve packets were received when we clicked the icon and the certificates were from DigiCert High Assurance CA-3 and DigiCert High Assurance EV Root CA. Next we captured the network traffic coming from "addons.dynect. mozilla.net" and "services.addons.mozilla.org" with the observed IP of 63.245.216.132 and 63.245.216.134 over the port 443 respectively. Both certificates were issued by DigiCert High Assurance EV CA-1. The marketplace was prompted for installation once we clicked the icon. The moment we accepted the application installation, we received the packet from "*.akamai. net" and "*.edgesuite.net" with the observed IP of 176.255.203.* over the port 80 and 443 simultaneously. This IP belongs to Facebook and the certificates were issued by Baltimore CyberTrust Root, GTE CyberTrust Global Root, and Cybertrust Public SureServer SV CA. We also detected network traffic from "marketplace.firefox.com" and "*.cdn.mozilla.net" over the port 443 during the Facebook application installation. As usual, the Facebook icon was created at the home screen as soon as the installation has finished.

Next when we opened the Facebook application, we received the packets again from "m.facebook.com." The Facebook application directed us to the login page and we used the prepared Facebook account to login. The login process for the Facebook application caught our attention. Immediately after we clicked the login button, the traffic were encrypted and the packet captured were from "safebrowsing.cache.l.google.com" with the observed IP of 90.222.188.* over the port 443. The certificates were issued by Google Internet Authority G2, GeoTrust Global CA, and Equifax Secure Certificate Authority. These services were used to check malicious activities that downloaded and installed malicious software without the user consent. Repeating login process multiple times showed randomness of checking process as we could observe the packets only twice!

After successfully authenticating our test account, we scrolled down to the Facebook news-feed and we identified the captured packet again came from "*.akamai.net," "fbcdn-profile-a. akamaihd.net," and "fbcdn-photos-c-a.akamaihd.net.edgesuite.net" with the observed IP of 176.255.203.* over the port 80 and 443. Various issuer of certificates such as from Cybertrust Public SureServer SV CA, GTE Cybertrust Global Root, and Baltimore Cybertrust Root were identified. The packets from this server were carrying Facebook images, text, as well as other encrypted communications. We performed several Facebook activities such as post a status, post a picture, comment, and like a friend's status, send Facebook private message, received private message, user search, and post an emoticon. All of these activities came from "*.akamai.net," "fbcdn-profile-a.akamaihd.net," and "fbcdn-photos-c-a.akamaihd.net.edgesuite.net." On the other hand, network traffic from Google services such as Google Analytic and Google Internet Authority were captured; starting from the moment we open the marketplace until the end of our experiment. The same network traffic was also observed in the Ubuntu experiment. Table 4 shows the summary of our observed IPs together with their registered organization, country of origin, and certificate issuers for the Facebook experiment.

TABLE 4 Observed IP and Registered Organization for Facebook Experiment

Registered Organization	Observed IP	Country Origin	Certificate Issuers
Mozilla	63.245.216.131 63.245.216.132 63.245.216.134	United States United States United States	– DigiCert SHA2 Extended Validation Server CA – DigiCert High Assurance EV Root CA
	68.232.34.191	United States	– DigiCert High Assurance CA-3
Google	216.58.210.46	United States	– Google Internet Authority G2 – GeoTrust Global CA – Equifax Secure Certificate Authority
	90.222.188.0– 90.222.188.255	United Kingdom	– Google Internet Authority G2 – GeoTrust Global CA – Equifax Secure Certificate Authority
Facebook	31.13.90.2	Ireland	– DigiCert High Assurance CA-3 – DigiCert High Assurance EV Root CA
	90.223.223.0– 90.223.223.255 176.255.203.0– 176.255.203.255	United Kingdom United Kingdom	– Cybertrust Public SureServer SV CA – GTE Cybertrust Global Root – Baltimore Cybertrust Root

3.2 Network Analysis on Twitter

A network analysis of the Twitter application followed the same steps as the Facebook application; it consisted of three stages starting from the application installation, credential login, and communication activities using the Twitter application in FxOS. VM disks were created for the installation, credential login, and communication activities stages for ease of organizing and monitoring purposes. We again needed to access the FxOS marketplace in order to install the Twitter application. The packets were captured again from "marketplace.firefox.com" with the observed IP of 63.245.216.131 over the port 80 and 443 simultaneously. For encrypted packets, the certificates were issued by DigiCert SHA2 Extended Validation Server CA and DigiCert High Assurance EV Root CA. Similarly, we also detected network traffic from the Google Internet Authority with the observed IP of 216.58.210.78 for this case. These services were encrypted, whereas their certificates were issued by Google Internet Authority G2, GeoTrust Global CA, and Equifax Secure Certificate Authority.

Likewise we again saw the network traffic from "*.cdn.mozilla.net" with the observed IP of 68.232.34.191 over the port 443 when we browsed the application list in Mozilla Marketplace and the certificate was issued by DigiCert High Assurance CA-3. However, we captured a different source of packets when we clicked on the Twitter icon. The packets we received were from "mobile.twitter.com" with the observed IP of 185.45.5.37 and 185.45.5.48 over the port 443. Both IP's certificates were issued by Symantec Class 3 Secure Server CA-G4 and Symantec Class 3 Public Primary Certification Authority-G5. We also managed to capture the network traffic from "addons.dynect.mozilla.net" and "services.addons.mozilla.org" with the observed IP of 63.245.216.132 and 63.245.216.134 over the port 443 respectively, which were the same packets at the same stage during our previous experiment. At the point we accepted for application installation, we received the packets from "ocsp.ws.symantec.com. edgekey.net" and "ss.symcd.com" with the observed IP of 23.54.139.27 over the port 80. This server was transmitting the application data from the server hosted by Akamai Technologies, a cloud service provider based in the United States. As usual, network traffic came from Google services, in addition traffic from "marketplace.firefox.com" and "*.cdn.mozilla.net" over the port 443 were also detected during the Twitter application installation. The Twitter icon was created at the home screen as soon as the installation was finished.

Next when opening the Twitter application, we received the packets again from "mobile. twitter.com." Furthermore, we also managed to capture the packets from "cs139.wac.edge-castcdn.net" and "*.twimg.com" with the observed IP of 68.232.35.172 over the port 443. The certificates were issued by DigiCert High Assurance EV Root CA and DigiCert SHA2 High Assurance Server CA. From our investigation these servers belong to Twitter. Similar to Facebook application, the Twitter application also directed us to the login page and we used the preprepared Twitter account to login. For the Twitter application, immediately after we clicked login button, the traffic was encrypted and we also managed to capture the packet from "safebrowsing.cache.l.google.com" with the observed IP of 90.222.188.* over the port 443. The certificates were issued by Google Internet Authority G2, GeoTrust Global CA, and Equifax Secure Certificate Authority. These services were used to check downloaded and installed malicious software without user consent. In contrast to Facebook, we managed to capture this packet every time we login to the Twitter application. We continually received a packet from "mobile.twitter.com" while the login process taking place.

After successfully logged into our test account, we then scrolled down to the Twitter newsfeed and managed to capture the packets from "*.twimg.com" with the observed IP of 199.96.57.7 over the port 80 and 443 simultaneously. Previously we identified the packets from "*.twimg.com" but the source IP was different. The certificates were also issued by DigiCert High Assurance EV Root CA and DigiCert SHA2 High Assurance Server CA. The packet from this server carried Twitter images, text, as well as other encrypted communication. Next we performed several Twitter activities such as tweet, reply tweet, retweet, follow, and unfollow user, direct message, view profile, create hashtag, and perform user search. All of these activities came from "mobile.twitter.com" and "*.twimg.com." Similar to the Facebook application, network traffic from Google services such as Google Analytic and Google Internet Authority were captured starting from the moment we opened the marketplace until the end of our experiment. Table 5 shows the summary of our observed IP together with their registered organization, country of origin, and certificate issuers for the Twitter experiment.

TABLE 5   Observed IP and Registered Organization for Twitter Experiment

Registered Organization	Observed IP	Country Origin	Certificate Issuers
Mozilla	63.245.216.131 63.245.216.132 63.245.216.134	United States	– DigiCert SHA2 Extended Validation Server CA – DigiCert High Assurance EV Root CA
	68.232.34.191	United States	– DigiCert High Assurance CA-3
Google	216.58.210.78	United States	– Google Internet Authority G2 – GeoTrust Global CA – Equifax Secure Certificate Authority
	90.222.188.0– 90.222.188.255	United Kingdom	– Google Internet Authority G2 – GeoTrust Global CA – Equifax Secure Certificate Authority
Akamai Technologies	23.54.139.27	United States	– N/A
Twitter	68.232.35.172 199.96.57.7	United States	– DigiCert High Assurance EV Root CA – DigiCert SHA2 High Assurance Server CA
	185.45.5.37 185.45.5.48	United States	– Symantec Class 3 Secure Server CA-G4 – Symantec Class 3 Public Primary Certification Authority-G5

3.3 Network Analysis on Telegram

Telegram was the only instant messaging application that we used in our experiment. Following the same steps for Facebook and Twitter application, this experiment also consists of three stages starting from the application installation, credential login, and communication activities using Telegram application in FxOS. VM disks were created again for the installation, credential login, and communication activities stages to ease the organizing and monitoring purposes. During installation of the Telegram application, the packets were captured again from "marketplace.firefox.com" with the observed IP of 63.245.216.131 over the port 80 and 443 simultaneously when we opened Mozilla Marketplace application from the FxOS simulator. For encrypted packets, the certificates were issued by DigiCert SHA2 Extended Validation Server CA and DigiCert High Assurance EV Root CA.

Next when we browsed and searched the Telegram application in Mozilla Marketplace, we saw again the network traffic from "*.cdn.mozilla.net" with the observed IP of 68.232.34.191 over the port 443 with the certificate was issued by DigiCert High Assurance CA-3. When we clicked the Telegram icon, we received the installation data from "download.cdn.mozilla.net" with the observed IP of 93.184.221.133 over the post 80. We also managed to capture the network traffic from "addons.dynect.mozilla.net" and "services.

addons.mozilla.org" with the observed IP of 63.245.216.132 and 63.245.216.134 over the port 443 respectively, which were the same packets at the same stage during our previous experiment. The same as previous experiment, network traffic from "marketplace.firefox. com" and "*.cdn.mozilla.net" over the port 443 have also been detected during Telegram application installation. The Telegram icon was created at the home screen as soon as the installation finished.

Next we then opened the Telegram application and to our surprise, we received the packet from "marketplace.firefox.com" with the observed IP of 63.245.216.131. Normally this packet is received when we clicked on the Mozilla Marketplace icon. When the application was executed, we proceeded with the Telegram phone number registration. The moment the phone number and country were selected, we received a packet from "addons-blocklist-single1.vips.phx1.mozilla.com" with the observed IP of 63.245.217.113 over the port 80. Then clicking the next button and while the Telegram application was generating the registration key, we received the network traffic from "telegram.org" with the observed IP of 149.154.167.51 over the port 80. A registration code was received and our network capturing software recorded incoming network traffic again from "telegram. org" but with different observed IP which was 149.154.167.91 over the port 80. At the same time we also received the network traffic from "*.us-west-2.compute.amazonaws. com" with the observed IP of 52.24.145.20 over the port 443. The certificates were issued by DigiCert Global Root CA and DigiCert SHA2 Secure Server CA. When we repeated our experiment with Ubuntu, the same traffic came through when we received registration key for Telegram. Therefore we can conclude that this server was used to push and generate the registration key for Telegram. In contrast to the Facebook and Twitter network analysis, we were no longer received the network traffic from "safebrowsing. cache.l.google.com" with the observed IP of 90.222.188.* during our experiment. This is because Telegram is only involved with messaging services and no browsing mechanisms were included.

After the registration process was completed, we performed several communication activities such as creating a new contact, opening chat windows, creating group, and sending messages to other contacts. During these activities, we received the network traffic from "telegram.org" with the observed IP of 149.154.171.* over the port 80. When we received a message from another contact, incoming traffic was from "github.map.fastly.net" with the observed IP of 185.31.19.133 over the port 443. The certificates were issued by DigiCert High Assurance EV Root CA and DigiCert SHA2 High Assurance Server CA. We then continued our experiment by sharing our location to our contact and the network traffic was recorded from Google Internet Authority with the observed IP of 216.58.209.234 over the port 443. These services were encrypted, whereas their certificates were issued by Google Internet Authority G2, GeoTrust Global CA, and Equifax Secure Certificate Authority. Finally we ended our experiment by playing the song received from another contact and again, we received the network traffic from "*.us-west-2.compute.amazonaws.com" with the observed IP of 52.24.145.203 over the port 443. Table 6 shows the summary of our observed IP together with their registered organization, country of origin and certificate issuers for Telegram experiment.

TABLE 6 Observed IP and Registered Organization for Twitter Experiment

Registered Organization	Observed IP	Country Origin	Certificate Issuers
Mozilla	63.245.217.113	United States	N/A
	63.245.216.131 63.245.216.132 63.245.216.134	United States	– DigiCert SHA2 Extended Validation Server CA – DigiCert High Assurance EV Root CA
	68.232.34.191	United States	– DigiCert High Assurance CA-3
	93.184.221.133	United States	N/A
Google	216.58.209.234	United States	– Google Internet Authority G2 – GeoTrust Global CA – Equifax Secure Certificate Authority
Telegram	149.154.167.51 149.154.167.91	United States	N/A
	149.154.171.0– 149.154.171.255	United States	N/A
Github	185.31.19.133	Unknown	– DigiCert High Assurance EV Root CA – DigiCert SHA2 High Assurance Server CA
Amazon	52.24.145.20 52.24.145.203	United States	– DigiCert Global Root CA – DigiCert SHA2 Secure Server CA

4 CONCLUSION AND FUTURE WORKS

Network analysis is a vital piece in conducting mobile forensics. In this paper, we have successfully presented the network analysis of two popular social networking applications (Facebook and Twitter) and one instant messaging application (Telegram) on FxOS. The findings of this study reported valuable forensics evidence such as image files, communication texts, and authentication credentials detectable in the network traffic. Fortunately, the captured credentials were not in plaintext. Communications in Telegram were transmitted over port 80 in plain text. However, all communication activities in Facebook and Twitter were encrypted and transmitted over port 443. The other conclusion drawn from this research was that not all service providers are storing client data on their servers, i.e., Twitter is using the cloud services from Akamai Technologies to store their installation files. Multiple certificates were carved from the packets namely Mozilla used the certificates from DigiCert; Google from Google Internet Authority; Facebook and Twitter from DigiCert.

This research has brought about many questions in need of further investigation. More information of the FxOS applications investigation would help us to establish a greater degree of network traffic forensic accuracy. Further research opportunities include undertaking the process outlined in this research for cloud storage services. Previous forensic investigation on cloud storage services generally used the cloud storage applications on Apple iOS and Google Android as case studies. Therefore the presence of FxOS will increase in-depth study of FxOS forensics in the cloud storage forensic area. In addition, this research is the first forensic investigation to use the phone simulator in order to monitor network traffic on mobile phone. A future study of investigating network traffic on other mobile OS using phone simulator would be very interesting.

References

[1] Mozilla Corporation, Mozilla announces global expansion for Firefox OS, Available from: http://blog.mozilla.org/press/2013/02/firefox-os-expansion/, 2013.

[2] S. Mohtasebi, A. Dehghantanha, A Mitigation Approach to the Privacy and Malware Threats of Social Network Services, Springer, Berlin Heidelberg, 2011. pp. 448–459. http://dx.doi.org/10.1007/978-3-642-22410-2_39.

[3] F.N. Dezfouli, A. Dehghantanha, R. Mahmod, N.F. Mohd Sani, S. Shamsuddin, A data-centric model for smartphone security, Int. J. Adv. Comput. Technol. 5 (2013) 9–17, http://dx.doi.org/10.4156/ijact.vol5.issue9.2.

[4] M. Damshenas, A. Dehghantanha, R. Mahmoud, A survey on digital forensics trends, Int. J. Cyber-Secur. Digit. Forensics 3 (2014) 1–26.

[5] D. Quick, K.K.R. Choo, Dropbox analysis: data remnants on user machines, Digit. Investig. 10 (2013) 3–18, http://dx.doi.org/10.1016/j.diin.2013.02.003.

[6] Hjelmvik, E., Network Miner 1.6.1, 2014.

[7] Combs, G., Wireshark, 2013.

[8] D. Quick, K.K.R. Choo, Digital droplets: Microsoft SkyDrive forensic data remnants, Futur. Gener. Comput. Syst. 29 (2013) 1378–1394, http://dx.doi.org/10.1016/j.future.2013.02.001.

[9] D. Quick, K.K.R. Choo, Google drive: forensic analysis of data remnants, J. Netw. Comput. Appl. 40 (2014) 179–193, http://dx.doi.org/10.1016/j.jnca.2013.09.016.

[10] B. Martini, K.K.R. Choo, Cloud storage forensics: OwnCloud as a case study, Digit. Investig. 10 (2013) 287–299, http://dx.doi.org/10.1016/j.diin.2013.08.005.

[11] J. Farina, M. Scanlon, M.T. Kechadi, BitTorrent Sync: first impressions and digital forensic implications, Digit. Investig. 11 (2014) S77–S86, http://dx.doi.org/10.1016/j.diin.2014.03.010.

[12] B. Blakeley, C. Cooney, A. Dehghantanha, R. Aspin, Cloud storage forensic: hubiC as a case-study, in: IEEE 7th International Conference on Cloud Computing Technology and Science (CloudCom), 2015, pp. 536–541. http://dx.doi.org/10.1109/CloudCom.2015.24.

[13] M. Shariati, A. Dehghantanha, K.-K.R. Choo, SugarSync forensic analysis, Aust. J. Forensic Sci. 48 (2015) 95–117, http://dx.doi.org/10.1080/00450618.2015.1021379.

[14] T.Y. Yang, A. Dehghantanha, K.-K.R. Choo, Z. Muda, Windows Instant Messaging App forensics: Facebook and Skype as case studies, PLoS ONE 11 (2016), e0150300. http://dx.doi.org/10.1371/journal.pone.0150300.

[15] F. Daryabar, A. Dehghantanha, K.-K.R. Choo, Cloud storage forensics: MEGA as a case study, Aust. J. Forensic Sci. (2016) 1–14, http://dx.doi.org/10.1080/00450618.2016.1153714.

[16] F. Daryabar, A. Dehghantanha, B. Eterovic-Soric, K.-K.R. Choo, Forensic investigation of One Drive, Box, Google Drive and Dropbox applications on Android and iOS devices, Aust. J. Forensic Sci. (2016) 1–28, http://dx.doi.org/10.1080/00450618.2015.1110620.

[17] D. Quick, K.K.R. Choo, Forensic collection of cloud storage data: does the act of collection result in changes to the data or its metadata? Digit. Investig. 10 (2013) 266–277, http://dx.doi.org/10.1016/j.diin.2013.07.001.

[18] M.N. Yusoff, R. Mahmod, M.T. Abdullah, A. Dehghantanha, Mobile forensic data acquisition in Firefox OS, in: The Third International Conference on Cyber Security, Cyber Warfare, and Digital Forensic (CyberSec2014), 2014, pp. 27–31.

[19] I.I. Androulidakis, Mobile Phone Security and Forensics—A Practical Approach, Springer, New York, 2012. PhD Proposal. http://dx.doi.org/10.1017/CBO9781107415324.004 .

[20] VMware, VMware Workstation, 2013.

[21] Microsoft, Microsoft Network Monitor, 2010.
[22] M.N. Yusoff, R. Mahmod, M.T. Abdullah, A. Dehghantanha, Performance measurement for mobile forensic data acquisition in Firefox OS, Int. J. Cyber-Secur. Digit. Forensics 3 (2014) 130–140.
[23] M.N. Yusoff, R. Mahmod, A. Dehghantanha, M.T. Abdullah, An approach for forensic investigation in Firefox OS, in: The Third International Conference on Cyber Security, Cyber Warfare, and Digital Forensic (CyberSec2014), IEEE, 2014, pp. 22–26.
[24] M.N. Yusoff, R. Mahmod, A. Dehghantanha, M.T. Abdullah, Advances of mobile forensic procedures in Firefox OS, Int. J. Cyber-Security Digit. Forensics 3 (2014) 141–157.

6

Mobile Phone Forensics: An Investigative Framework Based on User Impulsivity and Secure Collaboration Errors

M. Petraityte*, A. Dehghantanha*, G. Epiphaniou†

*University of Salford, Salford, United Kingdom †University of Bedfordshire, Luton, United Kingdom

1 INTRODUCTION

The issues with mobile device security have been under the radar of scholars and security researchers for a while now. As convenient as mobile devices have become, their versatile interaction with the environment and their users have vulnerabilities that have received attention from multiple researches [1–7]. For a long time social engineering and flaws with user behavior online was associated with computers [8]. However, as technology evolves, users now face another challenge as mobile devices have evolved to become powerful tools that are connected to the Internet and also cheap enough to be available to a large population of users that may be unable to afford a laptop and broadband service. It is thought that "10% of Americans own a smartphone but do not have broadband at home, and 15% own a smartphone but say that they have a limited number of options for going online other than their cell phone," where "smartphone dependent" individuals are likely to be people with a low income and less education, or young adults [9]. Furthermore, Kaspersky Lab reported an intensive growth in mobile malware since 2011, and in 2013 there were more than 148,327 items of mobile malware [3,10]. Therefore it is very likely that users will regularly face threats related to mobile devices, yet they are likely to be unable to recognize them because of poor security awareness. Under such circumstances, it is not likely that users will manage the security of their mobile device very well. Another factor that contributes to poor hygiene when it comes to mobile security is that users do not seem to significantly value their privacy prior to its loss. The proliferation of mobile malware has also increased the attack surface and complexity in this paradigm causing traditional defense mechanisms to adapt slower than the overall attack evolution. Also, network convergence allowed criminals from different areas and backgrounds to gather into the same space with a variety of attack techniques and motives. This allowed for more decentralized, multistaged cyber attacks that demand a different approach in terms of prediction, detection, and response.

Moreover, digital forensics investigators often face challenges investigating a variety of mobile devices that differ from one another and they also have to make sure that the key principles of collecting evidence is adhered to [11]. As a result, researchers come up with a variety of methods and tools that help to solve existing issues, such as suggesting possible investigative frameworks for analysis of devices [6,12–14], applications [2,15,16] as well as malware [3,11,17–19]. However, understanding the factors that influence the behavior of mobile device users and the common mistakes behind the compromise of their mobile devices can be helpful for the forensics investigators and could potentially shorten the time spent on the investigation of possible breach scenarios as forensic and allows forensics analysts to conduct a risk-aware investigation. This is especially worthwhile because the digital forensics related to mobile devices is of growing importance to researchers and scientists [20].

This paper aims to address this issue by conducting a scenario-based role-play experiment that investigates how mobile users respond to social engineering via mobile device and to use the result of this experiment for a guided mobile phone forensics investigation method that could facilitate the work of digital forensics investigators while analyzing the data from mobile devices. This experiment also helps to identify the trends and emerging challenges that have an impact on mobile device users and gives suggestions for ways of tackling this problem.

For the purposes of this experiment QR code images were used to mimic social engineering and phishing fraud because QR codes are potentially perfect tools for such attacks and their malicious use has been already observed in the past [21,22]. Essentially, QR code could be as dangerous as clicking on a link or downloading an attachment in a phishing email, as the scanned code redirects the user to a fake website, which could also be contaminated with malware.

The rest of this paper is structured as follows. The first section presents the overview of literature and summarizes the previous research that has been conducted and explains how this research positions itself to address some of the gaps in the literature. This is followed by an explanation of the research method and details about the survey questionnaire in the second section. Finally the last section presents and discusses the results and suggests the investigative framework for digital forensics. Limitations of this research as well as conclusions to what has been presented are outlined in sections six and seven, respectively.

2 REVIEW OF RELATED WORK

Users trust their mobile devices by using them for a wide variety of purposes with the help of the available applications—from communicating with family and friends to shopping and maintaining their finances online [23,24]. This makes mobile devices a very good, yet poorly protected, source of valuable information [25]. Naturally, the more users trust their mobile devices, the more attractive these devices become to attackers with malicious intents [19,21,26].

Just like malware for the traditional computers, the malware of mobile devices can be developed to perform a variety of tasks [18], such as collecting valuable information, monitoring user activity or performing tasks on behalf of the user with the help of spyware, worms, rootkits, bots, and Trojans [17,18,21]. This shifting landscape of the cyberspace is clearly manifested by the number of new users or "electronic citizens" joining the Internet on a daily basis. End users are now being actively targeted using the emergence of new mobile devices and applications as a core attack vector. Technical solutions have proven only partially effective to evolving threats, rendering static security controls ineffective as more users use their own IT devices.

In spite of efforts to protect users against social engineering and phishing emails in traditional computing platforms [8,27], there is very little attention paid for security awareness of mobile device users. Many users jailbreak their devices with no apparent understanding of why this should not be done. To them, a jailbroken device simply looks like a third party provides a legitimate software, only outside the app store. And it may look like there is nothing wrong with that [28,29]. In fact, users may even think that the app stores actually put unnecessary constrains on downloading and using the applications, while somewhere else they exist for free and with added functionalities [29]. Users, however, are unaware that malware is what usually comes as an added feature, too, with significant privacy and financial losses [17,28,30]. Users may feel that the access lock on the device is an inconvenience rather than protection [31] because the common understanding about security is that there is nothing to hide [32], yet it shows that users are unaware of what happens when the device is lost or stolen without having any access protection on it. Due to software development malpractices, software developers also create applications that request too many access permissions to the information on the mobile device which could lead to exploitation of the device [4,18]. However, users hardly ever pay attention to what access is required by the applications because the access provisioning is similar to the terms and conditions of software usage that nobody cares to read [29]. Moreover, due to limited screen size of mobile devices, it may be difficult to see all the content that pops up as potential fraud, only a part of a web address may be visible, which eventually make it difficult to differentiate between legitimate and malicious contents [8,29].

QR codes were originally created for a legitimate reason and have a useful purpose. However, attackers have realized that QR codes could serve as a perfect social engineering tool that can be used for redirection to fake websites and the installation of malware onto a user's mobile devices [21,22]. While QR codes are a fairly new feature in the world of technology and their popularity is growing steadily [21,33], they are bringing up a new route for malware to spread. QR codes are often associated with promotions, discounts, or coupons that users expect to receive when they interact with the QR code and the destination website [33]. This is an ideal way to spread fraud as users actually expect to receive something by scanning a QR code, therefore the request to install a malicious application could be perceived as part of a reward process [22,33]. As a consequence, mobile device users could be particularly susceptible to frauds utilizing QR codes.

On the other side there is a lack of a unified approach for the investigation of mobile devices and hardly any consideration of user behavior that led to the compromise of a mobile device [6]. Many researchers focused on collecting evidence of forensics value from mobile phones based on the potential location of the evidences. Other forensics investigators, especially those investigating the iOS platform, suggested the collection and preservation of data from cloud platforms connected to the mobile device [2,14,16,34–36]. However, there is yet any approach to conduct an investigation of mobile devices based on common security risks that mobile device users are facing because of their own mistakes.

This paper analyzes the role that the users' behavioral factors play in the overall users' perception of mobile device security and then proposes a guideline for conducting forensics investigations of mobile devices on the basis of common security mistakes of mobile users.

3 EXPERIMENT DESIGN

An online web-based questionnaire was created to assess the user interaction with QR codes. It was accessible through an online invitation from the researcher. The questionnaire was divided into three parts. The first part was an assessment of 10 QR code images, which were carefully created by the research team. Half of these images contained a genuine URL and the other half was bogus URLs. The 10 QR codes were carefully selected to represent a range of topics that are associated with common day-to-day activities, such as shopping, advertising, product labeling, and sites for information. The second part of the questionnaire contained demographic information about the participants in order to evaluate their familiarity with smartphone security. It consisted of age, gender, current employment status, and level of education. The third part of the questionnaire was used for cognitive reflection test (CRT) to measure the cognitive impulsivity of the test participants. The reason for arranging these parts in such a way is to ensure that the demographic questions would not alert the participants that they were involved in a mobile security study until after they had completed their assessment of the 10 QR codes.

A total of 100 participants consisting of university students, lecturers, and staff participated in the experiment. The participants were divided into two groups to complete the questionnaire in two different sessions. Each session took around 30 min and was facilitated by a member of the research team who explained the purpose of the study to participants. In the first session participants were informed that they were participating in a study that aims to understand the user's behavior with regards to QR code without explaining about its possible malicious use. In the second session participants were informed that the study investigates potentials for exploiting some aspects of user's security using QR codes and what is the definition of an "exploit." The users were asked to act on behalf of a made-up character and their task was to determine if the QR code was genuine or not and, if they could, provide the reasons, in their opinion, of why the code was fake. The reason of this approach was to measure the factor of the users' expectancy and how does that affect the results, if at all.

The research aimed to analyze the following variables:

(1) *Familiarity with the security of smartphones.* The participants were not directly asked to rate their familiarity with mobile devices, as their judgment would only show their own opinion. The variable was created using the Predictive Analytics Software (PASW) syntax coding to predict the average score of the demographic questionnaire.

(2) *Cognitive impulsivity.* To measure cognitive impulsivity participants completed the CRT, which consisted of three questions. Due to the nature of CRT, the participants had to think before providing an answer as the most obvious response was not the correct one.

Participants received 1 score for a correct answer; the higher the score, the better the person was at controlling their impulsivity. This test was chosen as it is likely that the predictive validity of this measure is equal or above other cognitive tests that claim to measure cognitive impulsivity. This measure was included in this study to investigate if impulsivity could lead to wrong identification of fake or genuine QR code.

(3) *Behavioral response.* Participants were given the question with answers below. The way they responded was used to measure their behavioral response.

How would you deal with this QR code?

(a) Scan the QR code and click on the URL.
(b) Scan the QR code and verify the URL.
(c) Scan the QR code and leave it.
(d) Never scan the QR code.

Two behavioral answer variables of each participant were calculated using the previously used PASW software, both for a genuine QR code behavior score and a genuine QR, as follows. If the QR code being evaluated was genuine:

- the participant would score 10 for response;
- 1 5 for response;
- 1 2.5 for response; and
- 1 0 for response.

If the QR code being evaluated was fake:

- the participant would score 0 for responses;
- 1 2.5 for response;
- 1 5 for response; and
- 1 10 for response.

Participants could score a maximum of 100 and a minimum of 0 for each type of QR code.

4 RESULTS AND DISCUSSION

Table 1 sums up the average scores for both categories of managing fake QR codes and the genuine ones. The results show that those participants that knew about the purpose of the questionnaire and the study scored higher than those who did not know the purpose of the questionnaire. Based on these findings, there was a small difference between the two groups of participants. Overall, the genuine QR code was managed better than the fake one.

TABLE 1   Result of Questionnaires

Description	Mean Score of Questionnaire Findings
Total point accumulated for 100 participants	4611
Total score for 100 participants	329.326
Mean score for 1 participant	3.29

4.1 Familiarity With Smartphones Security

According to the findings of the questionnaire, the more familiar users were with smartphone security, the better they dealt with the QR code assessments. This finding was statistically significant and somewhat predictable as people who are familiar with smartphone security are likely to be more aware of the risks and consequences associated with fake QR code rather than people who do not use such devices very often.

TABLE 2   Average Behavioral Score for Managing QR Codes

	Not Informed	Informed	Total
Fake QR code	22.1	29.2	25.65
Genuine QR code	30.65	31.1	30.875

Table 1 shows that the total score of the online questionnaire survey is 3.29 out of 5. It is fair to conclude that the majority of the participants were familiar with smartphone security. This had no significant impact for dealing with the genuine QR codes but as it is shown in Table 2 it impacted the way the participants treated the fake QR codes.

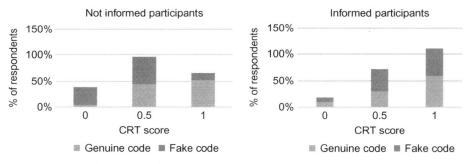

FIG. 1   The comparison of CRT scores between the participants that were informed and not informed about the survey and the impact of CRT on how the participants managed the codes.

4.2 Cognitive Impulsivity

Less impulsive people who did not know what the purpose of this test was (those with a higher CRT score) responded better, as shown in the Fig. 1. Participants with higher CRT scores were less likely to click on the URL held inside the fake QR code. The cognitive impulsivity did not show any significant difference on the participants who were informed of the purpose of the study.

5 FORENSICS INVESTIGATION GUIDELINE

The performed experiment shows how susceptible users are to downloading and installing a piece of software on their mobile device. Even those participants who knew that they should be careful about the QR codes that were presented to them still did not pay enough attention while making decisions in using the mobile device. This suggests that apart from user education in smartphone security, cognitive impulsivity is the key component in the decision making of users. A logical assumption suggests that the highest potential to act without a second thought arises when a user experiences any kind of social engineering or when they do not pay enough attention while performing other tasks. Depending on the method of the attack a user may be exposed to some social engineering attack attempts before they get tricked into downloading and installing a malware. It could also be that a user does not have a full view of the advertisement or a pop-ups that open together with a legitimate website and could accidentally click on it while trying to switch it off. However, a lot of the common mobile device user mistakes come from conscious decision making and owner's actions.

The suggested forensics investigation guideline that is shown in Fig. 2 prioritizes forensics investigator actions with regard to the common mistakes that arise from social engineering of end users, where gradient colors indicate the level of social engineering involved and the next step in the flowchart.

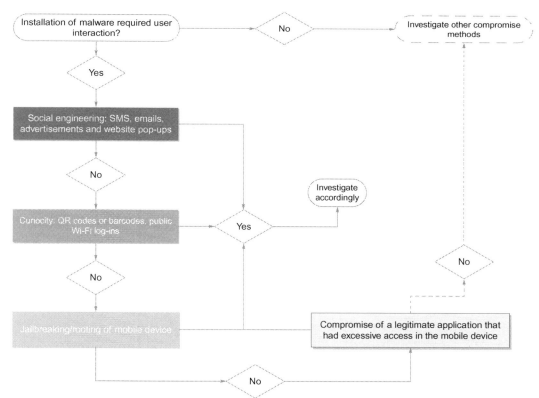

FIG. 2 Suggested forensics investigation guideline based on users' common security mistakes.

Social engineering is understood as tricking someone into "breaking security policies," where spam is an example of social engineering [37]. Lately there are various types of spam, such as junk emails, phishing, SMSing, annoying advertisements, and pop-ups while browsing the Internet [38]. All types of this spam is relevant to mobile devices and their users when mobile devices allow website content. A user may accidentally click on any of them simply because of their design and lack of full visibility on the screen of a mobile device. Also, it is possible to accidentally click on a pop-up or advertisement just by trying to switch it off and get rid of it as well as being tricked into thinking that it is a part of a legitimate website that a user tried to open. It is probably the most popular way for malware to spread and attack mobile device users. For this reason, as well as potentially the highest likelihood of cognitive impulsivity impact, it is suggested to consider this group of items first when conducting a digital investigation.

Second comes a group of actions that contain social engineering, yet a user must make a conscious decision to perform an action. Those are likely to be mistakes that a user performs out of curiosity, convenience, or benefit. Logging into a compromised public Wi-Fi and a scan of a QR code or a barcode could be a few examples of such behavior that may lead to the exploitation of the mobile device.

The next step is to check if a user has jailbroken the mobile device. Users jailbreak their mobile devices seeking a variety of benefits without realizing that the third party software may contain malware. This action requires a conscious decision and is therefore one of the least impulsive actions that a user may take. Information sharing about third party software repositories and decentralized threat management systems is more prominent than ever, which contrasts to the traditional approaches in cyber/computer security principles related to restrictions in input data and controlling human behavior. The paradigm is shifted towards monitoring and studying human aspects in users' interaction with their mobiles as part of the formal actions and decision making processes within adversarial clusters.

The last step is to detect if a user is using legitimate applications that require excessive permissions on a mobile device and the mobile device gets exploited due to compromise of such application, for example via infected application update. Users hardly understand the permissions that are required by various applications and to what they are given access. Possibly even fewer users think twice before installing such applications or at least consider disabling the unnecessary access requests.

These common mistakes of mobile device users contain a certain level of impulsivity which, according to the role-play experiment, is an important factor that leads to the highest likelihood of mobile device exploitation and end user security flaws. Certainly, other ways of exploiting mobile devices that do not require user interaction are also possible, yet they should be analyzed using other available investigation methods.

6 LIMITATIONS

This study has limitations, just like any other study. Firstly QR codes are only one threat among others in the spectrum of mobile device exploit possibilities and there could be other equally valid threats associated with mobile devices. However, the phishing-type of social engineering that users are accustomed to seeing as emails can be easily replicated by QR codes on mobile devices and therefore QR codes served well for the purpose of the experiment.

Secondly the study was based on a role-play experiment that required users to analyze the given information and provide advice. However, participants were not required to scan a QR code from an unknown source, website, or station and therefore results may not imply real-world scenarios.

Moreover, the participants of this study did not have the contextual information that would often influence decision making. For example, they did not know what was the occupation of the fictitious character on behalf of whom they were acting, neither how technology-savvy that person is, nor whether she liked to use the QR code technology.

Another limitation of this research relates to the sample of participants. The total of 100 participants in this study were all members of one university—students, lecturers, and staff. A sample of this kind is likely to be biased in terms of age, education, familiarity with mobile security apps and various other factors. Therefore the conclusions of this experiment are not necessarily representative of the general population of the mobile device users.

7 CONCLUSION AND FURTHER RESEARCH

The aim of this paper is to conduct a scenario-based role-play experiment that investigates how mobile users respond to social engineering via a mobile device and to use the result of this experiment for a guided mobile phone forensics investigations that could facilitate the work of digital forensics investigators while analyzing the data from mobile devices. For the purposes of this research the fraud was a QR code and the findings indicate that the genuine QR codes were managed better than the fake ones and this did not depend on how much informed the participants were given about the experiment.

Although informed participants performed better in managing both types of QR codes, they were significantly better in managing the fake ones. This implies that educated mobile device users are much better at managing the security of their phones. The users should be continuously reminded that the QR codes could contain malware that may infect their devices, yet it is only one aspect of mobile device security. This experiment simply shows that increased user awareness helps to improve secure user behavior.

This research also analyzed a few other factors that have impact on users when they face a QR code. The survey results indicate that controlled impulsiveness is associated with improved performance in managing fake QR codes in users who were not informed about the purpose of this study. However, these factors did not have a significant impact when users were informed about the purpose of the study, but on the other hand their familiarity with mobile device security helped them to recognize the fake QR codes. This shows that when users are well informed and become aware of social engineering they may be more impulsive in their decision making towards mobile device security.

As a result, a forensic investigation guideline was suggested in accordance with common security mistakes of mobile device users. The guideline suggested to focus on possible remnants of user activities resulting from user impulsivity, lack of knowledge, and understanding during a forensics investigation. This research only briefly touched the aspect of application permissions and malware on mobile devices, therefore future research could further investigate users' perception of application permissions on their device and the limits of intrusion that users allow for the applications and suggest an investigation guideline based on users' awareness and their ability to recognize malware on their mobile devices.

References

[1] F.N. Dezfouli, A. Dehghantanha, R. Mahmod, N.F.B.M. Sani, S. bin Shamsuddin, A data-centric model for smartphone security, Int. J. Adv. Comput. Technol. 5 (9) (2013).

[2] F.N. Dezfouli, A. Dehghantanha, B. Eterovic-Soric, K.-K.R. Choo, Investigating social networking applications on smartphones detecting Facebook, Twitter, LinkedIn and Google+ artefacts on Android and iOS platforms. Aust. J. Forensic Sci. 48 (4) (2016) 469–488, http://dx.doi.org/10.1080/00450618.2015.1066854.

[3] M. Damshenas, A. Dehghantanha, K.-K.R. Choo, R. Mahmud, M0Droid: an android behavioral-based malware detection model, J. Inf. Priv. Secur. 11 (3) (2015).

[4] H. Shewale, S. Patil, V. Deshmukh, P. Singh, Analysis of Android vulnerabilities and modern exploitation techniques, ICTACT J. Commun. Technol. 6948 (2014) 863–867.

[5] X. Hei, X. Du, S. Lin, Two vulnerabilities in Android OS kernel, in: 2013 IEEE International Conference on Communications (ICC), Budapest, 2013, pp. 6123–6127, http://dx.doi.org/10.1109/ICC.2013.6655583.

[6] S. Mohtasebi, Smartphone forensics: a case study with Nokia E5-00 mobile phone, Int. J. Digit. Inf. Wirel. Commun. 1 (3) (2011) 651–655.

[7] P. Tripp, Dynamic detection of inter-application communication vulnerabilities in Android, in: R. Hay, O. Tripp, M. Pistoia (Eds.), Proceedings of the 2015 International Symposium on Software Testing and Analysis – ISSTA 2015, ACM Press, New York, ISBN: 9781450336208, 2015, pp. 118–128, http://dx.doi.org/10.1145/2771783.2771800.

[8] K. Shah, T. Shenvi, K. Desai, R. Asrani, V. Jain, Phishing: an evolving threat, Int. J. Stud. Res. Technol. Manage. 3 (1) (2015) 216–222.

[9] A. Smith, U.S. Smartphone Use in 2015 | Pew Research Center, Available from: http://www.pewinternet.org/2015/04/01/us-smartphone-use-in-2015/, 2015 (accessed 17.12.15).

[10] R. Costin, D. Emm, Securelist | Kaspersky Security Bulletin 2013. Malware Evolution—Securelist, Securelist, Available from: https://securelist.com/analysis/kaspersky-security-bulletin/57879/kaspersky-security-bulletin-2013-malware-evolution/, 2013 (accessed 09.12.15).

[11] M. Damshenas, A. Dehghantanha, R. Mahmoud, A survey on digital forensics trends, Int. J. Cyber-Security Digit. Forensics 3 (4) (2014) 209–235.

[12] P.N. Ninawe, S.B. Ardhapurkar, Design and implementation of cloud based mobile forensic tool, in: 2015 International Conference on Innovations in Information, Embedded and Communication Systems (ICIIECS), 2015, pp. 1–4.

[13] E.R. Mumba, H.S. Venter, Mobile forensics using the harmonised digital forensic investigation process, in: 2014 Information Security for South Africa, 2014, pp. 1–10.

[14] S. Parvez, A. Dehghantanha, H.G. Broujerdi, Framework of digital forensics for the Samsung Star Series phone, in: 2011 3rd International Conference on Electronics Computer Technology, vol. 2, 2011, pp. 264–267.

[15] D. Quick, K.-K.R. Choo, Dropbox analysis: data remnants on user machines, Digit. Investig. 10 (1) (2013) 3–18.

[16] T.Y. Yang, A. Dehghantanha, K.-K.R. Choo, Z. Muda, Windows instant messaging app forensics: Facebook and Skype as case studies, PLoS ONE 11 (3) (2016) e0150300.

[17] F. Daryabar, A. Dehghantanha, Investigation of malware defence and detection techniques, Int. J. Digit. Inf. Wirel. Commun. 1 (3) (2011) 645–650.

[18] M. Damshenas, A. Dehghantanha, R. Mahmoud, A survey on malware propagation, analysis and detection, Int. J. Cyber-Security Digit. Forensics 2 (4) (2013) 10–29.

[19] K. Shaerpour, A. Dehghantanha, R. Mahmod, Trends in Android malware detection, J. Digit. Forensic Secur. Law 8 (3) (2013) 21–40.

[20] F.F.N. Dezfoli, A. Dehghantanha, R. Mahmoud, N.F.B.M. Sani, F. Daryabar, Digital forensic trends and future, Int. J. Cyber-Security Digit. Forensics 2 (2) (2013) 48–76.

[21] A. Kharraz, E. Kirda, W. Robertson, D. Balzarotti, A. Francillon, Optical delusions: A Study of Malicious QR Codes in the Wild, in: 2014 44th Annual IEEE/IFIP International Conference on Dependable Systems and Networks, Atlanta, GA, 2014, pp. 192–203, http://dx.doi.org/10.1109/DSN.2014.103.

[22] K. Krombholz, P. Frühwirt, P. Kieseberg, I. Kapsalis, E. Weippl, QR code security: a survey of attacks and challenges for usable security, Hum. Asp. Inf. Secur. Privacy Trust 8533 (2014) 79–90.

[23] A. Dehghantanha, R. Ramli, A user-centered context-sensitive privacy model in pervasive systems, in: IEEE, no. 2010 Second International Conference on Communication Software and Networks, 2010, pp. 78–82.

[24] A. Aminnezhad, A. Dehghantanha, M.T. Abdullah, A survey on privacy issues in digital forensics, Int. J. Cyber-Security Digit. Forensics 1 (4) (2012) 311–323.

[25] M.N. Yusoff, R. Mahmod, M.T. Abdullah, A. Dehghantanha, Mobile forensic data acquisition in Firefox OS, in: 2014 Third International Conference on Cyber Security, Cyber Warfare and Digital Forensic (CyberSec), 2014, pp. 27–31.

[26] K. Qian, C.-T. Dan Lo, M. Guo, P. Bhattacharya, L. Yang, Mobile security labware with smart devices for cyber-security education, in: IEEE 2nd Integrated STEM Education Conference, 2012, pp. 1–3.

[27] M. Pattinson, C. Jerram, K. Parsons, A. McCormac, M. Butavicius, Why do some people manage phishing emails better than others? Inf. Manag. Comput. Secur. 20 (1) (2012) 18–28.

[28] J. Imgraben, A. Engelbrecht, K.-K.R. Choo, Always connected, but are smart mobile users getting more security savvy? A survey of smart mobile device users, Behav. Inf. Technol. 33 (12 December 2014) (2014) 1347–1360, http://dx.doi.org/10.1080/0144929X.2014.934286.

[29] S. Mansfield-Devine, Mobile security: it's all about behaviour, Netw. Secur. 2014 (11) (2014) 16–20.

[30] Q. Do, B. Martini, K.-K.R. Choo, A forensically sound adversary model for mobile devices, PLoS ONE 10 (9) (2015) e0138449.

[31] A. Sabeeh, A.H. Lashkari, Users' Perceptions on Mobile Devices Security Awareness in Malaysia, in: 2011 International Conference for Internet Technology and Secured Transactions (ICITST), Abu Dhabi, 2011, pp. 428–435.

[32] R. Coustick-Deal, Open Rights Group—Responding to 'Nothing to hide, Nothing to fear', Available from: https://www.openrightsgroup.org/blog/2015/responding-to-nothing-to-hide-nothing-to-fear, 2015 (accessed 18.12.15).

[33] MHG, QR Code Usage Survey: The Impact of QR Codes on Advertising Recall, MGH, Baltimore, MD—Washington, DC, 2011.

[34] M. Shariati, A. Dehghantanha, B. Martini, K.-K.R. Choo, Chapter 19—Ubuntu one investigation: detecting evidences on client machines, in: R.K.-K.R. Choo (Ed.), The Cloud Security Ecosystem, Syngress, Cambridge, MA, 2015, pp. 429–446.

[35] M. Shariati, A. Dehghantanha, K.-K.R. Choo, SugarSync forensic analysis, Aust. J. Forensic Sci. 48 (1) (2016) 95–117.

[36] F. Daryabar, A. Dehghantanha, B. Eterovic-Soric, K.-K.R. Choo, Forensic investigation of OneDrive, Box, GoogleDrive and Dropbox applications on Android and iOS devices, Aust. J. Forensic Sci. (2016) 1–28.

[37] J.W.H. Bullee, L. Montoya, W. Pieters, M. Junger, P.H. Hartel, The persuasion and security awareness experiment: reducing the success of social engineering attacks, J. Exp. Criminol. 11 (1) (2015) 97–115.

[38] M. Iqbal, M.M. Abid, M. Ahmad, F. Khurshid, Study on the effectiveness of spam detection technologies, Int. J. Inf. Technol. Comput. Sci. 8 (1) (2016) 11–21.

Performance of Android Forensics Data Recovery Tools

B.C. Ogazi-Onyemaechi*, A. Dehghantanha*,
K.-K.R. Choo[†,‡]

*University of Salford, Salford, United Kingdom †University of Texas at San Antonio,
San Antonio, TX, United States ‡University of South Australia, Adelaide, SA, Australia

1 INTRODUCTION

Smart mobile devices, particularly smartphones, are increasingly popular in today's Internet-connected society [1–4]. For example, few years ago in 2010, shipments of smartphone grew by 74% to 295 million units [3,4]. Unsurprisingly, sales of smartphones have been increasing since then [5,6], and it has been estimated that 1.5 billion smartphones will be sold by 2017 and 1 billion mobile subscribers by 2022 [7–15].

Such devices are generally used to make phone calls, send SMS messages, web browsing, locate places of interests, map navigation, image and video capture, entertainment (e.g., gaming and lifestyle), business and economic transactions (e.g., internet banking), take notes, create and view documents, etc. [6,16–18]. Due to their widespread adoption in corporate businesses, these devices are a rich source of information (e.g., corporate data and intellectual property) [19–22]. The potential to target such devices for criminal activities (e.g., malware such as banking Trojans) or be used as an attack launch pad (e.g., used to gain unauthorized access to corporate data) [19,23–29], makes it important to ensure that we have the capability to conduct a thorough investigation of such devices [22,30,31,18,32–35].

While there are a small number of forensic tools that can be used in the forensic investigation of smart mobile devices [36], the extent to which data can be recovered varies, particularly given the wide range of mobile devices and the constant evolution of mobile operating systems and hardware [37,38]. For example, recovering data from the internal memory of a smartphone remains a challenge [34,39,40]. Further to these challenges is the requirement to create forensically sound and effective tools and procedures [36,20,41].

Therefore it is essential that the forensic community keeps pace with forensic solutions for smart mobile devices [42,43,2–4]. This is the focus of this chapter. Specifically, we study the effectiveness of five popular mobile forensics tools, namely: Phone Image Carver, AccessData FTK (Forensic Tools Kit), Foremost, Recover My Files, and DiskDigger, in recovering evidential data from a factory-restored Samsung Galaxy Note 3 running Android Jelly Bean version 4.3.

The structure of this chapter is as follows. Section 2 reviews related work. Section 3 outlines the methodology and our experiment setup. Section 4 presents our findings, and Section 5 concludes this chapter.

2 RELATED WORK

The present investigation is conducted based on the current acquisition method on smartphones and the extent of available forensic techniques and tools on the analysis of evidence. Smartphones have many profound sections of where and how evidence is collected when it is dealing with a crime occurrence [44]. Therefore with the ever-increasing features and utility, it becomes much more complicated to collect evidences from a smartphone [43,45]. Consequently, there are different acquisition methods on different architectures and software that a smartphone operates on [18,39]. These differences in the architecture make it extremely difficult to perform similar acquisition method on different devices and operating systems [23]. However, NIST created guidelines for Computer Forensics Tools Testing (CFTT) to provide for the differences in architecture [45]. Therefore mobile device forensics has been defined as the science of recovering digital evidence from a mobile device under forensically sound conditions using accepted methods. Notwithstanding, mobile device forensics is considered an evolving specialty in the field of digital forensics [23,25]. The procedures for the validation, preservation, acquisition, examination, analysis, and reporting of digital information had been discussed [25]. Although there had been an established program and guidelines, mobile device forensics, like any other evolving field, still has its own forensics challenges [26]. Evolvement on different areas of usage for mobile phones provides even further challenges in their investigation. For example, investigation of cloud applications on mobile phones [44,46–48], malwares on smartphones, [49–51], and investigating mobile phones as part of botnets [52] and SCADA [53] systems are all challenging forensics research areas. In view of the evolving nature of mobile device forensics, it is suggested that forensic practitioners who rely primarily on general-purpose mobile forensic toolkits might find that no single forensic tool could recover all relevant evidence data from a device [6]. Therefore researchers are working to establish the best forensic tools and procedures that are reliable for mobile device's investigation [27,31,33,46,54].

Investigations conducted in the field of mobile device forensics still show variations in research opinions on the effectiveness and reliability of different forensic tools when applied to different mobile device architectures [23]. The removal of internal memories from a mobile device or their mirroring procedure is evasive and complex because of difficulties in having direct hardware access [16]. To resolve such challenges, five mobile device forensic scenarios were studied; and a method to perform data acquisition of an Android smartphone regardless of the architecture was proposed. The method was validated using Motorola Milestone II A953, Sony Ericson Xperia X10 miniPro, Motorola Defy, Samsung Galaxy S 9000a, Motorola II, and Motorola Milestone A853 [16]. These architecture-based difficulties were confirmed by investigating Symbian- and Windows-based mobile devices [23]; which revealed that tools for forensic investigation of smartphone mobile devices always would pose challenges in forensic investigation because of the continual evolving nature of the technology [23,40]. The data recovery capabilities of EnCase, FTK, Recuva, R-Studio, and Stellar Phoenix from a desktop Windows XP were compared [36]. The comparison revealed that EnCase, FTK, Recuva, and R-Studio performed identically when recovering marker files from most images [36,53]. The experiment showed also that Stellar Phoenix corrupted two bytes in each of two text files (even when these files had not been deleted) and added a padding of zeroes at the end of another file that had not been deleted [36]. Nonetheless, the study concluded that no two tools produced identical results [36]. Further to this, a different study conducted on Samsung Star 3G phone used TK file Explorer 2.2, MOBILedit 4, and Samsung PC studio for logical acquisition of different data files for analysis, and this was to create a framework for forensic investigation of Samsung Star 3G device [17]. Evidence collection and analysis conducted on a Nexus 4 phone discovered a flaw that allowed access to all data on the device without a device wipe that occurs when the bootloader is unlocked [55]. The challenges of smartphone forensics continue to expand even with the emergence of Linux-based Firefox OS, which has no procedure yet for forensic investigation [56].

To ensure a sound forensic investigation, care should be taken to preserve and retrieve the volatile data inside the memory of the mobile device [47]; hence, a backup and acquisition process was proposed to work on windows mobile phones, android mobile phones, and iPhones [47]. The recovery of information held on a Windows Mobile smartphone was investigated using different approaches to acquisition and decoding, accepting AccessData FTK and DD imagers. The investigation concluded that no one technique recovers all information of potential forensic interest from the device [35]. Further work on mobile device forensics shows that a diverse collection of smartphone forensic tools has been introduced; however, these studies do not guarantee data integrity, which is required for digital forensic investigation [48]. Therefore, Android device acquisition utilizing Recovery Mode was investigated to analyze the Android device Recovery Mode variables that compromise data integrity at the time of acquisition. Consequently, an Android data acquisition tool that ensures integrity of acquired data was developed [48]. It was noted there was not yet specific procedures or rules to collect evidence from a smartphone [7]. Therefore, forensic investigators use existing procedures in the acquisition of digital evidence [7]. Furthermore, it was suggested that the relative amount of important evidence that could be gathered from the smartphone differ based on different versions of software system that runs on the smartphone. However, nothing was done on the acquisition of evidence on a formatted android device—where it was claimed that all data and applications were erased [7].

The challenges of data recovery for forensic investigation extends to cloud computing environment [46]. Therefore, utilizing TPM in hypervisor [42], implementing multifactor authentication and updating the cloud service provider policy to provide persistent storage devices are proposed to overcome the difficulties in Cloud forensics [51,57]; which include limited access to obtain evidence from the cloud, seizure of physical evidence for integrity validation, evidence presentation, or rulings on data saved in different locations [46]. In a cloud-related forensic investigation, Guidance Encase and AccessData forensic Toolkit were evaluated; and the tools show that they can successfully return volatile and nonvolatile data from the cloud [50]. Thus, a foundation is laid for the development of new acquisition methods for the cloud that will be trustworthy and forensically sound [50]. To ensure a reliable cloud-based forensic investigation, a step-by-step technique for evidence data collection was proposed [55]. There was a review of 7 years of research into forensic investigation of various smartphone mobile device platforms, data acquisition scheme and information recovery methods in order to provide comprehensive reference material to enhance future research [33]. Prior to the advancement of forensic tools, the traditional method of memory acquisition focused on the physical memory. This procedure most often requires the removal of the memory chip from the chipboard. These methods put valuable evidence at risk because during the removal process there might be loss or damage of essential evidence.

Emphasizing on the need for accurate and reliable forensic tools and procedures, there was a warning against unfair application of wrong forensic techniques and evidence to secure conviction in fervour of the prosecution [52]. Notably, some challenging areas include "erroneous allegations of knowledgeable possession, misuse of time stamps and metadata, control and observation of the discovery process." Other challenging areas include "authentication issues, deficiencies and the lack of verification for proprietary software tools, deliberate omission or obfuscation of exculpatory evidence and inadvertent risks resulting from the use of legitimate services" [52].

The foregoing review shows there is need to investigate the recovery performance of Phone Image Carver, AccessData FTK, Foremost, Recover My Files, and DiskDigger from FTK and DD images acquired from Android mobile smartphones.

3 EXPERIMENT SETUP

In our experiments, we used the popular Samsung Galaxy S2 i9100 as the case study device. The device has an internal memory of 16 GB, random access memory (RAM) of 1 GB, running Android Gingerbread version 2.3.4 operating system (OS) (Android OS, Ice Cream Sandwich version 4.0.3). The focus of our study was on the internal memory; thus, no memory card was inserted in the phone. Prior to the experiments, the phone was preloaded with Enron dataset [58–64], which is considered similar to data collected for fraud detection. Therefore, it is a good dataset for the present investigation. The device was subsequently factory reset before taking images on the phone (see Fig. 1). The reason for factory resetting the phone was to wipe all preloaded data and investigate the effectiveness of the forensic tools in recovering the data erased from the device.

Fig. 1 shows that two different image acquisition processes, logical and physical image acquisition, were conducted after the device was restored to default factory state. AFLogical forensic tool was used for logical Image acquisition on the formatted disk (device). The tool captures the call-log calls, contacts phones, MMS, MMS-Parts, and SMS, which were contained in the preloaded Enron dataset. It stores this information in a zip folder named forensics.zip within the device itself. The .zip folder contains .csv files, which hold the logs of the

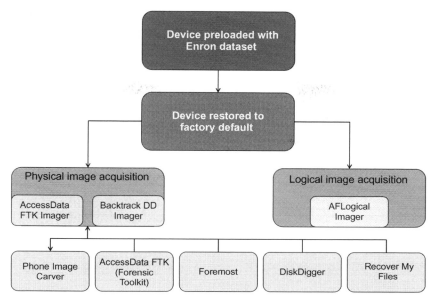

FIG. 1   Schematic representation of processes conducted on the case study device.

device. However, when opened .cvs files show blank suggesting that logical acquisition of data is not executable in a reformatted device. Comparing to another investigation, analysis of logical image, bb file, from Blackberry PlayBook device did not produce direct data files of user activity. However, it produced some key files that can assist to further trace device usage [33,53,65]. Related studies confirm also that Encase and FTK forensic tools could not recover all data from NTFS-formatted logical disk partitions [34,52].

On the other hand, AccessData FTK Imager 3.1.3.2 and Backtrack dd Imager were used for physical acquisition of images. Subsequently, Phone Image (Carver v1.6.0), AccessData FTK, Foremost, DiskDigger, and Recover My Files (v4.7.2) were employed to analyze the two different physical images.

During the image creation process using AccessData FTK Imager 3.1.3.2, the backup option was not selected. This was to ensure that no backup data was available. The physical memory of the device was imaged and analyzed using several tools. The resulting image revealed that the tool created only 2.227 GB image file compared to the 16 GB physical memory capacity of the device. This means that AccessData FTK imager recovered only 14% of the device memory capacity. The imager separated the physical drive into eight images. The size of the first seven images is 1.46 GB and the eighth image is 767 MB. This experiment compares with another study where AccessData FTK Imager recovered a higher average of 86.4% of the physical disk capacity from the various image segments [34].

Another image was acquired from the case study device using .dd imager in Backtrack. This tool converts the memory into a disk dump. Similar to the acquisition of image using AccessData, the dd imager used command line prompt in Backtrack dd Imager without any filter. The image size converted by this tool shows only 11 GB of the 16 GB memory capacity of the device, which translates to 68.75% recovery of the device capacity. The remaining memory was ignored due to slack spaces, which is the disk space between the end of the file content and the end of the last cluster in which the file is saved [34]. Two types of disk dumps were created after imaging the device. One of the disk dumps uses the access data FTK images, while the other uses backtrack dd image. Subsequently, several recovery tools were used to perform analysis on the images to determine the effectiveness of these tools. Prior to analysis, validation checks were conducted on the images using hash calculation for integrity checking [48] as shown in Table 1. Image numbers S2.001–S2.008 in column one of Table 1 are the validation and integrity check identification numbers for each of the eight images acquired by AccessData FTK imager. DD, on the other hand is the validation and integrity check ID number for the DD image that was acquired as a single image. The corresponding MD5 sums and SHA1 values are given in columns two and three of Table 1.

TABLE 1   Validation and Integrity Check of Images

Image	MD5	SHA1
S2.001	df14a97ed884e959f79d718a4a3e8de0	838f1291740988d86e2b2b22625646e20e9e535a
S2.002	334bc971671ad78a09abadd81aa2419f	aa42e0269f4cb2fd53b065f0aea56823fb770d88
S2.003	53393c41f197b08a693db24600b2eab1	35cc22977e11e6c966c569260812fde04471401e
S2.004	4396a40fb1825166db005e39d211b5a8	fecb8eabff34ea01ad4a84cc283625af5ca0319f
S2.005	6e9a8fc2cc1235da1d33a51d73a53c30	1b03158408ae5e567d6a7e27993ab46ecd8fe686
S2.006	Ab49d0350af243d6d3d6df1791adb58f	Eb7a722cc1b14fc8bdf06c81390df45ab34f5a50
S2.007	35d8479c1dc29edacb33ad9dcaa07d5b	Eac0ba1a3e4e8ef8b0195ab682081c4d12d9d36e
S2.008	01a5c72710d2223d012e8e7b71e9055c	C782fb92564990314de7baefa2db748ac186aa7b
DD	1eeac023329e6d70ffcc78e7230c1ca7	76ae66d29894ae6b21f73bac87578c9dd1202c77

4 RESULTS AND DISCUSSIONS

Two types of image acquisition namely logical image and physical image acquisition were conducted. AFLogical was used to acquire the logical disk image. The tool captures the call-log calls, contacts phones, MMS, MMS-Parts, and SMS that were contained in the preloaded Enron dataset. It stores this information in a zip folder named forensics.zip within the device itself. The .zip folder contains .csv files that holds the logs of the device. However, when opened the .cvs files show blank suggesting that logical acquisition of data is not executable in a reformatted device. This revelation agrees with particularly the respective findings of Buchanan-Wollaston and Mercuri. The blank .cvs files confirm that Encase and FTK were unable to recover some data from NTFS-formatted logical disk partitions, except by further procedure where the data acquired must be decoded [33–35,52,66].

Earlier on AccessData image and backtrack dd image were acquired for the physical disk of the device. The content of the FTK Image and BackTrack dd image of the target Samsung Mobile device were loaded on different forensic tools. Three different tools namely, Phone Image Carver v. 1.6.0, AccessData FTK (Forensic ToolKit 1.81.3), and dd Image FTK were used to analyze the images.

TABLE 2 Recovered Files Format Using Phone Image Carver

	File Format									
FTK image	DocX	HTML	JPG	MP3	SQLite	SWF Flash	Text	Text UTF-16	Text-Shift-JIS	Zip
Backtrack dd image	DocX	HTML	JPG	MP3	SQLite	SWF Flash	Text	Text UTF-16	Text-Shift-JIS	Zip

Table 2 shows the various files format recovered from the images using Phone Image carver. Phone Image Carver recovered evidence of many different formats of data, confirming that Phone Image Carver supports over 300 file types [35]. The present experiment supports the finding which suggests that .docx files were the only Office documents detected. However, it disagrees that Phone Image Carver did not detect .jpg files [35]. This study reveals that utilizing Phone Image Carver tool is extremely time-consuming and not efficient; suggesting that it is not suitable for real investigation. Phone Image Carver tool does not list out the deleted files according to file formats, however the information still exists within the image. It was noted that Phone Image Carver does not permit addition of further file types to its database, meaning that a number of file types from the data set would not be detected [35]. An additional feature of Phone Image Carver tool is that the activities performed in it are recorded in a log file. This offers a great opportunity for the analyst to go back and review his steps each time he uses Phone Image Carver tool.

The FTK and dd images acquired in Section 3 were analyzed using AccessData FTK. Analysis revealed that 12 [12] categories of files were recovered from each of the two images as shown in Fig. 2.

Fig. 2 shows minor differences in the recovery function of both FTK and dd images from the same restored device. The recovered files in Fig. 2 reveals that different images from different acquisition tools give different depth of evidence recovered in the analysis [34]. While FTK Image recovered total file items of 926, dd Image recovered far less number of 530 when the same FTK tool was used on both images (Tables 3 and 4). It is clear that entries in some of the file items are the same, some with zero entries (no recovery); however, few others show significant differences between both images. Worthy of note are the entries under FTK Image for "Unchecked items (926), Other thumbnails (18) and Filtered in (926)."

The analysis shows the corresponding entries for dd Image are lower, except for graphics and other thumbnails where dd Image and FTK Image recovered virtually equal numbers of files. This suggests that dd images provide negligently better recovery for graphic and thumbnail files. However, both images recorded similar values under File Status and File Category, except for Slack/free space where FTK Image had significantly higher value (869) than dd Image (471). The analysis suggests that in the event of recoverable evidences from slack spaces, FTK image gives more recovery files than dd image. In other words, slack spaces could contain deleted files, deleted file fragments, and hidden data [54,56]. The negative side of it is that recovering from it could result in a waste of time if there were no recoverable evidence in the slack spaces. It is worthy to note that files were not recovered from FTK Image 8, which contains the Slack/free spaces. On the percentage file recovery of FTK Image, Mercuri noted that CFTT Program tests revealed defects in the hard disk image preparation process on Windows XP OS [34,52]. Taken into account, the analysis revealed that defect might still have some drawback on the performance of FTK as an imager in the present study on smartphone.

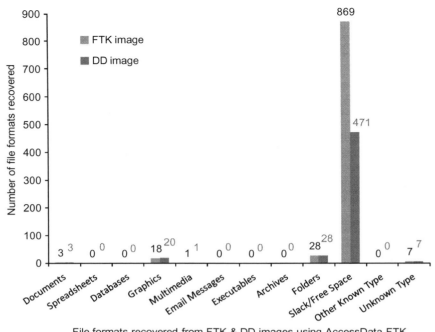

FIG. 2   Recovery and analysis of data from both FTK and dd images using FTK forensic toolkit.

TABLE 3   FTK Image Result Using FTK

File Items	No	File Status	No	File Category	No
Total file items	926	KFF Alert Files	0	Documents	3
Checked items	0	Bookmarked items	0	Spreadsheets	0
Unchecked items	926	Bad extension	18	Databases	0
Flagged thumbnails	0	Encrypted files	0	Graphics	18
Other thumbnails	18	From email	0	Multimedia	1
Filtered in	926	Deleted files	2	Email messages	0
Filtered out	0	From recycle bin	0	Executables	0
		Duplicate items	2	Archives	0
		OLE subitems	0	Folders	28
		Flagged ignore	0	Slack/free space	869
		KFF ignorable	0	Other known type	0
		Data carved files	0	Unknown type	7

TABLE 4 dd Image Result Using FTK

File Items	No	File Status	No	File Category	No
Total file items	530	KFF alert files	0	Documents	3
Checked items	0	Bookmarked items	0	Spreadsheets	0
Unchecked items	530	Bad extension	20	Databases	0
Flagged thumbnails	0	Encrypted files	0	Graphics	20
Other thumbnails	20	From email	0	Multimedia	1
Filtered in	530	Deleted files	2	Email messages	0
Filtered out	0	From recycle bin	0	Executables	0
		Duplicate items	2	Archives	0
		OLE subitems	0	Folders	28
		Flagged ignore	0	Slack/free space	471
		KFF ignorable	0	Other known type	0
		Data carved files	0	Unknown type	7

Further analysis was conducted on the FTK and Backtrack dd Images using Foremost in Backtrack forensic tool. The FTK Images (1–8) were analyzed in segments, the way they were imaged. Fig. 3 shows the numbers of various file formats recovered from the two images.

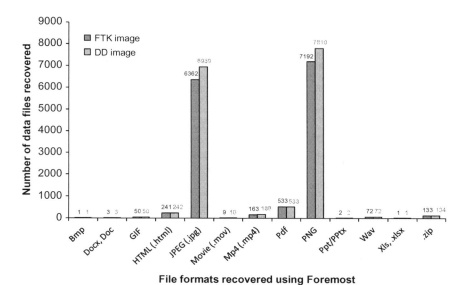

FIG. 3 Number of data files recovered from FTK and dd images using Foremost in Backtrack.

Unlike AccessData FTK, analysis conducted using Foremost showed format-specific files from both images. Apparently, Foremost recovered similar types of files from the two images, particularly, bmp, docx/doc, gif, html, movie, pdf, ppt/pptx, wav, xls/xlsx, and zip. The analysis showed that both images recovered the largest number of jpeg and png files. While analysis in Foremost showed that FTK image recovered 6362 jpeg and 7192 png files, dd image on the other hand recovered 6939 and 7810, respectively. The large number of graphics analyzed (recovered) suggests that the slack spaces contain more deleted graphic files, therefore foremost performed better in recovering them [54]. However, analysis in Foremost revealed a higher number of files from dd Image than it did from FTK image for jpeg/jpg, mp4, and png. Compared to the AccessData FTK, Foremost analyzed a higher number of file types. The recovery of high number of file types could be a result of high-performance of Foremost tool. The absence of slack/free spaces in the analysis suggests that Foremost performed better in recovering all deleted files, deleted file fragments, and hidden data files that were present in the slack/free spaces of the images, which AccessData FTK could not recover as shown in Fig. 2 [54,56].

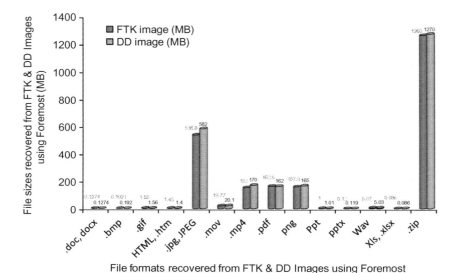

FIG. 4   Data file sizes recovered from FTK and dd images using Foremost in Backtrack.

The large sizes of data file shown in Fig. 4 further corroborates the suggestion that Foremost recovered deleted files, deleted files fragments, and perhaps hidden files that might be contained in the slack/free spaces which AccessData FTK could not recover as shown in Fig. 2 [54]. Comparing the data file sizes with the number of files recovered in Fig. 3, it is evident that Foremost forensic tool recovered more data from Backtrack dd Image than it recovered from FTK Image. This suggests also that Foremost forensic tool performs better in analyzing data files from Backtrack dd Image than FTK Image. The analysis reveals also that the zip, jpeg, mp4, png, and pdf files were the files most recovered using Foremost forensic tool. This result shows that Foremost performs better than AccessData FTK in recovering files from FTK and dd images, particularly dd image of a restored Android mobile smartphone device.

The next forensic tool to use in the analysis of the two images (FTK and dd acquired images) was Recover My Files version 4.2.7. The result of the analysis is shown in Fig. 5. The number of data files recovered from the two images shows no differences in the performance of Recover My Files as a forensic tool. The tool recovered 16,756 files from the FTK image, which is comparable with 16,758 files recovered from Backtrack dd image.

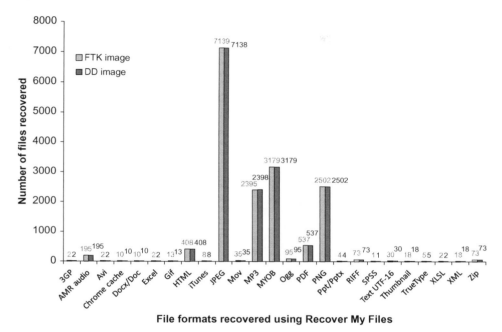

File formats recovered using Recover My Files

FIG. 5   Number of data files formats recovered from FTK and dd images using Recover My Files.

The results show also that jpeg, myob, png, mp3, pdf, html, and amr audio files were the most recovered in the order of listing. The tool has shown to recover more file formats and showed no slack/free space. The additional file formats it recovered include 3gp, amr audio, avi, chrome cache, itunes, mp3, myob, ogg, tif, spss, text UTF-16, thumbnails, and truetype. Similarity in the recovery function of Recover My Files on the two images is revealed further in Fig. 6. It is evident in Fig. 6 that the tool recovered equal sizes of data files from both FTK and dd images. The tool recovered 7.37 GB of data files for each file image confirming that mov, zip, jpeg, myob, mp3, avi, png, and pdf are among the most recovered files format.

Comparing Recover My File and Foremost in Figs. 7 and 8, the results show that Foremost recovered 14,762 and 15,985 data files from FTK and dd images respectively while Recover My File recovered 16,756 and 16,758 data files respectively from the same images. This recovery performance is repeated in the size of data files recovered, where Foremost recovered 2.35 and 2.38 GB of data files from FTK and dd images. On the other hand, Recover My File recovered 7.37 and 7.39 GB data files respectively from the same FTK and dd images.

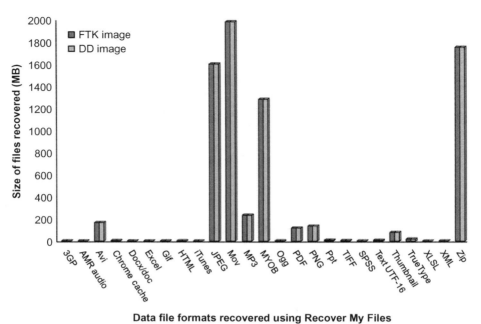

FIG. 6   Sizes of data files recovered from FTK and dd images using Recover My Files.

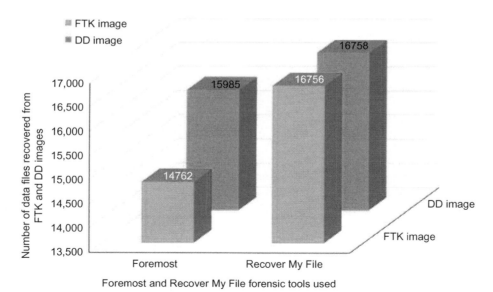

FIG. 7   Number of files recovered between Foremost and Recover My File.

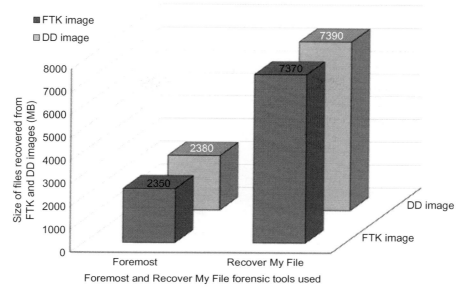

FIG. 8 Size of files recovered between Foremost and Recover My File.

Both the number and size of data files recovered could elaborate the huge difference in the recovery functions of the two forensic tools. While results show that foremost recovered large number of data files formats in jpeg (6939), png (7810), pdf (533), and hmtl (242) for FTK and dd Images, Recover my File recovered an average of jpeg (7139), myob (3179), png (2502), mp3 (2398), pdf (537), and html (408). Similarly, Foremost recovered an average size in jpeg (0.582 GB), zip (1.27 GB), mp4 (0.17 GB), pdf (0.162 GB), and png (0.165), while Recover My File recovered some phenomenal sizes in mov (1.98 GB), zip (1.75 GB), jpeg (1.6 GB), myob (1.28 GB), mp3 (0.2329 GB), and avi (0.1651 GB) for the two images. These analyzes reveal that Recover My File is more effective than Foremost in recovering data files from FTK and dd images of a restored device.

The superior performance of Recover My File over Phone Carver image, AccessData FTK and Foremost was exciting. Therefore, one more analysis was conducted on the acquired FTK and Backtrack dd Images using DiskDigger forensic tool. The analyzes are shown in Fig. 9.

Fig. 9 reveals that DiskDigger recovered also many different data files format. What is interesting here is that DiskDigger recovered equal number of data files from both FTK and DD Images. The figure shows that the largest numbers of files recovered from both images are from jpeg (7,178), tif (6939), png (2502), and mp3 audio (2398) files in the listed order. It is important to observe that DiskDigger tool did not record any slack/free space. This implies that the tool made deep recovery of all files in the two images. The distribution of the number of recovered data files (see Fig. 9) corresponds to the sizes of data files recovered from the images (see Fig. 10).

As shown in Fig. 10, the zip folder recorded the largest data file sizes, while jpeg, tif, mp3, avi, and mp3 followed in the same order.

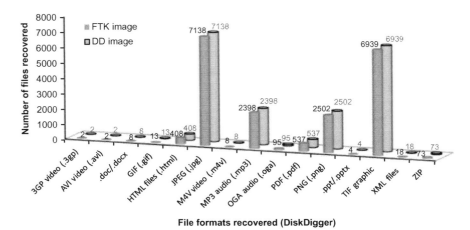

FIG. 9   FTK and DD image analysis of number of data files using DiskDigger tool.

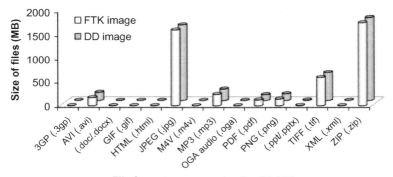

FIG. 10   FTK and DD image analysis of size of data files using DiskDigger tool.

The results in Fig. 10 suggest that Recover My File and DiskDigger show better recovery performance than Phone Image Carver and AccessData FTK. Although DiskDigger recovered 15 different file formats, Recover My File recovered 25 file formats, indicating a better deep recovery performance. However, DiskDigger recovered a greater total number of files (20,145) for both Images than the total number of files (16,758) recovered by Recover My File as shown in Fig. 11. The greater number of data files recovered from DiskDigger comes from the number of .tif files (6939) for both FTK and dd Images, which Recover My File did not recover.

Comparing Recover My File and DiskDigger in terms of data file size, it is clear that Recover My File recovered a larger file size (7.387 GB) than the data file size (4.596 GB) recovered by DiskDigger shown in Fig. 12. This difference is explained by the larger number of file formats recovered by Recover My File. These additional file formats and sizes (MB) include, amr audio (0.496 MB), chrome cache (2.6 MB), itunes (0.121 MB), mov (1980 MB),

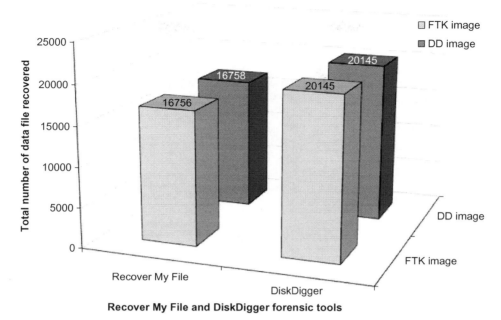

FIG. 11   Comparing data file number recovered using Recover My File and DiskDigger.

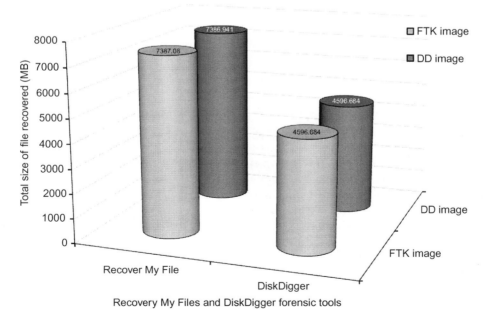

FIG. 12   Comparing data file size recovered using Recover My File and DiskDigger

myob (1280 MB), ogg (1.8 MB), spss (0.657 MB), text UTF-16 (7.3 MB), thumbnails (77.7 MB), and truetype (18.3 MB). It is evident that the two additional data file formats from Recover My File that made major contribution to the difference are .mov and .myob. The results suggest that DiskDigger performs better than Recover My File only in the area of the number of data files, particularly the .tif files (6939), recovered by each from the two images. Conversely, Recover My File performs better in terms of deep search for different data file formats, and the size of data files recovered.

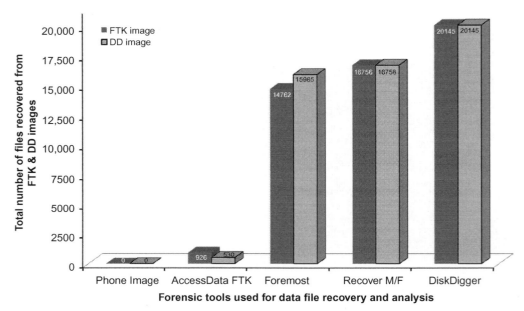

FIG. 13   Total number of files recovered from FTK & DD images using different forensic tools.

The summary of the recovery performance of the five forensic tools is shown in Figs. 13 and 14. The figures show that Phone Image Carver AccessData FTK did not perform well under the present experimental conditions as a forensic recovery tool. Foremost, on the hand recovered more file formats and appreciable large number of data files with corresponding data file size. However, Foremost shows to recover slightly higher number of data files (jpeg and png) from dd image than FTK image while the sizes of the data file recovered show no difference. DiskDigger appears to have performed well compared to Recover My File. It recovered many file formats that is still less than the number of data file formats recovered by Recover My File. DiskDigger proves to recover the highest number of data files but less than the size of data files recovered by Recover My File. Therefore, the study shows that Recover My File has the best recovery function as a forensic tool. It proved to have the deepest search penetration, recovered the highest number of data file formats, and recovered the largest size of data file formats, although it was less than DiskDigger in the number of data files recovered.

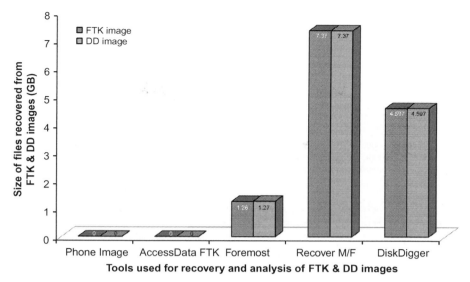

FIG. 14 Total size of data files recovered from FTK & DD images using different forensic tools.

5 CONCLUSION AND FUTURE WORKS

The increasing use of smartphone for various social-economic transactions led to a consequent increase in cybercrimes committed through smartphones. The nature of these devices and the variety of applications resided on them deemed challenging challenges to forensic investigators. To address these challenges, this paper investigated the use of different forensic tools for recovering data files from a restored Android mobile phone. The data was extracted using different forensic tools, namely AccessData FTK and Backtrack dd, on the physical image acquisition of the device. The focus of this paper was to investigate the data recovery functions of Photo Image Carver, AccessData FTK, Foremost, Recover My Files and DiskDigger in forensic investigation of FTK and DD images from smartphone mobile device. The study revealed that .dd images compare more favorably for android mobile forensic investigation than FTK images, judging from the size of evidence it holds. Moreover, the experiment revealed that Phone image carver recovered some file types including SQLite, SWF Flash, and Text-Shift JIS, which other tools could not recover. Phone Image Carver keeps log file record of activities performed in it, giving the analyst the opportunity to review his previous steps each time he uses the tool. Foremost proves to recover more number of files data than Phone Image Carver and AccessData FTK. On the other hand, Recover My Files and DiskDigger had greater percentage recovery performance than Foremost, Phone Image Carver, and AccessData FTK. Both Recover My Files and DiskDigger recovered many data file formats suggesting they had a deep penetration recovery capability. However, Recover My Files recovered more files of type mov, zip, JPEG, and MYOB than DiskDigger recovered. Recover My Files proves to recover the greatest percentage of evidence by recovering 3GP, AMR audio, avi, itunes, Myob, ogg, thumbnails, and truetype files, which no other tools recovered. Therefore, Recover My Files proves to be the best recovery tool in this study.

In conclusion, the analysis tools used in this experiment showed different levels of recovery performance. Most of the tools recovered major file formats that other tools did not recover, suggesting that no single forensic tool could recover all forensic evidences in a smartphone image. In future, further similar studies are suggested to be conducted on other mobile platforms such as iPhone and compare and contrast results with those presented in this paper.

References

[1] D. Bennett, The challenges facing computer forensics investigators in obtaining information from mobile devices for use in criminal investigations, Inf. Secur. J. Glob. Perspect. 21 (3) (2012) 159–168.

[2] A. Netstar, Research says shipments of smartphones grew 74 percent in 2010, European Communications, 10 March 2011, Available from: http://www.eurocomms.com/industry-news/7655-research-says-shipments-of-smart-phones-grew-74-percent-in-2010.

[3] Berg Insight, Research says shipments of smartphones grew 74 percent in 2010, News Archive, 2011.

[4] Berg Insight, Research says shipments of smartphones grew 74 percent in 2010, European Communications. Available from: http://www.eurocomms.com/industry-news/7655-research-says-shipments-of-smartphones-grew-74-percent-in-2010, 2011 (accessed 28.12.15).

[5] J.D. La Fuente, J. Santiago, A. Román, C. Dumitrache, D. Casasanto, When you think about it, your past is in front of you: how culture shapes spatial conceptions of time, Psychol. Sci. 25 (9) (2014) 1682–1690.

[6] Data I, Idc T, Quarterly W, Phone M, IDC: smartphone shipments to overtake feature phones worldwide in 2013, Available online at: http://thenextweb.com/insider/2013/03/04/idc-smartphone-shipments-to-overtake-feature-phones-worldwide-in-2013/#gref.

[7] A. Simão, F. Sícoli, L. Melo, F. Deus, R. Sousa Júnior, Acquisition and analysis of digital evidence in Android smartphones, Int. J. Forensic Comput. Sci. 6 (1) (2011) 28–43.

[8] B.D. Dilworth, Worldwide smartphone sales to Hit 1.5 billion in 2017: IHS report, 2017.

[9] Smartphone users worldwide will total mobile users pick up smartphones as they become more best practices in digital video advertising go beyond the articles: hear from our clients: want to learn more? Available from: http://www.emarketer.com/Article/Smartphone-Users-Worldwide-Will-Total-175-Billion-2014/1010536, 2014. (accessed 19.03.16).

[10] M. Neeraj, Smartphone sales 2015–2017: India will surpass the US [report], Available from: http://daze-info.com/2015/07/04/global-smartphone-sales-2015-2017-india-will-surpass-us-report/, 2015 (accessed 19.03.16).

[11] Gartner says worldwide device shipments to grow 1.5 percent, to reach 2.5 billion units in 2015, Newsroom. Available from: http://www.gartner.com/newsroom/id/3088221, 2015 (accessed 19.03.16).

[12] J. Gozalvez, Advances in wireless power transfer, IEEE Veh. Technol. Mag. 10 (2015) 14–32.

[13] Roland T, Trend B, Roland Berger Trend Compendium 2030 – Trend 2 Globalization and Future Markets, 2014, pp. 1–29, Retrieved July 27, 2016, from: https://www.rolandberger.com/publications/publication_pdf/roland_berger_trend_compendium_2030_trend_2_globalization_and_future_markets_20140501.pdf.

[14] P. Woodgate, I. Coppa, N. Hart, Global Outlook 2014: Spatial Information Industry, Australia and New Zealand Cooperative Research Centre for Spatial Information, 2014, pp. 1–25.

[15] R. Reynolds, Trends influencing the growth of digital textbooks in US higher education, Publ. Res. Q. 27 (2) (2011) 178–187.

[16] L. Aouad, T. Kechadi, J. Trentesaux, An open framework for smartphone, in: G. Peterson, S. Shenoi (Eds.), Advances in Digital Forensics VIII, IFIP AICT, 383, 2012, pp. 159–166. IFIP International Conference on Digital Forensics, Springer, Berlin, Heidelberg.

[17] N. Dezfouli Farhood, A. Dehghantanha, R. Mahmod, N.F.B. Mohd S, S.B. Shamsuddin, A data-centric model for smartphone security, Int. J. Adv. Comput. Technol. 5 (9) (2013) 9–17.

[18] S.H. Mohtasebi, A. Dehghantanha, Towards a unified forensic investigation framework of smartphones, Int. J. Comput. Theory Eng. 5 (2) (2013) 351–355.

[19] A. Hoog, Android and mobile forensics, in: J. McCash (Ed.), Android Forensics: Investigation, Analysis and Mobile Security for Google Android, 1st ed., Elsevier, Amsterdam, 2011, pp. 1–40 (Chapter 1).

[20] CBC News, Cybercrime moving to smartphones and tablets, say experts [Internet]. CBC News, 2013, Available from: http://www.cbc.ca/news/canada/manitoba/cybercrime-moving-to-smartphones-and-tablets-say-experts-1.1877058 (accessed 28.12.2015).

[21] A. Savoldi, P. Gubian, I. Echizen, A comparison between windows mobile and Symbian S60 embedded forensics, in: IIH-MSP 2009–2009 5th International Conference on Intelligent Information Hiding and Multimedia Signal Processing, 2009, pp. 546–550.

[22] L. Ablon, M.C. Libicki, A.A. Golay, Markets for Cybercrime Tools and Stolen Data: Hacker's Bazaar, National Security Research Division, Santa Monica, CA, 2014.

[23] S. Mohtasebi, A. Dehghantanha, A mitigation approach to the privacy and malware threats of social network services, in: V. Snasel, J. Platos, E. El-Qawasmeh (Eds.), Digital Information Processing and Communications, Springer, Berlin, 2011, pp. 448–459.

[24] F. Sabena, A. Dehghantanha, P.S. Andrew, A review of vulnerabilities in identity management using biometrics, in: Proc. 2nd International Conference on Future Networks, ICFN 2010, 2010, pp. 42–49.

[25] K. Nicolai, R. Carsten, A. Aaron, E.-P. Barbara, C. John, K. Thomas, On the creation of reliable digital evidence, in: Advances in Digital Forensics VIII, IFIP AICT 383, 2012, pp. 3–17.

[26] A. Rick, B. Sam, J. Wayne, Guidelines on Mobile Device Forensics, National Institute of Standards and Technology, United States, 2014, pp. 15–43.

[27] M. Damshenas, A. Dehghantanha, R. Mahmoud, A survey on digital forensics trends, Int. J. Cyber-Secur. Digit. Forensic 3 (4) (2014), 209–234.

[28] A. Dehghantanha, K. Franke, Privacy-respecting digital investigation, in: 2014 12th Annual International Conference on Privacy, Security and Trust (PST), 2014, pp. 129–138.

[29] A. Aminnezhad, A. Dehghantanha, M. Abdullah, A survey on privacy issues in digital forensics, Int. J. Cyber-Secur. Digit. Forensic 1 (4) (2012) 311–323.

[30] K. Shaerpour, A. Dehghantanha, R. Mahmod, Trends in Android malware detection, J. Digit. Forensic Secur. Law 8 (3) (2013) 21–40.

[31] F.N. Dezfouli, A. Dehghantanha, R. Mahmod, N.F.B.M. Sani, S.B. Shamsuddin, F. Daryabar, A survey on malware analysis and detection techniques, Int. J. Adv. Comput. Technol. 5 (2013) 42–51.

[32] J. Aycock, Computer viruses and malware, Advances in Information Security, vol. 22, Springer, US, 2006, pp. 25–29.

[33] K. Barmpatsalou, D. Damopoulos, G. Kambourakis, V. Katos, A critical review of 7 years of mobile device forensics, Digit. Investig. 10 (4) (2013) 323–349.

[34] J. Buchanan-Wollaston, T. Storer, W. Glisson, Comparison of the data recovery function of forensic tools, in: G. Peterson, S. Shenoi (Eds.), Advances in Digital Forensics IX, 9th IFIP WG 11.9 International Conference on Digital Forensics, IFIP Advances in Information and Communication Technology, vol. 410, Springer, Berlin, 2013, pp. 331–347.

[35] G. Grispos, T. Storer, W.B. Glisson, A comparison of forensic EVIDENCE recovery techniques for a windows mobile smart phone, Digit. Investig. 8 (1) (2011) 23–36.

[36] M. Damshenas, A. Dehghantanha, R. Mahmoud, A survey on malware propagation, analysis and detection, Int. J. Cyber-Secur. Digit. Forensic 2 (4) (2013) 10–29.

[37] C. Tassone, B. Martini, K.-K.R. Choo, J. Slay, Mobile device forensics: a snapshot, Trends Issues Crime Crim. Justice 460 (2013) 1–7.

[38] W.B. Glisson, T. Storer, J. Buchanan-Wollaston, An empirical comparison of data recovered from mobile forensic toolkits, Digit. Investig. 10 (1) (2013) 44–55.

[39] NIST, Have your computer forensics tools been tested? Computer Forensics Tool Testing Handbook, National Institute of Standards and Technology (NIST), 2015.

[40] R. Ayers, W. Jansen, S. Brothers, Guidelines on mobile device forensics, (NIST Special Publication 800-101 Revision 1) 2014, 85 pp.

[41] B.-W. Joe, S. Tim, G. William, Comparison of the data recovery function of forensic tools, in: Advances in Digital Forensics IX, IFIP AICT 410, 2013, pp. 331–347.

[42] M. Sidheeq, A. Dehghantanha, G. Kananparan, Utilizing trusted platform module to mitigate botnet attacks, in: 2010 International Conference on Computer Applications and Industrial Electronics (ICCAIE), 2010, pp. 245–249.

[43] K. Shaerpour, A. Dehghantanha, R. Mahmod, Virtualized honeynet intrusion prevention system in Scada, in: The International Conference on E-Technologies and Business on the Web (EBW2013), 2013, pp. 11–15.

[44] M.M.N. Umale, P.A.B. Deshmukh, P.M.D. Tambhakhe, Mobile phone forensics challenges and tools classification: a review, Int. J. Recent Innov. Trends Comput. Commun. 2 (2014) 622–626.

[45] M. Mulazzani, M. Huber, E. Weippl, Data visualization for social network forensics, in: G. Peterson, S. Shenoi (Eds.), Advances in Digital Forensics VIII, IFIP AICT, 383, Springer, Berlin, 2012, pp. 115–126. IFIP International Federation for Information Processing 2012.

[46] M. Damshenas, A. Dehghantanha, R. Mahmoud, S. Bin Shamsuddin, Forensics investigation challenges in cloud computing environments, in: Proc. 2012 Int. Conf. Cyber Secur. Cyber Warf. Digit. Forensic, CyberSec, 2012, pp. 190–194.

[47] F.N. Dezfouli, A. Dehghantanha, R. Mahmoud, N.F.B.M. Sani, S.bin. Shamsuddin, Volatile memory acquisition using backup for forensic investigation, in: Proc. 2012 Int. Conf. Cyber Secur. Cyber Warf. Digit. Forensic, CyberSec, 2012, pp. 186–189.

[48] N. Son, Y. Lee, D. Kim, J.I. James, S. Lee, K. Lee, A study of user data integrity during acquisition of Android devices, Digit. Investig. 10 (Suppl.) (2013) S3–S11.

[49] N. Kuntze, C. Rudolph, A. Alva, B. Endicott-popovsky, J. Christiansen, T. Kemmerich, On the creation of reliable digital evidence, in: G. Peterson, S. Shenoi (Eds.), Advances in Digital Forensics VIII, IFIP AICT, 383, Springer, Berlin, 2012, pp. 3–17. IFIP International Federation for Information Processing 2012.

[50] J. Dykstra, A.T. Sherman, Acquiring forensic evidence from infrastructure-as-a-service cloud computing: exploring and evaluating tools, trust, and techniques, Digit. Investig. 9 (2012) S90–S98.

[51] N. Borhan, A. Dehghantanha, A Framework of TPM, SVM and boot control for securing forensic logs, Int. J. Comput. Appl. 50 (13) (2012) 15–19.

[52] R. Mercuri, Criminal defense challenges in computer forensics, in: S. Goel (Ed.), Digit Forensics and Cyber Crime, First International ICST Conference, ICDF2C 2009, LNICST, vol. 31, Springer, Berlin, 2010, pp. 132–138.

[53] M. Al Marzougy, I. Baggili, A. Marrington, BlackBerry PlayBook backup forensic analysis, in: M. Rogers, K.C. Seigfried-Spellar (Eds.), Digit Forensics and Cyber Crime, 4th International Conference, ICDF2C 2012, Lecture Notes of the Institute for Computer Sciences, Social Informatics and Telecommunications Engineering, vol. 114, Springer, Berlin, 2013, pp. 239–252.

[54] S. Vandeven, B. Filkins, Forensic images: for your viewing pleasure, Inf. Secur. (2014) 1–38.

[55] Q. Do, B. Martini, K.-K.R. Choo, A cloud-focused mobile forensics methodology, IEEE Cloud Comput. 2 (4) (2015) 60–65.

[56] M. Mulazzani, S. Neuner, P. Kieseberg, M. Huber, S. Schrittwieser, E. Weippl, Quantifying windows file slack size and stability, in: G. Peterson, S. Shenoi (Eds.), Advances in Digital Forensics IX, 9th IFIP WG 11.9 International Conference on Digital Forensics, IFIP Advances in Information and Communication Technology, vol. 410, Springer, Berlin, 2013, pp. 183–193.

[57] M. Damshenas, A. Dehghantanha, R. Mahmoud, S. Shamsuddin, Cloud computing and conflicts with digital forensic investigation, Int. J. Digit. Content Technol. Appl. 7 (9) (2013) 543–553.

[58] J. Shetty, J. Adibi, The Enron Email Dataset—Database Schema and Brief Statistical Report, Inf. Sci. Inst. Tech. Report 2004.

[59] S.P. Hotel, N. Beach, Workshop on Link Analysis, Counterterrorism and Security at the SIAM International Conference on Data Mining Workshop on Link Analysis, Counterterrorism and Security, 2005.

[60] J. Shetty, J. Adibi, Discovering important nodes through graph entropy: the case of Enron email database, in: Proc. 3rd Int. Work Link Discov., 2005, pp. 74–81.

[61] J. Diesner, T.L. Frantz, K.M. Carley, Communication networks from the Enron email corpus "it's always about the people. Enron is no different", Comput. Math. Organ. Theory 11 (2006) 201–228 (abstract).

[62] B. Klimt, Y. Yang, The Enron Corpus: a new dataset for Email classification research, in: J.-F. Boulicaut, E. Floriana, G. Fosca, P. Dino (Eds.), European Conference on Machine Learning, Vol. 3201, Springer, Berlin, Heidelberg, 2004 September 20, pp. 217–226.

[63] J. Diesner, K.M. Carley, Exploration of communication networks from the Enron email corpus, in: Int. Conf. Data Mining Workshop Link Anal. Counterterrorism Secur., 2005.

[64] Y. Zhou, K.R. Fleischmann, W.A. Wallace, Automatic text analysis of values in the Enron email dataset: clustering a social network using the value patterns of actors, in: Proc. Annu. Hawaii Int. Conf. Syst. Sci., 2010.

[65] M. Al Marzougy, B. Ibrahim, M. Andrew, BlackBerry Playbook backup forensic analysis, in: M. Rogers, K.C. Seigfried-Spellar (Eds.), ICDF2C 2012, LNICST 114, 2013, pp. 239–252.

[66] F. Cruz, A. Moser, M. Cohen, A scalable file based data store for forensic analysis, Digit. Investig. 12 (2015) S90–S101.

Honeypots for Employee Information Security Awareness and Education Training: A Conceptual EASY Training Model

L. Christopher*, K.-K.R. Choo[†,‡], A. Dehghantanha[§]
*The Honeynet Project, Singapore Chapter, Singapore [†]University of Texas at San Antonio, San Antonio, TX, United States [‡]University of South Australia, Adelaide, SA, Australia [§]University of Salford, Salford, United Kingdom

1 INTRODUCTION

Information and communications technologies form the backbone of many aspects of the critical infrastructure sectors, particularly in technologically advanced countries such as Australia and Singapore. For example, the moment a system is connected to a public facing IP address (cyberspace), the system will be probed, scanned, or compromised almost immediately, as revealed in a 2014 study [1].

The challenges of securing a corporation's information security are increasingly interdisciplinary and multifaceted, as information security is defined not only by people, process, and technical perfection but rather by an ability to manage these imperfections. In addition, information security threats will continue to evolve into new forms. Technical solutions, while effective, cannot provide a comprehensive solution [2]. The Australian Signals Directorate [3] noted that

> even the best technical security measures can be defeated by inappropriate user behavior [sic]. Some users, in particular individuals and small businesses, are more vulnerable due to a general lack of awareness of cyber threats and relatively low resources devoted to information security.

Human factors are likely to remain one of the weakest links in attempts to secure systems and networks [4]. Although information security management is relatively mature, comprehensive statistics on patterns and trends in malicious cyber activities, particularly incidents involving private sector corporations, remain an elusive goal (e.g., due to unreported and undetected activities) [5].

One typical information security strategy is to create conditions unfavorable to security incidents, for example, by identifying, manipulating, and controlling the situational or environmental factors to limit the opportunities for offenders to engage in criminal behavior. The routine activity theory, for example, explains that crime is generally opportunistic, which occurs when a suitable target is in the presence of a motivated offender and is without a capable guardian [6]. Therefore to reduce security incidents, one could target each of these areas— (1 and 2) increasing the effort required to offend and the risk of getting caught, as well as (3) reducing the rewards of offending. One such strategy is employee information security awareness and education training (and user education is also one of the key cybercrime mitigation strategies identified by the Australian Signals Directorate) [3].

Employee information security awareness and education are critical in mitigating cyber threats as well as maintaining up-to-date knowledge of cybercriminal activities and mitigation measures available (e.g., to harden their systems, control access to facilities, and deflecting offenders). Major corporations generally include information security awareness programs in their corporation training. Effective awareness and education training can potentially reduce the numbers of vulnerable systems that can be exploited. However, fearing negative publicity and the resulting competitive disadvantage due to leakage of information about security breaches and monitoring metrics, information about such breaches (e.g., how they occur and what are the lessons learnt) is generally not shared with most employees.

In addition, postincident forensic investigations are not generally conducted [7]; hence, corporations may not have a complete picture of the security incident. Honeypots can be a useful tool to facilitate understanding of attack trends and attacker behaviors, as these systems are designed to emulate services of a typical server and capture attacker activities.

A number of studies [8–10] have highlighted the usefulness of honeypots in information security education, but they are usually discussed in the context of the higher education institution settings (i.e., educating university students) rather than in a real-world corporate environment. In this paper we study the feasibility of deploying honeypots with the aim of collecting attacker trends, behaviors and activities that can be used in information security awareness and education training in a corporate environment.

Both honeypots in our study were deployed on a low-cost embedded devices in a Private University based in Singapore. Applying the routine activity theory, we outline an employee information security awareness and education training that uses data collected from the honeypots.

The rest of the paper is organized as follows. The next section introduces our experiment setup. Findings from the Dionaea and Kippo are presented in Sections 3 and 4, respectively. We then describe how the routine activity theory can be used to design employee information security awareness and education training in Section 5. The last section concludes this paper.

2 EXPERIMENT SETUP

We set up two honeypots, namely Dionaea [11] and Kippo [12], using Raspberry Pi (see Table 1) running on Raspbian, which is a Debian-based operating system.

TABLE 1   Specifications

Raspberry Pi Model B	
Operating system	Raspbian
Processor	ARM1176JZF-S 700 MHz
Graphical user interface card	Broadcom VideoCore IV GPU
RAM	512 MB
Video out	Composite (PAL and NTSC), HDMI or Raw LCD (DSI)
Audio out	3.5 mm Jack or Audio over HDMI
Storage	SD/MMC/SDIO
Networking	10/100 Ethernet (RJ45)
Low-level peripherals	<ul><li>8 × GPIO</li><li>UART</li><li>I2C bus</li><li>SPI bus with two chip selects</li><li>+3.3 V</li><li>+5 V</li><li>Ground</li></ul>
Power requirements	5 V @ 700 mA via MicroUSB or GPIO Header

Dionaea is a low interaction honeypot that emulates services in order to collect malware targeting protocols such as Server Message Block (SMB). The SMB implementation on Dionaea is based on python and SMB emulation is based on mwcollectd. Dionaea also supports the uploading of files into the SMB shares and protocols such as:

- Hpertext Transfer Protocol (HTTP) although it does not capture any data transmitted via HTTP.
- File Transfer Protocol to create directories and allow the uploading and downloading of files.
- Trivial File Transfer Protocol for file transfer, Microsoft SQL Server.
- Voice over IP protocol to capture incoming SIP messages.

We make use of the libemu library [13] in the capturing of malware for our study. The medium interaction Kippo honeypot collects information about attempted brute force activities targeting Secure Shell (SSH) services.

Both honeypots were setup in a network zone protected by the firewall—see Fig. 1. As both systems are running low interaction and medium interaction honeypots, there is minimal risk of either honeypot being used as proxy to compromise other connected systems. The binary and logs are sent to a reporting server running on a virtual machine for further analysis. The data are extracted via SQLite for Dionaea and Mysql for kippo.

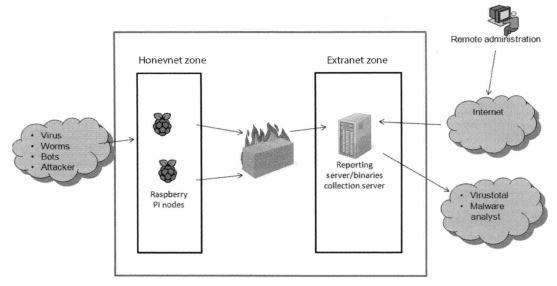

FIG. 1   Honeypot set up.

3 FINDINGS: DIONAEA

This honeypot was hosted from a local Internet service provider link, with a total of 115,882 IP connections to the honeypot. The data was collected over a period of 97 days, from Oct. 25, 2013 to Jan. 30, 2014.

Fig. 2 shows the breakdown of targeted ports on the Dionaea honeypot. The highest number of hits (77.52%) was on port 445 (SMB, the main protocol run by Dionaea). This is followed by port 139 (15.21%) and port 135 (5.21%).

3.1 Breakdown of Attacks by Time of Day

Fig. 3 shows the distribution of connection over the 24-h period. It was noted that connections followed a 9:00 a.m. to 5:00 p.m. GMT+8, peaking at 12:00 p.m. and a sharp drop at 5:00 p.m.

This could be because more machines are connected online during a typical work day cycle.

3.2 Breakdown of Attacks by IP Address

Table 2 presents a breakdown of detected successful connections by IP addresses. Of the six countries associated with the top 10 IP addresses, the United Kingdom accounted for close to three-quarter of detected successful connections. It was noted that this result does not imply that there are more attackers from the United Kingdom, as the IP address may be spoofed or belonged to a compromised computer based in the country. The spread of the different geo-location spread does, however, suggest that attacks could have originated from any part of the world.

Breakdown of targeted port

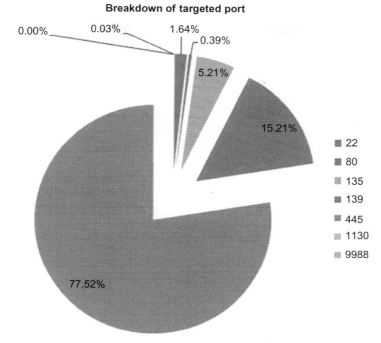

FIG. 2 Breakdown of detected attacks by ports (Dionaea honeypot).

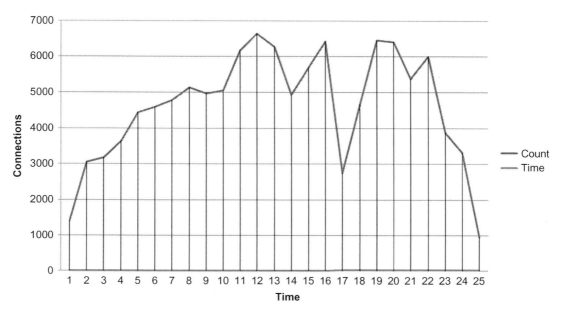

FIG. 3 Breakdown of detected attacks by time of day (Dionaea honeypot).

TABLE 2   Breakdown of Detected Successful Connections by Countries (Dionaea Honeypot)

Connections	IP	Country
58,609	176.227.xxx.xxx	United Kingdom, England, Gosport
4957	2.95.xxx.xxx	Russian Federation, Moscow City, Moscow
4937	78.61.xxx.xxx	Lithuania, Vilniaus Apskritis, Vilnius
2972	186.89.xxx.xxx	Venezuela, Bolivarian Republic of, Miranda, Petare
2627	186.89.xxx.xxx	Venezuela, Bolivarian Republic of, Miranda, Petare
2253	221.143.xxx.xxx	Korea, Republic of, Seoul-t'ukpyolsi, Seoul
1624	2.95.xxx.xxx	Russian Federation, Moscow City, Moscow
1334	93.183.xxx.xxx	Bulgaria, Khaskovo, Khaskovo
837	2.95.xxx.xxx	Russian Federation, Moscow City, Moscow
753	212.21.xxx.xxx	Bulgaria, Grad Sofiya, Sofia

Further analysis was carried out on the actual number of malware downloaded from the connections. As noted in Table 3, although the top connection was from Gosport in United Kingdom (a total of 58,609 connections), there were only 962 instances of malware downloaded. The high number of connections could be for reconnaissance purpose prior to the delivery of the malicious payload. It was also noted that connections originating from Korea did not result in any malware download. Similarly, these connections could be probing for specific information about the host prior to proceeding with an actual exploitation (which may not involve the use of malware).

TABLE 3   Further Analysis of Downloads From Top 10 Connections by Countries

Downloads	IP	Country
962	176.227.xxx.xxx	United Kingdom, England, Gosport
2400	2.95.xxx.xxx	Russian Federation, Moscow City, Moscow
2425	78.61.xxx.xxx	Lithuania, Vilniaus Apskritis, Vilnius
1423	186.89.xxx.xxx	Venezuela, Bolivarian Republic of, Miranda, Petare
1271	186.89.xxx.xxx	Venezuela, Bolivarian Republic of, Miranda, Petare
0	221.143.xxx.xxx	Korea, Republic of, Seoul-t'ukpyolsi, Seoul
794	2.95.xxx.xxx	Russian Federation, Moscow City, Moscow
652	93.183.xxx.xxx	Bulgaria, Khaskovo, Khaskovo
413	2.95.xxx.xxx	Russian Federation, Moscow City, Moscow
358	212.21.xxx.xxx	Bulgaria, Grad Sofiya, Sofia

3.3 Malware Captured by Dionaea

The majority of the captured malware from this honeypot were Conficker worm [14] exploiting the RPC vulnerability MS08-067 [15]. Fig. 4 shows the breakdown of the different variant of Conficker worm captured. The presence of Conficker proved its resiliency since it was first discovered in 2008. For example, a report by F-Secure noted that one-third of all detected threats were attributed to Conficker [16].

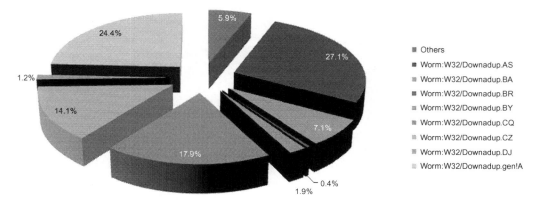

FIG. 4 Breakdown of detected successful connections by countries (Dionaea Honeypot).

4 FINDINGS: KIPPO

The dataset was collected over a period of 483 days, between Aug. 18, 2013 and Dec. 14, 2014. A number of **1,075,161** login attempts to the Kippo honeypot were recorded, and of which, **3762** single unique IP addresses were logged.

4.1 Top 10 Passwords Attempted

Passwords are analogous to our key to a locked door, and weak usernames and passwords are often a vector that can be targeted by attackers to gain entry into the system.

The most commonly passwords attempted were "admin," and the different variants of "password"—see Fig. 5. Other popular attempted passwords include common words (e.g., apple—1706, pass—1565, user—1017), common names (e.g., David—551, Peter—316, Sally—202), and common keyboard stroke (e.g., qwerty—2110, qazwsx—2111, q!w@e#r$—71).

The length of the passwords attempted generally ranged from six to nine characters (i.e., >50% of attempted passwords).

The two most commonly used usernames are root and admin. The former is the default username for a Unix based machine, while the latter is a commonly used username in routers or network devices. It was noted that oracle was among the top 10 usernames as it is a widely used database. Our findings echoed studies such as [17,18].

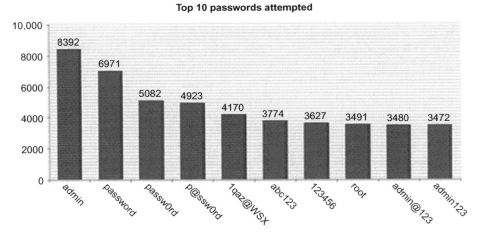

FIG. 5   Top 10 passwords attempted (Kippo honeypot).

Most organizations will not have a password policy that requires a long password [19], and in various studies [18] recent high profile breaches suggested that reusing usernames and passwords is not an uncommon practice among users. For example, a recent study found several hundred thousand leaked passwords from 11 web sites that "43–51% of users reuse the same password across multiple sites" [20]. Based on the findings, the authors designed a "cross-site password-guessing algorithm, which is able to guess 30% of transformed passwords within 100 attempts compared to just 14% for a standard password-guessing algorithm without cross-site password knowledge." Another recent study by Lu et al. [21] also demonstrated that it is relatively easy to identify online individual e-commerce customers by using the customers' usernames.

4.2 Top 10 IP Connections

The chart below outlined the top 10 unique IP addresses visiting the honeypot, where a majority of the IP connections were from Hong Kong and China. This is a similar observation reported by Cisco [22] but differs from recent studies undertaken by researchers from Aristotle University of Thessaloniki [23] and University of Ostrava [24]. In the first research a Dionaea honeypot was deployed between Feb. 19 and Mar. 11, 2012, Mar. 28 and Apr. 23, 2012, and Jan. 21 and Feb. 19, 2013. Similar to our research, Dionaea and Kippo honeypots were deployed. The top five attack countries varied between the three deployment periods in the first research. Unlike our findings, the top attack countries in both studies are dominated by European countries. This is, perhaps, due to the location of the deployed honeypots.

4.3 Top 10 Successful Commands

Kippo simulates a system with a limited command line. It allows the preconfiguration of username and password for login. In this setup, we used the default username "root" and password "admin" as the login username and password in order to gain a better understanding of attacker activities once they are logged into the compromised system. Such activities are captured in the database and allow real-time playback as shown in Fig. 10.

Fig. 11 listed the top 10 commands executed when an attacker was connected to the system. It was observed that the folder of interest appears to be /tmp, which stores temporary files which will automatically be deleted upon boot up. Attackers were observed to upload their artifacts or tools to the /tmp folder. The second most popular activity is the directory listing command, ls, which provides the attacker an overview of the system file structure.

4.4 Files Downloaded

There were a total of 93 unique files downloaded as shown in Fig. 6. We observed that a majority of the binaries are designed for 32-bit executables on MIPS or Intel platform. A handful of the captured binaries were compiled for ARM chipset.

Further analysis of the captured malware shows that a significant number of the binaries were designed to conduct denial of service attacks. The other popular captured malware were backdoors targeting Linux platform, which reflects the trend highlighted in the 2014 McAfee Labs Threat Report [25].

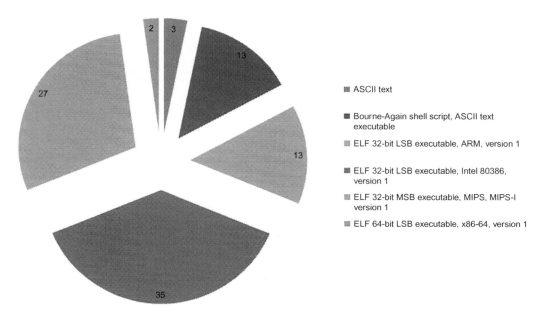

- ASCII text
- Bourne-Again shell script, ASCII text executable
- ELF 32-bit LSB executable, ARM, version 1
- ELF 32-bit LSB executable, Intel 80386, version 1
- ELF 32-bit MSB executable, MIPS, MIPS-I version 1
- ELF 64-bit LSB executable, x86-64, version 1

FIG. 6   Breakdown of captured malware type (Kippo honeypot).

5 A CONCEPTUAL EASY TRAINING MODEL

Most major corporations would have existing information security awareness and education training in place. The design of such training could be customized for individual corporate, although it would generally consist of three basic building blocks, namely: awareness, training, and education [26] (Fig. 7).

- Awareness typically begins by ensuring all employees within the organization have a basic understanding of cybercrime and the importance of information security, generally achieved via ongoing training and education—the other two building blocks.
- During training, participants (e.g., employees) will be taught relevant and up-to-date skills and competencies in order to contribute to a culture of security within the corporate.
- As aptly summarized in [26], education integrates all essential skills and relevant competencies into a common body of knowledge for information security specialists and professionals.

Enhancing or improving information security management in corporate has been studied by researchers. For example, Nersen, Rana, Mumtaz [27] identified several factors that could be included in awareness and education training. In another recent work, Martini and Choo [28] explained how the Situational Crime Prevention, a criminology theory, can be used as the underlying theoretical lens in the design of cybersecurity courses.

The routine activity theory [29] is another popular criminology theory that has been widely used to study cybercrime. The theory states that for crime to occur, there must be three elements, namely, a person motivated to commit the offense, a vulnerable victim who is available, and insufficient protection to prevent the crime. The theory draws on rational exploitation of "opportunity" in the context of the regularity of human conduct to design

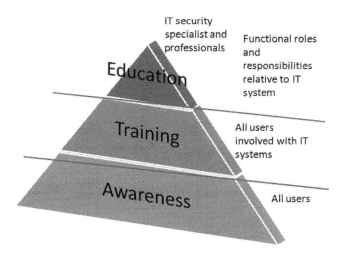

FIG. 7   The IT Security Learning Continuum. *(Adapted from Page 8, NIST-SP800-50.)*

crime prevention strategies, especially where terrestrial interventions are possible. Therefore to reduce the probability of the occurrence of a crime, we would need to:

- increase the effort required to offend;
- increase the risk of getting caught; and/or
- reduce the rewards of offending.

Our proposed engaging stakeholders, acceptable behavior, simple teaching method, yardstick (EASY) training model can be used with the routine activity theory to design training activities, which will increase the effectiveness of security awareness training and enhance the security culture within the corporate—see Table 4.

TABLE 4   Applying Routine Activity Theory to the Conceptual EASY Model

	Routine Activity Theory		
EASY Model	**Increasing the Effort Required to Offend**	**Increasing the Risk of Getting Caught**	**Reducing the Rewards of Offending**
Engaging stakeholders			
Engage senior management support	Yes	Yes	
Engage employee (including contractors and vendors)	Yes	Yes	
Engage with industrial partner s	Yes	Yes	
Acceptable behavior			
Reward good user behavior	Yes		Yes (particularly for insider-related threats)
Improved social support		Yes	
Improved feedback and assistance		Yes	
User ownership in detection and suspected incidents, compromises, or anomalies	Yes	Yes	
Simple teaching method			
Explore effective training methods	Yes		
Scalable and cost effective		Yes	
Yardstick			
Measurement through assessment	Yes		
Multiple channel feedback	Yes		

We now explain the four pillars of the model, as well as how honeypot data can be used in the model.

5.1 Engaging Stakeholders

A successful security awareness program requires commitment and support of all stakeholders, including senior management (e.g., the C-level executives). For example, a committed supportive senior management team who is able to lead by example (e.g., active participants in corporate training activities) will reinforce the importance of information security and set the right tone in ensuring a healthy security culture within the corporate. In addition, a clearly committed senior management will help ensure that the corporate's information security training program is adequately funded and implemented.

Employees are generally the frontline of information security threats and, therefore, active participation from employees will play a key role in early detecting and mitigation of information security threats (e.g., reporting of abnormalities which will lead to follow-up investigation and formulation of mitigation strategies). This would significantly increase the effort for an attacker to gain entry or increase the risk of detection. Security incident response teams should also consider join global alliances, such as Anti-Phishing Working Group and Forum for Incident Response and Security Teams, to facilitate timely sharing of information to better combat security threat.

Traditionally, security awareness training materials are delivered using presentation slides and e-learning platforms, which are generally nonengaging and information may not be up-to-date. The use of honeypot data could contribute to this gap.

In our model, we propose using interactive tools such as data visualization tools, as the latter has been shown to be an effective way to positively influence user [30]. Using real data collected from honeypots, materials delivered using data visualization tools can help ensure employees have an up-to-date and in-depth understanding of attacker trends. For example, the top attacks ports collected from both honeypots would allow participants to understand:

- attack vectors targeted by attackers (e.g., see Figs. 2–4 and 6);
- attack origins and time of attacks (e.g., see Fig. 3 and Tables 2 and 3);
- commonly attempted username and password combinations (e.g., see Figs. 5–9); and
- attacker activities on the system (e.g., see Figs. 10 and 11).

Such information would also allow the corporation to identify their vulnerable systems that can be exploited and ensure appropriate security measures are in place (e.g., turning off services that are not required to reduce the exposure). Employees would also be able to understand that attacks do not originate from one country or region, and attacks can originate from countries as far as Lithuania (in the context of the honeypot setup in this study). In addition, honeypot data would provide employees with up-to-date information on malware trends (e.g., what are the current malware targeting the corporate).

Honeypot data could also be used to provide senior management with an overview of the threat landscape (e.g., via a honeymap) as well as a real-time data visualization attack traffic to demonstrate how corporate systems are being targeted by attackers located in different places around the world (see Fig. 12).

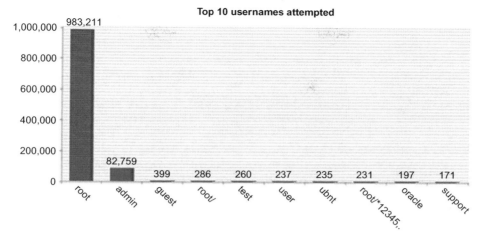

FIG. 8   Applying routine activity theory to the conceptual EASY model.

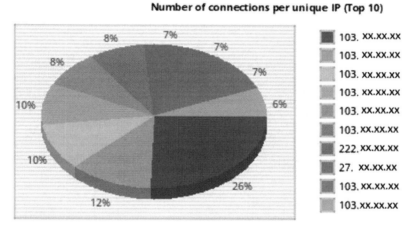

FIG. 9   Top 10 attacker IP (Kippo honeypot).

5.2 Acceptable Behavior

An important element to ensure the success of a security awareness initiative is to inculcate the correct user behavior towards information security. Every employee has their specific role and responsibilities within the company. We need to build a culture of ownership towards the responsibility of security among all employees. This could start with equipping employees with a good understanding of current cybercrime threats and trends (e.g., information about the latest phishing scam that may results in the employee system being compromised or

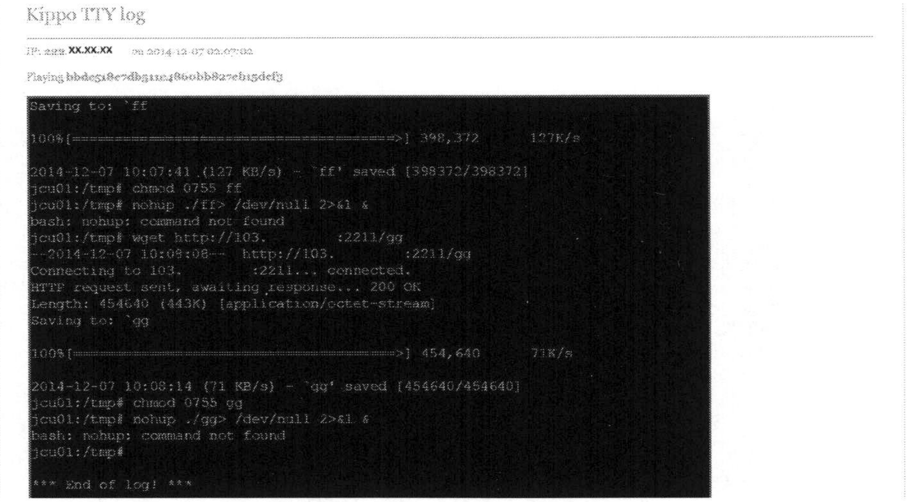

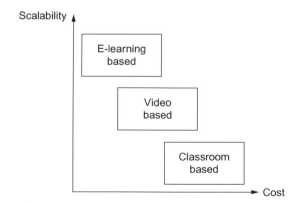

FIG. 10   Playback of the command used by attacker (Kippo honeypot).

ID	Input (success)	Count
1	cd /tmp/	30
2	ls	16
3	uname -a	15
4	exit	12
5	echo "WinSCP: this is end-of-file:0"	8
6	clear	4
7	pwd	3
8	ifconfig	3
9	chmod 0755 /tmp/java.13.2.8_11	3
10	wget http://119.188.8.74/zhi	3

FIG. 11   Top 10 commands (Kippo honeypot).

FIG. 12   Cost and scalability of the different delivery method.

their account credentials phished), the potential impact of a security breaches, and mitigation strategies.

Employees should also be educated about the importance of taking personal responsibility and ownership to ensure a secure environment and adopt cyber hygiene practices (e.g., not sharing username and password). This is also consistent with the Australian Government information security manual, which emphasized the importance of ensuring employees are familiar with their roles and responsibilities, understand and support security requirements, and learn how to fulfill their security responsibilities [31].

Employees could be motivated by using an appropriate reward system for employees demonstrating competency and walking the talk on security best practices. For example, we could organize a campaign to publicly identify the "most information security aware employee of the month" who demonstrates such values through nomination. We could also incorporate the use of the honeypot to influence user behavior. For example, we could demonstrate to end users how rapidly malware could infect the Dionaea honeypot when it is connected to the Internet and provide a preview through the playback action of what was done by attacker upon intrusion. We attempt to immerse the user through a live "hack" scenario and this could enrich the user's learning experience that was not found in conventional awareness training program.

Insider abuse has been the subject of academic research in the last few decades, but remains a concern area to corporates and governments. For example, Verizon data breach report 2014 [32] identified that the third most frequent data breach was caused by insider misuse. One deterrence strategy against insider abuse is to publish anonymized audit findings, for example, findings of unauthorized access by employees, to raise awareness and deter future offending. In addition, corporations should consider introducing employee counseling initiatives that include avoiding having disgruntled employee carrying out malicious act. This is enhanced by providing appropriate social support within employees to establish a positive environment condoning bad behavior and allow appropriate feedback channel for whistle blowing.

Security is often being regarded as the responsibility of the information technology and information security division within the corporation. Given the limited resources and wide threat surface, there are multiple entry points to a corporate system that can be exploited by cybercriminals. Therefore it is important to put in place reporting requirements for employees to report detected and suspected incidents, compromises, or anomalies. In addition, having an established corporate communication channel (e.g., an online incident reporting platform) and documentation of security best practices will enhance employee information security awareness and knowledge, and this could be reinforced using mock exercises with up-to-date data collected from honeypots.

5.3 Simple Teaching Method

Senior stakeholders in the organizations need to understand the importance of the right governance enablers and more importantly, to understand that information security is not only a cost or an IT issue, but it can facilitate economic exchange and deliver real business benefits. It is important for senior stakeholders in the organizations to be able to answer questions such as:

1. Who would benefit from having access to our information and systems?
2. What makes us secure against security threats?
3. Is the behavior of my staff enabling a strong security culture?
4. Are we ready to respond to an information security incident?
5. What would a serious information security incident cost our corporate?
6. How much effort will be needed to mitigate and recover from a serious cyber security incident?

The teaching method of the security awareness training must be simple and easy to use. Common methods include classroom-based, computer-based e-learning, and video-based learning, each requires different considerations on cost and scalability—see Fig. 13.

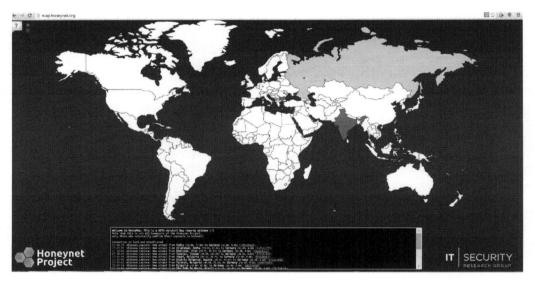

FIG. 13   The Honeynet Project's Honey Map.

It is also recommended that corporations consider putting classroom-based security training for new employees, and reenforcement training be delivered via video and/or e-learning based. Regardless of the delivery method, the principle of the teaching method should be simple, direct to the point, and easily understood by users with different backgrounds. Avoid using technical jargons and terminologies, which may not be easily understood by the employees. As previously explained, the training materials could be reinforced using live examples (e.g., live captured activities from the honeypot) to walk participants through the different aspect of security best practices.

We also designed a simple password checking application (see Fig. 14) where participants could key in their password to check against the data collected from the honeypots and other known sources (e.g., known databases of compromised username and passwords)

Total number of password collected: 1,075,161

FIG. 14 Password checking application.

to determine whether their password is one of those commonly attempted by attackers. This is a simple and cost-effective way to self-assess passwords as well as reinforcing the importance of having a strong password.

5.4 Yardstick

For any program to be successful, we need to be able to measure its outcome and monitor the progress. The monitoring should be done continuously so that gaps could be identified early and appropriate remediation could be applied. Therefore an appropriate feedback channel should be established such that improvement to the security awareness training could be made. This could be provided in the form of questionnaire surveys, evaluation forms, interviews and focus group, and success criteria need to be established (e.g., employee attendance rate and minimal score to pass assessment test).

6 CONCLUSION AND FUTURE WORK

Honeypot data can provide useful information that could be used in the understanding of attacker trends during employee information security awareness and education training. A better insight and knowledge of attacker trends will guide further responses at the operational level (e.g., effectiveness of existing controls) and contribute to management policy making and reform within the corporation.

- At a strategic level, will inform and help senior management and other key stakeholders to reach a level of consensus and decide on broad strategies, policies, and resources for the corporate in a timely fashion.

- At the operational level, findings about existing and emerging patterns of network activities will support policy makers and other key stakeholders in their decisions about focusing scarce resources in the most effective way (e.g., effect change to harden the environment),

It is also likely that corporations would be more likely to share such data internally considering the nonsensitive nature of the data, thus, allowing all employees to have up-to-date intelligence and ensuring that appropriate controls.

In this paper, we illustrated how the routine activity theory can be used as the underlying theoretical lens to design an employee information security awareness and education training, which incorporates real-world attack data (collected from honeypots). This approach has the potential to raise information security awareness within an organization as well as establishing a culture of security within the organization, and consequently, increase the effort required to offend, increase the risk of getting caught and reduce the rewards of offending.

Future work would include deploying honeypots in corporations and institutions in different countries located at different regions, as well as customized honeypot tools for specific security awareness themes (e.g., mobile security, web applications security, and industrial control system). We will also collaborate with like-minded researchers and practitioners to deploy our conceptual EASY model. This would allow us to receive practical feedback on the suitability of the various pillars in the model, which will provide the basis for the best practice (and the library of training methodologies and tools) recommendations. Face-to-face interviews will also be conducted with relevant stakeholders to determine the feasibility of the refined model and library of training methodologies and tools.

Acknowledgments

The views and opinions expressed in this article are those of the authors alone and not the organizations with whom the authors are or have been associated/supported. The authors would also like to thank the Private University in Singapore for deploying the two honeypots used in this study.

The authors declare that they have no competing financial or commercial interests.

References

[1] Y.G. Zeng, D. Coffey, J. Viega, How vulnerable are unprotected machines on the Internet? in: M. Faloutsos, A. Kuzmanovic (Eds.), Passive and Active Measurement, Lecture Notes in Computer Science, vol. 8362, Springer, Berlin, 2014, pp. 224–234.

[2] K.-K.R. Choo, A conceptual interdisciplinary plug-and-play cyber security framework, in: H. Kaur, X. Tao (Eds.), ICTs and the Millennium Development Goals—A United Nations Perspective, Springer, New York, NY, 2014, pp. 81–99.

[3] Australian Signals Directorate, 2014 Australian Government Information Security Manual: Executive Companion, Canberra, ACT, Australia.

[4] J. Imgraben, A. Engelbrecht, K.-K.R. Choo, Always connected, but are smart mobile users getting more security savvy? A survey of smart mobile device users, Behav. Inform. Technol. 33 (12) (2014) 1347–1360.

[5] K.-K.R. Choo, The cyber threat landscape: challenges and future research directions, Comput. Secur. 30 (8) (2011) 719–731.

[6] L.E. Cohen, M. Felson, Social change and crime rate trends: a routine activity approach, Am. Sociol. Rev. 44 (4) (1979) 588–608.

[7] N.H. Ab Rahman, A survey of information security incident handling in the cloud, Comput. Secur. 49 (2015) 45–69.

[8] J.K. Jones, G.W. Romney, Honeynets: an educational resource for IT security, in: Proceedings of the 5th Conference on Information Technology Education, ACM, New York, NY, 2004, pp. 24–28.

[9] R. Gandhi, C. Jones, W. Mahoney, A freshman level course on information assurance: can it be done? Here's how, ACM Inroads 3 (3) (2012) 50–61.

[10] K. Salah, Harnessing the cloud for teaching cybersecurity, in: Proceedings of the 45th ACM Technical Symposium on Computer Science education, ACM, New York, NY, 2014, pp. 529–534.

[11] Dionaea, https://github.com/rep/dionaea.

[12] Kippo, https://github.com/desaster/kippo.

[13] M. Koetter, Libemu library, http://www.honeynet.org/node/313.

[14] K. Burton, The Conficker worm, https://www.sans.org/security-resources/malwarefaq/conficker-worm.php.

[15] Microsoft, Microsoft security bulletin MS08-067—critical. https://technet.microsoft.com/library/security/ms08-067.

[16] F-Secure, Threat report H1 2014, https://www.f-secure.com/weblog/archives/Threat_Report_H1_2014.pdf, 2014.

[17] SANS Institute, SSH scanning activity, https://isc.sans.edu/ssh.html.

[18] R. Lichtenwalter, J.T. Lussier, N.V. Chawla, New perspectives and methods in link prediction, in: Proceedings of the 16th ACM SIGKDD International Conference on Knowledge Discovery and Data Mining, ACM, New York, NY, 2010, pp. 243–252.

[19] S. Komanduri, R. Shay, P.G. Kelley, M.L. Mazurek, L. Bauer, N. Christin, L.F. Cranor, S. Egelman, Of passwords and people: measuring the effect of password-composition policies, in: Proceedings of SIGCHI Conference on Human Factors in Computing Systems, ACM, New York, NY, 2011, pp. 2595–2604.

[20] A. Das, J. Bonneau, M. Caesar, N. Borisov, X. Wang, The tangled web of password reuse, in: Proceedings of the 21st Annual Network and Distributed System Security Symposium, Internet Society, 2014.

[21] C. Lu, H. Shuai, P.S. Yu, Identifying your customers in social networks, in: Proceedings of the 23rd ACM International Conference on Conference on Information and Knowledge Management, ACM, New York, NY, 2014, pp. 371–400.

[22] Cisco, Observations of login activity in an SSH honeypot, http://www.cisco.com/web/about/security/intelligence/ssh-security.html.

[23] I. Koniaris, G. Papadimitriou, P. Nicopolitidis, M. Obaidat, Honeypots deployment for the analysis and visualization of malware activity and malicious connections, in: Proceedings of IEEE Communications Software, Services and Multimedia Applications Symposium, IEEE, 2014, pp. 1819–1824.

[24] T. Sochor, M. Zuzcak, Study of internet threats and attack methods using honeypots and honeynets, in: A. Kwiecień, P. Gaj, P. Stera (Eds.), Computer Networks, Communications in Computer and Information Science, vol. 431, Springer, Berlin, 2014, pp. 118–127.

[25] McAfee, McAfee Labs Threat Report, Threat Statistics, Top Network Attacks, 2014, p. 36.

[26] M. Wilson, J. Hash, Building an Information Technology Security Awareness and Training Program, NIST Special Publication 800-50, National Institute of Standards and Technology, Washington, DC, 2003.

[27] N. Waly, R. Tassabehji, M. Kamala, Measures for improving information security management in organisations: the impact of training and awareness programmes, in: Proceedings of UK Academy for Information Systems Conference Proceedings, 2012, pp. 1–11.

[28] B. Martini, K.K.-R. Choo, Building the next generation of cyber security professionals, in: Proceedings of 22nd European Conference on Information Systems, 2014, pp. 1–14.

[29] R.A. Tewksbury, E. Ehrhardt Mustaine, Cohen, Lawrence E., and Marcus K. Felson: routine activity theory, in: F.T. Cullen, P. Wilcox (Eds.), Encyclopedia of Criminological Theory, Sage Publications, Thousand Oaks, CA, 2010. http://www.sagepub.com/schram/study/materials/reference/90851_03.2r.pdf.

[30] A. Manivannan, O. Nov, M.L. Satterthwaite, E. Bertini, The persuasive power of data visualization, New York University Public Law and Legal Theory working papers. Paper 474, http://lsr.nellco.org/nyu_plltwp/474, 2014.

[31] Australian Signals Directorate, 2014 Australian Government Information Security Manual: Controls, Canberra, ACT, Australia.

[32] Verizon, 2014 data breach investigations report, http://www.verizonenterprise.com/DBIR/2014/reports/rp_Verizon-DBIR-2014_en_xg.pdf.

Implications of Emerging Technologies to Incident Handling and Digital Forensic Strategies: A Routine Activity Theory

N.H. Ab Rahman*,†, *G.C. Kessler*‡,§, *K.-K.R. Choo**,¶

*University of South Australia, Adelaide, SA, Australia †Universiti Tun Hussein Onn Malaysia, Johor, Malaysia ‡Embry-Riddle Aeronautical University, Daytona Beach, FL, United States §Edith Cowan University, Joondalup, WA, Australia ¶University of Texas at San Antonio, San Antonio, TX, United States

1 INTRODUCTION

The rapid progression of emerging technologies over the years has transformed organizational users of technology into a more sophisticated workforce. Cloud-based services, for example, provide a simple way for users to create, process, and store their personal and business data on the Internet. The advantage of interconnected devices and data synchronization, additionally, causes easy collaboration as well as increased work productivity. The reliance on these emerging technologies, however, can be exploited by cybercriminals as a way to target their sensitive data.

There has been an increase in the volume and sophistication of cybersecurity attacks in recent years. For example, Symantec Corporation [1] reported that 70% of social media scams were manually shared, five out of every six large companies were targeted with spear phishing, ransomware attacks grew 113% between 2013 and 2014. In addition, 46 new families of Android malware were discovered. Of note, approximately one million Android applications were malicious [1]. The Australia Cyber Security Centre (2015) also reported that ransomware and spear phishing attack are likely to be an increasing threat to the confidentiality, integrity, and availability (CIA) of user data.

Consequences from cybersecurity incidents could have significant financial impacts, both directly and indirectly. For example, it was reported that approximately AUD 8 million were paid by more than 10,000 victims of the Cryptolocker ransomware attack in Australia [2]. Cybersecurity attacks could also result in physical harm to their victims, such as in the incident involving the Ashley Madison Website [3]. It is, arguably, critical that organizations have an effective and proactive incident handling plan in place to mitigate CIA risks and to attribute the source of a cyberattack. Such a plan will not only help the organization manage and coordinate the incident response but facilitate future incident responses and investigations.

Incident handling and digital forensics are established areas in the information security domain. As digital technologies continually evolve, however, incident handling and digital forensic strategies require improvements and adaptation in order to meet the increasing security demand. At any given point in time, a key issue is to determine whether current strategies apply to new emerging technology platforms and the threat landscape. Therefore, in this research, we seek to elicit the following information from experienced industry practitioners:

- What are the existing cyber threats faced by the industry?
- What are the impacts of emerging cyber threats to incident handling and digital forensic strategies?

We use the routine activity theory (RAT) as the underlying theoretical lens to study the impacts of emerging cyber threats to incident handling and digital forensic activity. RAT consists of three factors, namely: motivation, opportunity, and guardianship. RAT is described in more detail in the following section.

This paper is structured as follows. Background and related work are presented in Section 2. Section 3 describes our research methodology; and findings are discussed in Section 4. The discussion is presented in Section 5, and the last section concludes this paper.

2 BACKGROUND AND RELATED WORK

In this section we provide an overview of the current emerging technologies areas and the associated threats. We also introduce the RAT and related literature.

2.1 Emerging Technologies and Threats

Emerging technologies have evolved from technology advancement coupled with innovative approaches to delivering computing services [4]. According to a report from the European Network and Information Security Agency (ENISA), the seven emerging technology threat areas are cyber physical systems, mobile computing, cloud computing, trust infrastructure, big data, Internet of Things (IoT), and network/software virtualization; the top threats are malicious code, Web-based attacks, injection attacks, botnets, denial of service (DoS) attacks, spam, phishing, exploit kits, data breaches, physical damage, insider threats, information leakage, identity theft, cyber espionage, and ransomware [5]. Most of these threats are common to conventional computing infrastructures, although some threats may also have evolved in terms of sophistication, stealthiness, adaptability to responses, and unpredictability.

A thorough analysis of attack patterns at a given organization, such as those observed by Jang-Jaccard and Nepal [4], can potentially inform incident handling strategy and digital forensic practices and strategies. For example, forensic investigators need to have an in-depth understanding of the attack vectors in order to optimize the search for evidentiary data, and the preventative measures or mitigation strategies must be regularly reviewed and revised due to the constant evolving threat landscape [6].

2.2 Routine Activity Theory

RAT suggests that crime is based more on society's prosperity and criminal opportunity than on social causes, such as poverty and unemployment [7]. The theory also suggests that criminal victimization is likely to occur in the presence of a motivated attacker and a suitable target, and the lack of a capable guardian (e.g., inadequate legal and technical protections). In other words, the absence of one or more of these factors is likely to reduce the likelihood of a criminal activity [7]. As pointed out by Miró [8], fewer variations in patterns of daily activity—often the results of modern life—can increase the likelihood of crime. RAT focuses on how daily, routine activities of a victim could create a predictable pattern. For example, a burglar would observe the victim (e.g., when the property is likely to be vacant) to determine the best time to break into the property. The same could be true about other physical and cyber security operations.

Due to the increasing dependence of organizations on information and communication technologies (ICT), such as mobile devices and cloud services, ICT are a primary attack vector. By observing business activity patterns, for example, a cybercriminal may discover flaws and vulnerabilities in the people, process, and/or technical elements and exploit them successfully in a cyberattack. The lack of physical boundaries, unfortunately, complicates efforts to secure the cyberspace.

RAT has been widely used in the criminology literature to explain vandalism [9], fraud victimization [10], and lifestyle characteristics [11]; as well as in the security literature to explain cybercriminal behaviors, such as online harassment [12,13], cyber threats [14]; malware infection [15], and identity theft [16,17].

By way of example, consider the high profile Sony Pictures Entertainment (SPE) hacking incident in late 2014 through the perspective of RAT:

> The FBI has determined that the intrusion into SPE's network consisted of the deployment of destructive malware and the theft of proprietary information as well as employees' personally identifiable information and confidential communications. The attacks also rendered thousands of SPE's computers inoperable, forced SPE to take its entire computer network offline, and significantly disrupted the company's business operations … As a result of our investigation, and in close collaboration with other U.S. government departments and agencies, the FBI now has enough information to conclude that the North Korean government is responsible for these actions. Federal Bureau of Investigation [18].

In the context of this incident,

- Motivation—The attack appears to be state-sponsored and, ostensibly, because of the insult resulting from the release by Sony of a particular movie.
- Opportunity—Vulnerabilities in SPE's network which enabled the cybercriminal to intrude and inject malware.
- Guardian—It is likely that the inefficiency of the preventative measures or mitigation strategies, including network monitoring and detection, as well as user training, allowed the attack to be successful.

2.3 Related Work

Various scholars have argued that RAT is a useful tool in explaining cybercrime. Holt and Bossler [13], for example, found that routine computer use and physical guardianship had influence on the likelihood of a user being harassed while chatting online. A later study using a juvenile population showed that the use of social network sites, associating with peers who harass online, and posting sensitive information online could also increase online harassment victimization [12].

Focusing on malware infection, Holt and Bossler [15] reported that guardianship was a key predictor to victimization; users with higher computer skills were successfully attacked less often than those with lesser skills. Reyns [16] found a positive relationship between individuals' online routines (e.g., banking, shopping, downloading) and the likelihood of identity theft. Williams [17] observed that individual-level active personal guardianship and passive physical guardianship resulted in significantly reduced rates of online identity theft in Europe.

Adopting the RAT concept to inform cybercrime mitigation strategies, Choo [14] suggested that opportunities can be reduced by targeting each of these areas—"(1) increasing the effort required to offend; (2) increasing the risk of getting caught; and (3) reducing the rewards of offending." In a subsequent study undertaken by Choo [19], RAT has been incorporated as one of the theoretical components in a conceptual interdisciplinary plug-and-play cybersecurity framework.

However, to the best of our knowledge, there has been no attempt to use RAT to explain the impacts of emerging cyber threats to incident handling and digital forensic strategies. Therefore, in this paper, we seek to determine the utility of the theory to understand cyber security threats and inform incident handling and digital forensic strategies.

3 METHODOLOGY

This study was carried out using a self-administered online survey on the topics of cybersecurity incident trends, mitigation strategies, and key challenges of emerging technologies to cybersecurity. The majority of the questions were open-ended in order to obtain a detailed understanding of a respondent's own thinking [20]. A copy of the questionnaire is included in Appendix 1.

3.1 Data Collection

Using convenient sampling, we e-mailed the 10-question survey to members of an information security mailing list. We received 21 completed responses; one response had to be excluded due to poor data quality. More than half of the respondents were from government and nearly a third from the private sector. The distribution of the respondents' region and their industry type are shown in Table 1.

Fig. 1 shows the breakdown of respondents' job role. A quarter of the respondents were academicians, and just over the half were respondents who directly involve in digital forensic practices including Chief Information Officer (15%), Digital Forensic Specialist (15%), Digital Forensic Consultant (15%), and Law Enforcement Officer (10%). In the remainder of the paper, individual respondents are referred as R1, R2, etc.

TABLE 1   Region and Industry Type of Respondents

Region	Industry				
	Private Sector	Research Organization	Nonprofit Organization	Government	Total
North America	5	1	1	10	17
Europe		1			1
Oceania				1	1
Asia	1				1
Total	6	2	1	11	20

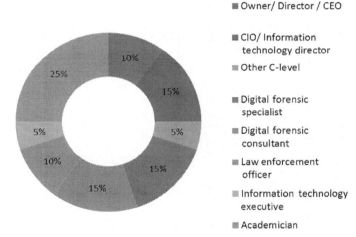

■ Owner/ Director / CEO

■ CIO/ Information technology director

■ Other C-level

■ Digital forensic specialist

■ Digital forensic consultant

■ Law enforcement officer

■ Information technology executive

■ Academician

FIG. 1   Job role of respondents.

3.2 Data Analysis

The data were analyzed primarily using qualitative methods. A coding process was applied in order to thematically analyze the textual content using the software tool, Atlas.ti.[1] Firstly, we analyzed the content to identify excerpts pertaining to motivation, opportunity, and guardianship—the main elements of RAT—as the three main codes. Secondly, similar excerpts from each of the codes were organized to analyze themes describing:

1. incident types and the associated motivation;
2. potential scenarios of cybercrime opportunity;
3. management and technical solutions to mitigate security risks; and
4. key challenges of incident handling and digital forensic practitioners faced due to emerging technologies development.

[1]http://atlasti.com/.

4 CYBER THREAT LANDSCAPE FROM A RAT PERSPECTIVE

This section presents the threat landscape identified by the survey respondents, from the perspectives of motivation, opportunity, and guardianship.

4.1 Motivation

A motivated threat actor can be any individual or group of individuals—external to the organization or an insider (e.g., employee, business partner, and vendor)—who is driven by criminal intent, ideology, financial gain, terrorism (state-sponsored or otherwise), or other causes (e.g., curiosity, fame, or attention) [19]. For example, half of the respondents reported that their organizations have encountered cybersecurity incidents and 60% indicated that criminally or financially motivated incidents posed significant risks to the organization. We categorize the incidents as content related (e.g., abusive content), information gathering (e.g., phishing), data availability (e.g., denial of service), data confidentiality (e.g., unauthorized use of data), data integrity (e.g., unauthorized modification), malicious code (e.g., ransomware), and intrusion attempts (e.g., unauthorized network access) (Fig. 2). A number of respondents specified that they have limited knowledge of the frequency or cause of attacks on their organization's systems. However, a small number of respondents were unable to disclose the information. Due to the sensitive nature of cybersecurity incidents, it is highly likely that the respondents underreported the number of incidents.

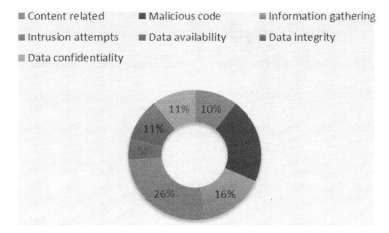

FIG. 2   Incident classification and number of informant.

Intrusion attempts and malicious code were the most common incidents reported. This is, perhaps, not surprising because over the half of the respondents agreed that financial motivation is a significant risk. Malicious code (usually spread via phishing attacks) is often financially motivated, such as the Zeus malware commonly used to steal banking information.

The motivations for other types of incidents were diverse. One participant (R3) reported that there was an incident involving university students accessing and deleting the university's network routing tables. This incident could be attributed to curiosity or attention seeking.

Furthermore, a cyberattack incident can be associated with more than one motivation. As one respondent (R11), who works for a government agency, explained: "Compromise of externally hosted websites by anonymous Indonesia and other criminal organizations ... post-incident analysis of some of the impacted machines showed traffic sniffing software and other Trojan software installed." This particular attack from a specific country against a government system was probably state-sponsored, or carried out by ideological or politically motivated cybercriminals. One participant (R2) also highlighted the potential for abuse of cyberspace to disseminate personal, religious, and political propaganda, such as incidents involving the dissemination of abusive content relating to hate crime.

4.2 Opportunity

Opportunities for malicious cyber activities can be broadly categorized into (i) industry profiling; (ii) emerging technologies, (iii) users; and (iv) rogue insiders.

Industry profiling: Every industry segment (e.g., education, retail, manufacturing, and finance) is characterized by a different set of sensitive information. The cybercriminal would find opportunity for exploitation by analyzing the business nature and data type associated with the industry sector of the organization. Academia, for instance, has personally identifiable information (PII) of students and parents, such as student identification numbers, social security numbers, date of birth, residency address, and parents' financial information, which could be used by cybercriminals to facilitate fraudulent activities. As respondent R1 observed, "Aside from grades, social security numbers and residence information, a university will also have access to students' financial information ...These forms also have financial information for parents, making the accessing of a university database a gold mine."

These sets of information could, directly or indirectly, lead to data privacy attacks. Government databases, healthcare institutions, financial institutions, entertainment companies, product designers, and manufacturers are likely to have network-accessible data that are attractive targets to cybercriminals. This can probably help explain the increasing number of phishing attacks. Respondent R11, for example, reported an increasing trend in attacks against government Web domain such as *gov.au*. Banking and retailing sites that deal mostly with financial information (e.g., credit or debit card data) are also frequently targeted by financially motivated cybercriminals (e.g., online fraud and phishing).

Emerging technologies: Emerging technologies could create opportunities for exploitation due to the interconnectedness of endpoint devices. IoT and Cloud of Things (CoT) devices, for example, have been targeted. CoT applications allow users to access data from any Internet location such as a desktop or laptop computer, mobile device, or any Web-enabled device, and any of these devices could be compromised to target systems that are connected to these devices. Two respondents (R9, R19) flagged point of sale (POS) devices as an attack vector that has been the subject of card skimming, RAM scraping, and Web-based attacks.

Users: Users increase cybercrime opportunities as humans have been known to be the weakest link in most information security chains. Security policies may be circumvented by internal users, either intentionally or accidentally (e.g., phishing); phishing is one widely used method to lure a victim to download a malicious program, open a malicious attachment, or click on a suspicious link. Despite the efforts in raising the awareness of users to phishing and other cyber threats, phishing remains a concern to many of the respondents. Four respondents (R11, R13, R16, and R20) explained that the techniques used in recent phishing attacks were observed to be more sophisticated (e.g., tools and social engineering tricks) and targeted. As one respondent (R16) rightly pointed out, "[m]orphing phishing attacks—no longer from hijacked e-mails, but from hijacked e-mail lists (so an e-mail appears via display name to be from someone we know, but the address is totally unfamiliar)."

Another information security trend that has been highlighted is ransomware, such as Cryptolock (R11). Once a device has been infected, the malware will seek to encrypt files stored on the device. Once a ransom (hence, the name ransomware) is paid, the decryption key will be provided to the victim so that the hard drive can be decrypted. For desperate victims, they are most likely to pay if the encrypted file contains important or sensitive information. In fact, in the absence of adequate backups, paying the ransom may be the only solution, particularly to small and medium-sized organizations.

Rogue insiders: Internal users who understand the internal system and have sufficient privileges to conduct malicious actions (e.g., undertaking internal network reconnaissance and data exfiltration) yet remain hidden or undetected as they are an authorized user. Addressing insider threats is somewhat tricky; an organization might provide a robust security protection. However, these protections might be ineffective if the rogue insider is familiar with the security system, explained one respondent (R11). The malicious acts are not limited to the CIA types of attack, but including the misuse of the organization's resources to distribute or host illegal data or media (R11).

4.3 Guardianship

The absence of a capable guardian, such as adequate ICT protections, increases the likelihood of a malicious cyber activity. Guardianship can include the implementation of security policies and procedures to safeguard the CIA elements of information assets using a given set of technical and management security strategies. Information security management addresses the design, implementation, and maintenance of policies, processes, and systems to ensure an acceptable level of risk to an organization's information assets [21]. A capable guardian, therefore, refers to adequate security strategies that fit the need of an organization's activities. In this section, we discuss the management and technical security solutions to mitigate the information security risks.

The majority of the survey respondents were not involved in the technical aspects of their organization's security posture and were unable to provide detailed information. Close to a quarter of the completed questionnaires had null responses to these questions. It is nevertheless interesting to observe how the remaining 75% of the respondents reported how their organization implements information security mitigation strategies. The themes identified for information security management elements are summarized in Table 2.

TABLE 2   The Identified Information Security Management Elements

Elements	Components	Respondents
Policy and procedures	ISO standards, Data Interchange Standard Association (DISA), Change management policy, acceptable use policy, organizational policies, mobile device management, authorization procedures	R6, R8, R11, R15, R16, R17
Security planning	Assume breach approach, defense in-depth	R12, R18
Personnel	Personnel's background checks	R14
Awareness and training	Training, security awareness program	R4, R15
Physical and environmental security	Physical security	R15
Audit	Internal and external audits	R11, R13, R14
Access control	Privileged account change, least privilege, separation of duties	R11, R14
Computer support and operations	Security support team, Incident response and forensic team	R2, R12, R16

The result as a whole demonstrated that basic elements of information security management are being adopted. To address emerging threats, proactive measures and up-to-date solutions, such as mobile device management (MDM), had been deployed by a number of the respondents' organizations. The proactive approach was echoed by a respondent (R18) who explained how defense in-depth was implemented in his organization:

> We have incorporated a multilevel set of applications, devices, etc. at the network level that protect the systems hosting our data. We have multiple security/monitoring applications running on the host operating system as well. We are also limiting access, the entire Engineering team constantly monitors and is responsible for securing the data, but we also have people from every department that assists/monitors/maintains systems and applications.

A good technical security strategy should implement both reactive and proactive security controls. Reactive strategies refer to response actions once a security incident is detected, such as the use of intrusion detection system (IDS). Proactive strategies, in contrast, are designed to detect and prevent incidents prior to an occurrence, such as regular vulnerability assessments and patch security updates. The technical solutions reportedly used by the respondents' organizations are listed in Table 3, and categorized as proactive or reactive. Endpoint protection and firewalls were the most reported proactive and reactive solutions, respectively. A possible explanation for this result could be simply because these are the two most common solutions. On the other hand, more sophisticated technical solutions, such as network segregation, may only be known or understood by a select few.

Overall, there appears to be a sense amongst respondents that capable technical guardianship is in place in terms of addressing security controls at the application, network, and data levels. That said, no particular mechanisms for managing emerging technologies (e.g., virtualization monitoring) was highlighted by respondents.

TABLE 3   The Identified Proactive and Reactive Technical Solutions

Proactive Measures	Respondents	Reactive Measures	Respondents
Cryptography, VPN	R1, R17	Logical access controls	R11
Endpoint protection	R2, R11, R13, R15, R16, R19	Logging	R11, R14
Network segregation	R11, R18	Firewalls	R2, R4, R9, R11, R13, R16, R17, R19
Offline and online backup of data	R1	Intrusion detection	R9, R15, R16, R17
Real time monitoring	R10, R11, R14,R18	Identification and authentication	R1
Data anonymization	R1		
Intrusion prevention	R11, R16		

One respondent (R11) explained about the technical measure against malicious insiders adopted by his organization:

> Logging and monitoring tools are deployed throughout the network. A document classification and Data Loss Prevention (DLP) solution is currently being rolled out. Most activities are traceable (post-incident) Encase Enterprise and FTK in use, Snare is in use for log capture and analysis. Endpoint protection is in place across the network, all email is securely archived.

Only a small number of respondents specifically expressed concern that their organization had inadequate security protections. For example, one respondent (R3) described a lack of support from top management and another (R10) commented on the absence of a dedicated information security support team. A small number of respondents mentioned poor mitigation strategies. For example, one respondent (R17) stated: "There are policies in place but are not followed. When an incident happens, if it involves client data, there is no mitigation ..." Less than half of the respondents (45%) indicated that their organization had contact with law enforcement authorities to receive advice on incident handling and digital forensic strategies.

When asked to highlight key challenges of incident handling and digital forensics from new emerging threats, most respondents identified cloud computing and mobile devices/platforms. A commonly cited challenge in cloud computing is the lack of tools and guidance to undertake forensic analysis and remote evidence collection, in addition to the concomitant issues of data ownership and scope of control over cloud resources. As most cloud services' data centers involve multiple locations in multiple countries on a clustered infrastructure, international laws—many inconsistent—come into play. One respondent (R16) commented on the need of understanding how cloud systems can be secured and locked down for forensic analysis, in comparison with mobile devices that can be reasonably controlled if one obtains physical control and can turn off network access. This view was echoed by another respondent (R4) in the context of forensic challenges for the examination of mainframe databases involving big data; a highly distributed environment of consumers with no security orientation can pose significant challenges to incident handling activities. Such challenges have also been noted in the literature (see [22]).

A common view amongst respondents about mobile devices was the concern of evidence acquisition, identifying potential evidence sources, data integrity on smart mobile devices, and bring your own device (BYOD) schemes where personally owned mobile devices can be one of the weakest links on an organization's network. One respondent (R3) explained that security risks due to mobile devices will not go away anytime soon and the need to be able to deal with such risks:

> Keeping up with them. We, as digital forensic examiners, will eventually need to specialize in the same way as the medical profession has. We will need to have people who are specialists in IOS devices, Android devices and desktop systems like the medical profession has cardiologists, neurologists and paediatricians.

Another respondent (R19) suggested the importance of digital forensic practitioners to be able to investigate different mobile platforms.

One respondent (R5) highlighted a risk that is not widely understood, that is the potential for intellectual property theft due to emerging technologies, such as 3D printers. Therefore forensic practitioners also need to be aware of and familiar with new sources and types of evidentiary data, including the specific acquisition procedures. As R5 stated, "Forensically, there will be new artifacts such as printer temporary files, and drawing files."

5 DISCUSSION

The survey findings provide a snapshot of the cyber threats faced by the respondents' organizations, as well as the common measures in place. We identify the following recurring themes.

Firstly emerging technologies are "supporting" an evolution in attack motivation and opportunity. There is an indication that financial gain is the most popular underlying motivation, which is consistent with the observations of Choo [14] (e.g., growing sophistication in the malware due to potential for illicit financial gain). Furthermore, most respondents observe that increasingly innovative and sophisticated, targeted attacks such as spear phishing, vishing, smishing, water hole attacks, and whaling are being detected, which is consistent with findings of ENISA [5]. Artifacts recovered during a digital forensic investigation (e.g., packet sniffing software or malware Command and Control code) would be significant to establishing the facts of the incident, and could be used in the attribution and prosecution of the perpetrators.

Cyberspace, such as social media, is a platform where one could "freely" distribute abusive content and facilitates hate crimes, cyberstalking, and cyberbullying. For example, social media plays a key role in the Arab Spring incident, where Facebook, Twitter, and other social media sites were the main medium of information exchange among those advocating for change [23]. Therefore social media applications have emerged as an important source of evidence in the investigation of cyberattacks and other forms of cybercrime, including cyberterrorism [24,25].

Secondly (technical) guardianship such as mitigation strategies need to keep pace with emerging technologies. The race between security solutions and cyber threats is evidenced in the increasing innovative security products on the market, such as tools for cloud monitoring, cloud identity management, and mobile security management. The increased use of social media applications, for example, and the many organizations that are currently allowing BYOD strategies, have increased the risks from untrusted mobile devices. MDM, therefore, becomes an important part of incident handling in order to enforce device registration and security policies in an enterprise mobility scenario. This observation is consistent with studies by Ab Rahman and Choo [6,26] which acknowledge that the needs of incident handling and digital forensics often overlap.

Maintaining an up-to-date forensic awareness and capability to deal with emerging technology apps is an ongoing challenge. The release of new software, in particular, complicates efforts to identify and recover data types, database formats, and location of potential evidence artifact sources. In cloud computing, for example, evidence artifacts may exist across cloud stacks (e.g., guest virtual machines or a server on the provider's site). Such concerns have also been raised by cloud forensic researchers [27,22], IoT forensic researchers [28], and mobile forensic researchers [29].

Legal and regulatory challenges have also received considerable attention, particularly in the investigations of transborder malicious cyber activities. Hooper et al. [30] suggested a need for harmonization of cyberlaws across jurisdictions in order to facilitate collaboration between law enforcement agencies. It is, undeniably, important for countries to establish legislation to facilitate transborder investigation. The Malaysia *Computer Crime Act 1997*, for example, addresses offenses committed by a person (regardless of nationality), inside or outside of Malaysia, and "if, for the offense in question, the computer, program or data was in Malaysia or capable of being connected to or sent to or used by or with a computer in Malaysia at the material time" [31].

Thirdly being proactive is key to improving the effectiveness of incident handling and digital forensic strategies. It is somewhat surprising that no clear evidence of digital forensic readiness was provided by the respondents. A likely interpretation for this might be that there is no mature standard implementation of such readiness, as evidenced by the recent publication of the Incident Investigation Principles and Processes standard [32]. It is important for an organization with any sort of interconnected network devices to be in such a proactive readiness state so that security incidents can be rapidly investigated, particularly difficult where incident artifacts must be correlated from various sources.

With multifaceted security issues, assuming that an attack has already occurred would be pragmatic advice for an incident handling team tasked with the design and improvement of their security strategies, as employed by Microsoft [33]. This indicates the need to be proactive, especially for a high security risk profile industry (e.g., finance and defense). In addition, active engagement in a cyber threat intelligence and information sharing community is one way to keep abreast of emergence threats. Indeed, not only must practitioners know their enemy, but must continually *think* like their enemy as they look at their own systems.

Finally poor implementation of systematic security strategies was an unanticipated finding in the survey. This poor planning is likely to be related to lack of support and enforcement from top management. Similar observation has been noted by Line [34] in the smart grids industry. This situation is somewhat astounding given the fact that cyber breaches across all sectors have been reported with increasing frequency over the last few years, and it is quite clear that a sophisticated cybercriminal can cause very serious direct and/or indirect damage. Recall the Sony Entertainment cyberattack described in Section 2.2; the attack was reportedly due to dissatisfaction (possibly by the government of one country) with one Sony movie that portrayed a sensitive national issue; the result was that the movie release was canceled and then that decision was reversed (and the release of the movie online) [18]. The impact in this incident was significant monetary loss, but also a more significant loss to the organization's reputation. A serious lesson learnt is therefore should be taken into account by all digital society.

6 CONCLUSION AND FUTURE WORK

Our study illustrated the current cyberthreat landscape due to emerging technologies as perceived by the survey respondents. We categorized the threats based on motivation, opportunity, and guardianship, the three factors of RAT. Emerging technologies result in significant—and new—motivations and opportunities to cybercriminals and, therefore, increases the challenges in incident handling and digital forensic to provide effective guardianship to mitigate the risks.

It might be argued that the current threat landscape transforms the strategic planning of incident handling and digital forensics to become more proactive in design, require better tactical tools, and cultivate a culture of information security amongst the practitioners. This study is somewhat limited due to undetailed information and a small number of respondents; further work is required to expand the sample size and refine our understanding in a bigger context.

APPENDIX 1 QUESTIONNAIRE ITEMS

(Q1) In the last calendar year (i.e., Jan. 1, 2013 to Dec. 31, 2013), has your organization encountered any cybersecurity incident (e.g., unauthorized access to your organization's computer systems or networks)? If yes, how many incidents and please briefly describe the nature of the incident(s), seriousness, loss or damage and mitigation strategies.	Estimated number of cybersecurity incidents encountered by your organization in the last calendar year (i.e., 1 Jan. 2013 to 31 Dec. 2013): _____ Description:

(Q2) Which cybersecurity incidents does your organization identify as significant risks? What steps have been taken to mitigate those threats? Incidents against (the confidentiality, integrity and availability of) data, computer systems or networks:	Cybersecurity incidents against the computer system of your organization (as a direct victim):	Please describe examples of the risk below, as well as mitigation steps:	Cybersecurity incidents committed by persons using computer infrastructure owned or operated by your organization:	Please describe examples of the risk below, as well as mitigation steps:

Computer-related
incidents for personal
or financial gain:

Specific computer-
related incidents:

(Q3) What are the trends in cybersecurity incidents
against the industry that your organization is in over
the past three calendar years (i.e., Jan. 1, 2011 to Dec. 31,
2013)? For example, new acts, emerging threats, or other
significant risks encountered by other organizations in
the same industry.
Please briefly describe its nature, seriousness, loss or
damage and/or potential mitigation strategies.

(Q4) What technical solutions are used by your organization to secure your organization's computer data, systems and network?	Committed against the computer system of your organization (as a direct victim)?	Committed by persons (including insiders) using computer infrastructure owned or operated by your organization?
(Q5) Please estimate the annual costs to your organization to implement the technical solution(s).		
(Q6) What procedural or management solutions are used by your organization to secure your organization's computer data, systems and network?	Committed against the computer system of your organization (as a direct victim)?	Committed by persons (including insiders) using computer infrastructure owned or operated by your organization?
(Q7) Please estimate the annual costs to your organization to implement the procedural or management solution(s).		
(Q8) In the last three calendar years (i.e., Jan. 1, 2011 to Dec. 31, 2013), has your organization had contact with law enforcement authorities concerning cybersecurity incidents or threats for the purposes of:	Please specify the frequency of the contacts with law enforcement authorities.	Please provide further details concerning the nature of the contacts with law enforcement authorities.

Receiving advice on prevention,
response to or general issues about
cybersecurity incidents or threats?

Reporting a cybersecurity incident or
threat?

Evidence gathering during a law
enforcement or forensic investigation?

Providing unpaid advice or assistance
(i.e., not consultancy work) to law
enforcement authorities?

Other (Please specify)

(Q9) What do you think are the three most important cybersecurity topics that need to be researched in the next few years?

Most important cybersecurity research topic: Why?

Second most important cybersecurity research topic: Why?

Third important cybersecurity research topic: Why?

(Q10) What are some of the key challenges that you see emerging technologies (e.g., smart mobile devices, cloud and big data) introducing to the field of digital investigation and/or forensics?

How is your organization/agency dealing with these challenges (if at all)?

References

[1] Symantec Corporation, 2015 Internet Security Threat Report, Symantec Corporation, 2015. http://www.symantec.com/security_response/publications/threatreport.jsp (accessed 09.09.15).

[2] Australian Cyber Security Centre, Australian Cyber Security Centre: 2015 Threat Report, Australian Government, https://acsc.gov.au/publications/ACSC_Threat_Report_2015.pdf, 2015 (accessed 11.09.15).

[3] Verge Staff, The Ashley Madison Hack: Everything You Need to Know, http://www.theverge.com/2015/8/19/9178965/ashley-madison-hacked-news-data-names-list, 2015 (accessed 24.09.15).

[4] J. Jang-Jaccard, S. Nepal, A survey of emerging threats in cybersecurity, J. Comput. Syst. Sci. 80 (5) (2014) 973–993.

[5] ENISA, ENISA threat landscape 2014: overview of current and emerging cyber-threats, ENISA Threat Landscape 2014, 2014. https://www.enisa.europa.eu/activities/risk-management/evolving-threat-environment/enisa-threat-landscape/enisa-threat-landscape-2014 (accessed 30.09.14).

[6] N.H. Ab Rahman, K.-K.R. Choo, A survey of information security incident handling in the cloud, Comput. Secur. 49 (2015) 45–69.

[7] L.E. Cohen, M. Felson, Social change and crime rate trends: a routine activity approach, Am. Sociol. Rev. 44 (4) (1979) 588–608.

[8] F. Miró, Routine activity theory. The Encyclopedia of Theoretical Criminology, John Wiley & Sons, Chichester, West Sussex, 2014, pp. 1–7, http://dx.doi.org/10.1002/9781118517390/wbetc198.

[9] R. Tewksbury, E.E. Mustaine, Routine activities and vandalism: a theoretical and empirical study, J. Crime Justice 23 (1) (2000) 81–110.

[10] K. Holtfreter, M.D. Reisig, T.C. Pratt, Low self-control, routine activities, and fraud victimization, Criminology 46 (1) (2008) 189–220.

[11] J. Miller, Individual offending, routine activities, and activity settings: revisiting the routine activity theory of general deviance, J. Res. Crime Delinq. (2012) 390–416, http://dx.doi.org/10.1177/0022427811432641.

[12] A.M. Bossler, T.J. Holt, D.C. May, Predicting online harassment victimization among a juvenile population, Youth Soc. 44 (4) (2012) 500–523.

[13] T.J. Holt, A.M. Bossler, Examining the applicability of lifestyle-routine activities theory for cybercrime victimization, Deviant Behav. 30 (1) (2008) 1–25.

[14] K.-K.R. Choo, The cyber threat landscape: challenges and future research directions, Comput. Secur. 30 (8) (2011) 719–731.

[15] T.J. Holt, A.M. Bossler, Examining the relationship between routine activities and malware infection indicators, J. Contemp. Crim. 29 (4) (2013) 420–436.

[16] B.W. Reyns, Online routines and identity theft victimization: further expanding routine activity theory beyond direct-contact offenses, J. Res. Crime Delinq. 50 (2) (2013) 216–238.

[17] M.L. Williams, Guardians upon high: an application of routine activities theory to online identity theft in Europe at the country and individual level, Br. J. Criminol. 56 (1) (2015) 21–48.

[18] Federal Bureau of Investigation, Update on Sony Investigation, National Press Release, https://www.fbi.gov/news/pressrel/press-releases/update-on-sony-investigation, 2014 (accessed 08.09.15).

[19] K.-K.R. Choo, A conceptual interdisciplinary plug-and-play cyber security framework, in: H. Kaur, X. Tao (Eds.), ICTs and the Millennium Development Goals—A United Nations Perspective, Springer, New York, 2014, pp. 81–99.

[20] M.E. Roberts, B.M. Stewart, D. Tingley, C. Lucas, J. Leder-Luis, S.K. Gadarian, B. Albertson, D.G. Rand, Structural topic models for open-ended survey responses, Am. J. Polit. Sci. 58 (4) (2014) 1064–1082.

[21] International Organisation for Standardisation, ISO/IEC 27001:2013 Information Technology—Security Techniques—Information Security Management Systems—Requirements, International Organisation for Standardisation, Geneva, 2013.

[22] D. Quick, B. Martini, K.-K.R. Choo, Cloud Storage Forensics, Syngress, Cambridge, MA, 2013.

[23] A.R. Ahmad, N.H. Hamasaeed, The role of social media in the Syrian civil war, in: Conference on Communication, Media, Technology and Design, 2014, pp. 284–289.

[24] A. Azfar, K.-K.R. Choo, L. Liu, An android social app forensics adversary model, in: Proceedings of 49th Annual Hawaii International Conference on System Sciences (HICSS 2016), 5–8 January 2016, IEEE Computer Society Press, 2016, 5597–5606.

[25] N.D. Farhood, A. Dehghantanha, B. Eterovic-Soric, K.-K.R. Choo, Investigating Social Networking applications on smartphones detecting Facebook, Twitter, LinkedIn and Google+ artefacts on Android and iOS platforms, Aust. J. Forensic Sci. 46(4) (2016), 469–488, http://dx.doi.org/10.1080/00450618.2015.1066854.

[26] N.H. Ab Rahman, K.-K.R. Choo, Integrating digital forensic practices in cloud incident handling: a conceptual cloud incident handling model, in: R. Ko, K.-K.R. Choo (Eds.), Cloud Security Ecosystem, Syngress, Cambridge, MA, 2015, 383–400, http://dx.doi.org/10.1016/B978-0-12-801595-7.00017-3.

[27] J. Dykstra, A.T. Sherman, Acquiring forensic evidence from infrastructure-as-a-service cloud computing: exploring and evaluating tools, trust, and techniques, Digit. Investig. 9 (2012) 90–98.

[28] E. Oriwoh, D. Jazani, G. Epiphaniou, P. Sant, Internet of things forensics: challenges and approaches, in: Proceedings of the 9th IEEE International Conference on Collaborative Computing: Networking, Applications and Worksharing, 2013, pp. 608–615.

[29] C. Tassone, B. Martini, K.R. Choo, J. Slay, Mobile Device Forensics: A Snapshot, in: Trends & Issues in Crime and Criminal Justice, 460, Australian Institute of Criminology, Canberra, 2013, pp. 1–7.

[30] C. Hooper, B. Martini, K.-K.R. Choo, Cloud computing and its implications for cybercrime investigations in Australia, Comput. Law Secur. Rev. 29 (2) (2013) 152–163.

[31] Laws of Malaysia, Act 563 Computer Crimes Act 1997, The Commissioner of Law Revision, Malaysia, 2006. pp. 1–15.

[32] International Organisation for Standardisation, ISO/IEC 27043:2015—Information Technology—Security Techniques—Incident Investigation Principles and Processes, International Organisation for Standardisation, Geneva, 2015.

[33] Microsoft, Microsoft Enterprise Cloud Red Teaming, http://download.microsoft.com/download/C/1/9/C1990DBA-502F-4C2A-848D-392B93D9B9C3/Microsoft_Enterprise_Cloud_Red_Teaming.pdf, 2014 (accessed 06.05.15).

[34] M.B. Line, A case study: preparing for the smart grids—identifying current practice for information security incident management in the power industry, in: 7th International Conference on IT Security Incident Management and IT Forensics, 2013, pp. 26–32.

Forensic Readiness: A Case Study on Digital CCTV Systems Antiforensics

A. Ariffin*, K.-K.R. Choo[†,‡], Z. Yunos*

*CyberSecurity Malaysia, Mines Resort City, Malaysia †University of Texas at San Antonio, San Antonio, TX, United States ‡University of South Australia, Adelaide, SA, Australia

1 INTRODUCTION

With the increasing use of digital closed-circuit television (CCTV) systems, it is not surprising that the importance of digital CCTV forensics in ensuring that reliability and admissibility of photographic (and video) evidence has been noted by a number of practitioners and researchers, including Porter [1] who proposed a theoretical digital forensics framework to deal with photographic evidence. One of the first activities in cases involving digital CCTV (and other multimedia) systems is to recover the video evidence from the storage media in a forensically sound manner, as demonstrated in our previous work [2–5].

However, case exhibits involving electronic systems such as digital CCTV systems may be damaged and/or tampered with by the suspect or other individuals who have a reason to hide or obfuscate their tracks. Antiforensic techniques to foil postincident investigations include removing, hiding and corrupting the electronic evidence, and damaging the hardware (e.g., storage media) [6].

Common antiforensic techniques to permanently delete digital evidence include overwriting the location of the digital evidence on storage media a few times with zeros or alternatively using random data (e.g., using a random number generator) and other media sanitization procedures (see [7]). However, if the motivation is to mislead a postincident investigation, other much more subtle techniques such as manipulation of timestamp information and metadata [8] are more likely to be used to create doubt or fabricate an alibi for the suspect. Therefore it is important for surveillance devices such as digital CCTV systems to have forensics readiness in their technologies.

Antiforensics are not new and they are unlikely to go away anytime soon. Therefore it is critical for investigators and forensic practitioners to be up-to-date on forensically sound procedures (e.g., in data recovery) as well as ways in which modern forensic tools and technologies can be circumvented by criminals using antiforensic techniques.

The contributions of this chapter are threefold:

- Demonstration of an antiforensics framework for digital CCTV systems, which allows permanent deletion of multimedia files based on selected timestamp including a proof of concept (POC) antiforensic prototype tool for automation purposes.
- Through this work, digital forensic practitioners would be able to understand and detect the antiforensic techniques as to provide better explanations on the residual digital evidence in the court of law. Concurrently, the antiforensics framework can also be technically referred to for forensic purposes in identification, preservation, analysis, and reporting of digital CCTV systems.
- Provide insights on the importance for manufacturers to include forensic readiness, which should be an integral part of their digital CCTV systems.

The remainder of this chapter is structured as follows: Section 2 outlines our proposed antiforensics framework for digital CCTV systems. In Section 3 the antiforensic techniques were demonstrated using two digital video recorder (DVR) hard disks, an iPhone, and technical discussions on a POC antiforensics tool for automation. The last section concludes the paper by emphasizing on the importance of digital CCTV forensic readiness.

2 OUR PROPOSED ANTIFORENSICS FRAMEWORK FOR DIGITAL CCTV SYSTEMS

2.1 An Overview of Digital CCTV Systems

Digital CCTV systems typically consist of analog cameras (Fig. 1; camera 1, 2, 3 and 4 for a 4-channel system), a DVR, and a monitor to view the captured events. These systems are also capable of connecting to smartphones for mobile monitoring through a network connection [9].

2.2 Development of Antiforensics Framework for Digital CCTV Systems

Permanently deleting multimedia files based on selected timestamp from digital CCTV systems can be exceptionally complex. Analysis of data stream for any general information such as file system type and digital CCTV system brand, identification of video file signatures, file system and image file encryption is part of our proposed antiforensic techniques.

Some technical information such as the video file signature can be learned, say, by reading the technical specifications of the manufacturer's manual. As explained by Kessler [10], if a file system is not referred, video file searching of DVR storage media should be based on file signatures.

Once we have identified the video file signature (note that our proposed antiforensic techniques do not require referring to the file system, particularly when the system is proprietary), we then need to search, locate, carve, and find the appropriate player with the right codec to replay the video file with timestamp for the antiforensics operation.

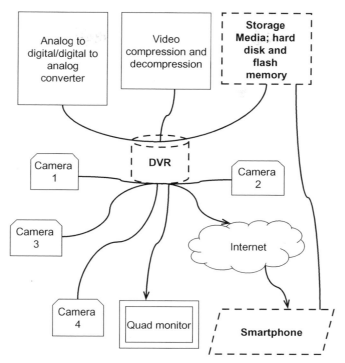

FIG. 1   A typical digital CCTV system.

Replay of the carved video file(s), an optional step, helps to ensure that the correct eviden-tial data is digitally destroyed. To replay the carved video file(s), the codecs of the video file(s) must be identified so that we can choose the right player.

To perform antiforensics on the mobile devices connected to the digital CCTV system used for monitoring, the individual needs to be familiar with the relevant technical specifications. In the case of an iOS device, for example, the individual would need to be familiar with the iOS file system (e.g., how image file metadata is embedded and that a unique per-file key is used to encrypt image files). For example, the catalog and journal files of the iOS device file system would have to be analyzed to search and locate the image file of a CCTV video streaming screenshot (Fig. 2).

After the restoration of the image file, its unique per-file key can then be obtained from the attribute file for decryption and viewing to confirm that it is the right file for permanent dele-tion. Once the per-file key associated with the target image file has been obtained, the per-file key can be manipulated, for example, performing a mathematical XOR operation with an-other randomly selected string of the same length so that the image file cannot be recovered (i.e., permanently deleted) [6]. Alternatively, the metadata of the image file in the catalog or journal file (reference for deleted image files of iOS device) can be purged to permanently delete the image file.

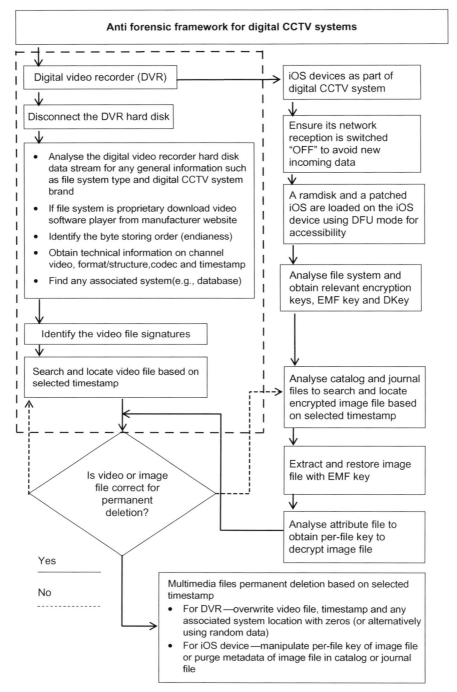

FIG. 2 Antiforensics framework for digital CCTV systems.

Therefore, we need to:

- For DVR—develop techniques to identify video files with timestamps based on file signatures without referring to a file system.
- For iOS device—develop techniques to identify encrypted image files with timestamps based on file system information and to decrypt them.

By analyzing the DVR and iOS device connected to the digital CCTV system, one would be able to obtain information such as the technologies used in the subsystems such as operating and file systems [11] and their technical operations. File system is an important subsystem used to manage the storage media of electronic devices.

Analyzing DVR and iOS device will allow us to:

- For DVR—identify the byte storing order used (endianess), channel video, format, codec and timestamp, and any other associated system (e.g., database).
- For iOS device—determine whether a standard file system such as hierarchical file system (HFS) with encryption is used.

Once the digital CCTV system's multimedia files are identified, it would be prudent to confirm before permanently deleting them. Antiforensic techniques would need to be developed to ensure that the multimedia files once deleted are impossible to recover.

3 CASE STUDIES

Two DVR hard disks and an iPhone 4 were selected as test devices (see Table 1). Both DVR hard disks contained video recordings and the iPhone had three CCTV video streaming screenshots captured using AVTECH's EagleEyes mobile monitoring application.

In our experiments, we choose to use open source tools (Table 2) wherever possible, as commercial forensic tools are generally costly and may not be available to individuals outside law enforcement agencies.

TABLE 1   Antiforensics Test Devices

No.	Test Devices	Product Brand	Purpose
1.	Test-device-DVR1	AVTECH CCTV hard disk	• To demonstrate permanent deletion of a CCTV video file based on timestamp
2.	Test-device-DVR2	Unknown CCTV hard disk brand	• Including technical discussions on timestamp manipulation
3.	Test-device-iPhone	iPhone 4 iOS 6.1.2	• To demonstrate permanent deletion of an image file, a CCTV video streaming screenshot • Including technical discussions on timestamp manipulation

TABLE 2 Antiforensic Tools of Test Devices

No.	Antiforensic Tools of Test Devices
1.	Autopsy forensic browser 2.24, SQLite database browser 2.0b1 and SMplayer 06.9+SVN-r3607, WinHex 14.5, EnCase 6.7, and FTK 3.0
2.	MacBook Pro laptop with Windows XP virtual system for Windows based software
3.	Redsn0w 0.9.9b5, to load custom ramdisk and patched iOS kernel

3.1 Test-Device-DVR1

During the visual inspection of test-device-DVR1, we obtained some technical information about the product from its manual and undertake further research on the device in order to gain an in-depth understanding of its technical specifications such as the evidential data's potential location and format and how the device stores its video data captured by the CCTV camera.

We then prepare the necessary tools to undertake the antiforensic activities. We used WinHex 14.5 to analyse the file system and determined that test-device-DVR1's file system was Ext3.

Examination of test-device-DVR1's data stream found several folders labeled with dates (e.g., 20110606, which represents Jun. 6, 2011). In these folders, there were directories named "Video" with subfolders labeled after the number of the channel (e.g., channel 1 is subfolder "1" and channel 2 is subfolder "2").

Each channel subfolder, for instance "1," had video files with stream as its file extension and a database, that is, video.db. The size of each video file, 11.stream, 12.stream, 13.stream, and 14.stream varies and the database was 397 KB.

The format/structure of video file and database were then analyzed at byte-level for the location of video files and databases. All the video files and database were found to have their own file header,[1] file signature (Table 3).

TABLE 3 Subfolder 1 Video Files and Database File Signatures

Video Files and Database	Header File Signature
11.stream	\0xF4\0xBE\0xEC\0x4D\0xAB\0x65\
12.stream	\0x40\0xC1\0xEC\0x4D\0x1D\0x6B\
13.stream	\0x50\0xCF\0xEC\0x4D\0x87\0x24\
14.stream	\0x60\0xD0\0xEC\0x4D\0x88\0x28\
video.db	\0x53\0x51\0x4C\0x69\0x74\0x65\0x20\0x66\0x6F\0x72\0x6D\0x61\ 0x74\0x20\0x33\0x00\

[1] A video file header can be regarded as a unique signature, and is important for identification when a search is performed for antiforensics.

Based on the file signatures, it was found that all video files were stored in sequence with zero-paddings to separate them from the next file with a database as the last file in a particular channel video subfolder.

The database was then analyzed using SQLite Database Browser 2.0b1, and we found it consisted of several records, primarily video frame identity (ID) number and its corresponding UNIX timestamp, and offset location. The latter would allow us to determine the size of the video file as explained in Fig. 3.

Because we were able to determine from our earlier analysis at byte-level using WinHex that the database type was SQLite, we located two hits on the database file signature. We found the first database (1) at offset 0x482E6000 and the second database (1) at offset 0xDO1F3000, and both databases had the same size of 397 KB.

From this point onward, it is quite straightforward to use the above findings to select and remove the video files permanently, based on timestamp. The databases of the test-device-DVR1 were an additional important piece of information, which did not rely much on the file system information for metadata.

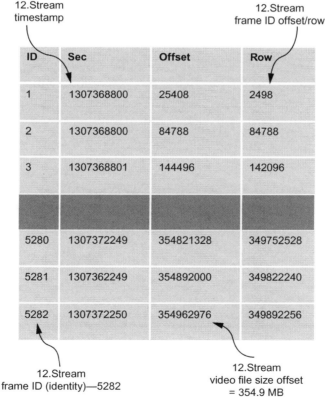

FIG. 3   Analysis of test-device-DVR1 database.

As an example, we chose to permanently delete a video file (known to us) recorded on Apr. 19, 2011 18:01:12. We first need to convert this timestamp information into the UNIX timestamp format (i.e., 1303236072). We then searched and found one of the databases with the timestamp record of 1303236072, which corresponded to 14.stream video file. Because the location and size of the 14.stream video file was identifiable through its file signatures (Table 4), it was trivial to permanently delete the targeted video file by overwriting the video file and database blocks with zeros (or random data) using WinHex so that any data recovery effort is unattainable.

TABLE 4   Permanent Deletion of Test-Device-DVR1 Video File Based on Timestamp

File	File Signature	Timestamp	Method of Deletion
Database 1	\0x53\0x51\0x4C\0x69\0x74\ 0x65\0x20\0x66\0x6F\0x72\ 0x6D\0x61\0x74\0x20\0x33\0x00\	Apr. 19, 2011 18:01:12 (1303236072)	Permanent deletion based on selected timestamp while system is not in operation. Only using CCTV hard disk
14.stream video file	\0x60\0xD0\0xEC\0x4D\0x88\0x28\		

Before the 14.stream video file was permanently deleted, it was carved based on its file signature and size for replay to ensure that it was the right video file for deletion. The video file hexadecimal data was then analyzed with WinHex to identify the codec required for the replay.

The video codec was identified as H.264 from the file signature of \0x32\0x36\0x34\ and this finding was consistent with our reading of test-device-DVR1's manual. We then used SMPlayer (version 06.9+SVN-r3607) to decode the carved 14.stream video file and confirmed that it was the (known) video file recorded on of Apr. 19, 2011 18:01:12.

Once the 14.stream video file deletion was deleted, we mounted test-device-DVR1 and were unable to locate any trace of 14.stream video file (i.e., the deleted video file). Moreover, the deletion transaction was not captured in the log of the system as the device was not in operation when the deletion was undertaken.

	ID	Sec
1	1	1303236066
2	2	1303236067
3	3	1303236068
4	4	1303236068
5	5	1303236069
6	6	1303236070
7	7	1303236070
8	8	1303236071
9	9	1303236072
10	10	1303236072
11	11	1303236073
12	12	1303236073

FIG. 4   Timestamp manipulation of test-device-DVR1 database.

Instead of deleting the video file, we can also edit the timestamp record to mislead any postincident investigation; test-device-DVR1 relies on its databases for video timestamps. Because the location and size of the databases were known, the actual video timestamps can be easily changed to another time and date including file system metadata. For example, we can change the timestamp of video frame ID1 and all subsequent video frames (Fig. 4) using an automated tool (e.g., increase timestamp of video frame ID1 and all subsequent video frames by 1).

3.2 Test-Device-DVR2

Test-device-DVR2 was a CCTV hard disk of unknown brand and to further compli-cate matters, we had no information about the actual digital CCTV system.[2] Therefore we were unable to research on the technical specifications or obtain any information about the file system used. We assume that test-device-DVR2 used a proprietary file system.

For a CCTV hard disk with a proprietary file format, there are a few technical issues that need special attention. Firstly the byte storing order of the CCTV hard disk must be deter-mined. Forensic examiners would need to analyse whether the byte storing order is little or big endian. Once the byte storing order had been determined, the file signatures can be identified and this technical information can be used to correlate every file signature to a channel video, depending whether it is 4-channel or 8-channel that recorded the scenes with timestamps.

Because test-device-DVR2 was assumed to have a proprietary file system, the video file codec would also be of a proprietary format. At this point of time, we were unable to locate an appropriate proprietary software player or to download from the manufacturer website because the brand of the CCTV system was unknown. The carved video files with time-stamps, for confirmation before permanent deletion, would not be able to be replayed using a standard video player.

Two commercial forensic software, EnCase 6.7 and FTK 3.0, installed on the MacBook run-ning Windows XP operating system were used to check and confirm whether the file system of the test-device-DVR2 was proprietary. As expected, both tools were not able to recognize the file system and any video files.

WinHex 14.5 was then used to conduct further analysis on the data stream of test-device-DVR2. Using WinHex, we found that at offset 0 where sector 0 onwards is the typical loca-tion of file system information, the file system was unknown. Hence, it was confirmed that the file system of test-device-DVR2 was proprietary, that is not employing a standard and recognizable file system such as Linux Ext3 or NTFS. Unlike Poole et al. [12], no further analysis was undertaken on the file system of test-device-DVR2 as it would have been time consuming and impractical.

[2] If a complete digital CCTV system is available, it is possible to check its time setting and determine the offset with the actual time. The time offset is beneficial for verification in the court of law against the actual time of incident. In the event that digital forensic examiners do not have access to a complete digital CCTV system, the timestamps obtained from the CCTV hard disk are reliable provided that they had not been tampered with.

Next, each sector of the cloned CCTV hard disk was analyzed to determine and confirm the brand and byte storing order used. "aRipOd S" text string was found at offset 4A85D55C00, which indicated that the brand of test-device-DVR2 was RapidOS. The text string arrangement did not directly match because of its byte storing order. Test-device-DVR2's system stores data in a reverse 16-bit byte little endian. This finding was useful for further analysis of the unknown content format; which would help both digital forensic and antiforensic efforts in understanding how the test-device-DVR2 stores its data.

Test-device-DVR2 was then analyzed for any recognizable file signatures. For instance, repetitive hexadecimal patterns must be identified because the channel video (1, 2, 3, and 4; or it can be more for 8-channel digital CCTV system) and timestamp tracks interleaved with each other.

Repetitive hexadecimal patterns were found as follows: (1) \0xF9\0x01\0x00\0x40\, (2) \0xF9\0x01\0x00\0x41\, (3) \0xF9\0x01\0x00\0x42\, (4) \0xF9\0x01\0x00\0x43\, (5) \0xFA\0x01\0x01\0x00\, and (6) \0xF0\0x7E\0x4B\0x0B\ (the first two bytes change frequently in successive tracks), and no other standard file signature was found.

Based on the brand information found (i.e., RapidOS), we were able to download relevant product manuals and video player software. According to the product manuals, it appeared that the video files from test-device-DVR2 could be replayed using its T3000-4 viewer software, and the video file format was VVF[3] (i.e., most players will not be able to replay VVF files).

100 GB of data were then extracted from test-device-DVR2; 16-bit byte swapped using WinHex 14.5 and replayed with the T3000-4 viewer. 4-channel CCTV videos with timestamps were replayed accordingly. Based on the video replay, it was determined that test-device-DVR2 was a 4-channel digital CCTV system and further analysis was made on the repetitive interleaving hexadecimal signatures of the 100 GB data. The video and timestamp file signatures were then interpreted as follows (Table 5).

TABLE 5   Interpretation of Test-Device-DVR2 File Signatures

No.	File Signatures	Interpretation
1.	\0x01\0xF9\0x40\0x00\	Channel 1 video header file signature
2.	\0x01\0xF9\0x41\0x00\	Channel 2 video header file signature
3.	\0x01\0xF9\0x42\0x00\	Channel 3 video header file signature
4.	\0x01\0xF9\0x43\0x00\	Channel 4 video header file signature
5.	\0x01\0xFA\0x00\0x01\	Footer file signature
6.	\0x7E\0xF0\0x0B\0x4B\	UNIX 32-bit little endian hexadecimal timestamp

---

[3] VVF file format is typically dedicated for CCTV videos and we were unable to locate further technical specifications online.

Once we have obtained the above findings, it was possible to permanently delete video files based on selected timestamp from test-device-DVR2. In our case study, we chose to permanently delete a channel video as outlined in Table 6.

TABLE 6   Permanent Deletion of Test-Device-DVR2 Channel Video Based on Timestamp

No.	Item	File Signature	Timestamp	Method of Deletion
1.	Channel 3 video	\0x01\xF9\x42\x00\	May 14, 2009 at	Permanent deletion based
2.	Footer	\0x01\0xFA\0x00\0x01\	10:20:42 → \0x7A\0xF0\0x0B0\ x4A\	on selected timestamp while system is not in operation. Only using CCTV hard disk

The Channel 3 video header and footer file signatures, and UNIX 32-bit hexadecimal timestamp were converted to test-device-DVR2's 16-bit byte little endian format as follows: (1) \0xF9\ x01\x00\x42\ → Channel 3 video header file signature, (2) \0xFA\x01\x01\x00\ → Footer file signature, and (3) \0xF0\0x7A\0x4A\0x0B\ → Timestamp of May 14, 2009 at 10:20:42.

WinHex 14.5 was used to search and carve the channel video based on the file header and footer, and selected timestamp for confirmation before permanent deletion. The channel video file with timestamp was 16-bit byte swapped and converted into VVF file format for replay using the T3000-4 viewer.

Once we had reviewed that the replayed video file was the target, we then permanently deleted the video by overwriting its data blocks (512 bytes) with zeros using WinHex.

Because the file signature of the timestamps was known, it was trivial for us to manipulate the channel video timestamps accordingly.

3.3 Test-Device-iPhone

Similarly to the previous two test devices, we studied the electronic components and system operations of test-device-iPhone. We found that the camera in iPhone 4 captures a scene through its charge-coupled electronic component and the electronic signals are converted to digital data using an analog-to-digital converter. The digital data (i.e., image of the scene) is formatted in a file container with a specific codec (e.g., jpeg) and it is encrypted with a 256-bit per-file key; the same process is applied for a CCTV video streaming screenshot. The per-file key is then wrapped with a data protection class key called DKey and it is stored in the attribute file of the file system as metadata.

AVTECH's EagleEyes application was installed on test-device-iPhone to enable mobile monitoring. Mobile users are also able to take a video streaming screenshot using the application. For instance, if there is an intruder in their premise, a video streaming screenshot can be taken and used as evidential material in a court of law.

In our case study, three CCTV video streaming screenshots were taken using test-device-iPhone (test-device-iPhone was reset earlier to avoid any remnant data).

Test-device-iPhone was visually inspected and the system time checked.[4] If test-device-iPhone was already switched "ON", we will have to ensure that its network reception is

---

[4] Step 1 is crucial in a real-world situation.

switched "OFF." This procedure is taken to prevent data contaminating or corruption (e.g., via a remote wipe command).

In order to search, locate and permanently delete one of the encrypted video streaming screenshot image files based on selected timestamp, test-device-iPhone was accessed using SSH (secure shell) connection via redsn0w 0.9.9b5.[5] Test-device-iPhone user partition was then mounted, /dev/disk0s1s2, to access the folder, DCIM/100APPLE/, which contains the image files. During this process the journaling system of the test-device- iPhone was disabled to avoid the file system logging our antiforensic activities.

The three video streaming screenshot image files were found in the DCIM/100APPLE/ folder (IMG_0001.JPG, IMG_0002.JPG and IMG_0003.JPG) and their timestamps were Jul. 9, 2013 at 15:31:25, 15:33:12, and 15:34:16. The image files were also viewed for confirmation that they were the right files. We chose to permanently delete IMG_0001.JPG file (Table 7).

We now repeated the above experiment with the two remaining images except that we did not disable the journaling system this time. In this second experiment, we deleted IMG_0002. JPG file and took a copy of the entire test-device-iPhone user partition.

The partition copy was checked using Autopsy Forensic Browser 2.24 to identify test-device-iPhone's file system and it was confirmed that the file system was HFS+. WinHex 14.5 (and other tools) could also be used to determine the file system.

Because the file system of test-device-iPhone was known to be HFS+, the journal file[6] was analyzed to search and locate both deleted files (i.e., IMG_0001.JPG and IMG_0002.JPG). Note that information on deleted image files can only be found in the journal file whereas the catalog file is for current image files.

We were unable to find any information on IMG_0001.JPG file in the journal file. The IMG_0001.JPG file reference/metadata in the catalog file was purged immediately by the HFS+ file system of test-device-iPhone once it was deleted, and this activity was not logged by the journal file because the journaling system was disabled when the IMG_0001.JPG was deleted.

TABLE 7   Permanent Deletion of Test-Device-iPhone CCTV Video Streaming Screenshot Image Files Based on Timestamp

No.	Item	Per-File Key	Timestamp	Method of Deletion
1.	IMG_0001.JPG file	Not needed	Jul. 9, 2013 at 15:31:25	Permanent deletion based on selected timestamp while system is in operation
2.	IMG_0002.JPG file	B6FDC5555ECA5 6742BCDEF32187 ACDEF44BAC345 21BBCDED33456 CEA675BB34D	Jul. 9, 2013 at 15:33:12	Permanent deletion based on selected timestamp of system user partition copy

---

[5] An iPhone tool to upload custom ramdisk and patched iOS kernel to bypass the security checks.

[6] Its function is to record iPhone's system activities; for example, file deletion.

As expected, we managed to find IMG_0002.JPG's filename and metadata[7] in the journal file (as the journaling system was not disabled during the deletion), which implies that IMG_0002.JPG file had been deleted but still recoverable. IMG_0002.JPG file can still be permanently deleted by purging its metadata in the journal file. However in this experiment, we will now show that we can recover IMG_0002.JPG file because the information on its location and size was available in the journal file of test-device-iPhone.

We managed to verify the timestamp[8] of IMG_0002.JPG file by referring to its metadata. The hexadecimal value of CE01F9D8 obtained from IMG_0002.JPG file's metadata in the journal file (Mac format) was converted into standard timestamp format. According to the timestamp, the IMG_0002.JPG file was recorded on Jul. 9, 2013 at 15:33:12, which was consistent with the date and time when the screenshot was taken by the authors. This finding can also be used to manipulate the IMG_0002.JPG file's timestamp by changing the hexadecimal value of CE01F9D8.

Although the deleted IMG_0002.JPG file had been located, it cannot be viewed as it was encrypted. The wrapped per-file key was required to calculate its per-file key in order to decrypt the image file. Because the CNID of the IMG_0002.JPG file was known to be 00000DAA, the wrapped per-file key can be located in the protect structure of the attribute file, part of the HFS+ file system. Two other associated encryption keys were also fetched from the "Effaceable Storage" of test-device-iPhone, namely EMF Key[9] and DKey.[10] Test-device-iPhone uses Advanced Encryption Standard 256-bit crypto engine to encrypt and decrypt files stored on the device (Apple 2012). In order to decrypt the recovered (encrypted) IMG_0002.JPG file, we would now compute the 256-bit per-file key used to protect the image file (Fig. 5).

The restoration done by reencrypting the IMG_0002.JPG file blocks using the EMF key was necessary due to the decryption of test-device-iPhone's file system and content by the EMF key during the SSH connection. The EMF key was decrypting the data partition of the test-device-iPhone to reveal the file system information. We obtained the catalog, journal, and attribute files of the HFS+ file system and metadata of the contents from this process that was imperative in locating information (e.g., CNID, first location of blocks, size, timestamp, and wrapped per-file key) of the deleted and encrypted IMG_0002.JPG file. The per-file key and the calculated initialisation vectors based on all logical block addressing were used to decrypt the IMG_0002.JPG file. The decrypted image file could then be viewed using a standard image application.

We verified that the IMG_0002.JPG file was the right file to be permanently deleted based on the selected timestamp. The next step was overwriting IMG_0002.JPG file metadata in the journal file with zeros so that it will not be recoverable. Alternatively, we can also manipulate the IMG_0002.JPG's 256-bit wrapped per-file key with a 256-bit randomly generated number. Without the right per-file key, it would not be possible to recover IMG_0002.JPG file.

---

[7] Searching using WinHex is recommended because it performs better and easy to use.

[8] The timestamp is important should the image file be tendered in a court of law.

[9] EMF key is the data partition encryption key.

[10] NSProtectionNone class key used to wrap file keys for always accessible file on the data partition.

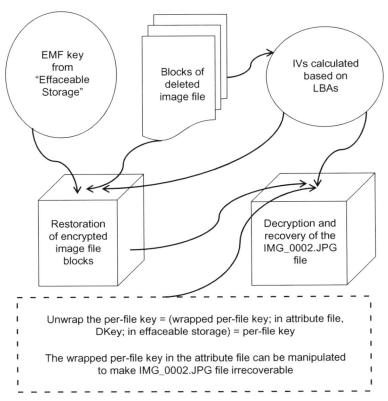

FIG. 5 Test-device-iPhone's IMG_0002.JPG file recovery for confirmation before antiforensic techniques are applied based on selected timestamp.

3.4 Prototype Tool

We have provided a step-by-step approach to conducting antiforensics on the above three test items, which demonstrated the practicability of our proposed antiforensic techniques. However, the time taken for the above antiforensic process can be shortened considerably if the searching and permanent deletion of the CCTV video files with timestamps were automated—the aim of our prototype tool.

As discussed earlier, video/image file formats have their own file header[11] and metadata structure. A JPEG file, for example, has a file structure that includes information such as the timestamp and (camera) device information. Such information is also known as metadata tags and is stored in EXIF format—a standard that specifies the formats for images, sound, and ancillary tags used by digital cameras including smartphones.

Without file signatures, it would not be possible to search CCTV video files with timestamps; without referring to file systems. Therefore developing a file signature database is a core component of the antiforensics prototype tool for digital CCTV systems. Similar to

---

[11] Possibly footer, in hexadecimal value and it is unique.

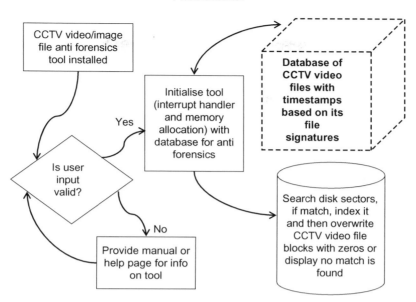

FIG. 6   Software architecture and operations of our prototype tool.

antivirus software, the file signature database needs to be updated whenever there is a new video file format.

Fig. 6 shows the software architecture and operations of the prototype tool. The tool is based on Linux operating system, and has system call functions to read/write from/to storage media of digital CCTV systems, for instance, searching of file signatures. CCTV video files with timestamps and metadata are permanently deleted when the tool finds a matching file signature in the database (similar to how an antivirus software works—the software will either delete or quarantine the malware if a matching signature is found). The tool if installed in a digital CCTV system on a Linux platform will wait for the user input to search and delete the target video image files based on timestamps.

4 CONCLUSION

We demonstrated the utility of our antiforensics framework for digital CCTV systems and iOS devices using two DVRs and an iPhone as case studies. A prototype tool was then developed to automate the searching and permanent deletion of the CCTV video files with timestamps; thus, reducing the time required for the process. This work was able to be conducted by studying the underlying technologies of all the devices.

And, with the same technical knowledge, a suspect or other individuals are able to hide or obfuscate their tracks in order to foil postincident investigations. The technologies within the devices could, therefore, be manipulated even though basic security features were deployed.

Hence, we demonstrated that the security features are not foolproof and digital CCTV systems could be susceptible to permanent deletion. Timestamp information could also be modified, which complicates a forensics investigation.

Therefore it is important for the manufacturers to include the element of forensic readiness in their products, especially during the design of digital CCTV systems. It is a dilemma for digital forensics practitioners to deal with existing technologies that were developed without forensics readiness. The most likely available evidence after antiforensic work is performed would be to study the remaining patterns such as timestamps as to proof the incident did occur supported by facts proving that there was tampering, however, this would not be adequate in the court of law. The importance of ensuring forensics readiness was also echoed by Ab Rahman and Choo [13]. Ab Rahman et al. [14] also proposed a conceptual forensic-by-design framework and explained how such a framework could be incorporated in the design of a cyber-physical cloud system.

Future work includes extending the framework to other popular digital CCTV systems and devices connected to such systems, with the aims of refining the model and validating the prototype tool.

References

[1] G. Porter, A new theoretical framework regarding the application and reliability of photographic evidence, Int. J. Evid. Proof 15 (1) (2011) 26–61.
[2] A. Ariffin, C. D'Orazio, K.-K.R. Choo, J. Slay, iOS Forensics: how can we recover deleted image files with time-stamp in a forensically sound manner? in: International Conference on Availability, Reliability and Security, Prague (ARES 2013), 2–6 September 2013, University of Regensburg, Germany, 2013, 375–382.
[3] A. Ariffin, K.-K.R. Choo, J. Slay, Digital camcorder forensics, in: Australasian Information Security Conference (ACSW-AISC 2013), Adelaide, South Australia, Volume 138 of the ACS Conferences in Research and Practice in Information Technology (CRPIT) Series, Australian Computer Society, 2013, pp. 39–47.
[4] A. Ariffin, J. Slay, K.-K.R. Choo, Data recovery from proprietary formatted CCTV hard disks, in: IFIP WG 11.9 International Conference on Digital Forensics, National Center for Forensic Science, Orlando, FL, USA. Advances in Digital Forensics IX, Springer, 2013, 213–223.
[5] D. Quick, K.-K.R. Choo, Data reduction and data mining framework for digital forensic evidence: storage, intelligence, review, and archive, Trends & Issues in Crime and Criminal Justice 480, 2014, pp. 1–11.
[6] C. D'Orazio, A. Ariffin, K.-K.R. Choo, iOS anti-forensics: how can we securely conceal, delete and insert data? in: Proceedings of 47th Annual Hawaii International Conference on System Sciences (HICSS 2014), IEEE Computer Society Press, 2014, pp. 4838–4847.
[7] R. Kissel, M. Scholl, S. Skolochenko, X. Li, Guidelines for Media Sanitization. Draft NIST Special Publication 800-88 Revision 1, National Institute of Standards and Technology, Gaithersburg, MD, 2012.
[8] B. Blunden, Anti-Forensics: The Rootkit Connection, 2009. Black Hat USA, http://www.blackhat.com/presentations/bh-usa-09/BLUNDEN/BHUSA09-Blunden-AntiForensics-PAPER.pdf.
[9] M. Esteve, C.E. Palau, J. Martinez-Nohales, B. Molina, A video streaming application for urban traffic management, J. Netw. Comput. Appl. 30 (2007) 479–498.
[10] G. Kessler, File Signatures Table. Available online: http://www.garykessler.net/library/file_sigs.html, 2011.
[11] E. Huebner, D. Bema, C. Kai, Data hiding in the NTFS file system, Digit. Investig. 30 (4) (2006) 211–226.
[12] N.R. Poole, Q. Zhou, P. Abatis, Analysis of CCTV digital video recorder hard disk storage system, Digit. Investig. 5 (2009) 85–92.
[13] N.H. Ab Rahman, K.-K.R. Choo, A survey of information security incident handling in the cloud, Comput. Secur. 49 (2015) 45–69.
[14] N.H. Ab Rahman, W.B. Glisson, Y. Yang, K.-K.R. Choo, Forensic-by-design framework for cyber-physical cloud systems, IEEE Cloud Comput. 3 (1) (2016) 50–59.

Forensic Visualization: Survey and Future Research Directions

C. Tassone*, B. Martini*, K.-K.R. Choo*,†

*University of South Australia, Adelaide, SA, Australia †University of Texas at San Antonio, San Antonio, TX, United States

1 INTRODUCTION

Over the last couple of decades electronic devices have evolved from storing simple data types (i.e., text documents, photos, and videos) consisting of basic metadata, detailing useful information such as created/modified/accessed dates and original device/user name information to more personalized devices now encompassing large amounts of sensitive and personally identifiable information, such as social media, communication applications, multimedia (e.g., pictures and videos), holding advance metadata functionally providing geolocation, user name, device name, and camera aperture. In fact, portable electronic devices such as tablets, laptops, and cell phones can now contain more sensitive and personally identifiable information data than a typical personal computer [1–3]. This is not surprising. For example, according to the Australian Communications and Media Authority [4], it was noted that "[m]obile services in operation (including voice and data) reached 27 million, a 2% increase since June 2014 as of May 2015, 74% were estimated to be using a smartphone compared to 67% last year." Similar trends were also observed in other developed countries such as USA where 91% of the population reportedly owns mobile phones [5], and UK at 81% [6] and developing countries such as South Africa with over two-third of the population having mobile phones [7].

With the increasing prevalence of portable devices, forensic evidence extracted from mobile/electronics devices can be an invaluable evidence source for investigators in both civil litigation (e.g., investigation of an employee) and criminal prosecution. Digital forensics is evolving at a pace significantly faster than traditional forensic sciences, mainly due to the rapid development of information and communications technologies (ICT) and its ready adoption by the public and by criminals [8]. Mckemmish [9] defines digital forensics as a four-stage process, comprising identification, preservation, analysis, and presentation.

Quick and Choo [10] highlighted the impacts of increasing volume of digital forensic data on digital forensic laboratories, such as increasing backlogs of evidence awaiting analysis. They also observed that "[t]he capability of a human examiner to understand the massive volume of data is not able to keep pace with the ability to gather and store the data." The resulting amount of information that needs to be sifted through also highlighted the importance of visualization software which can be deployed to facilitate presentation of forensic analysis (e.g., provide a more effective way of communicating the forensic investigation findings to the investigator or the judiciary). Digital forensics and e-Discovery software (e.g., XRY, Nuix, EnCase, and Oxygen) generally use basic tables and search functionality alongside different visualization methodology, and despite the importance of visualization in forensic software, this appears to be an understudied area. For example, we were not able to locate any survey or review paper on forensic visualization. This is the gap we seek to contribute to in this paper.

In this chapter we focus mainly on portable electronic device forensics, due to the increasingly popularity of mobile devices in forensic investigations. In Section 2 we explain the role of forensics software based on several court transcripts and identify challenges faced by forensic practitioners while trying to find "trophy items" (i.e., items that will proved substantial evidence when presented to court), which highlight the need for more effective forensic visualization. Section 3 we investigate current literature highlighting the need for visualization, and extract the known visualization methodology utilized by current forensic and e-discovery software and then survey existing survey literature comparing over 294 visualization techniques published in the since 2010 in Section 4. Defines a set of rules based upon Mckemmish [9] four forensic principles for the selection of a visualization methodology to meet to be able to be useful to a forensic practitioner. Then utilizing visualization criteria to extract useful methodologies from survey papers to analysis there viability for utilization in digital forensic datasets while providing examples.

2 DIGITAL FORENSICS

Forensically sound procedures play an important part in the collection, analysis, and presentation of evidence in a court of law. There are a number of digital forensic procedures (also known as models and frameworks). For example, a widely used digital forensic framework in Australia is that of Mckemmish [9], who described the process as: "identifying, preserving, analyzing, and presenting digital evidence in a manner that is legally acceptable."

- During *Identification*, practitioners need to gather information about the case exhibits and the potential data types and storage information (e.g., capacity and how data is stored) [11]. This will help to determine the appropriate extraction methodology [12].
- *Preservation* of digital evidence requires that the methodology used preserves the evidence preventing changes to the original data by performing a logical or physical extraction [13].
  - Logical extraction copies the logical storage objects from the electronic device (e.g., directories and files) [14,15].
  - Physical extraction performs a bit-for-bit copy of the entire physical storage. Unlike logical extraction, physical extraction may be able to acquire remnants of deleted data [15,16].

- *Analysis* of the cloned data from the first two elements is usually done within the forensic extraction software resulting in report/s being generated to present the evidence to the courts.
- *Presentation* is the communication of the analysis findings to the court (e.g., in the form of a forensic examination report) [17].

2.1 Examples of Cases Involving Evidence From Portable Devices

Due to the increasing popularity of portable electronic devices, the number of court cases involving evidential data from these devices is increasing. Examples of such cases are discussed in the following section.

The *United States of America* v *David Burgess* (*2012*) *No. 08-8053* (Aug. 11, 2009) case reinforces the importance of using a forensically sound software to perform physical extraction of the evidence and view images on the mobile device without the risk of modifying the original source. In this particular case, the practitioner had to search approximately 166,000 images, including movies and texts over two devices, and it was estimated that between 30 and 45% of the files were child abuse materials.

In *Western Australia*, (*2012*) *WASCA 153*, the supreme court of Western Australia in the matter of Bevan v The State of Western Australia presented the forensic analysis of a seized red Nokia mobile telephone and a blue Nokia mobile telephone which contained incriminating text messages consistent with drug dealing. The defendant tried to make the evidence extracted from the two mobile phones admissible, calming that the two forensic software tools utilized (XRY and Cellebrite) were not reliable however the judge stated "The workings of the instrument need not be given and it seems to me that in this case the notes of the experienced officer, the evidence that this software is regularly used by him establishes the level of accuracy and in his notes at the time that he was—successfully used the program seems to me to meet the tests as they were stated in Bevan's case." This case makes important note that performing an extraction of mobile devices should be done using a forensically sound software that is accepted by local law. This particular case also showed the trust that judges have with forensic software that have been to be validated to be forensically sound by local practitioners, the detective who extracted the data did not have any qualifications for utilizing the forensic software however has had previous experience it was for this reason that most forensic extractions are performed by authorized personal who are competent (her Honor; "Data obtained in this way will be admissible if there is evidence from a suitably qualified person to prove that the process produces accurate results as well as evidence to show that the downloading was properly carried out on the particular occasion in question"). Due to this situation the people who perform the extraction are backlogged with cases that need to be processed and when the evidence takes the practitioner away from their work resulting in more backlogs.

In *Georgiou* v *Spencer Holdings Pty. Ltd.* (2011) FCA 1222 (Oct. 28, 2011) (Adelaide, South Australia), pictures and text messages were provided as evidence. The forensic consultant used "XRY" to perform a logical extraction of the mobile phone that was submitted as evidence, expressing his own opinion that the forensic application would have a great deal more data than that shown in the document which the applicant had discovered. The applicant made a request to obtain the second respondent's mobile phone for cross examination. However, there is very few forensic software out there that provide cross examination allowing two or more forensic data sets to be compared in the same interface or to allow the comparison from different forensic software.

In *State of North Carolina* v *Jose Alberto Beiza Tapia* (Feb. 21, 2012) (No. COA11-461) (Court of Appeals of North Carolina), the officer utilized a forensic tool "Cellebrite," extracting evidence from the suspect's phone and obtaining electronic information such as call history, incoming calls, outgoing calls, and missed calls. The officer then generated a report presenting useful information to the court of law. This report provides easier navigation of evidence during the proceedings (e.g., not valid to pass the phone around which could result in the evidence being altered or changed). This is one of the main reasons why forensic software are utilized to provide multiple copies of the evidence without the fear of alterations.

A memorandum opinion by Paul W. Grimm, District judge title *United States of America* v *Ali Saboonchi et al.* (Apr. 7, 2014) (No. PWG-13-100) elaborates on how mobile forensic software such as XRY work by creating a copy of the data stored on the device through a logical or physical extraction, points out some of the unique benefits and issues with forensic extraction. Even if the extraction is performed, the search and analysis could take place long after the device itself has been returned to its owner and therefore is unbounded by time. Second the software can recover a vast amount of information even after it has been deleted. It has the ability to create an image of the device providing all files, the slack space, master file table, and metadata as a precise copy of the original device. This prevents the alteration or loss of the data as a result of the operation of a computer, it also clearly show pornography and privacy in plain view. Whereas a manual search of the device may result in the evidence being compromised due to damaged hardware, data loss, or poor forensic analysis.

In *United States of America,* Plaintiff-Appellee v *Adrian Alvarado,* Defendant-Appellant (2012) No. 11-40771 (Aug. 15, 2012) (United States of America), suspect was arrested for possession of narcotics, while under arrest the authorities seized the phone and the suspect was released on bond. During forensic analysis of the mobile phone the authorities discovered that his phone contained a video of a minor engaged in a sexually explicit act and text messages between the minor and the suspect. In requesting the video, this new evidence resulted in the suspect being arrested 5 weeks after the initial incident.

The People, Plaintiff and Respondent v *Gregory Diaz*, Defendant and Appellant (2011) No. S166600 (Jan. 3, 2011) (United States of America), the Sheriff looked at the phone text message folder and discovered evidence that the suspect was dealing with illegal narcotics. However, this was a manual search and the officer "had to manipulate the phone and go to several different screens to access the text message folder." Making special note that phone data is dynamic and the data could have been affected or changed by accident (e.g., while the officer was conducting the search, the phone was on and connected to the network so any incoming calls could have replaced important evidence or it could have been wiped remotely) resulting in the evidence being inadmissible.

Further cases mentioning mobile forensic data, include

- *United States of America* v *Trevin Rounds* (2014) No. 12-51081 (Apr. 9, 2014) (United States of America), forensic practitioner provided several new text messages to strengthen the prosecution of the suspect.
- *United States of America* v *Abel Flores-Lopez* (2012) No. 10-3803 (Feb. 29, 2012) (United States of America), expressed the importance of not needing a warrant to obtain the ability to search a mobile phone, due to the ability of the user wiping the phone.

- *State of Iowa* v *Jacque Louis Miller* (2012) No. 2-498/11-1064 (Jul. 25, 2012) (United States of America), crime prevention officer utilized a forensic tool to search and find incriminating evidence, the evidence was produced to the court in the form of a report that was generated by the forensic tool.
- *United States of America* v *Jeremy Halgat et al.* (2014) No. 2:13-cr-241-APG-VCF (Apr. 22, 2014) (United States of America), important conversations between officers and the informants were stored on the undercover agents' phones, they utilized the forensic tool to prevent the loss or damage of the evidence.
- *United States of America* v *David Burgess* (2009) No. 08-8053 (Aug. 11, 2009) (United States of America), investigator highlights that phones, especially ones that contain flash drives, can hold vast amounts of information from images to data files.
- In *United States of America* v *Adrian Alvarado* (Aug. 15, 2012) (No. 11-40771) (United States of America), text messages requesting pornographic video from a minor and the resulting video were forensically extracted from the suspect's personal mobile phone. This resulted in the suspect being arrested for a child pornography offense.

Cases involving the mention of different forensic software and tools

- In *United States of America* v *Jae Shik Kim, Karham Eng. Corp.* (2015) No. 13-0100 (May 8, 2015) (United States of America), the forensic practitioner utilized the forensic software tool EnCase to export files from the suspect's computer, and also used another program Intella to process the files after the extraction due to providing more advanced capabilities to search the text of emails that are no otherwise searchable.
- In *United States of America* v *Christopher D. Rarick* (2016) No. 14-4212 (Jan. 7, 2016) (United States of America), the investigating officer utilized the forensic tool Susteen to generate a report based on the suspect's phone, which included technical information about the phone itself, call logs, contacts, pictures, audio files, video files, and other data. The officer identified from the thumbnails that the pictures contained child pornography.
- In *Malibu Media, LLC* v *John Doe* (2015) No. 14-1280 (Feb. 2, 2015) (United States of America), the investigating officer required use of different forensic software programs to analyze the suspect's hard-drives, utilizing two version of EnCase version 6 and 7 and Internet Evidence Finder to be able to acquire the evidence that was split over multiple devices.
- In *United States of America* v *Richard Cyr* (2015) No. 2:14-cr-19 (Aug. 12, 2015) (United States of America), the investigating officer used Forensic Toolkit (FTK) to make a forensic copy of the digital evidence, then created a searchable index for the investigation, that allowed a search and a record of the frequency of words and other groups of letters and numbers.
- In *Malibu Media LLC* v *Mike Cuddy* (2015) No. 1:13-cv-02385-WYD-MEH (Jan. 26, 2015) (United States of America), the investigator utilized Oxygen Forensic Analyst 2014 for supported phones/tables. However, in this case the judge gave the officer permission to utilize the mobile device's manufacturer-endorsed backup solutions to capture data stored on the mobile device.
- In *Peter Clarke* v *Great Southern Finance Pty. Ltd* (2014) VSC 516 (Dec. 11, 2014) (Australia), involving the use of Nuix, Visual Analytics provided the investigator with an effective means to search approximately 10 million electronic files to help identify trophy items.

- In *State of North Carolina, v Jose Alberto Beiza Tapia* (2012) No. COA11-461 (Feb. 21, 2012) (United States of America), the defendant objected to testimony referring to the report generated by Cellebrite, claiming that the report generated was inadmissible, however, the judge overruled the defendant's claim due to finding no errors by the investigating officer in the process.
- In *State of Louisiana* v *Keith Martin* (2015) No. 49,700-KA (Apr. 15, 2015) (United States of America), the forensic practitioner testified he examined a number of phones owned by the suspects, collecting and verifying calls logs, text messages, calendar events, notes, WiFi information, Map locations, and a dictionary. The practitioner explained that his office utilizes a device called Cellebrite to process mobile phones and that he is also required to use Lantern software to process iPhones, thus finding incriminating messages between the two suspects.
- i2 Analysts Notebook by IBM (i2).

As outlined, there are court cases in which data contained within electronic devices have been used as evidence. While the matters outlined above have mentioned that a simple message could be the tipping of the scales during prosecution, there is little discussion in the court transcripts in relation to whether additional analysis was undertaken to extract items from the evidence source. There have also been instances where practitioners need to utilize multiple forensic software tools to acquire all of the information.

2.2 Challenges

Court transcripts only show the final result of the forensic process, and do not outline the time required to perform the analysis after the extraction of data. Forensic practitioners usually utilize the same software for analytical work using inbuilt functions to search, filter, and identify trophy items with different visualization methodologies, if provided. Mobile forensic visualization is a relatively new subdiscipline of forensics science, and has incorporated many of the same principles used in digital forensics (also known as computer forensics, forensic computing, etc.) However, unlike computer forensics, portable devices have seen a rapid evolution in capability, which has raised some concerns and identified major differences. Jansen, Delaitre, and Moenner [18] pointed out that portable devices such as mobile phones are special purpose appliances that perform a set of tasks using software defined by their vender and operating system. In addition, hardware used in mobile devices differs from its computer counterparts, and consequently, traditional digital forensic techniques may not be entirely appropriate [19]. Hence, there are commercial forensic software tools that are dedicated to mobile forensics (see [20,21]). Due to the constant advances in ICT (e.g., new mobile devices, mobile operating systems, portable tablets running a verity of software venders, and tailored applications to each version), the challenge is for forensic practitioners and software tools to keep pace with these new advances in technology. For example, it would take time to update and upgrade forensic software in order to meet the expanding range of electronic devices, and coupled operating systems and applications. It is unlikely that every tool will have the capacity to support all devices. Findings from various studies have highlighted the difficulty of extracting data from a variety of different portable device operating systems using both validated commercial and open source mobile forensic software [22–25].

Glisson et al. [20] identified major concerns with the increasing amounts of data being generated by mobile devices, suggesting the inability for mobile forensic software companies in maintaining the reliability of the evidence being extracted from these devices. Their study looked into benchmarking mobile devices against different digital forensic software suites, due the different methodologies being utilized by the mobile forensic software companies to perform their extraction and analysis of the data resulting in different quantities of data being extracted from the same mobile device. They believe forensic practitioners may need to utilize multiple mobile forensic software programs to obtain a more complete data set. They also noted the difficulty they faced when it came to the comparison of the extracted data between the three mobile forensic software tools was due to the different methods for visualizing datasets. The mobile forensic software used in this research included Cellebrite's Universal Forensic Extraction Device, XRY Forensics' Examination Kit, and Radio Tactics' Aceso.

3 VISUALIZATION IS KEY

3.1 Related Work

Information visualization in its broadest definition provides information as an organized form of interpretation through a variety of different methods. These methods can vary from static or dynamic text, tables, images, graphs, and even maps providing a visual representation of large-scale collections of nonnumerical information [26]. The earliest forms of visualizations were composed of geometric diagrams of positions of celestial bodies in relations to one's own location and geographical maps to aid in navigations as early as 6200 BC [27]. Friendly and Denis [27] continue to provide an in-depth history of visualization over the century, providing timelines for the adoption of digital information representation and defining data visualization as "information that has been abstracted in some schematic form, including attributes or variables for the units of information." Providing humans with the ability to comprehend data, for example, in the form of mental image(s) [28] is particularly beneficial in visualizing large amount of data [29–31]. The large amount of data generated by digital devices now highlights the importance of visualization, providing an integral part in the analytical process.

Kim and Un [32] presented a paper on digital forensic visualization with mobile phone data. They noted that important evidence may be contained on a devices and developed a visualization application that allowed meaningful forensic evidence to be identified using a variety of visualization methods. This would allow the forensic practitioner to effectively analyze extracted data for comparison in tabular forms.

However visualization is not a simple process, you just do not have the ability to say, "Here is data, now visualize." Therefore not all visualization methodologies can visualize that same types of data, for example, timeline based mythologies require a date value to be usable. There are a variety of different visualization techniques that can be used for rendering and visualizing data. These include tree layouts (i.e., Tree-map, H-tree, etc.), balloon view, radial view, line graphs, bar charts, and x-y plots [33]. These visualization techniques could be used to represent data statistics such as modification, creation, accessed dates/times, and location [34].

This becomes highly effective when dealing with large data sets, Herman et al. [35] identified some of the issues with rendering large data sets, such as compromises in performance and also reaching the limits of the viewing platform, so even if you can place a thousand items onto a simple graph the user would not be able to interpret or locate important items. Current forensic/e-discover software using common methods for displaying data like tables now incorporate filters and search capability, allowing the user to sift through the large data sets. This is now a required feature in today's software providing the user with the ability to analyze the filtered visualized datasets and hopefully allow them to identify the required information, which they seek.

In the context of digital forensics, visualization can facilitate or ease the process of identifying and understanding vital evidence from the raw data generated by forensic software. Schrenk and Poisel [36], studies have confirmed that visualization can improve the efficiency of investigator and forensic practitioners by allowing sorting and filtering of data at a visual level reducing the time required during the analysis stage. Similarly, various other studies have found that visualization of (raw) data sets generally improve the user's understanding compared to traditional interfaces [36,37].

Noting that existing visualization software is not normally interoperable (i.e., cannot read output from another forensic tool), previous studies [19,21,38] demonstrated that no single tool can be used to extract the evidence from different digital devices (i.e., XRY used for mobile devices and EnCase used for hard-drive for the same case) and may not serve some particular needs of the forensic community [39]. The ever changing environment of digital forensics and e-Discovery software tools that specialize in the extraction process now allow practitioners to visualizes extracted dataset with a variety of different visualization methodologies, providing practitioners with the ability for refinement and ease of identification of key trophy items.

There are many papers that look into the benefits for visualizing data allowing for faster human interpretation and how this data is presented in the forensic field. In addition, visualizing data could also provide a positive effect on trust of the information by highlighting important relationships between data and items. The following papers provide an important background with the importance of visualization and how it will aid with the interpretation of data extracted from for electronic devices that contain vast amounts of unique data types.

Osborne and Turnbull [40] highlighted the need to develop architectures to provide forensic practitioners with the ability to visualize forensic data that will aid with digital forensic investigations. The development of such architectures would provide practitioners with the ability to visualize forensic data in a form that is familiar and can provide further insight. The developed architectures need to provide algorithms that can identify relationship identification, normalization of data, multiple sources incorporation, and the ability to provide effective visualization methods.

Becker et al. [41] conducted an experiment to test the effect of visualizing security and privacy data for an internet and cloud service provider to increase the trust that they have with their users, elaborating that most companies in the industry usually represent these values through textual statistics. This experiment noted that the visualization of information provides a positive affect; the knowledge about how to design and select of the visualization may have dramatically different effects on the data you are trying to represent, as everyone has their own interrelation of data.

Goodall [37] conducted a comparative evaluation between a visualization application and traditional user interface for analyzing network data. The study found that when users used the visual application they performed significantly more accurately and performed faster compared to the text-based application, allowing them to identify patterns and anomalies in the data more effectively, especially for novice users attempting to learn how to use the application, which is used to aid in training professionals [42]. Thomson et al. [43] research looks further into the comparison between text and visualization-based analysis for monitoring log files for network intrusion. Showing that different visualization methodologies could affect users' workload when analyzing data, using the information acquired, they developed a prototype to visualize log files from multiple sites (multiple network logs allowing for cross analysis of information), identify continuous timeline, and attack patterns extracted out of a dataset from a list. This visualization provides users with a reduced cognitive when interpreting the complex information.

Further studies have been undertaken to identify time-based visualization methods that are effective at different applications. Aigner et al. [44] systematic review for visualizing time-oriented data provides researchers the ability to identify suitable visual methodologies to conduct analytics on datasets, however, due to an abundance of approaches for visualizing time-based data sets, each method has only been validated to a specific task within the domain. The result is that it is almost incomprehensible to consider the complexity of all aspects involving time-based visualization.

In relation to digital forensics Olsson and Boldt [39] developed a prototype to provide investigating officers with the ability to view all of the evidence that has been extracted from a computer hard-drive, then plot the items that have been extracted onto a graphical timeline view enforcing the benefits as stated above by: "visualizing evidence on a forensic timeline increases the examiners' ability to see correlation between different events on a computer, which definitely could prove valuable in a digital crime investigation" and allowed users to locate evidence that is coherent in time. Teerlink and Erbacher [45] investigated how important the analysis proves through visualization, pointing out that software tools need to reduce the tedious amounts of information that forensic practitioners need to search with relations to large hard-drives and the large amount of time is spent trying to interpret the data while maintain high levels of patience and tolerance for errors. They develop a prototype to show directory hierarchies in conjunction with block views of files on filtered tree-maps. They achieved this by utilizing the output capacities generated by EnCase, allowing their research to be based on a forensically sound process. Kim and Un [32] discussed how they obtained extracted data from a portable forensic tool (tool name not given) for USB device analysis that allowed them to import a comma separated values (CSV) data file for visualization on their prototype comparing visualization to text-based analysis, however, clear images are not provided for the different visualization methods and text-based analysis.

Catanese and Fiumara [29] developed a prototype to analyze mobile phones by graphically representing the relationships among mobile phone users with a node-line layout on a radial tree, the prototype was developed to explore the structure of large graphs, and provided them with the ability to measure the connectivity between users, providing fast search and the identification of relationships between groups of people (e.g., shows connections between the suspect and known criminals). However, even though current forensic software and researches are starting to adopt visual solutions for large forensic datasets this can still result in information overload. Osborne et al. [46] "Explore, Investigate, and Correlate" (EIP) conceptual framework prevents such an issue by addressing scalability and comprehension of digital evidence. The framework is broken up into three phases as outlined by the title. When the framework produces an output it provides the practitioner with the ability to save its state allowing for faster transversal of visualization states. The explore phase provides an overview of the different types of data contained in the imported source/s and context-based type filtering. The investigate phase allows the practitioner to perform a deeper analysis of the information by utilizing functions to further filter (e.g., keyword search), zoom (e.g., search within a particular time frame), and read particular items (e.g., read a single SMS). This helps remove nonessential data from the visual view. The correlate phase provides the ability to add new sources or saved EIP states into the visualization while maintaining the current filtered, search, and zoom settings. Osborne and Slay [38] developed a prototype based on their EIP conceptual framework to evaluate the effectiveness of the approach to analysis and presentation of large digital datasets. Highlighting an ongoing user study and how they designed a large data set with a digital forensics complexity, to use in their user study comparing a typical text-based analysis and the visualization approach based on the EIP process. The results for the developed prototype were captured from a variety of quantitative studies (e.g., open-ended question usability surveys) and qualitative studies (e.g., participant's performance and accuracy were measured) allowing the author to test their model in the real-world environment [47].

3.2 Popular Commercial Forensic and e-Discovery Software

To undertake research into different visualization methodologies utilized by current commercial forensic and e-Discover software, we set a couple of different criteria that needed to meet to include in this study.

1. Need to be a commercial, this prevents open sources software that does not need to be liable for any inconsistencies.
2. Need to have been used in a court transcript unless has been officially provisioned to a government organization for use in criminal investigations.
3. Must provide a form of usable visualization.
4. And due to the confinements of this research all forms of visualization must be public knowledge through websites/brochures/online video demonstrations.

The 11 forensic and e-Discover were identified for our study:

- Nuix: Visual Analytics (Nuix)
- Micro Systemation: XAMN/XRY (XAMN)
- Cellebrite's UFED Link Analysis (UFED)
- EnCase Analytics (EnCase)
- Oxygen Forensic Suite 2015 Analyst (Oxygen)
- Katana Forensics Lantern (Katana)
- Susteen Secure View 3 (Susteen)
- Forensic Toolkit FTK AccessData (FTK)
- Internet Evidence Finder IEF Magnet Forensics (IEF)
- Intella Vound (Intella)
- i2 Analysts Notebook by IBM (i2)

The variety of forensic and e-Discovery software provided their own interpretation of the data visualization using proprietary names for common visualization methodologies. If a name for a visualization has not been provided, then a genetic name will be chosen. Some of the following commercial tools providers provide a variety of software, however, only one product has been selected from each see Table 1.

TABLE 1   Forensic and e-Discovery Software Visualization

Visualization	Software
Horizontal chart	EnCase
Stacked horizontal chart	Nuix, EnCase
Pie chart	Nuix, XAMN, Oxygen, FTK
Line chart	Nuix
Bar chart	FTK
Tag cloud/word cloud	Nuix
Venn diagram	Nuix
Map/geographic	Nuix, XAMN, UFED, EnCase, Oxygen, Susteen, FTK, IEF, I2
Pivot table	Nuix,
List/table view	Nuix, XAMN, UFED, Oxygen, Katana, Susteen, FTK, Intella, I2
Time lines	XAMN, UFED, EnCase, Susteen, FTK, IEF, Intella
Activity matrix	Oxygen
Social graph	Oxygen, Intella
Link analysis graph	Katana
Link graph	Susteen
Social analyzer/bubble chart	FTK
Bubble chart	EnCase
Connections/group view	XAMN, UFED
Prime # List	Susteen
Activity map	Susteen
Web activity	Susteen
Social networking analysis	Susteen
Heat maps	FTK
Cluster map	Intella
Word lists	Intella
Tree-map	FTK
Histogram view filtering	I2
Activity view	I2
Heat matrix view	FTK, I2
Social network (vis is called: K-Cores)	I2
Tree view (could be tree-map)	Intella

The field of academic research has always utilized basic visualization methodologies (e.g., line, bar, column, pie, etc.) providing the author with the ability to portray qualitative and quantitative research. These methodologies provide basic overview showing the quantity or frequency of their data sets. The academic world consists of many research fields and each field leans upon its chosen visualization methodology to provide readers with the best ability to interpret their findings. Over the last few years researchers have begun to develop or use a variety of visualization methodologies providing different views for interpretation.

According to existing literature surveys published in the last 5 years [48–70] investigating 294 visualization techniques, the popular techniques are shown below that had three or more overlapping methodologies see Table 2.

TABLE 2 Academic Selected Visualization

Visualization	Application Context
Tree-maps	Computer graphics and information visualization [48,51,52,56,65,69], human-computer interaction [49], big data [50], software engineering [57,63], data base [59], security and communication networks [62]
Basic charts and graphs	Computer graphics and information visualization [48,52,68–70], human-computer interaction [49,67], big data [50], quantitative approaches in management [53], science and technology [54], archeology [55], software engineering [57], data mining [58], data base [59]
Word clouds/tag clouds	Computer graphics and information visualization [48,60,65,68], big data [50], data mining [58]
Scatter plots	Computer graphics and information visualization [48,61,68–70], big data [50], quantitative approaches in management [53], data base [59]
Parallel coordinates	Computer graphics and information visualization [61,69,70], human-computer interaction [49,67], big data [50], data base [59]
Timeline	Computer graphics and information visualization [48,64,65], human-computer interaction [49], big data [50]
ThemeRiver	Computer graphics and information visualization [60], human-computer interaction [49], data mining [58]
Map/geographic	Computer graphics and information visualization [48,61,68], science and technology [54], archaology [55]
Cone trees	Software engineering [57,63], data base [59]
Glyph	Computer graphics and information visualization [48,65], archeology [55]
Horizon graph	Human-computer interaction [49,67], big data [50]
DocuBurst	Computer graphics and information visualization [60,64], data mining [58]

The diversity of visualization techniques investigated to produce Table 2 illustrates the overlap with techniques providing a basis to analyze the compatibility of the techniques to provide expectable means of visualizing forensic data.

4 FORENSIC VISUALIZATION SELECTION CRITERIA

Before visualizing any forensic data we must first establish some rules based upon Mckemmish's [9] four forensic principles, which ensure admissibility of the digital forensic process:

Rule 1—Minimal handling of the original. This is ensured by cloning the data stored on the electronic device, which is performed by a forensic software. By importing the extracted data into visualization software we can ensure rule one is met. However, Mckemmish points out that because we are using a copy of the data that is generated by one of the output capabilities from the forensic software we can ensure that access to the original data will be kept to a minimum. This also points out an issue with utilizing a separate software tool, not only does this include additional steps in the process for analyzing but also for storing the duplicated data. If the time taken to perform this extraction step will allow the practitioner the ability to identify trophy items within a shorter time then the process is justified.

Rule 2—Account for any changes. All changes must be recorded with adequate reasoning. If changes are required for the importation of data to the database or to the visualization application, a clear log needs to be provided, along with the changes made (e.g., altering the original timestamp format in the dataset to conform to the database or applications format). If this occurs then the original format must be shown side-by-side with the altered version.

Rule 3—Comply with the rules of evidence. This is normally organization specific ensuring that the process complies with local judicial requirements. Also the manner in which the evidence is presented should accurately represent the original data.

Rule 4—Do not exceed your knowledge. Digital forensic practitioner/s should not exceed the limits of their knowledge, the same process should be utilized for the interpretation of different visualization techniques, as some of the methods are newly discovered. There should be supported documentation provided with the application to allow the examiner the necessary material to improve their knowledge to allow them to interpret the dataset that is visualized.

The application of these rules needs to be applied, not only to the development of forensic and e-discovery software, but also to the suitable visualization techniques. We have identified a number of different visualization techniques from a variety of academic papers (see Table 2). To evaluate each technique for suitability for digital forensic data representation we have selected supportive criteria. The criteria will be based on Mckemmish's [71] categories for classifying the process as being forensically sound; *Meaning, Errors, Transparency,* and *Experience* and [39] Timeline representation of data.

Meaning—the interpretation of evidence remains unaltered by the visualization technique. This can be broken down further two steps.

1. *Repeatability* allows the dataset to be visualized without the concern that data would be changed or altered, allowing the data to be revisualized at different times or locations without change. Such a feature is a requirement for forensic visualization when communicating with other investigators or users.
2. *Lucidity* is the clarity and obscurity-free understanding of the visualized method, each visualized method that is generated needs to be easily understood by the audience (e.g., forensic practitioner, investigating officer). Clarity of the method chosen is also limited by

the user's understanding of the methodology; careful selection is required for each data time to select the most appropriate method to match the visualization type.

Errors—need to be identified and accounted for to prevent evidence from being taking into question.

3. *Anomaly* detection provides the user with the ability to identify unusual datasets and to highlighting imported datasets that may have an unsupported format also identifying outliers.

Transparency—provides the ability to examine and verified all of the data. This can be achieved with granularity and Filterability.

4. *Granularity* is the ability to go into greater detail as opposed to some visualization methods will provide an overview of usage of an device like a pie chart showing the percentage of each service used on the device. However, it will not show all the details of the items that generate that pie chart, e.g., viewing individual text messages inside of the pie chart rather than with a table it will show the user all of the available data for each item (e.g., number, message, time stamp, etc.).
5. *Filterable* allows the visualized method to be refined down to key items by means of text searches or by date stamps. Providing such functionality will allow the practitioner to isolate the data to around the incident time or even by location, which will provide a faster means of identifying key evidence for the prosecution. The filtering can be processed before the visualization is generated.

Experience—This particular process links up with the four rules, as outlined above by the four forensic principles that ensure admissibility of the digital forensic process. This particular step encompasses all of the criteria but cannot be defined by the different visualization techniques. This can, however, be aided by a timeline. By providing a timeline the user may have the ability to see how the data flows over a period of time, allowing interpretation of large datasets.

6. *Timeline* The view shows users the events that occurred within a specific timeframe. In most situations the investigating officers is only looking at a specific moment in time that the crime could have occurred. This limits the amount of data that the user needs to focuses on while trying to find the evidence required before broadening the scope of the timeframe. This is especially important in cases where the suspect's mobile phone may have items from when the suspect started using the phone. For example, in most situations people keep and maintain their mobile phones for two years before upgrading in Australia.

To analyze the differences between the software and the academic survey papers, we produced Table 3, which is broken up into three parts.

The table illustrates that the vast majority of techniques do not meet all criteria, the same applies for the visualization utilized by the forensic software. This is highlighted to show that the developers improved the individual weaknesses of the techniques by teaming them up with symbiotic relationships if deemed necessary. For example, with bubble charts the developers provided a click/hover ability to provide granularity functionality that is absent from bubble chart criteria showing greater detail when paired up with another technique (e.g., table, bar, list, etc.).

TABLE 3   Forensic Visualization Criteria

	Visualization Method	Requirement			Timeline View	Filterable	Granularity
		Repeatability	Lucidity	Anomaly			
Application context	Tree-maps		✓	✓		✓	
	Scatter plots	✓	✓	✓		✓	
	Parallel coordinates	✓	✓	✓		✓	
	ThemeRiver	✓	✓	✓	✓	✓	
	Cone trees	✓	✓	✓		✓	
	Glyph	✓	a	a	a	a	a
	DocuBurst	✓	✓	✓		✓	✓
Cross over	Word/tag clouds	✓	✓	✓		✓	✓
	Timeline	✓	✓	✓	✓	✓	✓
	Horizon graph	✓	✓	✓	✓	✓	
	Map/ geographic	✓	✓	✓		✓	
	Line graphs	✓	✓	✓	a	✓	
	Bar graphs	✓	✓	✓	a	✓	
	Pie chart's	✓	✓	✓		✓	
Software	Venn diagram	✓	✓	✓		✓	
	Pivot table	✓	✓		a	✓	✓
	List/table view	✓	✓			✓	✓
	Stacked horizontal chart	✓	✓	✓		✓	
	Activity matrix	✓	✓	✓		✓	
	Social graph	✓	✓	✓		✓	
	Link analysis graph	✓	✓	✓		✓	
	Link graph	✓	✓	✓		✓	
	Social analyzer	✓	✓	✓		✓	

Continued

TABLE 3   Forensic Visualization Criteria—cont'd

Visualization Method	Requirement			Timeline View	Filterable	Granularity
	Repeatability	Lucidity	Anomaly			
Bubble chart	✓	✓	✓		✓	
Connections/group view	✓	✓	✓		✓	
Prime # List	✓	✓			✓	✓
Activity map	✓	✓		✓	✓	✓
Web activity	✓	✓		✓	✓	✓
Social networking analysis	✓	✓	✓		✓	✓
Heat maps	✓	✓	✓		✓	✓
Cluster map	✓	✓	✓		✓	✓
Word lists	✓	✓	✓		✓	✓
Tree-map	✓	✓	✓		✓	✓
Histogram view filtering	✓	✓	✓	✓	✓	
Activity view	✓	✓	✓	✓	✓	✓
Heat matrix view	✓	✓	✓	✓	✓	
Social network	✓	✓	✓		✓	
Tree view	✓	✓	✓		✓	

Notes: The software reviewed sometimes uses the same visualization methodologies, however, the product names are different, for this report they have been listed based on their commercial name.

[a] May be able to do depending on the developer implemented that functionality.

The above table also highlights the three criteria that need to be met in order to successfully be used to represent forensic data reliability, lucidity, and filterability. And must also provide at least one main functionalities such as anomaly detection, timeline view, or granularity.

4.1 Identified Forensic Visualization Possibilities

The previous sections identified key visualization methodologies from the academic field that are currently not utilized for the identified digital forensic visualization software and e-Discovery software. This section will provide background and current academic papers utilizing these methodologies while also providing justification and use case scenarios for forensic investigations based on digital evidence.

Tree-maps were first presented by Carrier and Spafford [72] back in 2004 as a novel method for visualizing hierarchically structured information. One of the benefits allows 100% utilization of the allocated space by partitioning off the area into a collection of different colored rectangular boxes. The rectangles could be used to represent size, number, and location. There have been a number of softwares that currently utilize this methodology to provide a visual overview of files stored on a personal computer, providing a fast and effective method to locate and clean your storage device (e.g., kDirStart, WinDirStart, etc.). Tree-maps could provide a high-level overview of each of the categories stored on phones/HDD or any form of storage, providing practitioners with the ability to identify unusual storage of files such as pictures stored in an android root directory as well as providing a basic overview of the major feature of the device by looking at the quantity of apps/music/videos.

Scatter plots basic construction was first published by Herschel as identified by Friendly and Denis [73] and was originally used to smooth empirical bivariate data. However, it was not commonly used until the early 1900s. Scatter plots are used to plot data points on a horizontal and a vertical axis in an attempt to show how much one variable is affected by another. Each row in the data table is represented by a marker whose position depends on its values in the columns set on the X and Y axes. Scatter plots plot data points on a horizontal and a vertical axis showing how one variable is affected by another. Each row in the data table is represented by a marker whose position depends on its values in the columns set on the X and Y axes, a third variable utilizing a different color or size of the marker. Scatter plots can allow practitioners to determine whether there is a correlation between two variables, if there is a correlation, and the strength of that correlation. In reference to a mobile phone this could be used to identify at what time of the day the phone is most used showing correlation or even identifying outliers that my hold important information.

Parallel coordinates is a widely used multidimensional visualization technique providing the ability to plot individual data items across many dimensions allowing the differences to be compared side-by-side [74]. This provides an effective way to show relationships between pairwise dimensions. Each dimension corresponds to a vertical axis and each data item is displayed as a series of connected points along the dimensions [75]. Parallel coordinates are more often used in scientific and academic studies but have yet to be utilized in the forensic and e-discovery fields. Parallel coordinates could provide practitioners with a tool to compare similar case items and their usages against each other, comparing their usages (e.g., SMS, MMS, Email, etc.) to see if a patterns occurs between known convictions.

ThemeRiver was introduced as a prototype system to visualize a large collection of documents detailing the thematic variation over time [76]. Allowing the discovery of patterns illustrating relationships, structure, and anomalies in the dataset allows users the ability to prove hypotheses and provide new insights. ThemeRiver is a collection of data represented by a "river" flowing from left to right imposed on a timeline. The widening or narrowing represents changes in the amount of that data items at that point in the timeline each of the different data times are represented by a different color depicting currents within a river. A ThemeRiver can provide a basic overview of the usage of the suspect's device to simulate to a timeline graph. It also provides the ability to see combined peaks in device usage and inactivity. However, one of the downsides is the ease of identifying the individual quantities of data at a particulate time.

Cone Trees is a three-dimensional representation of hierarchical information. The hierarchy is presented in 3D to maximize the effective use of available screen space and enable visualization of the whole structure. The node of the tree is located at the apex of the cone and all its subnodes are arranged around the circular base of the cone in 3D, providing advanced functionality by allowing any node to be brought to the front by clicking on it and rotating the tree [77]. The head node of the hierarchy is placed at the top with its child-nodes placed evenly spaced along its basenoting that each cone is semitransparent so that it can be perceived, yet not block the view of cones behind it. Cone trees are normally utilized to represent directory structures and company charts, allowing this ability to transfer over to visualize the file structure of investigating items or the ability to show the links between different case items and suspects.

Glyph are used for multivariate data visualization and are commonly referred to as icons, providing the ability convey one or more data values through the use of different attributes (e.g., color, shape, size, and position on display area) [78]. Glyphs are normally laid out in a space-based area on the values for data variable mapping to special coordinates. However, one of the major flaws with glyphs is that if two or more glyphs have the same or similar icon due the overlapping values, they could coincide or overlap hindering information that could impede a forensic investigation and can also slow down the rendering process [79]. Glyphs have been used in a number of different fields and used as stars, trees, boxes, faces, arrows, wheels to other forms of glyph-based visualization methodologies such as Docubursts. Practitioners could utilize glyph-based techniques as an overlay of a geographical map using unique map legends to represent usage locations or even comparing different case items on a cone tree by different icons.

DocuBurst provides a sunburst visualization of hierarchical links between words, as described in Collins, Carpendale and Penn [80]. DocuBursts represented by a radial space filling layout similar to sectors on a Hard Disc Drive. DocuBurst are ordered from the center topic to the outer edges where each of the related topics are shown as a child topic. Each of the child topics can have children of their own up to a limit of 25 [81]. The size of each of the topics reflects the number of times the word appears in a document and color is used to differentiate between documents. DocuBursts have the potential to assist in providing a basic overview of the data that has been extracted and the ability to identify common patterns in the types of messages (e.g., emails, SMS, notes, etc.) having the potential to pick up common conversation tactics such as referring to a place or location in a message to a particular person showing a common meeting spot between two suspects.

The assumptions for the practicality uses of different visualization methodologies can only provide a glimpse into the future possibility of untapped potential. It will not be until a software developer attempts to implement a new technique that the validity can be conformed to provide a benefit.

5 CONCLUSION AND FUTURE RESEARCH

In this chapter, we investigated a variety of forensic and e-Discovery software tools, identifying a number of visualization methodologies currently being used today and a number of unique visualization methodologies that are currently being developed and utilized in the academic field.

We identified a number of court cases that contained incriminating digital evidence that resulted in prosecution; we highlighted the type of device and the quantity of data different practitioners are faced with during the analysis stage of the forensic process. We also summarized a number of court cases that identified forensic software tools that were utilized during the investigation, we utilized these tools for comparison to visualization survey papers published in the academic field.

We identified a number of new visualization methodologies that could be used to visualize a number of different types of data based on the studies that have been published. We noted as there will always be a growing amount of data from new and future devices and that the forensic field will need to evolve at a parallel pace to create new and improved methods to allow the fastest and most effected form of data interpretation.

At the end of the day there is only so much information a visualization methodology can prove and it still solely relies on the practitioners understanding and capability that has been acquired of over the course of their career. No single visualization technique can be the one and only solution but by combining the use of multiple visualization techniques, we can provide the best features to identify and recorded trophy items.

Future work includes an analysis of the storage of extracted forensic datasets resulting in the development of a database schema for third-party forensic data storage and retrieval, prototype of schema, and proof of visualization concept. Followed by the development of a prototype to test the viability of the identified unutilized visualization methodologies identified in this chapter.

References

[1] N. Lim, A. Khoo, Forensics of computers and handheld devices identical or fraternal twins? Commun. ACM 52 (6) (2009) 132–135.

[2] D. Quick, K.-K.R. Choo, Digital droplets: Microsoft Skydrive forensic data remnants, Futur. Gener. Comput. Syst. 29 (6) (2013) 1378–1394.

[3] D. Quick, K.-K.R. Choo, Dropbox analysis: data remnants on user machines, Digit. Investig. 10 (1) (2013) 3–18.

[4] Australian Communications and Media Authority, Communications Report 2014–15, Australian Communications and Media Authority, Australia, 2015.

[5] A. Smith, Smartphone Ownership—2013 Update, Pew Research Center's Internet & American Life Project, Washington, DC, 2013.

[6] Behavioural Insights Team, Reducing Mobile Phone Theft and Improving Security, Behavioural Insights Team, London, 2014.

[7] R.I. Rotberg, J.C. Aker, Mobile phones: uplifting weak and failed states, Wash. Q. 36 (1) (2013) 111–125.

[8] K.-K.R. Choo, Harnessing information and communications technologies in community policing, in: Community Policing in Australia, Research and Public Policy Series 111, Australian Institute of Criminology, Canberra, 2011, 67–75.

[9] R. Mckemmish, What is Forensic Computing? Australian Institute of Criminology, Canberra, 1999. Australian Institute of Criminology Trends & Issues in Crime and Criminal Justice.

[10] D. Quick, K.-K.R. Choo, Impacts of increasing volume of digital forensic data: a survey and future research challenges, Digit. Investig. 11 (4) (2014) 273–294.

[11] V. Baryamureeba, F. Tushabe, The enhanced digital investigation process model, in: Proceedings of the Fourth Digital Forensic Research Workshop, 2004.

[12] M. Reith, C. Carr, G. Gunsch, An examination of digital forensic models, Int. J. Digit. Evid. 1 (3) (2002) 1–12.

[13] S.R. Selamat, R. Yusof, S. Sahib, Mapping process of digital forensic investigation framework, Int. J. Comput. Netw. Secur. 8 (10) (2008) 163–169.

[14] N.L. Beebe, J.G. Clark, A hierarchical, objectives-based framework for the digital investigations process, Digit. Investig. 2 (2) (2005) 147–167.

[15] G. Grispos, T. Storer, W.B. Glisson, A comparison of forensic evidence recovery techniques for a windows mobile smart phone, Digit. Investig. 8 (1) (2011) 23–36.

[16] M. Breeuwsma, M. de Jongh, C. Klaver, R. Van Der Knijff, M. Roeloffs, Forensic data recovery from flash memory, Small Scale Digit. Device Forensics J. 1 (1) (2007) 1–17.

[17] G.C. Kessler, Anti-Forensics and the Digital Investigator, Edith Cowan University, Mount Lawley, WA, 2007. p. 1.

[18] W. Jansen, A. Delaitre, L. Moenner, Overcoming impediments to cell phone forensics, in: Proceedings of the 41st Annual Hawaii International Conference on System Sciences, 2008, p. 483.

[19] S.L. Garfinkel, Digital forensics research: the next 10 years, Digit. Investig. 7 (2010) S64–S73.

[20] W.B. Glisson, T. Storer, J. Buchanan-Wollaston, An empirical comparison of data recovered from mobile forensic toolkits, Digit. Investig. 10 (1) (2013) 44–55.

[21] C. Tassone, B. Martini, K.-K.R. Choo, J. Slay, Mobile Device Forensics: A Snapshot, Australian Institute of Criminology, Canberra, 2013. Australian Institute of Criminology Trends & Issues in Crime and Criminal Justice, 460, 1–7.

[22] K. Fairbanks, K. Atreya, H. Owen, Blackberry IPD parsing for open source forensics, in: IEEE Southeastcon, 2009, pp. 195–199.

[23] Y.H. Guo, J. Slay, J. Beckett, Validation and verification of computer forensic software tools-searching function, Digit. Investig. 6 (2009) S12–S22.

[24] D. Irwin, R. Hunt, Forensic information acquisition in mobile networks, in: IEEE Pacific Rim Conference on Communications, Computers and Signal Processing (PacRim), 2009, pp. 163–168.

[25] S. Raghav, A.K. Saxena, Mobile forensics: guidelines and challenges in data preservation and acquisition, in: IEEE Student Conference on Research and Development (SCOReD), 2009, pp. 5–8.

[26] S.G. Eick, Graphically displaying text, J. Comput. Graph. Stat. 3 (2) (1994) 127–142.

[27] M. Friendly, D.J. Denis, Milestones in the History of Thematic Cartography, Statistical Graphics, and Data Visualization, Retrieved, 5(11), 2001, p. 2011.

[28] J.J. Thomas, K.A. Cook, Illuminating the Path: The Research and Development Agenda for Visual Analytics, National Visualization and Analytics Center, Richland, WA, 2005.

[29] S.A. Catanese, G. Fiumara, A visual tool for forensic analysis of mobile phone traffic, in: Proceedings of the 2nd ACM Workshop on Multimedia in Forensics, Security and Intelligence, 2010, pp. 71–76.

[30] G. Mohay, Technical challenges and directions for digital forensics, in: First International Workshop on Systematic Approaches to Digital Forensic Engineering, 2005, pp. 155–161.

[31] E. Vlastos, A. Patel, An open source forensic tool to visualize digital evidence, Comput. Stand. Interfaces 30 (1-2) (2008) 8–19.

[32] K. Kim, S.K. Un, Visual analysis of portable computer forensic data, in: Y.-H. Han, D.-S. Park, W. Jia, S.-S. Yeo (Eds.), Ubiquitous Information Technologies and Applications, Springer, Netherlands, 2013, pp. 453–459.

[33] S. Chavhan, S.M. Nirkhi, Visualization techniques for digital forensics: a survey, Int. J. Adv. Comp. Res. 2 (4) (2012) 74–76.

[34] S. Teelink, R.F. Erbacher, Improving the computer forensic analysis process through visualization, Commun. ACM 49 (2) (2006) 71–75.

[35] I. Herman, G. Melançon, M.S. Marshall, Graph visualization and navigation in information visualization: a survey, IEEE Trans. Vis. Comput. Graph. 6 (1) (2000) 24–43.

[36] G. Schrenk, R. Poisel, A discussion of visualization techniques for the analysis of digital evidence, in: Sixth International Conference on Availability, Reliability and Security (ARES), 2011, pp. 758–763.

[37] J.R. Goodall, Visualization is better! A comparative evaluation, in: Sixth International Workshop on Visualization for Cyber Security (VizSec), 2009, pp. 57–68.

[38] G. Osborne, J. Slay, Digital forensics infovis: an implementation of a process for visualisation of digital evidence, in: Sixth International Conference on Availability, Reliability and Security (ARES), 2011.

[39] J. Olsson, M. Boldt, Computer forensic timeline visualization tool, Digit. Investig. 6 (2009) S78–S87.

[40] G. Osborne, B. Turnbull, Enhancing computer forensics investigation through visualization and data exploitation, in: International Conference on Availability, Reliability and Security (ARES '09), 2009, pp. 1012–1017.

[41] J. Becker, M. Heddier, A. ÖKsuz, R. Knackstedt, The effect of providing visualizations in privacy policies on trust in data privacy and security, in: 47th Hawaii International Conference on System Sciences, 2014, pp. 3224–3233.

[42] G. Francia, M. Trifas, D. Brown, R. Francia, C. Scott, Visualization and management of digital forensics data, in: Proceedings of the Third Annual Conference on Information Security Curriculum Development, 2006, pp. 96–101.

[43] A. Thomson, M. Graham, J. Kennedy, Pianola—visualization of multivariate time-series security event data, in: Seventeenth International Conference on Information Visualisation, 2013, pp. 123–131.

[44] W. Aigner, S. Miksch, W. Müller, H. Schumann, C. Tominski, Visualizing time-oriented data—a systematic view, Comput. Graph. 31 (3) (2007) 401–409.

[45] S. Teerlink, F.R. Erbacher, Foundations for visual forensic analysis, in: IEEE Information Assurance Workshop, 2006, pp. 192–199.

[46] G. Osborne, B. Turnbull, J. Slay, The Explore, Investigate and Correlate' (Eic) conceptual framework for digital forensics information visualization, in: ARES 2010, Fifth International Conference on Availability, Reliability and Security, 15–18 February 2010, Krakow, Poland, 2010, pp. 629–634.

[47] G. Osborne, The Explore, Investigate and Correlate Process for Information Visualization in Digital Forensics, University of South Australia, Adelaide, SA, 2012.

[48] F. Wanner, A. Stoffel, D. Jäckle, B. Kwon, A. Weiler, D. Keim, K.E. Isaacs, A. Giménez, I. Jusufi, T. Gamblin, State-of-the-art report of visual analysis for event detection in text data streams, in: EuroVis 2014: The Eurographics Conference on Visualization, 9–13 June 2014, Swansea, UK, 2014, pp. 1–18.

[49] W. Aigner, S. Miksch, H. Schumann, C. Tominski, Survey of visualization techniques: visualization of time-oriented data, Springer, London, 2011. pp. 147–254.

[50] M. Krstajic, D.A. Keim, Visualization of streaming data: observing change and context in information visualization techniques, in: IEEE International Conference on Big Data, 2013, pp. 41–47.

[51] P. Caserta, O. Zendra, Visualization of the static aspects of software: a survey, IEEE Trans. Vis. Comput. Graph. 17 (7) (2011) 913–933.

[52] A. Shamim, V. Balakrishnan, M. Tahir, Evaluation of opinion visualization techniques. Inf. Vis. (2014), http://dx.doi.org/10.1177/1473871614550537.

[53] K. Miettinen, Survey of methods to visualize alternatives in multiple criteria decision making problems, OR Spectr. 36 (1) (2014) 3–37.

[54] G.-D. Sun, Y.-C. Wu, R.-H. Liang, S.-X. Liu, A survey of visual analytics techniques and applications: state-of-the-art research and future challenges, J. Comput. Sci. Technol. 28 (5) (2013) 852–867.

[55] P. Bernardes, J. Madeira, M. Martins, J. Meireles, The use of traditional and computer-based visualization in archaeology: a user survey, in: The 13th International Symposium on Virtual Reality, Archaeology and Cultural Heritage VAST, 2012.

[56] H. Schulz, S. Hadlak, H. Schumann, The design space of implicit hierarchy visualization: a survey, IEEE Trans. Vis. Comput. Graph. 17 (4) (2011) 393–411.

[57] A. Pleuss, R. Rabiser, G. Botterweck, Visualization techniques for application in interactive product configuration, in: Proceedings of the 15th International Software Product Line Conference, Volume 2, 2011, pp. 1–8.

[58] A.B. Alencar, M.C.F. De Oliveira, F.V. Paulovich, Seeing beyond reading: a survey on visual text analytics, WIREs Data Min. Knowl. Discovery 2 (6) (2012) 476–492.

[59] M.M. Dias, C. Franco, E. Rabelo, J.K. Yamaguchi, Visualization techniques: which is the most appropriate in the process of knowledge discovery in data base? InTech Open Access, Croatia, 2012.

[60] Q. Gan, M. Zhu, M. Li, T. Liang, Y. Cao, B. Zhou, Document visualization: an overview of current research, Wiley Interdiscip. Rev. Comput. Stat. 6 (1) (2014) 19–36.

[61] M. Abdelaziz, R. Nancy, S. Olivier, Survey of multidimensional visualization techniques, in: The proceedings of Computer Graphics, Visualization, Computer Vision and Image Processing (CGVCVIP'12), Lisbon Portugal, 2012.

[62] Y. Zhang, Y. Xiao, M. Chen, J. Zhang, H. Deng, A survey of security visualization for computer network logs, Secur. Commun. Netw. 5 (4) (2012) 404–421.

[63] B. Shneiderman, C. Dunne, P. Sharma, P. Wang, Innovation trajectories for information visualizations: comparing treemaps, cone trees, and hyperbolic trees, Inf. Vis. 11 (2) (2012) 87–105.

[64] Z. Geng, R.S. Laramee, T. Cheesman, A. Rothwell, D.M. Berry, A. Ehrmann, Visualizing translation variation of *Othello*: a survey of text visualization and analysis tools, in: Eurographics Conference on Visualization (EuroVis), 2011.

[65] C. Rohrdantz, M. Krstajic, M. El Assady, D. Keim, What's going on? How twitter and online news can work in synergy to increase situational awareness, in: 2nd IEEE Workshop on Interactive Visual Text Analytics "Task-Driven Analysis of Social Media" as part of the IEEE VisWeek 2012, Seattle, Washington, DC, 2012.

[66] W. Javed, B. Mcdonnel, N. Elmqvist, Graphical perception of multiple time series, IEEE Trans. Vis. Comput. Graph. 16 (6) (2010) 927–934.

[67] C. Perin, F. Vernier, J.-D. Fekete, Interactive horizon graphs: improving the compact visualization of multiple time series, in: Proceedings of the SIGCHI Conference on Human Factors in Computing Systems, 2013, pp. 3217–3226.

[68] C. Eun Kyoung, L. Bongshin, M.C. Schraefel, Characterizing visualization insights from quantified selfers' personal data presentations, IEEE Comput. Graph. Appl. 35 (4) (2015) 28–37.

[69] H.A. Basit, M. Hammad, R. Koschke, A survey on goal-oriented visualization of clone data, in: IEEE 3rd Working Conference on Software Visualization (VISSOFT), 2015, pp. 46–55.

[70] J. Johansson, C. Forsell, Evaluation of parallel coordinates: overview, categorization and guidelines for future research, IEEE Trans. Vis. Comput. Graph. 22 (1) (2016) 579–588.

[71] R. Mckemmish, When is digital evidence forensically sound? in: Advances in Digital Forensics IV, IFIP International Federation for Information Processing, vol. 285, Springer, New York, 2008, pp. 3–15, http://link.springer.com/chapter/10.1007%2F978-0-387-84927-0_1.

[72] B. Carrier, E.H. Spafford, An event-based digital forensic investigation framework, in: Digital Forensic Research Workshop, 2004.

[73] M. Friendly, D. Denis, The early origins and development of the scatterplot, J. Hist. Behav. Sci. 41 (2) (2005) 103–130.

[74] A. Inselberg, The plane with parallel coordinates, Vis. Comput. 1 (2) (1985) 69–91.

[75] T. Van Long, A new metric on parallel coordinates and its application for high-dimensional data visualization, in: IEEE International Conference on Advanced Technologies for Communications (ATC), 2015, pp. 297–301.

[76] S. Havre, B. Hetzler, L. Nowell, Themeriver: visualizing theme changes over time, IEEE Trans. Vis. Comput. Graph. 8 (1) (2002) 9–20.

[77] G.G. Robertson, J.D. Mackinlay, S.K. Card, Cone trees: animated 3d visualizations of hierarchical information, ACM, New York, 1991. pp. 189–194.

[78] R. Borgo, J. Kehrer, D.H. Chung, E. Maguire, R.S. Laramee, H. Hauser, M. Ward, M. Chen, Glyph-based visualization: foundations, design guidelines, techniques and applications, in: Eurographics State of the Art Reports, 2013, pp. 39–63.

[79] A. Komlodi, P. Rheingans, U. Ayachit, J.R. Goodall, A. Joshi, A user-centered look at glyph-based security visualization, in: IEEE Workshop on Visualization for Computer Security, 2005, pp. 21–28.

[80] C. Collins, S. Carpendale, G. Penn, Docuburst: Visualizing Document Content Using Language Structure, Wiley Online Library, 20091039–1046.

[81] T. Heuss, B. Humm, T. Deuschel, T. Fröhlich, T. Herth, O. Mitesser, Semantically guided, situation-aware literature research, in: Linked Data and User Interaction, Series 162, IFLA, The Hague, 2015, pp. 66.

Investigating Storage as a Service Cloud Platform: pCloud as a Case Study

T. Dargahi*, A. Dehghantanha†, M. Conti‡
*Islamic Azad University, Tehran, Iran †University of Salford, Salford, United Kingdom
‡University of Padua, Padua, Italy

1 INTRODUCTION

The usage of cloud storage, among individuals and companies, is increasing day by day. Due to the recent report of the Forbes (2015), *"47% of marketing departments will have at least 60% of their applications on a cloud platform by 2017"* [1], and *"cloud market cap will pass $500 billion by 2020"* [2]. Even though cloud storage offers several advantages compared to traditional and local storage of data, cloud users are concerned about the integrity of stored data, security, and user privacy issues [3, 4]. There exist several solutions that could be considered by security experts in order to protect the stored data and preserve privacy of the cloud users [5–8]. Adopting security mechanisms is useful in protecting data against being modified and accessed by unauthorized users, and make it difficult for the attackers to abuse the data. However, the artifacts which potentially remain on the cloud storage servers could threaten the privacy of the cloud users. In such a case, security mechanisms might not suffice to preserve users' privacy. As a result, protecting the sensitive data against cloud storage services, which leak the privacy of the users, is trending as an issue to the law enforcement agencies and other digital forensic investigators. Moreover, it should be contemplated that organized cyber criminals are always able to find new ways of evading the rules [9, 10]. This motivated several researchers to conduct a number of cloud storage forensic investigations on various cloud services and applications (apps) [11, 12]. However, with the ever increasing introduction of such cloud services and technologies, having an up-to-date understanding of possible data remnants after using new cloud storage apps is fundamental for forensic practitioner [13].

185

In this chapter we consider *pCloud*[1] as a case study to identify the possible evidential data that may remain after the use of pCloud on several different computer systems. pCloud is a free online cloud storage service (founded in 2013 in Switzerland) that has over four million users right today [14]. pCloud users are able to store, sync, and share their files, as well as make backup from other cloud services such as Dropbox. pCloud provides client-side encryption such that the data, which are leaving the client's system, are encrypted. Moreover, pCloud has the Quality Management Systems (ISO 9001:2008) and Information Security Management Systems (ISO 27001:2013) certificates. Due to the increasing use of the pCloud, and several good reviews that it received from the cloud expert reviewers [15–17], we are focusing on probable privacy issues of pCloud in this chapter. To the best of our knowledge, this is the first forensics investigative study of pCloud. In particular, We will answer the following questions in the rest of the chapter:

- What data (and the location of the data) can be found on *Windows*, *Ubuntu*, *Android*, and *iOS* operating systems when using pCloud services?
- What data can be leaked while accessing the pCloud using *Google Chrome* and *Internet Explorer* browsers on Windows operating systems?
- What data of forensic interest can be discovered in live memory on the aforementioned platforms?
- What data can be captured from network traffic?

Before introducing our research methodology and contribution of the chapter, we provide a brief literature review on forensic investigation of cloud storage services.

1.1 Related Work

Computer system users produce a great deal of digital data day by day in such a way that by 2020, the amount of produced data will exceed 40 zettabytes [18]. Therefore in order to store such a data on cloud, we need to have more fast and secure synchronization between servers and PCs; for which services such as *BitTorrent* are very common these days. In [19], Farina et al. conducted a forensic investigation on the BTSync client app and recognized the digital artifacts and network findings that could be then used by digital forensic examiners as evidence. Due to the increasing use of cloud computing and cloud storage services, researchers believe that cloud computing is more vulnerable to security and privacy issues, such as information theft [20–23], in particular considering online cloud services [24]. Thus there is a surge of interest by forensic professionals and privacy experts in cloud forensic analysis in recent years. In this section we briefly review the state-of-the-art in digital forensics investigation of cloud privacy.

Compared to the other aspects of computer analysis, only a few research studies have been conducted on cloud storage privacy investigation. Martini and Choo [25] were the first to carry out the cloud forensics investigation. They analyzed the *ownCloud* as a case study in order to find client and server side artifacts that could be useful as evidential data for forensics practitioners in performing cloud analysis. With the gradual increase of Cloud storage services, there is a growing tendency among individuals and organizations in using such a

---

[1] https://www.pcloud.com/

service in order to store and access several different kinds of data. Therefore most of the investigations on cloud context are concentrated on analyzing the privacy leakage probability of the widely used cloud storage services. For example, Quick and Choo analyzed the process of gathering data, browsing of data, and the synchronization of files focusing on *Dropbox* [26], *Microsoft SkyDrive* [27], and *Google Drive* [28]. In [27], the authors found the terrestrial artifacts that are left behind when using SkyDrive on different devices such as mobile phones and desktop computers. Similarly, Quick and Choo studied the possible data remnants on a Windows 7 computer and an Apple iPhone 3G when a user adopts *Dropbox* [26] or *Google Drive* [28] in order to store, upload, and access data in the cloud.

Along the same line of study, Hale [29] analyzed the digital artifacts remnant on a computer after accessing or manipulating *Amazon* Cloud Drive. They could recover several information, such as installation path, and upload/download operations. In [30], Chung et al. presented new method in order to analyze the digital artifacts left on all accessible devices, such as Mobile phones (e.g., iPhone and Android smartphone) and Desktop systems, running different OS (e.g., Windows and Mac) while using Amazon S3, Google Docs, Dropbox, and Evernote. Contrary to most of the cloud storage services that are based on open source platforms, Apple users have their own special cloud storage called *iCloud*. Oestreicher [31] investigated particularly iCloud service in order to find leftover digital droplets when using native Mac OS X during system synchronization with the cloud. There are also various research studies on several different cloud storage services that we summarized in Table 1. We refer the interested reader to [32, 33] for a comprehensive survey in this regard.

TABLE 1 A Brief Overview of the Existing Cloud Storage Forensics Research Studies

Cloud Services	Public Cloud	Private Cloud
Dropbox	[12, 26, 30, 34–37]	[35]
Amazon S3	[30]	
Evernote	[30]	
Google Drive	[12, 28, 30, 34, 37, 38]	
SkyDrive	[12, 27, 34]	
Box	[35, 37]	[35]
SugarSync	[35, 39]	[35]
Amazon Cloud Drive	[29]	
OneDrive	[36, 37]	
ownCloud	[36]	[25]
Flicker	[38]	
PicasaWeb	[38]	
iCloud	[31]	
UbuntuOne	[40]	

Continued

TABLE 1   A Brief Overview of the Existing Cloud Storage Forensics Research Studies—cont'd

Cloud Services	Public Cloud	Private Cloud
hubiC	[41]	
Mega	[42]	
Hadoop		[43]
Amazon EC2		[44]
vCloud		[45]
XtreemFS		[46]
Eucalyptus		[47]
Amazon AWS	[48]	

Outline. The rest of the chapter is organized as follows: in Section 2 we explain the research methodology and experimental setup. Section 3 presents the results of our experimental analysis on pCloud. We answer the question "What data can be captured from network traffic?" in Section 4. Finally, Section 5 concludes the chapter.

2 RESEARCH METHODOLOGY

In order to conduct a reliable digital forensic analysis, we should follow a forensic investigation guideline [49, 50]. In this research study we performed our forensic investigation based on the framework introduced by Martini and Choo [51], which is composed of four important stages (Fig. 1):

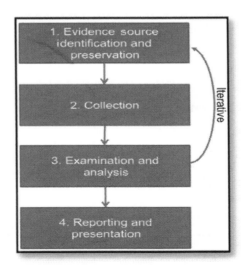

FIG. 1   Cloud forensics framework of Martini and Choo [51].

- *Evidence source identification and preservation.* In this phase we detect potential sources of evidences. We used *VMware Workstation 10.0.2 build 1744117* to create the virtual machines (VMs) for the experiments. We configured each VM with 1 GB of RAM, and 2 GB hard disk space for Android VM, 15 GB for Ubuntu VM, and 40 GB Windows VM.
- *Collection.* In this phase we collected the potential data resources and files in a forensically sound manner.
- *Analysis.* In this phase we analyzed the data obtained from the previous phase. We considered keywords such as *"account," "password,"* and *"files"* to search for evidence in the memory. This chapter is mainly focused on presenting analysis results of pCloud platform, however, we highlighted the collection and preservation approaches as deemed necessary!
- *Reporting and presentation.* This phase presents the collected evidences in such a way that would be acceptable by the court of law. As this chapter is only focused on presenting potential evidences, we briefly discussed this stage in our conclusion.

2.1 Experimental Setup

We conducted our experiments on four different operating systems: a 64 bit Windows 8, Ubuntu 14.04.1 LTS, Android 4.4.2, and iOS 8.1. We considered two different browsers: *Internet Explorer 10.0.9200.16384* and *Google Chrome 39.0.2171.71 m*. We carried out our experiments using the digital forensic research workshop challenge 2013 dataset (DFRWS[2]). We downloaded the dataset on December 8, 2014, and evaluated the hash of the dataset to ensure the integrity of the data. The dataset contains a main folder called `test` including ten directories namely: `au`, `b`, `img`, `js`, `ml`, `msx`, `pdf`, `txt`, `vid`, `z`. We carried out our investigation taking into account all the files included in all directories.

We utilized *Wireshark 1.12.3* to capture network traffic in all of the platforms and experimental tasks running on them. Furthermore, we used *NetworkMiner 1.6.1* to further analyze the captured network traffic. We captured physical memory in Ubuntu using *memdump 1.01-6-i386*. We used *Hex Workshop 6.7* (6.8.0.5419/Sep. 1, 2014) to analyze the captured physical memory of the VMs, after the successful execution of each task. One of the main goals of examining this type of app is to determine the possible remnants on different platforms using certain tools, which we explain in the following. Apart from the *sqlitebrowser 3.4.0*, we also adopted *iphonebackupbrowser-r38* for Android and iOS.

2.1.1 Windows

In order to investigate pCloud remnants on a Windows operating system, we considered two different research directions: (i) Windows web browser-based analysis and (ii) Windows app-based analysis.

As for the web browser-based investigation, we installed two popular browsers: *Microsoft Internet Explorer 10.0.9200.16384*, and *Google Chrome 39.0.2171.71 m* on four VMs, and performed different tasks specifically to the VM. Fig. 2 shows the web browser-based tasks on the Windows VM. We updated Microsoft Internet Explorer and installed Google Chrome

[2] http://www.dfrws.org/2013/challenge/index.shtml

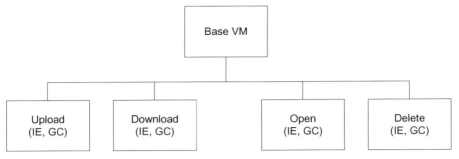

FIG. 2   Windows browser-based VMs.

on the base machine. We then cloned to four other machines for the following tasks: *upload*, *download*, *open*, and *delete*. Since it is a browser-based experiment, installation of pCloud was not required, as the experiment will be directly focusing on interacting with the pCloud in the web browser. We used all the folders and files from the DFRWS dataset during each task. For example, we first uploaded all the files during the upload task, and then downloaded back during the download task. Moreover, we captured network traffic during all the tasks.

The main artifacts that are recoverable from web browsers are from their cache and history folders. Therefore after performing the four aforementioned operations (i.e., upload, download, open, and delete) using the dataset, we analyzed the cache using *NirSoft IECacheview v 1.53* for Internet Explorer and *NirSoft ChromeCacheView v 1.61* for Google Chrome.

In order to conduct the windows app-based investigation, we adopted *Windows 8.1 Pro build 9600* with pCloud drive 2.0. We performed six different tasks as it can be seen in Fig. 3.

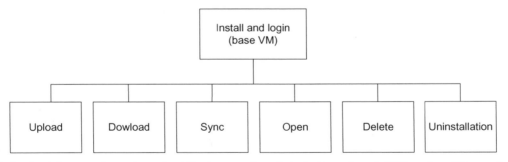

FIG. 3   Six different tasks performed on Windows app-based, Android app-based, iOS-based, and Ubuntu-based VMs. It should be noted that, since we performed the same operations for all of the four operating systems, we demonstrated all in one figure.

2.1.2 Android

In order to access the system folders on Android, the OS needs to be rooted. Without the root access, there is no way of accessing the data that are required to perform the experiments and capturing the internal memory. Also having the root access, we will be able to run certain commands and access system protected files. To interact with the given Android machine, we used a terminal called *Android emulator 1.0.5*. We accessed the system protected files using an app called *Root Browser 2.2.3*. With the help of this file browser, we were able to locate different critical artifacts related to the pCloud, such as databases and log files. We used a terminal emulator in order to capture the processes that were running in the internal memory (RAM Capture) and also to copy the captured file to the main investigation machine. We carried out six different experiments on an Android-based app (Android 4.4.2), which are depicted in Fig. 3.

2.1.3 iOS

In order to conduct experiments on iOS, we adopted an iPad mini running *iOS 8.1*. However due to some authentication issues from the owner, we were unable to jail break. We used *iTunes 12.0.1.26*, 64 bit, to back up the files after performing the tasks that are shown in Fig. 3. After completion of each task, we took a backup of the whole iPad using *iTunes* with the use of *iPhone Backup Browser 1.2.0.6* (by Google project). We were able to track the changes which was made during the installation procedure of the pCloud.

2.1.4 Ubuntu

We adopted the *Ubuntu 14.04.1 LTS* (Trusty Tahr) to carry out our investigation. We installed the pCloud drive 2.0 through the Ubuntu software center. We also performed the uninstallation process through the Ubuntu software center. We installed the pCloud drive on a main VM which was the "install and login." We also cloned this VM for the other tasks: upload, download, sync, open, delete, and uninstallation (see Fig. 3). In fact, we cloned these machines in order to avoid the virtual memory being overwritten by the execution of the next task, which would erase the evidence of the previous task with the new evidence of the next task.

The DFRWS dataset contained various types of files, and we used all of them in the experiments. For example, during upload, we uploaded all the folders and files. After the successful execution of each task, we captured the live memory using *memdump 1.01-6*. During carrying out all the tasks, we also captured the network traffic using *Wireshark 1.12.3*.

3 ANALYSIS AND FINDINGS

In this section we present our experimental findings along with the data analysis. In order to analyze the live memory we accessed the VM folders while the VM was powered on. We analyzed this memory, using *Hex Workshop*, after the corresponding task was successfully performed on the VM. It should be noted that, if we do not mention a specific action (such as download, upload, sync, or delete), it means there was no evidence that could be used by a forensic investigator for further analysis of that action.

3.1 Windows Browser-Based Experiments

We first set up the base VM in order to conduct the Window Browser-based experiments. As all the clones had the latest version of the Internet Explorer and Google Chrome, we avoided installing and updating the browsers when conducting experiments. We started the experiments with the "upload" VM, leading to the "download" VM, and after that "open" and "delete" VMs.

3.1.1 Upload

We were able to acquire information such as uploaded file names and the user names, which was used to upload the data to the pCloud, using Internet Explorer. As Fig. 4 shows, we could discover the folder path from the memory.

FIG. 4   Windows Browser-based—uploaded files.

3.1.2 Install and Login

As it can be seen in Fig. 5, the passwords and the email address are clearly discoverable from the physical memory, along with the interested file names and directories. These information are valuable for a forensic examiner.

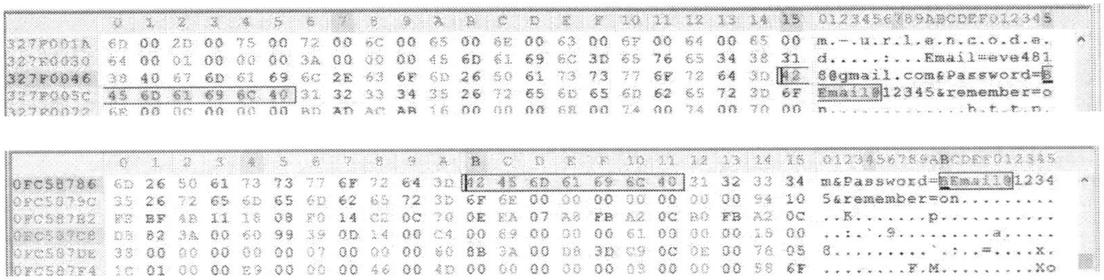

FIG. 5   Windows Browser-based—install and login.

We utilized *NirSoft IEPassView 1.32* in order to analyze the saved data files by the Internet Explorer. We found out that Internet Explorer saves the pCloud credentials in the registry. However, search results do not reveal any kind of information regarding the credentials in the Internet Explorer cache files, for which we used *IECacheview* to perform analysis. Obtained results indicate that all the uploads went through an encrypted server, making it difficult to gather much information about the uploads.

We also analyzed the memory image focusing on the Google Chrome browser. We were able to retrieve remnants such as username and password that were used to access pCloud (Fig. 6). We could also find evidential data through *ChromeCacheView* for Google Chrome cache, along with the links which were accessed during the tasks.

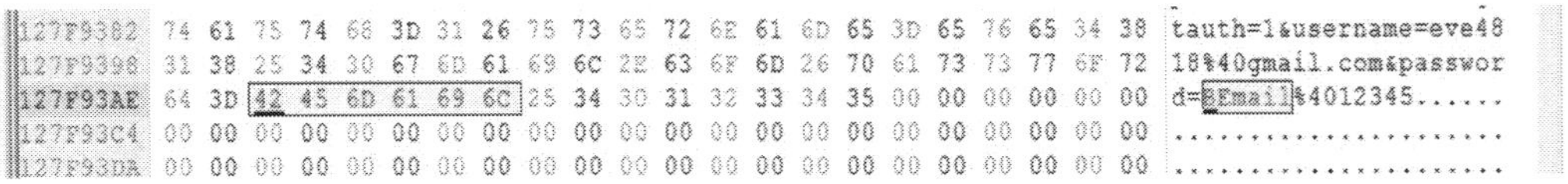

FIG. 6   Chrome—pCloud credentials.

3.2 Windows app-Based Experiments

In this section we discuss the evidential data we obtained while analyzing the pCloud app installed on Windows OS. We explain three different tasks: install and login, delete, and uninstall.

3.2.1 Install and Login

Upon the first installation of the pCloud on Windows, we have traced down the changes that the app made on both file system and the registry of the computer. The pCloud client created and modified the following address on the disk drive: `Users\User\Documents\ pCloud Sync`. This address is used to store the pCloud client files, the configuration, and some other necessary files. Other than the system's disk drive, pCloud has created entries in the registry of the Windows. The Registry entries can be found in the following locations:

- `HKEY_CURRENT_USER\Software\pcloud`
- `HKEY_CURRENT_USER\Software\pcloud LTD\pCloud Drive`
- `HKEY_CURRENT_USER\Software\Microsoft\Windows\CurrentVersion\Run`
- `HKLM\SOFTWARE\Wow6432Node\Microsoft\Windows\CurrentVersion\ Uninstall\ {3e0d7412-ce78-4007-a287-f4a4b42460b2}\DisplayName: ''pCloud Drive''`
- `HKLM\SOFTWARE\Wow6432Node\Microsoft\Windows\CurrentVersion\Uninstall\ {3e0d7412-ce78-4007-a287-f4a4b42460b2}\DisplayVersion: ''2.0.3.0''`
- `HKLM\SOFTWARE\Wow6432Node\Microsoft\Windows\CurrentVersion\ Uninstall\ {3e0d7412-ce78-4007-a287-f4a4b42460b2}\Publisher: ''pCloud LTD''`
- `HKLM\SYSTEM\CurrentControlSet\Services\SharedAccess\Parameters\ FirewallPoli cy\FirewallRules\ {9CB654A6-21A1-46DA-A953 -0FCB19FE13CA}: ''v2.22|Action=Allow|Active=TRUE|Dir=In| Protocol=6|App=% ProgramFiles(x86)% pCloud Drive\pCloud.exe| Name=pCloud|Edge=TRUE|''`
- `HKLM\SOFTWARE\Microsoft\Windows\CurrentVersion\Installer\ UserData\ S-1-5-18\Products\2CB735048C972D445A5864132F3A0314\ InstallProperties\ DisplayName: ''pCloud Drive''`
- `HKLM\SOFTWARE\Microsoft\Windows\CurrentVersion\Installer\ UserData\ S-1-5-18\Products\2CB735048C972D445A5864132F3A0314\ InstallProperties\ Publisher: ''pCloud LTD''`
- `HKLM\SOFTWARE\Wow6432Node\Microsoft\Windows\CurrentVersion\ Uninstall\ {3e0d7412-ce78-4007-a287-f4a4b42460b2} \ QuietUninstallString: ''%ProgramData% PackageCache\ {3e0d7412-ce78-4007-a287-f4a4b42460b2} \pCloud Drive.exe / uninstall /quiet''`
- `HKLM\SOFTWARE\Microsoft\Windows\CurrentVersion\Installer\ UserData\ S-1-5-18\Components\B8991F4234EFEBC4F8A2180B2B003A2C\ 2CB735048C972D445A5864132F3A0314: ''01:\Software\pCloud\AppPath''`
- `HKLM\SOFTWARE\Classes\CLSID\{0b73fac-351f-3948-9d8a-1dad9d870193} \InprocServer32\CodeBase:file:///%ProgramFiles(x86)%pCloudDrive/ ContextMenuHandler.DLL`

We found out that pCloud creates some files in the *Run* and also *Uninstall* folders of the registry. Other than changes in the registry and local hard drive, we noticed changes in the rules for Windows Firewall in order to solve the issues that may happen while connecting to the pCloud Servers (Fig. 7).

FIG. 7   Windows app-based registry changes in firewall folder.

After reviewing the memory dump images from the Windows machine, which pCloud client was installed on, we found out that we are unable to find any sort of plain text passwords. However, we have successfully found usernames within the memory dump.

3.2.2 Delete

In order to analyze the effect of the "Delete" action, we deleted some files. We recognized that it is still possible to find some traces of the deleted file names within the memory dump (Fig. 8).

```
02F26080   2B 30 30 30 30 22 2C 0A 09 09 09 22 64 69 66 66   +0000",...."diff
02F26090   69 64 22 3A 20 37 35 32 2C 0A 09 09 09 22 6D 65   id": 752,...."me
02F260A0   74 61 64 61 74 61 22 3A 20 7B 0A 09 09 09 09 22   tadata": {....."
02F260B0   6E 61 6D 65 22 3A 20 22 67 72 6F 75 6E 64 20 74   name": "ground-t
02F260C0   72 75 74 68 22 2C 0A 09 09 09 09 22 63 72 65 61   ruth",.....,"crea
02F260D0   74 65 64 22 3A 20 22 54 75 65 2C 20 31 36 20 44   ted": "Tue, 16 D
02F260E0   65 63 20 32 30 31 34 20 31 30 3A 31 32 3A 31 31   ec 2014 10:12:11
02F260F0   20 2B 30 30 30 30 22 2C 0A 09 09 09 09 22 69 73   +0000",......"is
```

FIG. 8   Windows app-based deleted files.

3.2.3 Uninstall

After the uninstallation process of the pCloud from the VM, we detected two registry entries (Fig. 9).

FIG. 9   Windows app-based uninstall registry change.

Other than the changes in registry, there were some files left on the disk after uninstallation of the app, which were located at: `\User\AppData\local\pCloud`. Moreover, we found out that pCloud client stores every information such as "account information" and the "files summery" in a database called *Data.db* on the computer. This database uses *sqlite dbms* system. From this database file, we were able to extract different kinds of data such as "uploaded file names," and "usernames" which the client used to access the pCloud. Moreover, by analyzing the database, we found a table called "file" that keeps all the stored files names. We could find all the files, which we created on our pCloud account. Furthermore, we were able to recover our pCloud account information, such as "userid" and "username" in a table called "settings."

3.3 Android app-Based Experiments

In this section we provide our experimental results related to the pCloud app when using Android OS. We considered three tasks: install and login, upload, and uninstall.

3.3.1 Install and Login

Once the pCloud was installed on the Android platform, the following two folders were created:

- `/Device/data/data/com.pcloud.pcloud`
- `/emulated/0/.pcloud/`

By using "Root Browser," it is possible to locate those folders after completion of the installation process. Moreover, an examination of the memory capture revealed useful information other than user login details, such as folder paths, its database location, and other pCloud related information. We recognized that the database for pCloud was stored in the following locations:

- `/data/data/com.pcloud.pcloud/databases/PCloudDB/`
- `/data/data/com.pcloud.pcloud/databases/PCloudDB-journal/`

Analyzing the database using *Sqlitebrowser 3.4.0*, it is possible to find "usernames," "email quota," and "tables," which are related to pCloud communications. Once the pCloud was installed, we logged in from the account that we previously created. Then the system analyzer dumped the whole memory of Android and sent it to analysis machine for further analysis. We analyzed the memory using *Hex Workshop 6.7*. In order to find data related to the user account, we used a search string (i.e., "account="). This way, we could identify the account which we had registered for the cloud storage (Fig. 10).

Upon finding the registered account, we used it in order to check if it is possible to find more credentials' details. Fig. 11 shows the extracted artifacts highlighted in yellow.

3.3.2 Upload

Considering the upload task we could recover some of the files, which were uploaded to the pCloud, from the memory capture. To this end, we used the search string "file." A part of the files are demonstrated in Fig. 12 (the highlighted parts).

3.3.3 Uninstall

In order to investigate the possible evidential data that could be remained on the memory after uninstallation of the app, we uninstalled the pCloud app and captured the memory.

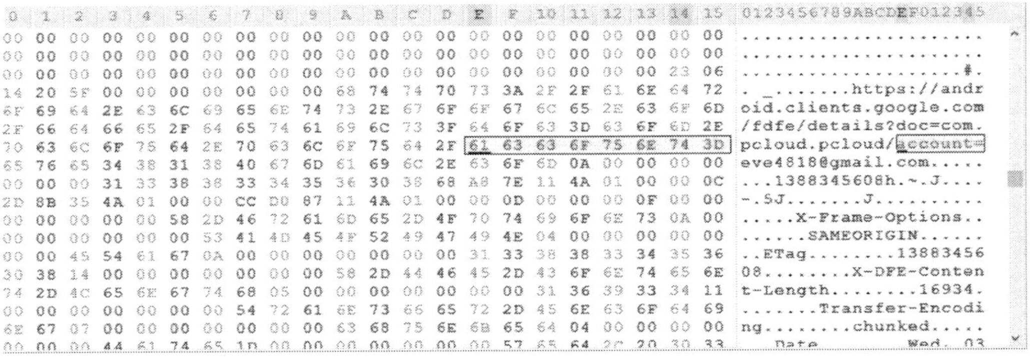

FIG. 10   Android—account details.

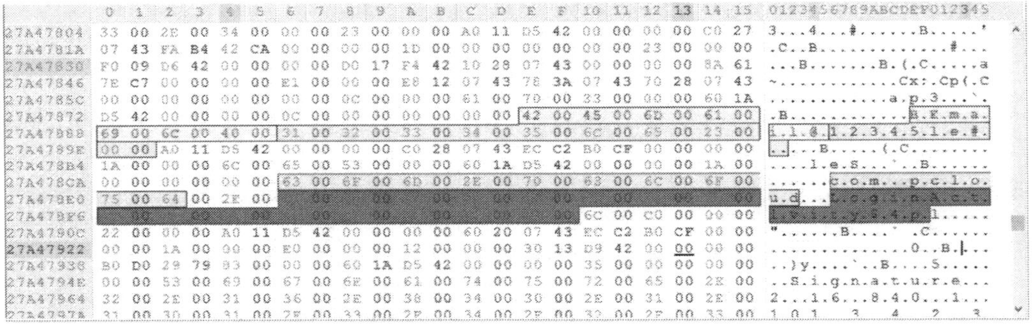

FIG. 11   Android—pCloud suspected credentials (highlighted part).

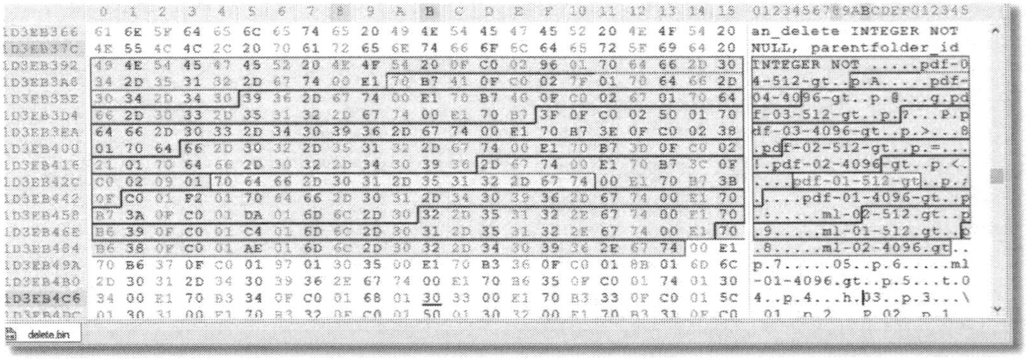

FIG. 12   Android based—uploaded files.

We could recover some of the folders that were already created in the installation process. We were also able to recover some of the details by accessing the default browser in Android. We logged into the pCloud service using Android default web browser, then we analyzed the cache file and browser history. We could recover evidences such as website information, and some cookie files regarding the access of pCloud (Fig. 13).

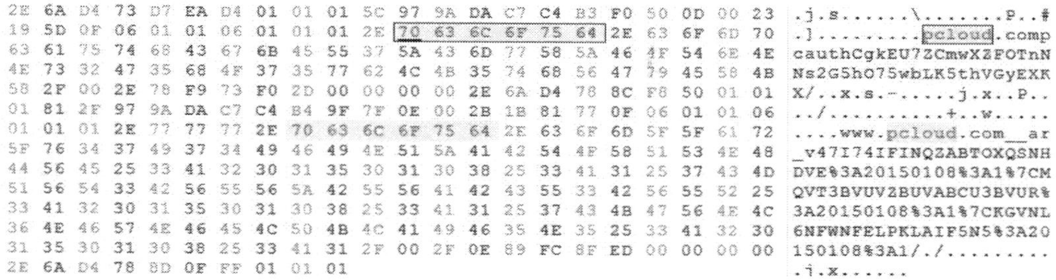

```
2E 6A D4 73 D7 EA D4 01 01 01 5C 97 9A DA C7 C4 B3 F0 50 0D 00 23   .j.s......\.......P..#
19 5D 0F 06 01 01 06 01 01 01 2E [70 63 6C 6F 75 64].2E 63 6F 6D 70   .].........pcloud.comp
63 61 75 74 68 43 67 6B 45 55 37 5A 43 6D 77 58 5A 46 4F 54 6E 4E   cauthCgkEU7ZCmwXZFOTnN
4E 73 32 47 35 68 4F 37 35 77 62 4C 4B 35 74 68 56 47 79 45 58 4B   Ns2G5hO75wbLK5thVGyEXK
58 2F 00 2E 78 F9 73 F0 2D 00 00 00 00 2E 6A D4 78 8C F8 50 01 01   X/..x.s.-.....j.x..P..
01 81 2F 97 9A DA C7 C4 B4 9F 7F 0E 00 2B 1B 81 77 0F 06 01 01 06   ../.........+..w.....
01 01 01 2E 77 77 77 2E 70 63 6C 6F 75 64 2E 63 6F 6D 5F 5F 61 72   ....www.pcloud.com__ar
5F 76 34 37 49 37 34 49 46 49 4E 51 5A 41 42 54 4F 58 51 53 4E 48   _v47I74IFINQZABTOXQSNH
44 56 45 25 33 41 32 30 31 35 30 31 30 38 25 33 41 31 25 37 43 4D   DVE%3A20150108%3A1%7CM
51 56 54 33 42 56 55 56 32 42 55 56 41 42 43 55 33 42 56 55 52 25   QVT3BVUV2BUVABCU3BVUR%
33 41 32 30 31 35 30 31 30 38 25 33 41 31 25 37 43 4B 47 56 4E 4C   3A20150108%3A1%7CKGVNL
36 4E 46 57 4E 46 45 4C 50 4B 4C 41 49 46 35 4E 35 25 33 41 32 30   6NFWNFELPKLAIF5N5%3A20
31 35 30 31 30 38 25 33 41 31 2F 00 2F 0E 89 FC 8F ED 00 00 00 00   150108%3A1/./.........
2E 6A D4 78 8D 0F FF 01 01 01                                        .j.x......
```

FIG. 13   Android based—cookies and web page info.

3.4 iOS-Based Experiments

Examining iOS for finding possible pCloud artifacts was difficult due to the complexity of the OS, compared to other operating systems. Moreover, we were unable to jail break iOS. Therefore we adopted backup investigation method to detect the exact location of the installed pCloud.

Upon installation of the pCloud on iOS, the folders/files which are depicted in Fig. 14 were created in the following locations:

- Library/Preferences/com.pcloud.pcloud.plist
- Library/googleanalytics-v2.sql
- Library/googleanalytics-v3.sql
- Library/Application Support/p.db

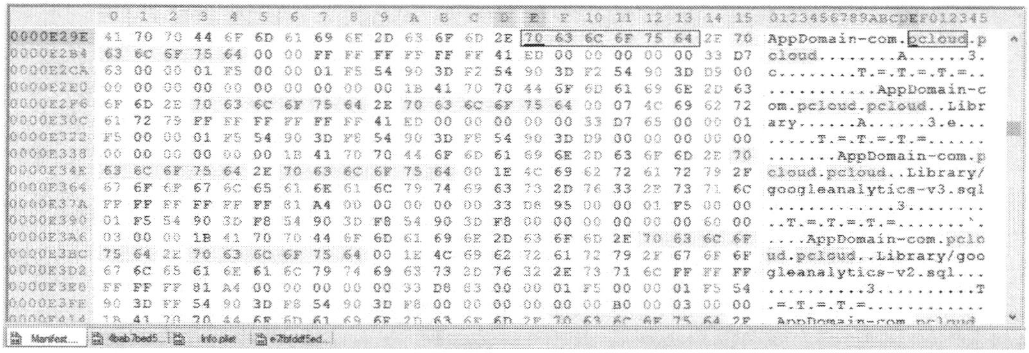

```
         0  1  2  3  4  5  6  7  8  9  A  B  C  D  E  F  10 11 12 13 14 15   0123456789ABCDEF012345
0000E29E 41 70 70 44 6F 6D 61 69 6E 2D 63 6F 6D 2E [70 63 6C 6F 75 64].2E 70   AppDomain-com.pcloud.p
0000E2B4 63 6C 6F 75 64 00 00 FF FF FF FF FF FF 41 ED 00 00 00 00 00 33 D7   cloud.......A......3.
0000E2CA 63 00 00 01 F5 00 00 01 F5 54 90 3D F2 54 90 3D F2 54 90 3D D9 00   c.........T.=.T.=..
0000E2E0 00 00 00 00 00 00 00 00 00 1B 41 70 70 44 6F 6D 61 69 6E 2D 63   ..........AppDomain-c
0000E2F6 6F 6D 2E 70 63 6C 6F 75 64 2E 70 63 6C 6F 75 64 00 07 4C 69 62 72   om.pcloud.pcloud..Libr
0000E30C 61 72 79 FF FF FF FF FF FF 41 ED 00 00 00 00 00 33 D7 65 00 00 01   ary......A......3.e...
0000E322 F5 00 00 01 F5 54 90 3D F8 54 90 3D F8 54 90 3D D9 00 00 00 00 00   .....T.=.T.=.T.=..
0000E338 00 00 00 00 00 00 1B 41 70 70 44 6F 6D 61 69 6E 2D 63 6F 6D 2E 70   .......AppDomain-com.p
0000E34E 63 6C 6F 75 64 2E 70 63 6C 6F 75 64 00 1E 4C 69 62 72 61 72 79 2F   cloud.pcloud..Library/
0000E364 67 6F 6F 67 6C 65 61 6E 61 6C 79 74 69 63 73 2D 76 33 2E 73 71 6C   googleanalytics-v3.sql
0000E37A FF FF FF FF FF 81 A4 00 00 00 00 00 33 D8 95 00 00 01 F5 00 00 01   ............3.......
0000E390 01 F5 54 90 3D F8 54 90 3D F8 54 90 3D F8 00 00 00 00 00 00 60 00   ..T.=.T.=.T.=......`.
0000E3A6 03 00 00 1B 41 70 70 44 6F 6D 61 69 6E 2D 63 6F 6D 2E 70 63 6C 6F   ....AppDomain-com.pclo
0000E3BC 75 64 2E 70 63 6C 6F 75 64 00 1E 4C 69 62 72 61 72 79 2F 67 6F 6F   ud.pcloud..Library/goo
0000E3D2 67 6C 65 61 6E 61 6C 79 74 69 63 73 2D 76 32 2E 73 71 6C FF FF FF   gleanalytics-v2.sql...
0000E3E8 FF FF FF 81 A4 00 00 00 00 00 33 D8 63 00 00 01 F5 00 00 01 F5 54   ........3.c.......T
0000E3FE 90 3D FF 54 90 3D F8 54 90 3D F8 00 00 00 00 00 00 B0 00 03 00 00   .=.T.=.T.=.........
0000E414 1B 41 70 70 44 6F 6D 61 69 6E 2D 63 6F 6D 2E 70 63 6C 6F 75 64 2F   AppDomain-com.pcloud
```

FIG. 14   iOS pcloud folder paths.

During the analysis process of the iOS backup files, we did not find any login details related to pCloud. However, we obtained some information such as "session ID" (type of cookie which the web servers store for a specific user for a duration of time), and "API key" (a code passed to the computer to identify the calling program to its user), which then could be useful for forensic investigations (see Fig. 15). Furthermore, we could obtain information such as pCloud installation directory location.

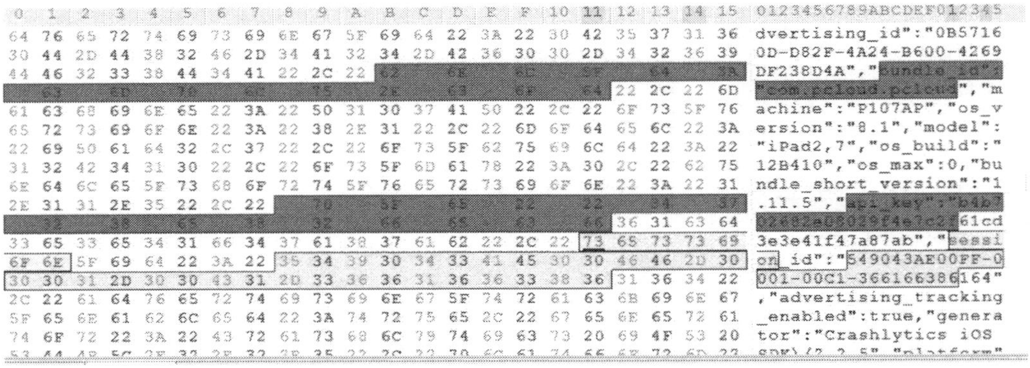

FIG. 15   iOS based—API key, session ID findings.

3.4.1 Upload and Uninstallation

Even though we did not obtain pCloud login details on iOS, we could detect some useful information such as "uploaded files names" (as highlighted in Fig. 16). Moreover, upon un-installation we could recover some of the deleted files. In order to access such information, we used several search strings such as common file types, for instance ".jpg" and ".pdf."

3.5 Ubuntu app-Based Experiments

During the experimental study on Ubuntu, we installed the pCloud drive 2.0 on base VM, and logged in. Then we cloned it for several tasks, which we carried out in the following sequential manner: upload, download, sync, open, delete, and uninstall. We analyzed all the acquired memory dump files using *hex workshop*. We found quite a number of evidences in the memory. These evidences are clearly useful for digital investigators in order to get to know the "username," "password," and "files names" of the victim or suspects.

As it is demonstrated in Fig. 17, it is possible to recover the "username" and "password" of the user during installation and login process. These information have high forensic value to the forensic examiners as it shows the credentials of the victims/suspects. Moreover, as Fig. 18 shows, we can retrieve the uploaded file names and the file path from the memory dump. We could also retrieve the same evidences as the ones extracted from the "upload VM memory dump, during the sync and download tasks. As it is depicted in Fig. 19, after the deletion of the files from the app, it is possible to recover "username" from the memory dump. This evidence can also help the forensic examiners to identify the credentials that were used.

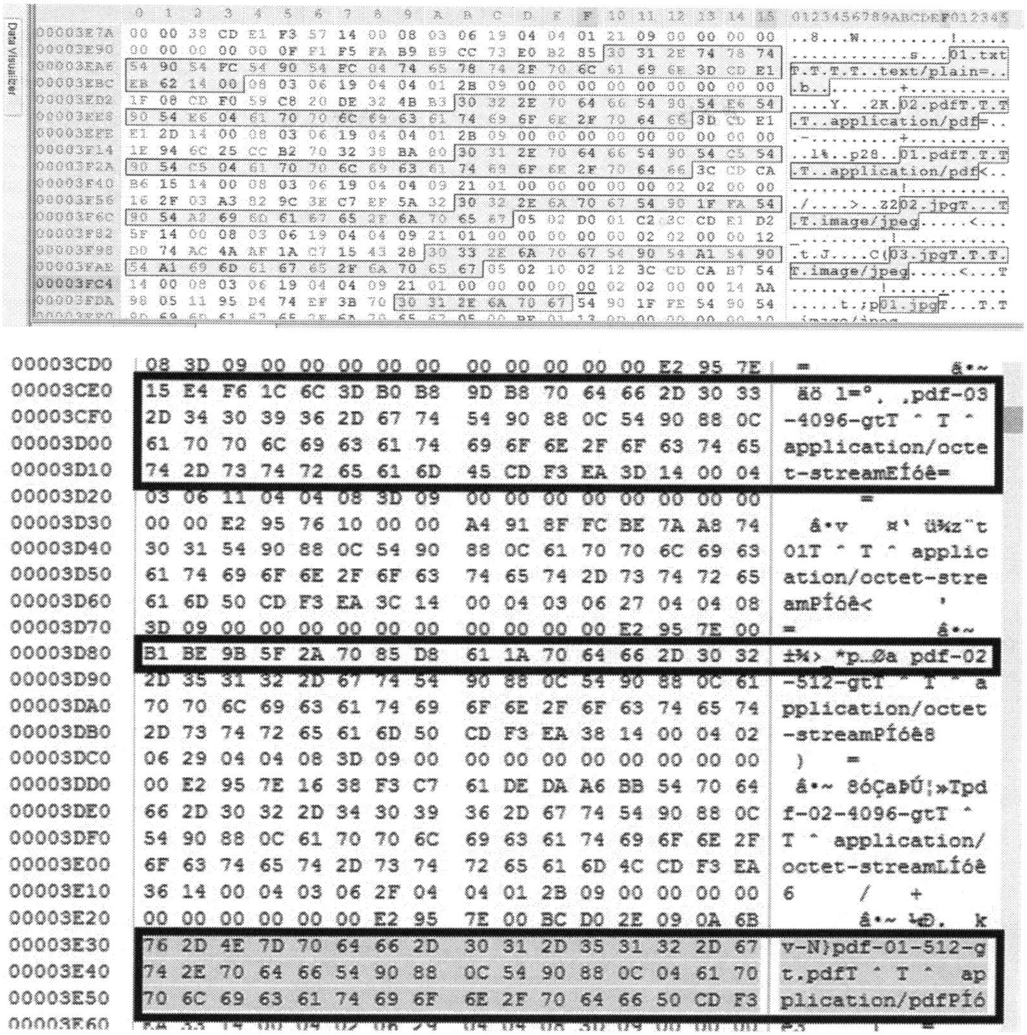

FIG. 16   iOS-based uploaded file names found in the backup files.

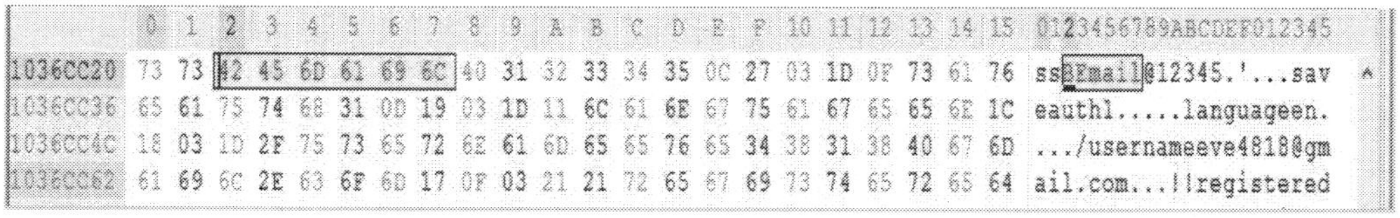

FIG. 17   Ubuntu—revealed credentials during install and login tasks.

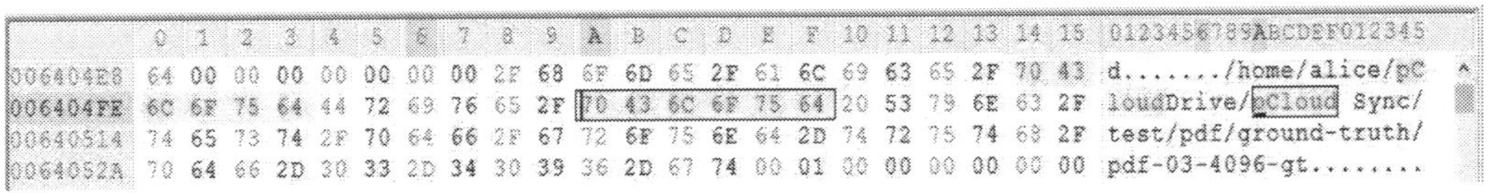

FIG. 18   Ubuntu—extracted information during upload process.

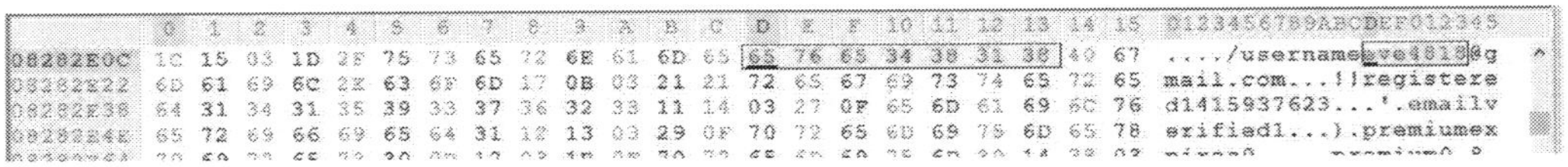

FIG. 19   Ubuntu—recovered username after deletion task.

4 NETWORK TRAFFIC

Compared to the evidential data recovered from the storage and memory, we could obtain a relatively limited amount of data by analyzing the network traffic. This is mostly because pCloud uses encrypted connections, such as *TLSv1.2* and *HTTPS* over *SSL* certificates, which are then provided by external vendors. During the download and upload tasks, an encrypted connection is established with protocol HTTPS.

In Table 2, we show some relevant IP addresses to pCloud, which we could recover during the Internet Explorer experiment. We can conclude that all the connections to these hosts were over TCP port 443, and used a *TLSv1.2* Encryption. Apart from these IP addresses, we were able to track the service providers for SSL certificates, along with the main login IP address/ URL which we could use as forensic investigators for further analysis. The recovered SSL Certificate providers list is as follows:

- http://silver-server-g2.ocsp.swisssign.net/
  nD3446FD9FE7AFCDEAC1C7AA2210D64FA65B0D782
- http://crl.swisssign.net/D3446FD9FE7AFCDEAC1C7AA2210D64FA65B0D782
- http://directory.swisssign.net/
  \\CN=D3446FD9FE7AFCDEAC1C7AA2210D64FA65B0D782%\\2CO=SwissSign2CC=
  CH?certificateRevocationList?base?objectClass=cRLDistributionPoint

5 CONCLUSION

In this chapter, by analyzing pCloud as a case study we demonstrated the possibility to re-cover a numerous amount of residual evidences from this platform. We analyzed the pCloud on several operating systems (i.e., Windows, Android, iOS, Ubuntu) considering different tasks (such as, install, login, upload, download, uninstall). We showed that all the pCloud credentials could be extracted along with the files that were used for storage. Even though the network connections were encrypted, some of the credentials used in almost all platforms were in plain text format which is an added advantage for forensic investigators. However,

TABLE 2 Recovered IP Addresses During the Internet Explorer Experiments

IP Address	Host Name	Activity
74.120.8.17/25/18/24/23/26	`binapi.pcloud.com`	Install and login
74.120.8.24/25/17/18/23/26	`binapi.pcloud.com`	Uninstall
74.120.8.56	`C47.pcloud.com`	
74.120.8.26/25/24/18/23/17	`binapi.pcloud.com`	Upload
74.120.8.28	`C1.pcloud.com`	
74.120.8.41	`C19.pcloud.com`	
74.120.8.56	`C47.pcloud.com`	
74.120.8.64	`C54.pcloud.com`	
74.120.8.73	`C61.pcloud.com`	
74.120.8.89	`C72.pcloud.com`	
74.120.8.92	`C75.pcloud.com`	
74.120.8.96	`C79.pcloud.com`	
74.120.8.100	`C82.pcloud.com`	
74.120.8.133	`C94.pcloud.comb`	
74.120.8.77	`a2.pcloud.com, translate.pcloud.com`	Upload
74.120.8.15/7/6/12/13	`api.pcloud.com, my.pcloud.com`	
74.120.8.14	`api.pcloud.com, my.pcloud.com, api8.pcloud.com`	
74.120.8.77	`a2.pcloud.com, translate.pcloud.com`	Open
74.120.8.15/7/6/12/13	`api.pcloud.com, my.pcloud.com`	
74.120.8.14	`api.pcloud.com, my.pcloud.com, api8.pcloud.com`	
74.120.8.34	`c15.pcloud.com`	
74.120.8.15/7/6/12/13	`api.pcloud.com, my.pcloud.com`	Delete
74.120.8.14	`api.pcloud.com, my.pcloud.com, api8.pcloud.com`	
74.120.8.34	`c15.pcloud.com`	

we were only able to collect login credentials by capturing the live memory at the time of installation of the pCloud service. So it is highly recommended for forensic investigators to capture the memory at the time of installation.

Our presented research study in this chapter may pave the way for forensics examiners investigating pCloud and other cloud storage platforms. In the future researchers can use similar investigation method to retrieve other cloud platforms remnants. For example, extending a presented approach for detecting evidences of different platforms over cloud, such as investigating mobile devices connected to the cloud [52, 53], and the investigation of cloud-based social networking platforms [54, 55], and cloud malware forensics [56, 56–59] would be interesting future works. Moreover, analyzing legal and privacy implications of conducting cloud forensics [60, 61] and developing relevant solutions could further opportunities for real-world utilization of cloud investigation techniques.

References

[1] L. Columbus, Predicting the future of cloud service providers, 2015. http://www.forbes.com/sites/louiscolumbus/2015/04/05/predicting-the-future-of-cloud-service-providers/ (Accessed June 27, 2015).

[2] A. Konrad, Report: cloud market cap to pass $500 billion by 2020, 2015. http://www.forbes.com/sites/alexkonrad/2015/06/18/byron-deeter-state-of-the-cloud/ (Accessed June 27, 2015).

[3] D. Chen, H. Zhao, Data security and privacy protection issues in cloud computing, in: Proceedings of the International Conference on Computer Science and Electronics Engineering, ICCSEE'12, 1, IEEE, 2012, pp. 647–651.

[4] C.A. Ardagna, M. Conti, M. Leone, J. Stefa, An anonymous end-to-end communication protocol for mobile cloud environments, IEEE Trans. Serv. Comput. 7 (3) (2014) 373–386.

[5] H. Takabi, J.B. Joshi, G.-J. Ahn, Security and privacy challenges in cloud computing environments, IEEE Secur. Priv. (6) (2010) 24–31.

[6] A. Mathew, Survey paper on security & privacy issues in cloud storage systems, in: Proceedings of the Electrical Engineering Seminar and Special Problems B, 571, 2012.

[7] S. Hosseinzadeh, S. Hyrynsalmi, M. Conti, V. Lepp, Security and privacy in cloud computing via obfuscation and diversification: a survey, in: Proceedings of the Seventh International Conference on Cloud Computing Technology and Science (CloudCom'15), IEEE, 2015, pp. 529–535.

[8] M.R. Memarian, M. Conti, V. Leppanen, EyeCloud: a BotCloud detection system, in: Proceedings of the Fifth IEEE International Symposium on Trust and Security in Cloud Computing, TSCloud'15, 1, IEEE, 2015, pp. 1067–1072.

[9] K.-K.R. Choo, R.G. Smith, Criminal exploitation of online systems by organised crime groups, Asian J. Criminol. 3 (1) (2008) 37–59.

[10] K.-K.R. Choo, Organised crime groups in cyberspace: a typology, Trends Organized Crime 11 (3) (2008) 270–295.

[11] D. Quick, B. Martini, R. Choo, Cloud Storage Forensics, Syngress, Cambridge, MA, USA, 2013.

[12] D. Quick, K.-K.R. Choo, Forensic collection of cloud storage data: does the act of collection result in changes to the data or its metadata? Digit. Investig. 10 (3) (2013) 266–277.

[13] F. Daryabar, A. Dehghantanha, N.I. Udzir, A review on impacts of cloud computing on digital forensics, Int. J. Cyber-Secur. Digit. Forensics (IJCSDF) 2 (2) (2013) 77–94.

[14] pCloud, about the company, https://www.pcloud.com/company/about.html (Accessed April 2016).

[15] Cloudswave awards 2015: introducing the 10 best document management software, 2015. http://www.cloudswave.com/blog/cloudswave-awards-2015-introducing-the-10-best-document-management-software/ (Accessed July 1, 2015).

[16] F. Barton, pCloud Drive 3.0: FindMySoft Editor's Review, 2014. http://pcloud-drive.findmysoft.com/ (Accessed July 1, 2015).

[17] S. Fisher, pCloud Review, 2015. http://freebies.about.com/od/computerfreebies/fl/pcloud-review.htm (Accessed July 1, 2015).

[18] L. Mearian, By 2020, there will be 5,200 GB of data for every person on Earth, 2012. http://www.computerworld.com/article/2493701/data-center/by-2020-there-will-be-5-200-gb-of-data-for-every-person-on-earth.html (Accessed July 9, 2015).

[19] J. Farina, M. Scanlon, M.-T. Kechadi, BitTorrent Sync: first impressions and digital forensic implications, Proceedings of the First Annual DFRWS Europe Digital Investigation 11 (2014) S77–S86.

[20] K.-K.R. Choo, Cloud computing: challenges and future directions, Trends Issues Crime Criminal Justice 400 (2010) 1–6.

[21] J. Galante, O. Kharif, P. Alpeyev, Sony network breach shows Amazon cloud appeal for hackers, Bloomberg News 16 (2011). http://www.bloomberg.com/news/2011-05-15/sonyattack-shows-amazon-s-cloud-service-lures-hackers-at-pennies-an-hour.html (Accessed June 5, 2014).

[22] Symantec, The Trojan. Hydraq incident: analysis of the Aurora 0-day exploit, 2011. http://www.symantec.com/connect/blogs/trojanhydraq-incident-analysis-aurora-0-day-exploit (Accessed November 20, 2014).

[23] A. Duke, 5 Things to know about the celebrity nude photo hacking scandal, 2014. http://edition.cnn.com/2014/09/02/showbiz/hacked-nude-photos-five-things/ (Accessed November 18, 2014).

[24] M. Taylor, J. Haggerty, D. Gresty, D. Lamb, Forensic investigation of cloud computing systems, Network Security 2011 (3) (2011) 4–10.

[25] B. Martini, K.-K.R. Choo, Cloud storage forensics: ownCloud as a case study, Digit. Investig. 10 (4) (2013) 287–299.

[26] D. Quick, K.-K.R. Choo, Dropbox analysis: data remnants on user machines, Digit. Investig. 10 (1) (2013) 3–18.

[27] D. Quick, K.-K.R. Choo, Digital droplets: Microsoft SkyDrive forensic data remnants, Future Gener. Comput. Syst. 29 (6) (2013) 1378–1394.

[28] D. Quick, K.-K.R. Choo, Google drive: forensic analysis of data remnants, J. Network Comput. Appl. 40 (2014) 179–193.

[29] J.S. Hale, Amazon cloud drive forensic analysis, Digit. Investig. 10 (3) (2013) 259–265.

[30] H. Chung, J. Park, S. Lee, C. Kang, Digital forensic investigation of cloud storage services, Digit. Investig. 9 (2) (2012) 81–95.

[31] K. Oestreicher, A forensically robust method for acquisition of iCloud data, Digit. Investig. 11 (2014) S106–S113.

[32] B. Martini, K.-K.R. Choo, Cloud forensic technical challenges and solutions: a snapshot, IEEE Cloud Comput. 1 (4) (2014) 20–25.

[33] A. Pichan, M. Lazarescu, S.T. Soh, Cloud forensics: technical challenges, solutions and comparative analysis, Digit. Investig. 13 (2015) 38–57.

[34] C. Federici, Cloud data imager: a unified answer to remote acquisition of cloud storage areas, Digit. Investig. 11 (1) (2014) 30–42.

[35] G. Grispos, W.B. Glisson, T. Storer, Using smartphones as a proxy for forensic evidence contained in cloud storage services, in: Proceedings of the 46th Hawaii International Conference on System Sciences (HICSS), IEEE, 2013, pp. 4910–4919.

[36] B. Martini, Q. Do, K.-K.R. Choo, Mobile cloud forensics: an analysis of seven popular Android apps, in: R. Ko, K.-K.R. Choo (Eds.), Cloud Secur. Ecosyst., Syngress, Cambridge, MA, 2015, pp. 309–345. http://dx.doi.org/10.1016/B978-0-12-801595-7.00015-X.

[37] F. Daryabar, A. Dehghantanha, B. Eterovic-Soric, K.-K.R. Choo, Forensic investigation of OneDrive, Box, GoogleDrive and Dropbox applications on Android and iOS devices, Aust. J. Forensic Sci. (2016) 1–28. http://dx.doi.org/10.1080/00450618.2015.1110620.

[38] F. Marturana, G. Me, S. Tacconi, A case study on digital forensics in the cloud, in: Proceedings of the International Conference on Cyber-Enabled Distributed Computing and Knowledge Discovery (CyberC'12), IEEE, 2012, pp. 111–116.

[39] M. Shariati, A. Dehghantanha, K.-K.R. Choo, SugarSync forensic analysis, Aust. J. Forensic Sci. 48 (1) (2016) 95–117.

[40] M. Shariati, A. Dehghantanha, B. Martini, K.-K.R. Choo, Ubuntu One investigation: detecting evidences on client machines, In: R. Ko, K.-K.R. Choo (Eds.), The Cloud Security Ecosystem, Syngress, Cambridge, MA, USA, 2015, pp. 429–446.

[41] B. Blakeley, C. Cooney, A. Dehghantanha, R. Aspin, Cloud storage forensic: hubiC as a case-study, in: Proceedings of the Seventh International Conference on Cloud Computing Technology and Science (CloudCom'15), IEEE, 2015, pp. 536–541.

[42] F. Daryabar, A. Dehghantanha, K.-K.R. Choo, Cloud storage forensics: MEGA as a case study, Aust. J. Forensic Sci. (2016), 1–14. http://dx.doi.org/10.1080/00450618.2016.1153714.

[43] C. Cho, S. Chin, K.S. Chung, Cyber forensic for hadoop based cloud system, Int. J. Secur. Appl. 6 (3) (2012) 83–90.

[44] J. Dykstra, A.T. Sherman, Acquiring forensic evidence from infrastructure-as-a-service cloud computing: exploring and evaluating tools, trust, and techniques, Digit. Investig. 9 (2012) S90–S98.

[45] B. Martini, K.-K.R. Choo, Remote programmatic vCloud forensics: a six-step collection process and a proof of concept, in: Proceedings of the 13th International Conference on Trust, Security and Privacy in Computing and Communications (TrustCom'14), IEEE, 2014, pp. 935–942.

[46] B. Martini, K.-K.R. Choo, Distributed file system forensics: XtreemFS as a case study, Digit. Investig. 11 (4) (2014) 295–313.

[47] F. Anwar, Z. Anwar, Digital forensics for eucalyptus, in: Proceedings of the Frontiers of Information Technology (FIT'11), IEEE, 2011, pp. 110–116.

[48] R. Marty, Cloud application logging for forensics, in: Proceedings of the ACM Symposium on Applied Computing, ACM, 2011, pp. 178–184.

[49] ACPO, Good Practice Guide for Computer Based Electronic Evidence V5, Association of Chief Police Officers (ACPO), National Hi-Tech Crime Unit (NHTCU), London, 2011.

[50] K. Kent, S. Chevalier, T. Grance, H. Dang, Guide to integrating forensic techniques into incident response, NIST Special Publication (2006).

[51] B. Martini, K.-K.R. Choo, An integrated conceptual digital forensic framework for cloud computing, Digit. Investig. 9 (2) (2012) 71–80.

[52] S. Mohtasebi, A. Dehghantanha, H.G. Broujerdi, Smartphone forensics: a case study with Nokia E5-00 mobile phone, Int. J. Digit. Inform. Wireless Commun. (IJDIWC) 1 (3) (2011) 651–655.

[53] S. Parvez, A. Dehghantanha, H.G. Broujerdi, Framework of digital forensics for the Samsung Star Series phone, in: Proceedings of the Third International Conference on Electronics Computer Technology (ICECT'11), 2, IEEE, 2011, pp. 264–267.

[54] S. Mohtasebi, A. Dehghantanha, Defusing the hazards of social network services, Int. J. Digit. Inform. Wireless Commun. (IJDIWC) 1 (2) (2011) 504–515.

[55] F. Norouzizadeh Dezfouli, A. Dehghantanha, B. Eterovic-Soric, K.-K.R. Choo, Investigating social networking applications on smartphones detecting Facebook, Twitter, LinkedIn and Google+ artefacts on Android and iOS platforms, Aust. J. Forensic Sci. 48(4) (2016) 469–488. http://dx.doi.org/10.1080/00450618.2015.1066854.

[56] F. Daryabar, A. Dehghantanha, H.G. Broujerdi, Investigation of malware defence and detection techniques, Int. J. Digit. Inform. Wireless Commun. (IJDIWC) 1 (3) (2011) 645–650.

[57] K. Sharpour, A. Dehghantanha, R. Mahmod, Trends in android malware detection, J. Digit. Forensics Secur. Law (JDFSL) 8 (3) (2013) 21.

[58] F.N. Dezfouli, A. Dehghantanha, R. Mahmod, N. F. B. M. Sani, S.B. Shamsuddin, F. Daryabar, A survey on malware analysis and detection techniques, Int. J. Adv. Comput. Technol. 5 (14) (2013) 42.

[59] M. Damshenas, A. Dehghantanha, R. Mahmoud, A survey on malware propagation, analysis, and detection, Int. J. Cyber-Secur. Digit. Forensics (IJCSDF) 2 (4) (2013) 10–29.

[60] F. Daryabar, A. Dehghantanha, N.I. Udzir, M. Sani, S. bin Shamsuddin, F. Norouzizadeh, A survey on privacy impacts of digital investigation, J. Next Gener. Inform. Technol. 4 (8) (2013) 57–68.

[61] A. Dehghantanha, K. Franke, Privacy-respecting digital investigation, in: Proceedings of the 12th Annual International Conference on Privacy, Security and Trust (PST'14), IEEE, 2014, pp. 129–138.

Cloud Storage Forensics: Analysis of Data Remnants on SpiderOak, JustCloud, and pCloud

S.H. Mohtasebi*, A. Dehghantanha†, K.-K.R. Choo‡,§

*Shabakeh Gostar Ltd. Co., Tehran, Iran †University of Salford, Salford, United Kingdom
‡University of Texas at San Antonio, San Antonio, TX, United States §University of South
Australia, Adelaide, SA, Australia

1 INTRODUCTION

Cloud computing enables businesses and individual to access computing resources such as servers and storages on an on-demand basis, where resources can be quickly provisioned with minimal efforts and interaction with the service provider [1]. The National Institute of Standards and Technology (NIST) broadly categorized cloud computing services into three categories:

1. Software as a Service (SaaS): When an application is used to access shared infrastructure of the Cloud Storage Service Provider (CSSP). A popular example of SaaS is Storage as a Service (STaaS) cloud systems.
2. Platform as a Service (PaaS): Users may deploy their own applications on the CSSP's infrastructure
3. Infrastructure as a Service (IaaS): The CSSP provides the underlying computing resources for the deployment of software [including Operation System (OS)] by the users [1].

The increasing popularity of STaaS and the potential for such services to be criminally exploited have attracted the attention of policing and forensics scholars in recent years [2]. Many emerging and new platforms are now based on cloud services to operate. As noted by the NIST [3], cloud forensics is the application of scientific rules, technological exercises and approved methods to rebuild past events of crime committed in the cloud computing environment.

A number of researchers have reported data collection and preservation [4–9], cloud malware detection [10,11] analysis and even privacy [12–14] as main challenges during investigation of cloud platforms. As explained by Martini and Choo [15], "the large number of open challenges presented in a report by the NIST [3] demonstrates that, at the time of the research, cloud forensics remains an unresolved and somewhat under researched area of enquiry."

Although a number of STaaS have been examined (see Table 1), researchers [39,40] have posited that organized crime and cyber criminals are innovative and will constantly seek to "innovate" in order to evade the scrutiny and reach of law enforcement, such as using other STaaS to store incriminating evidence.

In this research, we study three popular STaaS that have not been examined in the literature, namely: SpiderOak, JustCloud, and pCloud.

Users of SpiderOak, JustCloud, and pCloud may download, upload, and access their data using a web-browser and client application (e.g., mobile app). The SpiderOak client application also enables users to create, schedule, and restore backups and share files via password-protected links. In addition, the Hive feature of the SpiderOak client application allows contents to be synced across all devices linked to the user's account. SpiderOak Zero-knowledge service reportedly encrypts all data stored on their servers. Such a service would be attractive to cybercriminals and individual users who want to ensure that their stored data will not be surrendered to law enforcement agencies by the cloud service provider.

JustCloud allows users to synchronize, create backups, and share files. In file synchronization, a folder is created on the user's desktop after JustCloud's client application is installed, which enables the user to access data stored on all devices where the client application has been installed.

Users may store, sync, and share their files using pCloud. A unique feature of this CSSP is the upload link. User can have files uploaded on their space by those who have access to the upload link. This CSSP is also capable of making backups from other services including Dropbox, Facebook, Instagram, and Picasa. Table 2 briefly compares the features of aforementioned services.

In this paper, we answer the following questions:

(1) What artifacts of forensic interest can be recovered from the random access memory (RAM) and the hard disk (HDD) of a Windows device after using SpiderOak, JustCloud, and pCloud services via Internet Explorer (IE), Firefox (Fx), and Google Chrome (GC) browsers?

(2) What artifacts of forensic interest can be recovered from the RAM and HDD of a Windows device after using SpiderOak, JustCloud, and pCloud services via the respective client Windows applications?

(3) What artifacts of forensic interest can be recovered from the internal memory and internal storage of an iPhone device after using SpiderOak, JustCloud, and pCloud services via the respective iOS applications?

(4) Whether the contents or the metadata of the investigated files change during the process of uploading and downloading, and whether the timestamp information of the downloaded files is reliable?

Research will be conducted on Windows 8.1 and iOS devices. At the time of research, Windows 8.1 is the latest version of Microsoft desktop OS and iOS is one of the most popular mobile platforms [41,42].

TABLE 1 A Snapshot of Existing Cloud Forensics Research

Model	Public Cloud	Private Cloud
SaaS (including STaaS)	Amazon S3, Dropbox, Evernote, and Google Docs [16]	Dropbox, Box, and SugarSync [17]
	Dropbox, Google Drive, and Microsoft SkyDrive [18]	ownCloud [19]
	Dropbox, Box, and SugarSync [17]	
	Amazon Cloud Drive [20]	
	Dropbox, OneDrive, and ownCloud [21]	
	Google Document, Flicker, and PicasaWeb [22]	
	iCloud [23]	
	Google Drive [24,25]	
	Dropbox [26]	
	SkyDrive [27]	
	Google Drive, Dropbox, and SkyDrive [28]	
	UbuntuOne [29]	
	hubiC [30]	
	SugarSync [31]	
	Mega [32,33]	
	OneDrive, Box, GoogleDrive, and Dropbox [32,33]	
IaaS		Hadoop [34]
		Amazon EC2 [35]
		vCloud [36]
		XtreemFS [37]
		Eucalyptus [38]

Adapted from B. Martini, K.-K. R. Choo, An integrated conceptual digital forensic framework for cloud computing. Digital Invest., 9 (2) (2012) 71–80. doi:10.1016/j.diin.2012.07.001.

TABLE 2   CSSPs Comparison Table

		SpiderOak	JustCloud	pCloud
Operating systems support	Windows	Y	Y	Y
	Linux	Y	Y	Y
	Mac OSX	Y	Y	Y
	iOS	Y	Y	Y
	Windows Phone	N	Y	N
	Android	Y	Y	Y
	BlackBerry	N	Y	N
Storage (by free)		2GB	15MB[a]	20GB
Maximum paid storage		100GB	Not Limited	1TB
Backup		Y	Y	N
Sync		Y	Y	Y
Encryption		Y	Y	Y
Sharing		Y	Y	Y

JustCloud free trial expires after 14 days.

The rest of the paper is organized as follows: In Section 2, we describe the forensic framework used to guide the research and the experiment setup. The findings from the analysis of SpiderOak, JustCloud, and pCloud are presented in Sections 3–5, respectively. Finally, the last section concludes this paper.

2 RESEARCH METHODOLOGY

2.1 Cloud Forensic Framework

When conducting a forensic investigation, the investigator should adopt best practices such as those of the Association of Chief Police Officers (ACPO). The ACPO specifies four principles for collecting and examining digital evidence [43]:

- Principle 1: Data which may subsequently be relied upon in a court of law should not be changed.
- Principle 2: In the event that a person needs to access the original data, that person must be suitably qualified and is able to justify and explain the implications of the actions.
- Principle 3: An appropriate auditing and record-keeping processes should be in place that would ensure that an independent third party would be able to examine the recorded processes and achieve the same result.
- Principle 4: The investigating officer needs to ensure that the law and these principles are upheld.

It is also common practice that a forensic framework be used to guide the investigation. In the context of our paper, we adopt the cloud forensic framework introduced by Martini and Choo [44]. This is, perhaps, the first digital forensic framework designed to conduct both client and server investigations of cloud services. The framework has also been validated by the authors using ownCloud [19], [37], [36], and by Thethi and Keane [45] on EC2 cloud. There are three stages in this framework, namely: evidence source identification, collection, and preservation; examination and analysis; and presentation for the collected digital evidence from the cloud environment.

1. *Evidence source identification, collection, and preservation.* In this phase, potential sources of relevant data are identified. Any device capable of connecting to STaaS, either via a browser or a client application, is considered a potential source of evidence. In this phase, the investigator should also ensure that ACPO principles are adhered to, wherever possible. During collection of evidence from storage media, particularly media belonging to external parties, the investigator should also ensure that relevant laws and regulations are followed [46].

   In this research, the .vmem and vmdk files of each virtual machine (VM) were collected with extension E0 using AccessData FTK Imager. The former was cloned while the VM was running, whereas the latter was duplicated after the VM was shut down. The logs of Wireshark, recording communications between VMs and the respective STaaS were also acquired at this stage. The MD5 hash checksum of collected evidence files were documented.
2. *Examination and analysis.* Information from acquired data is extracted in this phase. Methods to circumvent or bypass protection mechanism on the devices may be used to examine and analyze information collected and preserved from the previous phase (e.g., use of tools to brute-force password-protected data). During this phase, findings should also be reviewed with information or intelligence drawn from other sources and investigations (e.g., see metadata analysis described in Sections 3–5; and [24,25] before a conclusion is drawn.
3. *Presentation.* In the last phase findings are documented for presentation in a court of law [46].

2.2 Experiment Setup

2.2.1 Windows

The Windows-based experiments were implemented on VMs using VMware Player 6.0.1. The following files with forensic value were collected and examined:

- .vmem file: A paging file that includes the backup of the VM's main memory [47].
- .vmdk file: A virtual disk file that stores the contents of the VM's hard disk drive [47].

Windows 8.1 Build 9600 along with IE 11.0.9600.16384, Fx 33.0.2, and GC 38.0.2125.111 m were installed on a VM with 25GB hard disk and 1GB memory. In this research, 14 files from a dd image file developed by Carrier [48] were used as the dataset (see Table 3). The original dd image file was mounted on the VM using OSFMount 1.5.

From the base VM, the following snapshots were created:

- VM-W1: A SpiderOak account was created using IE.
- VM-W2: A SpiderOak account was created on Fx.
- VM-W3: A SpiderOak account was created using GC.

TABLE 3   Files Used in the Windows-Based Experiment

Name	MD5	Note
file1.jpg	75b8d00568815a36c3809b46fc84ba6d	A JPEG file with JPEG extension
file2.dat	de5d83153339931371719f4e5c924eba	A JPEG file with non-JPEG extension
file3.jpg	1ba4e91591f0541eda255ee26f7533bc	A nonimage file with JPEG extension
file4.jpg	c8de721102617158e8492121bdad3711	A nonimage file with JPEG header
file5.rtf	86f14fc525648c39d878829f288c0543	A file with 0xffd8 signature value in multiple locations of the file
file8.zip	d41b56e0a9f84eb2825e73c24cedd963	A ZIP file with ZIP extension containing a JPEG file named file8.jpg
file8.jpg	f9956284a89156ef6967b49eced9d1b1	A JPEG file inside of the ZIP file
file9.boo	73c3029066aee9416a5aeb98a5c55321	A ZIP file with non-ZIP extension containing a JPEG file named file9.jpg
file9.jpg	c5a6917669c77d20f30ecb39d389eb7d	A JPEG file inside the ZIP file
file10.tar.gz	d4f8cf643141f0c2911c539750e18ef2	A gzipped tar file containing a JPEG file named file10.jpg
file10.jpg	c476a66ccdc2796b4f6f8e27273dd788	A JPEG file inside the gzipped tar file
file11.dat	f407ab92da959c7ab03292cfe596a99d	A JPEG file with dat extension
file12.doc	61c0b55639e52d1ce82aba834ada2bab	A Word document with a JPEG file inside it
file13.dll:here	9b787e63e3b64562730c5aecaab1e1f8	A JPEG file within an alternate data streams (ADS)

- VM-W4: A JustCloud account was created using IE.
- VM-W5: A JustCloud account was created on Fx.
- VM-W6: A JustCloud account was created using GC.
- VM-W7: A pCloud account was created on IE.
- VM-W8: A pCloud account was created on Fx in this VM.
- VM-W9: A pCloud account was created using GC.
- VM-W10: The SpiderOak's client application was installed. Sample files were also uploaded and downloaded using the client application.
- VM-W11: The JustCloud's client application was installed, and a series of uploading and downloading of sample files using the client application was undertaken.
- VM-W12: The pCloud's client application was installed.
- VM-W16: A series of downloading of sample files using SpiderOak with IE.
- VM-W17: Sample file were downloaded using SpiderOak via Fx.
- VM-W18: A series of downloading of sample files using SpiderOak with GC.
- VM-W19: A series of downloading of sample files using JustCloud with IE.
- VM-W20: A series of downloading of sample files using JustCloud with Fx.
- VM-W21: A series of downloading of sample files using JustCloud with GC.
- VM-W22: A series of downloading of sample files using pCloud with IE.
- VM-W23: A series of downloading of sample file using pCloud with Fx.
- VM-W24: A series of downloading of sample files using pCloud with GC (Fig. 1).

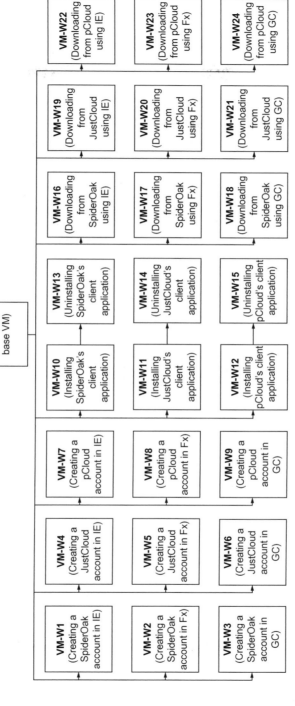

FIG. 1 Overview of Windows-based experiments.

Each of the STaaS accounts created was linked to a specific email address created for this research (see Table 4).

TABLE 4   Research Email Accounts

Email Address	First Name	Last Name
csforensics_1@yahoo.com	Johnny	Appleseed
csforensics_2@ yahoo.com	Mary	Major
csforensics_3@ yahoo.com	Richard	Miles

SpiderOak 5.1.8, JustCloud 1.4.0.28, and pCloud 1.3.2 were respectively installed on VM-W10, VM-W11, and VM-W12 and sample files were uploaded and downloaded using the respective client applications.

VM-W10, VM-W11, and VM-W12 were shut down and cloned respectively to VM-W13, VM-W14, and VM-W15. They were used for the investigation of data remnants after uninstallation of the client applications. On the last nine VMs (i.e., VM-W15 to VM-W24), the sample files were uploaded and downloaded using the respective browsers. On VM-W10, VM-W-11, and VM-W16 to VM-W24, MD5 checksum of the downloaded files were recorded and compared with the original ones.

In all our experiments, we configured the browsers and client applications to decline storing the passwords. In additional, prior to cloning each .vmem file, the corresponding browser was closed without the user signing out. The base VM was configured to create only one .vmdk file, and other VMs were generated by taking snapshots of the base .vmdk file. VMware Virtual Disk Manager Utility was used to merge the base .vmdk file with the snapshot files in order to make creating of the image file using FTK Imager possible.

2.2.2 iOS

In the iOS-based experiments, SpiderOak 3.1.1, JustCloud 1.3.11, and pCloud 1.11.15 apps were installed on an iPhone 5S device with iOS 8.1.1.

The following files were collected for further analysis on a personal computer (PC):

- Memory (.vmem file)
- Network logs collected by Wireshark (.PCAP files)
- Browsers' files
  - IE: %LocalAppData%\Microsoft\Windows\WebCache, %LocalAppData%\ Microsoft\Internet Explorer\, and %LocalAppData%\Packages\ windows_ie_ac_001\
  - Fx: %LocalAppData%\Mozilla\Firefox\Profiles\[Random Name].default\ and %AppData%\Mozilla\Firefox\Profiles\[Random Name].default\
  - GC: %LocalAppData%\Google\Chrome\User Data\Default
- Master file table (MFT) with $MFT file name and located in %SystemDrive%
- NTFS log ($LogFile) located in %SystemDrive%
- Prefetch folder located in %SystemRoot%\Prefetch\
- Registry
- Paging file with pagefile.sys filename in %SystemDrive%
- Swap file named swapfile.sys in %SystemDrive%

- Windows events located in %SystemRoot%\System32\winevt\Logs\
- Link files
- Thumbcache files located in %LocalAppData%\Microsoft\Windows\Explorer\
- Unallocated space

The above collected files were analyzed using following tools:

- Wireshark 1.12.1 was used to filter network traffic to detect IPs and ports used by the respective STaaS web-portal and client application.
- Autopsy Version 3.1.1 was used to conduct keyword search within E0 files linked to VMs' HDDs, and analyze browser cookies, browser histories and filtered files of E0 images.
- ESEDatabaseView v1.23 was used to analyze tables located in IE database. More specifically, for IE versions 10 and 11, the browser database is stored in an Extensible Storage Engine (ESE) file named WebCacheV01.dat [49]. The tables to be examined are contained in the ESE file located in %LocalAppData%\Microsoft\Windows\WebCache\.
- SQLite Manger was used to extract sqlite files of Fx and GC.
- DCode Date [50] was used for converting dates and times from hex, epoch, and WebKit formats to human readable format.
- Thumbcache Viewer 1.0.2.7 was used to extract thumbcache files.
- FTK Imager was used to analyze other files of interest.
- iExplorer was used for mounting and browsing iPhone backups.

Files from each of the E0 files that containing matching keywords were identified and filtered for further analysis—see Table 5.

3 FINDINGS: SPIDEROAK

3.1 Observations: SpiderOak's Account Created Using the Respective Browsers

We were able to recover various information associated with the creation of the SpiderOak's account using the respective browsers—see Tables 6–8.

3.2 Observations: SpiderOak's Application Program

Network traffics. Communications between the VM and SpiderOak's servers were made with IP addresses 38.121.104.79, 38.121.104.89, and 38.121.104.90 on port 443.
Memory. SpiderOak, the username, the email address, and the password of the created account along with the share ID (with the date and the time of creation), the shared URL and its password, the name of the shared folder, the name of the downloaded files, the name of the created sync and its folder on the host and on the target device, all were obtained from the collected vmem file (see Figs. 5 and 6).
Client application files. Client information such as the username, the share ID, RoomKey, the name of the shared folder, the name of the downloaded files, the name of the created sync and its folder on the host and on the target device as well as the date and the time of launched backup and synchronization were seen in %AppData%\SpiderOak\ spider_###############.log. In the log file, an IP address was found that appeared to

TABLE 5 Keyword Search Items

	VM-W1 to VM-W3	VM-W4 to VM-W6	VM-W7 to VM-W9	VM-W10	VM-W11	VM-W12	VM-W13	VM-W14	VM-W15	VM-W16 to VM-W18	VM-W19 to VM-W21	VM-W22 to VM-W24	The iPhone Device
Account email addresses	Y	Y	Y	Y	Y	Y	Y	Y	Y	Y	Y	Y	Y
Account names[a]	Y	Y	N/A	Y	Y	N/A	Y	Y	N/A	Y	Y	N/A	Y
Accounts ID[b]	Y	N/A	N/A	Y	NA	NA	Y	N/A	N/A	Y	N/A	N/A	Y
Account passwords	Y	Y	Y	Y	Y	Y	Y	Y	Y	Y	Y	Y	Y
CSSP names	Y	Y	Y	Y	Y	Y	Y	Y	Y	Y	Y	Y	N
Client applications' filenames	N	N	N	Y	Y	Y	Y	Y	Y	Y	Y	Y	N
Sample file names	N	N	N	Y	Y	Y	Y	Y	Y	Y	Y	Y	Y
Shared URLs	N	N	N	Y	N/A	N	Y	N/A	N	Y	N	Y	N
Share ID/Name	N	N/A	N/A	Y	N/A	Y	Y	N/A	Y	Y	N/A	Y	N
RoomKey	Y	N/A	N/A	Y	N/A	N/A	Y	N/A	N/A	Y	N/A	N/A	N
Shared files	N	N	N	Y	N/A	N	Y	Y	N	Y	Y	N	N
Shared URL password	N	N	N	Y	N/A	N/A	N/A	N/A	N/A	Y	N/A	N/A	N
Invitation message	N/A	N/A	N	N/A	N/A	Y	N/A	N/A	Y	N/A	Y	Y	N
Synchronization name	N	N	N	N	Y	N/A	N	Y	N/A	Y	Y	N/A	N
Downloading path	N	N	N	Y	Y	Y	Y	Y	Y	Y	Y	Y	N/A
Devices' names	N	N	N	Y	Y	Y	Y	Y	Y	Y	Y	Y	N
Integrity check	N	N	N	Y	Y	N/A	Y	N	N	Y	Y	Y	Y

The iPhone backups were also searched for user email address, name, IDs, and password.

[a] pCloud registration process does not ask for the name of the account.

[b] Accounts of JustCloud and pCloud do not have ID.

TABLE 6   Recovered Artifacts Associated With the Creation of the SpiderOak's Account Using IE

Location	Recovered Artifacts
Network traffic	IP address 173.223.11.89 on port 80 38.121.104.79 and 38.121.104.80 on port 443
Memory	Word "spideroak," the email address, the ID, and the name of the created account
Browser related files	The URL of SpiderOak visited during the creating of the account, in addition to the corresponding timestamp information of creation and access
Registry	URL of browsed webpages in HKEY_CURRENT_USER\Software\Microsoft\Internet Explorer\TypedURLs The Timestamp information in HKEY_CURRENT_USER\Software\Microsoft\Internet Explorer\TypedURLsTime
Paging	"spideroak.com" word

TABLE 7   Collected Artifacts With Regard to the Creation of the SpiderOak's Account Using Fx

Location	Recovered Artifacts
Network traffic	IP addresses 38.121.104.79 and 38.121.104.80 on port 443
Memory	The "spideroak" word, email address, ID, and name of the created account
Browser related files	The email address used in signing up process (see Fig. 2) The date and the UTC time of visiting
Unallocated space	The email address, the ID and the full name of the registered account (see Fig. 3)
Other files	SpiderOak's website was observed in a file located in %AppData%\Microsoft\Windows\Recent\CustomDestinations

TABLE 8   Recovered Artifacts Associated With the Creation of the SpiderOak's Account Using GC

Location	Recovered Artifacts
Network traffic	38.121.104.79 and 38.121.104.80 on port 443
Memory	"spideroak" word, the email address, the ID, the name, and the password of the created account (see Fig. 4)
Browser related files	Information about visited spideroak.com with the date and the UTC time of the last visit and "spideroak.com" word, the email address, the full name, and the ID of the created account
Unallocated space	The email address of the created account
Other files	SpiderOak's website was seen in a file in %AppData%\Microsoft\Windows\Recent\CustomDestinations

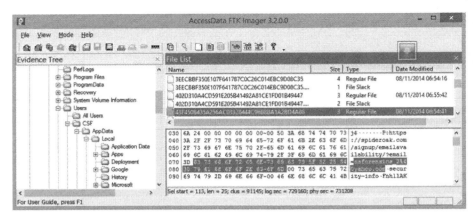

FIG. 2 The email address of the created account.

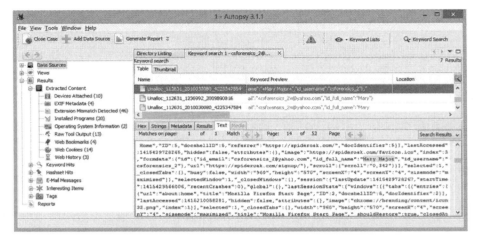

FIG. 3 The email address, the ID, and the full name of the created account.

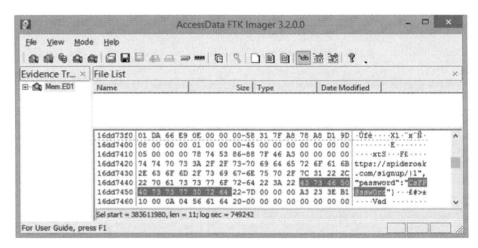

FIG. 4 Recovered password of the created account.

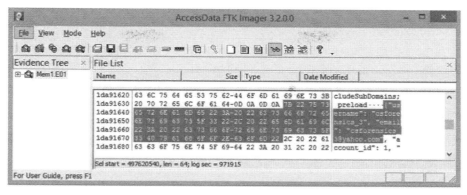

FIG. 5   The username and the email address of SpiderOak's account.

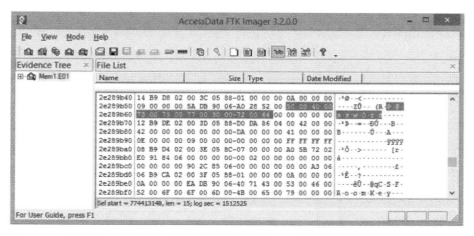

FIG. 6   The password of the created shared URL in VM-W10's vmem file.

be used for broadcasting on ports 21327 and 21328. The three first octals were the same as the device's IP address. In the oak_##############.log, similar events regarding the application along with the date and the time of occurrence were found. In %AppData%\SpiderOak\config.txt, the Hive path was observed. Files in %AppData%\SpiderOak\Sync contained the details of created syncs including the date and the time of their processing and source and destination paths, all, in SQLite format.

MFT. The sync name, the downloading folder name, and the installation filename were identified in the MFT$.

Registry. Installation filename and its storing path were found in the following keys:

- HKEY_CURRENT_USER\Software\Microsoft\Windows NT\CurrentVersion\AppCompatFlags\Compatibility Assistant\Store
- HKEY_USERS\S-1-5-21-1335463704-3291414260-3134846049-1001\Software\Microsoft\Windows NT\CurrentVersion\AppCompatFlags\Compatibility Assistant\Store

Moreover, SpiderOak's client application created inbound rules on both TCP and UDP protocols in Windows Firewall. The related keys' paths are as follow:

- [HKEY_LOCAL_MACHINE\SYSTEM\ControlSet001\Services\SharedAccess\ Parameters\FirewallPolicy\FirewallRules]
- [HKEY_LOCAL_MACHINE\SYSTEM\CurrentControlSet\Services\SharedAccess\ Parameters\FirewallPolicy\FirewallRules]

Prefetch. Installation filename was observed in Prefetch folder.
Paging file. The installation filename and the name of the downloaded files and their storing path were located in pagefile.sys.
Windows events. In the Application node, some records linked to the client application installation were located.
Link files. Two lnk files related to SpiderOak were located in %ProgramData%\Microsoft\ Windows\Start Menu\Programs\SpiderOak\.
Thumbcache. A thumbnail of file1.jpg was located in the Thumbcache folder.
Unallocated space. The name of the downloaded files, the installation filename, and spideroak.exe string were located in the unallocated space.
Other files. We located some information concerning the downloading folder and the name of the downloaded files in %ProgramData%\Microsoft\Search\Data\ Applications\Windows\GatherLogs\SystemIndex\SystemIndex.2.gthr and %LocalAppData%\Microsoft\Windows\Caches\{AFBF9F1A-8EE8-4C77-AF34- C647E37CA0D9}.1.ver0x0000000000000004.db, the Windows Indexing System and Windows File Caching respectively. The downloading folder name was also observed in NTUSER.DAT and ntuser.dat.LOG1, located in %UserProfile%, and the installation filename was observed in %SystemRoot%\AppCompat\Programs\Amcache.hve and %SystemRoot%\System32\config\SOFTWARE.LOG2. Also in %AppData%\ SpiderOak\fs_queue.db, synchronized files with the date and the UTC time were identified.

Spideroak.exe was observed in the following files:

- %SystemRoot%\System32\config\SYSTEM and SYSTEM.LOG1
- %SystemRoot%\System32\config\
- %SystemRoot%\System32\wdi\LogFiles\WdiContextLog.etl.002
- %SystemRoot%\Temp\AA9B36AA-758C-4EB0-94A6-C5AB9F4CEC2A\CompatProvider.dll
- %LocalAppData%\Local\Microsoft\Windows\appsFolder.itemdata-ms.bak
- %LocalAppData%\Local\Microsoft\Windows\appsFolder.itemdata-ms
- %LocalAppData%\Local\Microsoft\Windows\Explorer\TileCacheLogo-1736031_100.dat
- %LocalAppData%\Local\Microsoft\Windows\Caches/{3DA71D5A-20CC-432F-A115- DFE92379E91F}.1.ver0x000000000000000b.db
- %UserProfile%\ntuser.dat.LOG2
- %SystemRoot%\AppCompat\Programs\Amcache.hve.LOG1
- %SystemRoot%\Installer\24c05.msi

Based on the collected MD5 checksums, apart from file13.dll, the contents of other sample files were preserved by the CSSP. We were not able to restore alternate data stream (ADS) from file13.dll. Metadata of file12.doc such as Authors value remained the same as the original file.

It was also evident that the Modified value of downloaded files did not alter. However, we observed that the values of Created and Accessed fields were changed to the date and the time of downloading (see Fig. 7).

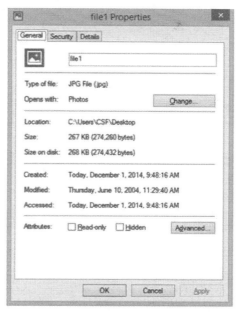

FIG. 7   General tab of file1.jpg after being downloaded by SpiderOak's client application.

3.3 Observations: Uninstalling SpiderOak's Application Program

Memory. Although the uninstall wizard asked for restart, restarting did not occur. Aside from the password of the shared URL, the result of memory analysis is similar to that reported in Section 3.2 (see Fig. 8).

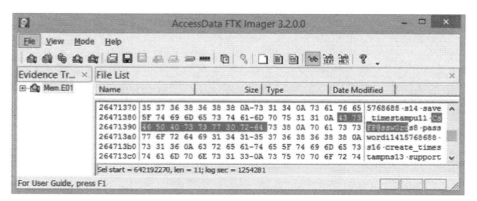

FIG. 8   Account's password in memory of VM-W13.

Client application files. After uninstalling SpiderOak on VM-W13, we observed that the Hive folder and its contents remained. We were also able to locate the files located in %AppData%\SpiderOak\ previously discussed in Section 3.2.

MFT and paging file. Both MFT and paging file contained spideroak word, the sync name, and downloading folder name.

NTFS log. "spideroak.exe" was observed in $LogFile.

Registry. The following keys pointed to spideroak.exe after uninstalling:
- [HKEY_CLASSES_ROOT*\shellex\ContextMenuHandlers\SpiderOak]
- [HKEY_CLASSES_ROOT\Directory\background\shellex\ContextMenuHandlers\ SpiderOak]
- [HKEY_CLASSES_ROOT\Directory\shellex\ContextMenuHandlers\SpiderOak]
- [HKEY_CLASSES_ROOT\Local Settings\Software\Microsoft\Windows\Shell\ MuiCache]
- [HKEY_CURRENT_USER\Software\Classes\Local Settings\Software\Microsoft\ Windows\Shell\MuiCache]
- [HKEY_CURRENT_USER\Software\Microsoft\Windows\CurrentVersion\Run]
- [HKEY_CURRENT_USER\Software\Microsoft\Windows\CurrentVersion\UFH\SHC]
- [HKEY_LOCAL_MACHINE\SOFTWARE\Classes*\shellex\ContextMenuHandlers\ SpiderOak]
- [HKEY_LOCAL_MACHINE\SOFTWARE\Classes\Directory\background\shellex\ ContextMenuHandlers\SpiderOak]
- [HKEY_LOCAL_MACHINE\SOFTWARE\Classes\Directory\shellex\ ContextMenuHandlers\SpiderOak]
- [HKEY_LOCAL_MACHINE\SYSTEM\ControlSet001\Services\SharedAccess\ Parameters\FirewallPolicy\FirewallRules]
- [HKEY_LOCAL_MACHINE\SYSTEM\CurrentControlSet\Services\SharedAccess\ Parameters\FirewallPolicy\FirewallRules]
- [HKEY_USERS\S-1-5-21-1335463704-3291414260-3134846049-1001\Software\Classes\ Local Settings\Software\Microsoft\Windows\Shell\MuiCache]
- [HKEY_USERS\S-1-5-21-1335463704-3291414260-3134846049-1001\Software\ Microsoft\Windows\CurrentVersion\Run]
- [HKEY_USERS\S-1-5-21-1335463704-3291414260-3134846049-1001\Software\ Microsoft\Windows\CurrentVersion\UFH\SHC]
- [HKEY_USERS\S-1-5-21-1335463704-3291414260-3134846049-1001_Classes\Local Settings\Software\Microsoft\Windows\Shell\MuiCache]

- *Prefetch folder.* "spideroak.exe" was observed in AgRobust.db, Layout.ini, Trace2.fx, RUNDLL32.EXE-125D4518.pf, RUNDLL32.EXE-F61C91E8.pf, and SPIDEROAK.EXE-CA2F0025.pf.

Windows events. In the Application node, Microsoft-Windows-Diagnostics-Performance%4Operational.evtx, Microsoft-Windows-Shell-Core%4Operational.evtx, and Microsoft-Windows-Windows Firewall With Advanced Security%4Firewall.evtx, we located records indicating the uninstalling of the client application. In addition, spideroak.exe was observed in WdiContextLog.etl.001, WdiContextLog.etl.002, and WdiContextLog.etl.003 which were located in %SystemRoot%\System32\wdi\ LogFiles\.

Link file. %ProgramData%\Microsoft\Windows\Start Menu\Programs\SpiderOak\ SpiderOak.lnk was linked to spideroak.exe.

Unallocated space. The spideroak word, the sync name, the sync folder name on the target machine, and downloading folder name were located in the unallocated space.

Other files. We located information indicating the name of the downloading folder in %ProgramData%\Microsoft\Search\Data\Applications\Windows\GatherLogs\ SystemIndex\SystemIndex.2.gthr and %LocalAppData%\Microsoft\Windows\ Caches\{AFBF9F1A-8EE8-4C77-AF34-C647E37CA0D9}.1.ver0x0000000000000004.db. Downloading folder name was also seen in NTUSER.DAT, and ntuser.dat.LOG1. The latter was located in %UserProfile%. Several other files we located also contained the spideroak.exe word.

3.4 Observations: Downloading From SpiderOak Using the Respective Browsers

We were able to collect information with forensic value associated with the downloading from SpiderOak using the respective browsers—see Tables 9–11.

According to the recorded MD5 checksums, the contents of the downloaded files, with the exception of file13.dll, remained intact. We were not able to restore ADS from file13.dll. Metadata of file12.doc such as Authors value remained the same as the original file. Unlike the result presented in Section 3.2, in addition to Created and Accessed fields, Modified value was also changed to the date and the time of downloading.

3.5 Observations: Browsing and Downloading From SpiderOak's iOS App

As shown in Fig. 13, a file named Cache.db-wal located in \Apps\SpiderOak\Library\ Caches\com.spideroak.SpiderOak\nsurlcache contained valuable information regarding the registered account and created backups and syncs.

Downloaded files were located in \Apps\SpiderOak\tmp\.caches, and \Apps\SpiderOak\ Library\Caches\com.spideroak.SpiderOak\nsurlcache\fsCachedData.

The dates and the times of Modified fields were identical to the date and the time of loading into the smartphone.

Apart from the file13.dll, the MD5 signatures of the sample files were the same as the original files. Modified date was pointing to the download time.

4 FINDINGS: JUSTCLOUD

4.1 Observations: JustCloud's Account Created in Using IE the Respective Browsers

Recovered information associated with the creation of the JustCloud's account using the respective browsers are presented in Tables 12–14.

TABLE 9 Recovered Artifacts Associated With Downloading From SpiderOak Using IE

Location	Recovered Artifacts
Network traffic	IP addresses 38.121.104.80, 80.157.17.91, and 204.79.197.200 on port 80 and 38.121.104.79 on port 443
Memory	The username and the device name were visible in the URL (see Fig. 9), shared title—the page was browsed-, and download folder name (SO Downloaded Files)
Browser logs	The URLs of SpiderOak that were visited along with the date and the UTC time of browsing, the downloading folder name and its path, the username stated in a URL, and the device name
MFT and NTFS log	The device name, the downloading folder name, the RoomKey, and the shared title (see Fig. 10)
Registry	In addition to Typed URL, the following keys pointed to spideroak.com: • HKEY_CLASSES_ROOT\Local Settings\Software\Microsoft\Windows\CurrentVersion\AppContainer\Storage\windows_ie_ac_001\Internet Explorer\DOMStorage\spideroak.com • HKEY_CURRENT_USER\Software\Classes\Local Settings\Software\Microsoft\Windows\CurrentVersion\AppContainer\Storage\windows_ie_ac_001\Internet Explorer\DOMStorage\spideroak.com • HKEY_USERS\S-1-5-21-1335463704-3291414260-3134846049-1001\Software\Classes\Local Settings\Software\Microsoft\Windows\CurrentVersion\AppContainer\Storage\windows_ie_ac_001\Internet Explorer\DOMStorage\spideroak.com HKEY_USERS\S-1-5-21-1335463704-3291414260-3134846049-1001_Classes\Local Settings\Software\Microsoft\Windows\CurrentVersion\AppContainer\Storage\windows_ie_ac_001\Internet Explorer\DOMStorage\spideroak.com
Paging	The shared title
Unallocated Space	Contained the device name and the shared title
Other files	The shared title was seen in: • %SystemRoot%\WinSxS\x86_microsoft-windows-twinui.resources_31bf3856ad364e35_6.3.9600.16384_en-us_c34c6f62bd449d58b\twinui.dll.mui • %LocalAppData%\Packages\windows_ie_ac_001\AC\INetCache\XSEVJ9WJ\shares[1].json • %SystemRoot%\System32\en-US\twinui.dll.mui Downloading folder name was observed in: • %UserProfile%\NTUSER.DAT and ntuser.dat.LOG1 • %SystemDrive%\$Extend/$UsnJrnl:$J • %SystemRoot%\System32\wdi/LogFiles\BootCKCL.etl • %LocalAppData%\Microsoft\Windows\UsrClass.dat and UsrClass.dat.LOG1 • %ProgramData%\Microsoft\Search\Data\Applications\Windows\GatherLogs\SystemIndex\SystemIndex.2.gthr Two files, one pointing to the downloading folder name and the other linked to the downloaded folder were found in %AppData%\Microsoft\Windows\Recent\.

TABLE 10   Recovered Artifacts Associated With Downloading From SpiderOak Using Fx

Location	Recovered Artifacts
Network traffic	IP addresses 38.121.104.80 on port 80 and 38.121.104.79 on port 443
Memory	The username and the device name in plaintext located in URL, and the shared title
Browser logs	Visited SpiderOak's URLs with the date and the UTC time were observed in cookies.sqlite; and places.sqlite located in %AppData%\Mozilla\Firefox\Profiles\[Random Name].default\ (see Figs. 10 and 11) The name of the downloaded file Both sessionstore.js and places.sqlite-wal were located in the same path contained the shared title and the username, and the shared title were located in several files in %LocalAppData%\Mozilla\Firefox\Profiles\[Random Name].default\cache2\entries\ and a file located in %AppData%\Microsoft\Windows\Recent\CustomDestinations\ The latter also included the username and the name of the downloaded file. The username was also found in %ProgramFiles%\Google\Update\1.3.25.5\goopdateres_is.dll As depicted in Fig. 12, in places.sqlite and the moz_annos table, the name of the downloaded file was observed
MFT	spideroak.com and the downloaded filename were seen in $MFT
NTFS log	The name of the downloaded file was seen in $LogFile
Link	The only related link file observed was %AppData%\Microsoft\Windows\Recent\e_.lnk, which referred to an archive of all sample files downloaded from SpiderOak
Unallocated space	spideroak.com, the device name, username were visible in the URL, and the downloaded filename were located in the unallocated space
Other files	The name of the downloaded file was observed in the below files: • %LocalAppData%\Microsoft\Windows\WebCache\V01.log and WebCacheV01.dat • %UserProfile%\NTUSER.DAT and ntuser.dat.LOG1 • %SystemDrive%\$Extend\$UsnJrnl:$J

TABLE 11   Recovered Artifacts Associated With Downloading From SpiderOak Using GC

Location	Recovered Artifacts
Network traffic	IP addresses 38.121.104.80 on port 80 and 38.121.104.79 on port 443
Memory	The username and the device name were visible in the URL
Browser logs	History and Cookies files contained information about visited spideroak URLs with the date and the UTC time of browsing. In the History file, the name of the downloaded file and its associated device name were observed. History Provider Cache, Cookies-journal, Shortcuts, Top Sites, Top Sites-journal, Favicons, Favicons-journal, Preferences, Current Tabs, and Current Session were located in %LocalAppData%\Google\Chrome\User Data\Default, which pointed to spideroak.com. The username and the device name were also observed in several files located in %LocalAppData%\Google\Chrome\User Data\Default\Cache\
MFT and NTFS log	"Spideroak.com" and the name of the downloaded file
Unallocated space	"spideroak" word
Other files	A file in %AppData%\Microsoft\Windows\Recent\CustomDestinations\ pointing to a URL containing the username in plaintext

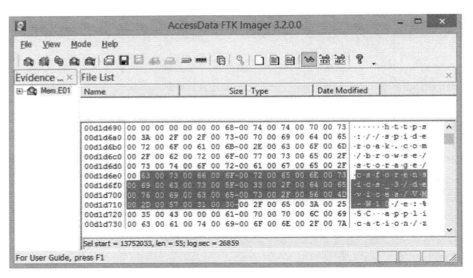

FIG. 9   The username and the device name in the collected vmem file from VM-W16.

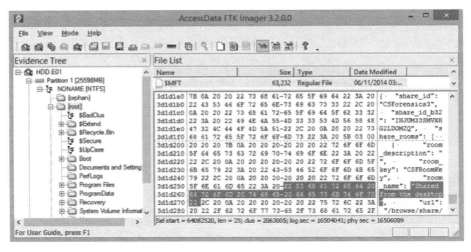

FIG. 10   RoomKey and shared message in the MFT.

4.2 Observations: JustCloud's Application Program

Network traffics. Communications between the client application and JustCloud's servers were made with IP addresses 54.231.64.4 and 184.154.150.133 on port 80.

Memory. The installation filename and its storing path, the name and the email address of the created account, the date and the time of account creation were observed in the memory (Fig. 14).

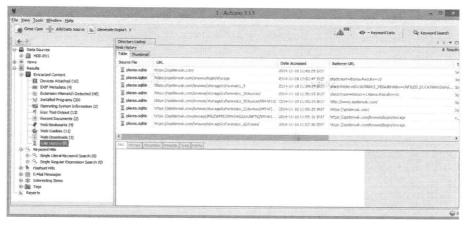

FIG. 11 The username and the device name in the URLs.

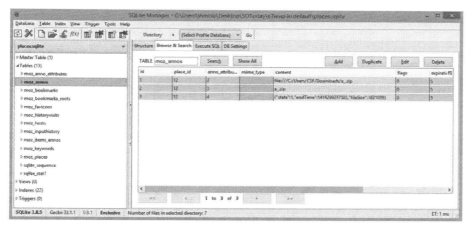

FIG. 12 The username and the device name in places.sqlite.

Client application files. In %ProgramFiles%\JustCloud\Database, the following files of forensic interest were identified:
- mpcb_settings.db contained the email address and the computer name used to log in.
- mpcb_backup_conf.db included the name of the files that were browsed to be backed up.

Also in %ProgramFiles%\JustCloud\log, the below key files were found:

- BACKUP.log contained a history of created backups along with the date and the time.
- LICENCE.log included the number of days that the account had been created and the name of the account.
- APPLICATION.log contained the date and the time of executing the program.
- DOWNLOADER.log included the details of a download failure occurred during downloading sample files.

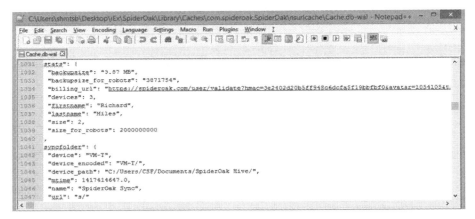

FIG. 13 Cache.db-wal containing some details of the account and created backups and syncs.

TABLE 12 Recovered Artifacts Associated With the Creation of the JustCloud's Account Using IE

Location	Recovered Artifacts
Network traffic	IP addresses 184.154.150.158, 37.252.162.208, 54.246.123.239, 74.125.230.154, 104.219.49.71, 94.31.29.154, 82.178.158.19, 74.125.230.132, 54.88.49.148, 217.163.21.35, 184.154.150.133, 173.194.67.95, 94.31.29.237, 82.178.158.18, 74.125.230.153, 23.251.138.168, and 10.10.34.34 on port 80. We also determined that some communications took place via IP address 184.154.150.158 on port 443. The email address used for creating the account was found in a packet with 184.154.150.158:80 destination
Memory	The "justcloud" word, the email address and the name of the created account
Browser related files	The JustCloud URLs visited, along with the date and the UTC time of browsing were found in WebCacheV01.dat The full name and the email address of the created account along with "justcloud" word in %LocalAppData%\Microsoft\Internet Explorer\Recovery\Last Active\{056F2E5F-67E5-11E4-9717-000C29B56A39}.dat and %LocalAppData%\Packages\windows_ie_ac_001\AC\INetCache\XSEVJ9WJ\account[1].htm
Registry	The URL of the visited webpages and the date and the UTC time of browsing respectively in TypedURLs and TypedURLsTime keys
Unallocated space	The name and the email address of the created account

- ONLINE_FOLDER.log contained the names of downloaded files.

MFT, Pagefile.sys, and unallocated. These contained the installation filename and JustCloud.exe.

NTFS log. The installation filename and JustCloud.exe were observed in $LogFile.

Prefetch folder. CONSENT.EXE-65F6206D.pf, JUSTCLOUD_SETUP.EXE-3C2F187F.pf, AgRobust.db,JUSTCLOUD.EXE-A4042D73.pf,RUNDLL32.EXE-125D4518.pf,andTASKENG. EXE-5BAF290C.pf located in %SystemRoot%\Prefetch\ included either the installation filename or JustCloud.exe. Layout.ini in the same path contained both mentioned files.

TABLE 13 Recovered Artifacts Associated With the Creation of the JustCloud's Account Using Fx

Location	Recovered Artifacts
Network traffics	IP addresses 184.154.150.158, 37.252.170.92, 54.75.236.238, 74.125.230.154, 94.31.29.154, 92.122.210.114, 74.125.136.95, 64.233.167.139, 54.164.48.8, 217.163.21.35, 104.219.49.71, 94.31.29.237, 74.125.230.141, 23.251.136.174, 184.154.150.133, and 10.10.34.34 on port 80. We also determined that some communications took place via IP address 184.154.150.158 on port 443. The email address used for creating the account was found in a packet with 184.154.150.158:80 destination
Memory	The "justcloud" word and the email address of the created account were observed in the collected vmem file
Browser related files	In %LocalAppData%\Mozilla\Firefox\Profiles\[Random Name].default\cache2\entries, the following files were indicating justcloud.com was browsed: • 09ACE8E5F96EFE3AA5A0CE0B5A5563299A0FDA44 • 1810CD15A41C6F610D8C7E8C4D39CDACB00E337A • 1BDE5F2D8D9F11EF0F335C5A9128DBE71382DA75 • 380C3CF91DFA451FBF740CA76A7DCB2BDBC0889C • 3E077C83363C5F69ACAEACB5C1994E04464AC18F • 446FF2398AF1F92765363BD3327D6D8CA4F77EC3 • 461025C8C3F848EBC71F9E28B9120ABF00A1E074 • 54872F69BC90AE690242ED63D0318EDA90D3557C • 553B5944009C5918AF6AF5A09812A8B0D17E6FBF • 5AF6B030BB839756C1D72CDB22A272BF2A618C22 • 6457C1BCEB28A521EE0ACC12400A002A8C1D1A8A • 7280D1006F4EA8E782FF4988DDACC2FE45E223CE • 7B44045EC0465D6CCFCB9E9FB691424E2E970466 • 7F74C3A115A0B08422A8409FC7494E00E9090F75 • 9252811649D77766E4FB7DC750D825FE68E4CF10 • 93B403780DF9FED67C2E7AE5EC879780BFAF41C1 • A721B51969F936D4EBAA8E4C6E3F99F8B703241B • AE3FAB291B124D80634CA386411F72B43E1B300D • C0EE83175D8130C265E78027748B480ABA944418 • C83034755D57A645F6FF927E13522DCA8EC5E39A • CDC7FBBA3E3BA42AFF33CD41F35C9EB8D63C0497 • CF49CBF7AD56117C73D75F827975BA8D9CFDF67B • D03FD20E97FDEE10EE8D20A4096B467ADB0B75B2 • E84B0DEA1E343D9D0C39D74D7D8AED548046BD3C • F0016B4F7C6CB097EA6FB493CB9F3070AA8ABA37 • F588D60C1323FF25E996F26CD45405D82D11C36E • F741938599B126A67F07C77106C86175D4F2DDBE • FC83C509516A560D495BCDD9C0C0025E0BB16907 Information regarding cookies and histories were found in cookies.sqlite, places.sqlite, and permissions.sqlite. The date and the UTC time of visiting were retrieved from the two first files
Unallocated space	The full name and the email address of the created account

TABLE 14   Recovered Artifacts Associated With the Creation of the JustCloud's Account Using GC

Location	Recovered Artifacts
Network traffics	IP addresses 184.154.150.158, 192.168.74.139, 68.67.128.156, 173.194.112.77, 54.246.114.22, 104.219.49.71, 217.163.21.34, 94.31.29.154, 74.125.136.95, 208.71.121.1, 195.59.150.17, 173.194.112.68, 107.21.26.11, 94.31.29.237, 23.251.128.113, 207.46.194.10, 204.79.197.200, 184.154.150.133, and 10.10.34.34 on port 80. It was also determined that communications also took place via IP address 184.154.150.158 on port 443
Memory	The "justcloud" word and the email address, the name, and the password of the created account
Browser files	History and Cookies files contained information about visited JustCloud's URLs with the date and the UTC time of browsing. Shortcuts, Top Sites, Favicons, Current Tabs, and Current Session all located in %LocalAppData%\Google\Chrome\User Data\Default also pointed to justcloud.com

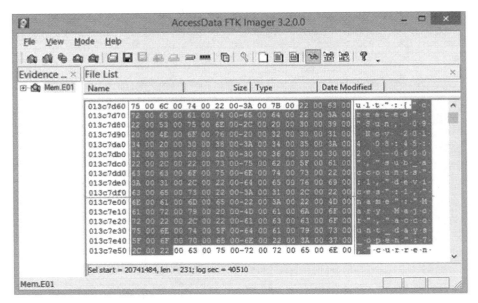

FIG. 14   The name of the registered account along with account creation date and time in vmem file of VM-W11.

Windows events. An event regarding JustCloud's backup service was located in the System log.

Link Files. Four relevant lnk files were found:

- %AppData%\Microsoft/Windows/Start Menu/Programs/JustCloud/JustCloud.lnk
- %AppData%\Microsoft/Windows/Start Menu/Programs/Startup/JustCloud.lnk
- %UserProfile%\Desktop\JustCloud.lnk
- %UserProfile%\Desktop\Sync Folder.lnk

Thumbcache files. JustCloud's icon was located in the thumbcache files.

Other files. A task named LaunchApp was created in %SystemRoot%\System32\Tasks\ and scheduled to run JustCloud.exe /windowlaunch command. We observed the installation filename in the following files:

- %LocalAppData%\IconCache.db
- %ProgramFiles%\JustCloud\spf.dat
- %SystemDrive%\$Extend\$UsnJrnl:$J
- %SystemRoot%\AppCompat\Programs\Amcache.hve and Amcache.hve.LOG1
- %SystemRoot%\System32\config\RegBack\SYSTEM
- %SystemRoot%\System32\config\SYSTEM, SYSTEM.LOG1, and SYSTEM.LOG2
- %SystemRoot%\System32\sru\SRU.log and SRUDB.dat
- %SystemRoot%\System32\wdi\LogFiles\BootCKCL.etl
- %UserProfile%\NTUSER.DAT and ntuser.dat.LOG1

The below files contained "JustCloud.exe":

- %SystemDrive%\$Extend\$UsnJrnl:$J
- %LocalAppData%\IconCache.db
- %LocalAppData%\Microsoft\Windows\Caches\{3DA71D5A-20CC-432F-A115-DFE9237 9E91F}.1.ver0x000000000000000c.db
- %UserProfile%\NTUSER.DAT and ntuser.dat.LOG1
- %SystemRoot%\AppCompat\Programs\Amcache.hve and Amcache.hve.LOG1
- %SystemRoot%\System32\config\RegBack\SOFTWARE
- %SystemRoot%\System32\config\SOFTWARE, SOFTWARE.LOG1, SOFTWARE.LOG2, SYSTEM, and SYSTEM.LOG1
- %SystemRoot%\System32\config\TxR\{b7bee95a-0b1a-11e3-93fc-90b11c043665}. TxR.0.regtrans-ms
- %SystemRoot%\System32\sru\SRU.log, SRU00008.log, and SRUDB.dat

From our experiments, we determined that JustCloud does not allow the uploading of files with an invalid extension and users attempting to do so will be presented with an error message—"*Failed: The remote server returned an error: (403) Forbidden.*". Recorded MD5 checksums showed that, the contents of sample files, with the exception of file13.dll, were preserved by this CSSP. Similar to the findings presented in Section 3.2, we were not able to restore ADS from file13.dll. Metadata of file12.doc were not altered. The values of Created, Modified, and Accessed fields were changed to the date and the time of downloading.

4.3 Observations: Uninstalling JustCloud's Application Program

Memory. With the exception of not being able to locate the email address of the account, the investigation result of the vmem file was the same as Section 4.2.
Client application files. Although the JustCloud folder was removed by the uninstalling process, they could be easily recovered using FTK Imager (see Fig. 15).
MFT and paging file. The installation filename and justcloud.exe were observed in MFT$ and pagefile.sys.
NTFS log. The installation filename and justcloud.exe were observed in $LogFile.
Registry. The following keys pointed to JustCloud.exe after uninstallation:

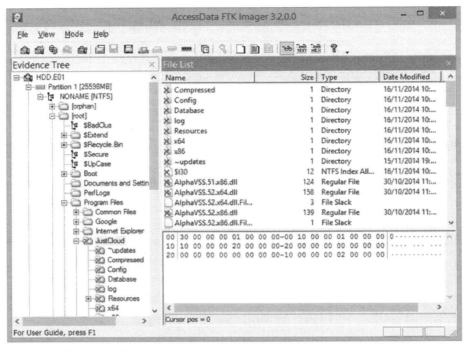

FIG. 15 Deleted folders of JustCloud.

- HKEY_CURRENT_USER\Software\Microsoft\Windows\CurrentVersion\UFH\SHC
- HKEY_CURRENT_USER\Software\Microsoft\Windows NT\CurrentVersion\AppCompatFlags\Compatibility Assistant\Store
- HKEY_LOCAL_MACHINE\SOFTWARE\Microsoft\Tracing\JustCloud_RASAPI32
- HKEY_LOCAL_MACHINE\SOFTWARE\Microsoft\Tracing\JustCloud_RASMANCS
- HKEY_USERS\S-1-5-21-1335463704-3291414260-3134846049-1001\Software\Microsoft\Windows\CurrentVersion\UFH\SHC
- HKEY_USERS\S-1-5-21-1335463704-3291414260-3134846049-1001\Software\Microsoft\Windows NT\CurrentVersion\AppCompatFlags\Compatibility Assistant\Store

Prefetch. In the Prefetch folder, CONSENT.EXE-65F6206D.pf, JUSTCLOUD_SETUP.EXE-3C2F187F.pf, and Layout.ini contained the installation filename. Also JustCloud.exe was included in AgRobust.db, BACKUPSTACK.EXE-831F34B6.pf, Layout.ini, TASKENG. EXE-5BAF290C.pf, RUNDLL32.EXE-125D4518.pf, and JUSTCLOUD.EXE-A4042D73.pf.

Windows events. A record in %SystemRoot%\System32\winevt\Logs\Microsoft-Windows-Diagnostics-Performance%4Operational.evtx pointed to justcloud.com.

Unallocated. The installation filename and the name of the account, backed up filenames with their paths, justcloud.com, and justcloud.exe were located in the unallocated space.

Other files. The scheduled task (LaunchApp) existed even after uninstallation. We observed the installation filename in the following files:

- %LocalAppData%\IconCache.db
- %ProgramFiles%\JustCloud\spf.dat
- %SystemDrive%\$Extend\$UsnJrnl:$J
- %SystemRoot%\AppCompat\Programs\Amcache.hve
- %SystemRoot%\System32\config\RegBack\SYSTEM
- %SystemRoot%\System32\config\SYSTEM and SYSTEM.LOG1
- %SystemRoot%\System32\sru\SRUDB.dat and SRUtmp.log
- %SystemRoot%\System32\wdi\LogFiles\BootCKCL.etl
- %UserProfile%\NTUSER.DAT and ntuser.dat.LOG1

Also the below files were pointing to JustCloud.exe:

- %SystemRoot%\System32\wdi\{86432a0b-3c7d-4ddf-a89c-172faa90485d}\{4d3b40fb-cace-4558-a9ad-cbd7532ac6e2}\snapshot.etl
- %SystemRoot%\System32\wdi\{86432a0b-3c7d-4ddf-a89c-172faa90485d}\S-1-5-21-1335463704-3291414260-3134846049-1001_UserData.bin
- %SystemRoot%\System32\wdi\{86432a0b-3c7d-4ddf-a89c-172faa90485d}\{fbde4aa3-f5b4-4dc2-8312-ae0f4e1228c8}\snapshot.etl
- %SystemRoot%\System32\wdi\{86432a0b-3c7d-4ddf-a89c-172faa90485d}\{73b44f2d-609e-4476-8a08-9342afe75051}\snapshot.etl
- %LocalAppData%\IconCache.db
- %LocalAppData%\Microsoft\Windows\Caches\{3DA71D5A-20CC-432F-A115-DFE92379E91F}.1.ver0x000000000000000d.db and {3DA71D5A-20CC-432F-A115-DFE92379E91F}.1.ver0x000000000000000c.db
- %UserProfile%\NTUSER.DAT, ntuser.dat.LOG1, and ntuser.dat.LOG2
- %SystemRoot%\AppCompat\Programs\Amcache.hve and Amcache.hve.LOG1
- %SystemDrive%\$Extend\$UsnJrnl:$J
- %SystemRoot%\System32\config\RegBack\SOFTWARE and SYSTEM
- %SystemRoot%\System32\config\ SYSTEM, SYSTEM.LOG1, SOFTWARE.LOG1, SOFTWARE.LOG2 and SOFTWARE
- %SystemRoot%\System32\config\TxR\{b7bee95a-0b1a-11e3-93fc-90b11c043665}.TxR.0.regtrans-ms
- %SystemRoot%\System32\sru\SRUDB.dat and SRUtmp.log
- %SystemRoot%\System32\wdi\LogFiles\BootCKCL.etl
- %SystemRoot%\System32\wdi\LogFiles\StartupInfo\S-1-5-21-1335463704-3291414260-3134846049-1001_StartupInfo2.xml, S-1-5-21-1335463704-3291414260-3134846049-1001_StartupInfo5.xml, and S-1-5-21-1335463704-3291414260-3134846049-1001_StartupInfo1.xml
- %SystemRoot%\System32\wdi\LogFiles\ WdiContextLog.etl.001, WdiContextLog.etl.002, and WdiContextLog.etl.003

4.4 Observations: Downloading From JustCloud Using the Respective Browsers

We were able to collect information with forensic value associated with the downloading from JustCloud using the respective browsers—see Tables 15–17.

Respecting the integrity check, the same result as Section 3.4 was obtained.

TABLE 15   Recovered Artifacts Associated With Downloading From JustCloud Using IE

Location	Recovered Artifacts
Network traffics	As shown in Fig. 16, for downloading, JustCloud transferred the user to http://capsa.storage.googleapis.com. Connections were made with IP addresses 23.67.70.64, 74.125.133.95, 74.125.136.100, and 94.31.29.154 on port 80, 184.154.150.133 on port 443, and 184.154.150.158 on ports 80 and 443
Memory	The sync name, the name of the account, and the device name
Registry	TypedURL and TypedURLTime respectively recorded justcloud.com's URLs and the date and the UTC time of visiting
Browser related files	Visited JustCloud's URLs with the date and the time of browsing in WebCacheV01.data The downloading folder name and its path, the email address of the account in a URL, and the device name in json extension were seen in one of WebCacheV01.data's tables The email address of the account in %LocalAppData%\Microsoft\Internet Explorer\Recovery\Active\{4924C995-702D-11E4-9719-000C29B56A39}.dat The name of the downloaded files in: • %LocalAppData%\Microsoft\Windows\INetCache\Low\IE\[Random Name]\with-others[1].htm (contained the device name as well) • %LocalAppData%\Microsoft\Windows\WebCache\ V01.log and WebCacheV01.dat • %ProgramData%\Microsoft\Windows Defender\Support\MpWppTracing-11202014-001654-00000003-ffffffff.bin
MFT	"justcloud.com" word
NTFS Log	"justcloud.com" word and the name of the downloaded files
Paging file	The name of downloaded files and their saving paths
Unallocated space	Device name

TABLE 16   Recovered Artifacts Associated With Downloading From JustCloud Using Fx

Location	Recovered Artifacts
Network traffics	IP addresses 74.125.133.95, 94.31.29.154, 173.194.45.170 and 173.194.41.40 on port 80 and 184.154.150.133, and 184.154.150.158 on port 443. We also determined connections also took place via IP address 184.154.150.158 on port 80
Memory	The email address and the password of the account (see Fig. 17), the names of downloaded files and the storing path
Browser related files	The URLs of JustCloud with the date and the UTC time of visiting in cookies.sqlite and places.sqlite located in %AppData%\Mozilla\Firefox\Profiles\[Random Name].default\. The name of downloaded files in WebCacheV01.dat and V01.log (see Fig. 18)
MFT and NTFS log	The name of downloaded files
Unallocated space	The email address of the account and the name of downloaded files with the path of storing
Other files	The name of downloaded files in %SystemDrive%\$Extend\$UsnJrnl:$J, %UserProfile%\ntuser.dat.LOG1 and NTUSER.DAT. justcloud.com in %ProgramFiles%\GUM5EFC.tmp\npGoogleUpdate3.dll

TABLE 17 Recovered Artifacts Associated With Downloading From JustCloud Using GC

Location	Recovered Artifacts
Network traffics	IP addresses 74.125.136.95 and 173.194.41.35 on port 80 and 184.154.150.133 and 184.154.150.158 on port 443. We also determined connections also took place via IP address 184.154.150.158 on port 80
Memory	The device name and the name of downloaded files with the path of storing
Browser related files	History and Cookies files contained information about visited JustCloud's URLs as well as the date and the UTC time of browsing. History Provider Cache, Cookies-journal, Shortcuts, Top Sites, Top Sites-journal, Favicons, Favicons-journal, Preferences, Current Tabs, Last Session, and Current Session all located in %LocalAppData%\Google\Chrome\User Data\Default also pointed to justcloud.com. The name of the downloaded files were seen in %LocalAppData%\Google\Chrome\User Data\Default\Cache\data_1
MFT, NTFS log, and paging file	They contained the names of downloaded files
Other files	The name of downloaded files in %ProgramData%\Microsoft\Windows Defender\Support\MpWppTracing-11202014-101334-00000003-ffffffff.bin

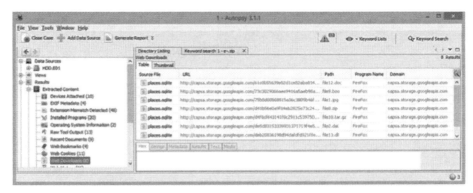

FIG. 16   For downloading JustCloud used googleapis.com.

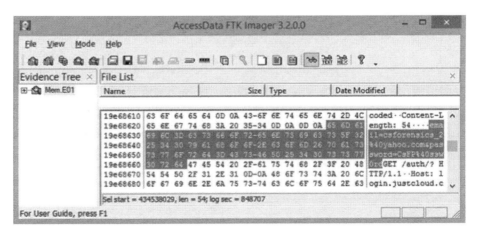

FIG. 17   Email address and password in vmem file.

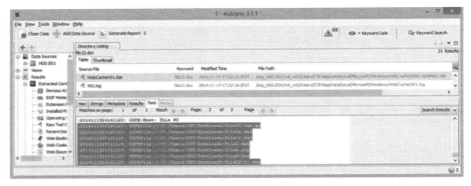

FIG. 18   The name of the downloaded files and their storing paths.

4.5 Observations: Browsing and Downloading From JustCloud's iOS App

In \Apps\JustCloud\Documents, a file named syncfolder.index contained the name of the sync folder and its files. Files located in \Apps\JustCloud\Documents\datacache downloaded files with different names were observed. In \Apps\JustCloud\Library\Preferences, a file contained account's user's email was located.

5 FINDING: pCLOUD

5.1 Observations: pCloud's Account Created in Using IE the Respective Browsers

We were able to recover various information associated with the creation of the pCloud's account using the respective browsers—see Tables 18–20.

5.2 Observations: pCloud's Application Program

Network traffics. Communications between the VM and JustCloud's servers were established with IP addresses 74.120.8.17, 74.120.8.25, 74.120.8.28, 74.120.8.71, 74.120.8.74, 74.120.8.98, 74.120.8.139, 74.120.8.153, and 74.120.8.157 on port 443.
Memory. The email address of the account, the email address of the person who was invited to have access to the shared URL, the message of the invitation, and the share title were observed in vmem file.
Client application files. In %LocalAppData%\pCloud\data.db, information regarding the synced files were observed. The file was in SQLite format and contained 25 tables that described files properties and folder names of synced data. For instance, as depicted in Fig. 20, the file table contained filenames and their creation and modification date and time in Unix-Numeric format. Also in the hashchecksum table, SHA1 hash values of synced files were recorded where their values matched with the original files' checksum.

TABLE 18 Recovered Artifacts Associated With the Creation of the pCloud's Account Using IE

Location	Recovered Artifacts
Network traffic	IP addresses 74.120.8.14 and 77.109.171.171 on port 80 and 74.120.8.7, 74.120.8.144, and 74.120.8.13 on port 443
Memory	The email address and the password of the registered account
Browser related files	pCloud related addresses along with the date and the UTC time of browsing in WebCacheV01.dat "pcloud" word in some files of %LocalAppData%\Microsoft\Internet Explorer\Recovery\Active\ and %LocalAppData%\Microsoft\Internet Explorer\Recovery\Last Active\ and in some subfolders of %LocalAppData%\Packages\windows_ie_ac_001\AC\INetCache\ and \Microsoft\Windows\INetCache\Low\IE\79IBA23G\qsml[1].xml
Registry	The URL of the visited webpages and the date and the UTC time of browsing respectively in TypedURLs and TypedURLsTime The following keys were pointing to pCloud: • HKEY_CLASSES_ROOT\Local Settings\Software\Microsoft\Windows\CurrentVersion\AppContainer\Storage\windows_ie_ac_001\Internet Explorer\DOMStorage\ • HKEY_CURRENT_USER\Software\Classes\Local Settings\Software\Microsoft\Windows\CurrentVersion\AppContainer\Storage\windows_ie_ac_001\Internet Explorer\DOMStorage\ • HKEY_USERS\S-1-5-21-1335463704-3291414260-3134846049-1001\Software\Classes\Local Settings\Software\Microsoft\Windows\CurrentVersion\AppContainer\Storage\windows_ie_ac_001\Internet Explorer\DOMStorage\
Unallocated space	"pcloud" word

TABLE 19 Recovered Artifacts Associated With the Creation of the pCloud's Account Using Fx

Location	Recovered Artifacts
Network traffic	IP addresses 74.120.8.14 on port 80 and 74.120.8.14, 74.120.8.6, 74.120.8.144, and 74.120.8.13 on port 443
Memory	pcloud.com and the email address and the password of the registered account
Browser related files	Files with random names indicating that pcloud.com was visited were located in %LocalAppData%\Mozilla\Firefox\Profiles\[Random Name].default\cache2\entries Information associated with cookies and histories in cookies.sqlite and places.sqlite and the date and the UTC time of browsing identified from aforementioned files "pcloud" word in permissions.sqlite, sessionstore.js, and places.sqlite-wal located in %AppData%\Mozilla\Firefox\Profiles\[Random Name].default\. The last two files also contained the email address.
Unallocated space	"pcloud" word and the email address of the created account

TABLE 20   Recovered Artifacts Associated With the Creation of the pCloud's Account Using GC

Location	Recovered Artifacts
Network traffic	IP addresses 74.120.8.14 on port 80 and 74.120.8.14, 74.120.8.6, 74.120.8.144, and 74.120.8.12 on port 443
Memory	The email address and the password of the registered account (see Fig. 19)
Browser related files	History and Cookies files contained information about the pCloud's URLs browsed with the date and the UTC time of browsing Shortcuts, Top Sites, Favicons, Current Tabs, History Provider Cache, Last Tabs and Current Session located in %LocalAppData%\Google\Chrome\User Data\Default\ pointed to pcloud.com. "pcloud" word and the email address discovered in %LocalAppData%\Google\Chrome\ User Data\Default\Cache\data_1
MFT, NTFS log, and unallocated space	The "pcloud" word

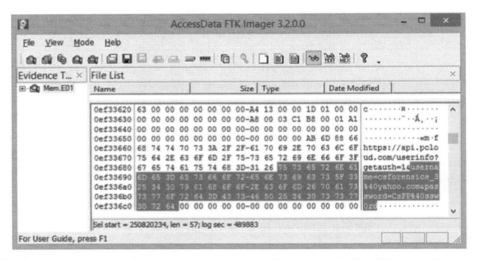

FIG. 19   The email address and the password of the created pCloud account in VM-W9's vmem file.

By using Autopsy, the invited email and the invitation message were found in the same file. We also observed the invited email in data.db-wal located in the same path.

Registry. pCloud's default storing folder path was located in HKEY_ CURRENT_USER\Software\pCloud\AppPFolders and HKEY_ USERS\S-1-5-21-1335463704-3291414260-3134846049-1001\Software\pCloud\ AppPFolders.

Windows events. In the Application node, records confirming the restore point creation and pCloud installation were located. Additionally, in Microsoft-Windows-Shell-Core%4Operational.evtx a record about pCloud was located.

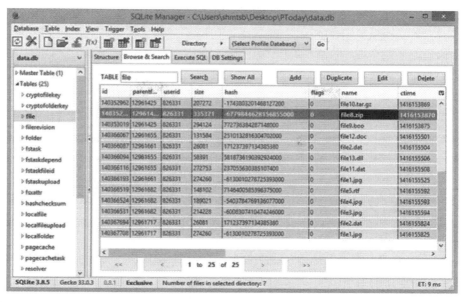

FIG. 20 The file table that contains filenames and their creation and modification date and time.

Link files. %ProgramData%\Microsoft\Windows\Start Menu\Programs\pCloudSync\
pCloud Drive.lnk pointed to pCloud's client application.
Thumbacache files. pCloud.exe was seen in TileCacheLogo-814531_100.dat.

The Installation filename was observed in MFT$, $LogFile, pagefile.sys, Prefetch folder,
the unallocated space, and below files:

- %LocalAppData%\Temp\pCloud_Drive_20141116195829.log
- %UserProfile%\NTUSER.DAT and ntuser.dat.LOG1
- %SystemRoot%\AppCompat\Programs\Amcache.hve, Amcache.hve.LOG1, and
  Amcache.hve.LOG2
- %SystemDrive%\$Extend\$UsnJrnl:$J
- %SystemRoot%\System32\config\SYSTEM, SYSTEM.LOG2, SOFTWARE, and
  SOFTWARE.LOG2
- %LocalAppData%\IconCache.db
- %SystemDrive%\ProgramData\Package Cache\{8527342e-b5b5-4274-8f1c-
  01a0320d3b7d}\state.rsm

5.3 Observations: Uninstalling pCloud's Application Program

Memory. Unlike the two other CSSPs studied, pCloud automatic signing in feature is
opt-in (i.e., only when a user opts to do so). Hence, no relevant evidence was located in
the vmem file.

Client application files. Uninstall process did not remove %LocalAppData%\pCloud\data. db and, therefore, we were able to recover information mentioned in Section 5.2.

MFT, NTFS log, paging file, unallocated space, and the below files contained references to pcloud.com:

- %LocalAppData%\IconCache.db
- %LocalAppData%\Microsoft\Windows\appsFolder.itemdata-ms, appsFolder. itemdata-ms.bak, and appsFolder.itemdata-ms~RF16c076.TMP
- %LocalAppData%\Microsoft\Windows\Caches\{3DA71D5A-20CC-432F-A115-DFE9 2379E91F}.1.ver0x000000000000000a.db and {3DA71D5A-20CC-432F-A115-DFE92379E 91F}.1.ver0x000000000000000b.db.
- %LocalAppData%\Microsoft\Windows\Explorer\TileCacheLogo-814531_100.dat
- %LocalAppData%\Temp\pCloud_Drive_20141116195829.log, pCloud_ Drive_20141116195829_1_pCloud_Drive.msi.log, pCloud_Drive_20141117112055.log, and pCloud_Drive_20141117112055_0_pCloud_Drive.msi.log
- %SystemDrive%\$OrphanFiles\16a88d.rbf and license.rtf
- %SystemDrive%\$Extend\$UsnJrnl:$J
- %SystemRoot%\AppCompat\Programs\Amcache.hve, Amcache.hve.LOG1, and Amcache.hve.LOG2
- %SystemRoot%\Installer\{5950DCB0-F15C-48E0-96D9-F5948DA2A419}\pCloud.exe
- %SystemRoot%\ServiceProfiles\LocalService\AppData\Local\lastalive0.dat
- %SystemRoot%\System32\config\RegBack\SOFTWARE and SYSTEM
- %SystemRoot%\System32\config\SOFTWARE, SOFTWARE.LOG2, SYSTEM, SYSTEM.LOG1, and SYSTEM.LOG2
- %SystemRoot%\System32\wdi\{86432a0b-3c7d-4ddf-a89c-172faa90485d}\{002d5213- d0d9-41a6-ae97-4c3b05d067f2}\snapshot.etl
- %SystemRoot%\System32\wdi\{86432a0b-3c7d-4ddf-a89c-172faa90485d}\{4c28eec8- 7733-4412-8c51-3088b62b54f0}\snapshot.etl
- %SystemRoot%\System32\wdi\{86432a0b-3c7d-4ddf-a89c-172faa90485d}\{f65e2d08- cfd5-4865-9d14-9b092616ddd1}\snapshot.etl
- %SystemRoot%\System32\wdi\{86432a0b-3c7d-4ddf-a89c- 172faa90485d}\S-1-5-21-1335463704-3291414260-3134846049-1001_UserData.bin
- %SystemRoot%\System32\wdi\LogFiles\BootCKCL.etl
- %SystemRoot%\System32\wdi\LogFiles\ StartupInfo\S-1-5-21-1335463704-3291414260-3134846049-1001_StartupInfo2.xml and S-1-5-21-1335463704-3291414260-3134846049-1001_StartupInfo3.xml
- %SystemRoot%\System32\wdi\LogFiles\WdiContextLog.etl.001, WdiContextLog. etl.002, and WdiContextLog.etl.003
- %UserProfile%\NTUSER.DAT, ntuser.dat.LOG1, and ntuser.dat.LOG2

Registry. The following keys pointed to pCloud:

- HKEY_CLASSES_ROOT\CLSID\{a0b73fac-351f-3948-9d8a-1dad9d870193}\ InprocServer32
- HKEY_CLASSES_ROOT\CLSID\{a0b73fac-351f-3948-9d8a-1dad9d870193}\ InprocServer32\1.0.0.0
- HKEY_CURRENT_USER\Software\Microsoft\Windows\CurrentVersion\UFH\SHC

* HKEY_CURRENT_USER\Software\Microsoft\Windows NT\CurrentVersion\
  AppCompatFlags\Compatibility Assistant\Store
* HKEY_CURRENT_USER\Software\pCloud\AppPFolders
* HKEY_LOCAL_MACHINE\SOFTWARE\Classes\CLSID\
  {a0b73fac-351f-3948-9d8a-1dad9d870193}\InprocServer32
* HKEY_LOCAL_MACHINE\SOFTWARE\Classes\CLSID\
  {a0b73fac-351f-3948-9d8a-1dad9d870193}\InprocServer32\1.0.0.0
* HKEY_LOCAL_MACHINE\SOFTWARE\Microsoft\Windows\CurrentVersion\
  Installer\Folders
* HKEY_USERS\S-1-5-21-1335463704-3291414260-3134846049-1001\Software\
  Microsoft\Windows\CurrentVersion\UFH\SHC
* HKEY_USERS\S-1-5-21-1335463704-3291414260-3134846049-1001\Software\
  Microsoft\Windows NT\CurrentVersion\AppCompatFlags\Compatibility Assistant\
  Store
* HKEY_USERS\S-1-5-21-1335463704-3291414260-3134846049-1001\Software\pCloud\
  AppPFolders

Prefetch. pcloud.exe was seen in AgAppLaunch.db, AgRobust.db, Layout.ini, MSIEXEC.
EXE-B5AFA339.pf, PCLOUD.EXE-42B26121.pf, and RUNDLL32.EXE-125D4518.pf
located in Prefetch folder.

Windows events. Records regarding the uninstallation were located in the Application node.
Also pcloud.exe was observed in Microsoft-Windows-Diagnosis-Scripted%4Operational.
evtx, Microsoft-Windows-Diagnostics-Performance%4Operational.evtx, Microsoft-
Windows-Shell-Core%4Operational.evtx, and Microsoft-Windows-Windows Firewall With
Advanced Security%4Firewall.evtx.

5.4 Observations: Downloading From pCloud Using the Respective Browsers

We were able to collect information with forensic value associated with the downloading
from SpiderOak using the respective browsers—see Tables 21–23.

We determined that the MD5 checksum of sample files, except file13.dll, were not altered
after downloading. However, we were not able to restore ADS from file13.dll. Metadata of
file12.doc such as Authors value remained the same as the original file. It was also observed
that Modified value of downloaded files was the date of uploading. The values of Created and
Accessed fields were, on the other hand, changed to the date and the time of downloading.

5.5 Observations: Browsing and Downloading From pCloud's iOS App

A file named p.db located in \Apps\pCloud\Library\Application Support contained table and data similar to those discussed in Section 5.2. We located file12.doc as one of the files
opened in the pCloud app in \App\pCloud\Library\Caches\com.pcloud.pcloud.cache.
Although the name of the located file was different, the MD5 signature indicated that the
contents of the file had not been changed. The metadata of the file was identical to the original one. The only other sample file found in the pCloud's app folder was file1.jpg, but had a

TABLE 21   Recovered Artifacts Associated With Downloading From pCloud Using IE

Location	Recovered Artifacts
Network traffics	IP addresses 74.120.8.7, 74.120.8.12, 74.120.8.13, 74.120.8.14, 74.120.8.15, 74.120.8.86, and 74.120.8.144 on port 443 and 80.239.230.147 on 80. We also determined connections with cloudfront.net were established with IP addresses 54.230.14.77 and 54.192.15.86 on port 443
Memory	The email address of the account, the invited email address, and the name of the downloaded file and its storing path
Registry	In addition to TypedURL, the following keys were pointing to pcloud.com: • HKEY_CURRENT_USER\Software\Microsoft\Internet Explorer\LowRegistry\DOMStorage\my.pcloud.com • HKEY_CURRENT_USER\Software\Microsoft\Internet Explorer\LowRegistry\DOMStorage\pcloud.com • HKEY_CURRENT_USER\Software\Microsoft\Internet Explorer\LowRegistry\DOMStorage\www.pcloud.com • HKEY_USERS\S-1-5-21-1335463704-3291414260-3134846049-1001\Software\Microsoft\Internet Explorer\LowRegistry\DOMStorage\my.pcloud.com • HKEY_USERS\S-1-5-21-1335463704-3291414260-3134846049-1001\Software\Microsoft\Internet Explorer\LowRegistry\DOMStorage\pcloud.com • HKEY_USERS\S-1-5-21-1335463704-3291414260-3134846049-1001\Software\Microsoft\Internet Explorer\LowRegistry\DOMStorage\www.pcloud.com
Browser related files	Visited pCloud's webpages with the date and the UTC time of browsing in WebCacheV01.data The email address of the invited person in %LocalAppData%\Microsoft\Windows\INetCache\Low\IE\O0RJ133M\listshares[1].json (see Fig. 21) The email address of the account in the below files: • %LocalAppData%\Microsoft\Windows\INetCache\Low\IE\[Random Name]\userinfo[1].json and userinfo[2].json • %LocalAppData%\Microsoft\Internet Explorer\Recovery\Last Active\{3B7526CF-70B3-11E4-9719-000C29B56A39}.dat Browsed uploaded filenames in the following file with the date and the time of creation and modification: • %LocalAppData%\Microsoft\Windows\INetCache\Low\IE\[Random Name]\listfolder[1].json Several js and json files located in the above path as well as the below files were pointing to pcloud.com: • %LocalAppData%\Microsoft\Windows\INetCookies\Low\ZY2FBEQ8.txt • %LocalAppData%\Microsoft\Windows\WebCache\V01.log • %UserProfile%\NTUSER.DAT and ntuser.dat.LOG1
MFT and the unallocated space	The "pcloud.com" and the email address of the account with the date of registration (see Fig. 22)

TABLE 22 Recovered Artifacts Associated With Downloading From pCloud Using Fx

Location	Recovered Artifacts
Network traffics	IP addresses 74.120.8.6, 74.120.8.7, 74.120.8.12, 74.120.8.15, 74.120.8.86, and 74.120.8.144 on 443, and IP address 74.120.8.15 on port 80. We also determined that communications with cloudfront.net were established on IP addresses 54.230.26.16, 54.230.26.91, 54.230.229.182, and 54.230.229.204 on port 443
Memory	The name of the downloaded file along with its storing path, the email address of the account, account creation date and time, the shared folder, its recipient and access permissions, and the date and the time of sharing (see Fig. 23)
Browser related files	Visited pCloud's URLs with the date and the UTC time of browsing in cookies. sqlite and places.sqlite located in %AppData%\Mozilla\Firefox\Profiles\ [Random Name].default\ The name of the downloaded file in places.sqlite and its moz_annos table The email address of the account, the shared folder name, access permissions, and the recipient in some files located in %LocalAppData%\Mozilla\Firefox\ Profiles\[Random Name].default\cache2\entries\[RandomFolderName]\ and %LocalAppData%Mozilla\Firefox\Profiles\[Random Name].default\cache2\ trash14488\
MFT, NTFS log, and pagefile.sys	pcloud.com and the name of the downloaded files and its saving path
Link files	%AppData%\Microsoft\Windows\Recent\archivedwl-740.lnk pointing to a downloaded archive that contained all sample files
Unallocated space	The email address of the account with the date of account registration, the names of downloaded files, the shared folder names, access permissions, and their recipients
Other files	The names of downloaded files in: • %AppData%\Microsoft\Windows\Recent\ CustomDestinations\6824f4a902c78fbd.customDestinations-ms. • %LocalAppData%\Microsoft\Windows\WebCache\ WebCacheV01.dat and V0100036.log • %SystemDrive%\$Extend\$UsnJrnl:$J • %UserProfile%\ NTUSER.DAT, ntuser.dat.LOG1, and ntuser.dat.LOG2 • %ProgramData%\Microsoft\Search\Data\Applications\Windows\ GatherLogs\SystemIndex\SystemIndex.3.gthr Also pcloud.com was seen in two mum files located in %SystemDrive%\$OrphanFiles\

TABLE 23   Recovered Artifacts Associated With Downloading From pCloud Using GC

Location	Recovered Artifacts
Network traffics	IP addresses 74.120.8.6, 74.120.8.7, 74.120.8.13, 74.120.8.14, 74.120.8.15, 74.120.8.86, and 74.120.8.144 on 443 were identified as pCloud servers' IPs. Connections to 74.120.8.14 were made on port 80, and communications established with cloudfront.net took place via IP addresses 54.230.26.21 and 54.230.26.96 on port 443
Memory	The name of the downloaded file and its storing path, the email address of the account, the password of the account, the creation date and time of the account, the name of the shared folder, the recipient of the shared folder, permissions, and the date and the time of sharing
Browser related files	History and Cookies files contained information about visited pCloud's webpages with the date and the UTC time of browsing The name of the downloaded file in History History Provider Cache, Cookies-journal, Shortcuts, History-journal, Top Sites, Top Sites-journal, Favicons, Favicons-journal, Preferences, Current Tabs, and Current Session, all located in %LocalAppData%\Google\Chrome\User Data\Default were pointing to pcloud.com The email address of the account and the invited email addresses in %LocalAppData\Local\Google\Chrome\User Data\Default\Cache\data_1
MFT and NTFS log	The name of the downloaded file
Other files	The name of the downloaded file in $Extend\$UsnJrnl:$J

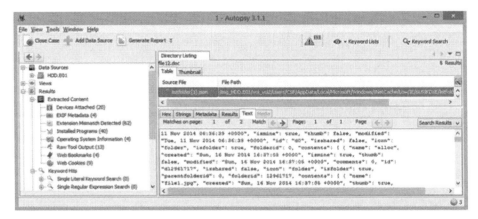

FIG. 21   The invited email address in a json file.

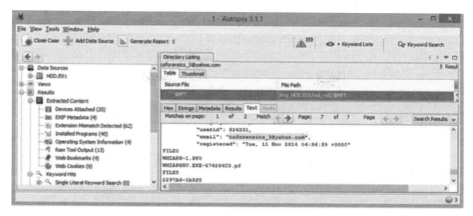

FIG. 22   Account email with the date of registration.

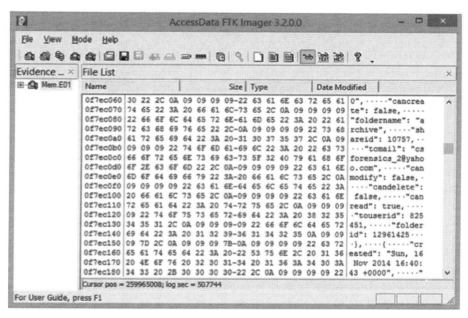

FIG. 23   The email address of the account with the date of registration.

different name and MD5 hash. Due to the lack of collected data, we were not able to draw a conclusion regarding the integrity verification in pCloud's mobile application.

6 CONCLUSION AND FUTURE WORK

In this research, we located and described various artifacts of forensic when SpiderOak, JustCloud, and pCloud were used with IE, Fx, and GC browsers, client application, and mobile application on Windows machines and iOS devices. The recovered artifacts include email addresses, the ID, and the name of the created account and the name of the uploaded and downloaded files. Our findings also suggested that user's credentials could be recovered from memory, and the checksums of sample files after being downloading from investigated CSSPs remained identical to the original. However, we noted that none of the investigated CSSPs could prevent the timestamp and the ADS of files from being changed. Our findings also indicated that metadata of the doc file examined in this study was not altered which could be another piece of useful information in forensic investigation.

Future work would extending our work to examining machines running Linux and other less popular operation systems.

References

[1] P. Mell, T. Grance, The NIST Definition of Cloud Computing Recommendations of the National Institute of Standards and Technology, The National Institute of Standards and Technology, U.S Department of Commerce, 2011, http://nvlpubs.nist.gov/nistpubs/Legacy/SP/nistspecialpublication800-145.pdf.

[2] M. Damshenas, A. Dehghantanha, R. Mahmoud, S. bin Shamsuddin, Forensics investigation challenges in cloud computing environments, in: 2012 International Conference on Cyber Security, Cyber Warfare and Digital Forensic (CyberSec), 2012, pp. 190–194. http://dx.doi.org/10.1109/CyberSec.2012.6246092.

[3] The National Institute of Standards and Technology, NIST Cloud Computing Forensic Science Challenges (Draft), 2014, http://safegov.org/media/72648/nist{_}digital{_}forensics{_}draft{_}8006.pdf.

[4] A. Aminnezhad, A. Dehghantanha, M.T. Abdullah, M. Damshenas, Cloud forensics issues and opportunities. Int. J. Inf. Process. Manage. 4 (4) (2013) 76–85. http://dx.doi.org/10.4156/ijipm.vol4.issue4.9.

[5] M. Damshenas, A. Dehghantanha, R. Mahmoud, S. Shamsuddin, Cloud computing and conflicts with digital forensic investigation. Int. J. Digit. Content Technol. Appl. 7 (9) (2014) 543–553. http://dx.doi.org/10.4156/jdcta.vol7.issue9.65.

[6] F. Daryabar, A. Dehghantanha, A review on impacts of cloud computing and digital forensics, Int. J. Cyber-Sec. Digit. Forensics 3 (4) (2014) 183–199. Society of Digital Information and Wireless Communications (SDIWC).

[7] G. Hogben, M. Dekker, Procure secure: A guide to monitoring of security service levels in cloud contracts, European Union Agency for Network and Information Security, 2012.

[8] C. Hooper, B. Martini, K.-K.R. Choo, Cloud computing and its implications for cybercrime investigations in Australia. Comp. Law Sec. Rev. 29 (2) (2013) 152–163. http://dx.doi.org/10.1016/j.clsr.2013.01.006.

[9] D. Quick, B. Martini, K.-K.R. Choo, Cloud Storage Forensics, Syngress, Cambridge, MA, 2013.

[10] M. Damshenas, A. Dehghantanha, R. Mahmoud, A survey on malware propagation, analysis and detection, Int. J. Cyber-Sec. Digit. Forensics 2 (4) (2013) 10–29.

[11] F. Daryabar, H.G.B. Ali Dehghantanha, Investigation of malware defence and detection techniques, Int. J. Digit. Inf. Wireless Commun. 1 (3) (2011) 645–650.

[12] A. Aminnezhad, M.T.A. Ali Dehghantanha, A survey on privacy issues in digital forensics, Int. J. Cyber-Sec. Digit. Forensics 1 (4) (2012) 311–323. Retrieved from http://sdiwc.net/digital-library/a-survey-on-privacy-issues-in-digital-forensics, .

[13] F. Daryabar, A. Dehghantanha, N.I. Udzir, N. Fazlida, A survey on privacy impacts of digital investigation, J. Next Gener. Inf. Technol. 4 (8) (2013) 57–68.

[14] A. Dehghantanha, K. Franke, Privacy-respecting digital investigation, in: 2014 Twelfth Annual International Conference on Privacy, Security and Trust, 2014, pp. 129–138. http://dx.doi.org/10.1109/PST.2014.6890932.

[15] B. Martini, K.-K.R. Choo, Cloud forensic technical challenges and solutions: a snapshot. IEEE Cloud Comput. 1 (4) (2014) 20–25. http://dx.doi.org/10.1109/MCC.2014.69.

[16] H. Chung, J. Park, S. Lee, C. Kang, Digital forensic investigation of cloud storage services. Digit. Investig. 9 (2) (2012) 81–95. http://dx.doi.org/10.1016/j.diin.2012.05.015.

[17] G. Grispos, W.B. Glisson, T. Storer, Using smartphones as a proxy for forensic evidence contained in cloud storage services, in: 46th Hawaii Int'l Conf. System Sciences (HICSS), 2013, pp. 4910–4919.

[18] C. Federici, Cloud Data Imager: a unified answer to remote acquisition of cloud storage areas. Digit. Investig. 11 (1) (2014) 30–42. http://dx.doi.org/10.1016/j.diin.2014.02.002.

[19] B. Martini, K.-K.R. Choo, Cloud storage forensics: ownCloud as a case study. Digit. Investig. 10 (4) (2013) 287–299. http://dx.doi.org/10.1016/j.diin.2013.08.005.

[20] J.S. Hale, Amazon cloud drive forensic analysis, Digit. Investig. 10 (3) (2013) 259–265.

[21] B. Martini, Q. Do, K.-K.R. Choo, Mobile cloud forensics: an analysis of seven popular android apps, in: R. Ko, K.-K.R. Choo (Eds.), Cloud Security Ecosystem, Syngress, Cambridge, MA, 2015, pp. 309–345.

[22] F. Marturana, G. Me, S. Tacconi, A case study on digital forensics in the cloud, in: 2012 International Conference on Cyber-Enabled Distributed Computing and Knowledge Discovery (CyberC), 2012, pp. 111–116. http://dx.doi.org/10.1109/CyberC.2012.26.

[23] K. Oestreicher, A forensically robust method for acquisition of iCloud data, Digit. Investig. 11 (2014) S106–S113. http://dx.doi.org/10.1016/j.diin.2014.05.006.

[24] D. Quick, K.-K.R. Choo, Data reduction and data mining framework for digital forensic evidence: storage, intelligence, review, and archive, Trends Issues Crime Crim. Justice 480 (2014) 1–11, http://www.aic.gov.au/media_library/publications/tandi_pdf/tandi480.pdf.

[25] D. Quick, K.-K.R. Choo, Google Drive: forensic analysis of data remnants. J. Netw. Comput. Appl. 40 (2014) 179–193. http://dx.doi.org/10.1016/j.jnca.2013.09.016.

[26] D. Quick, K.-K.R. Choo, Dropbox analysis: data remnants on user machines. Digit. Investig. 10 (1) (2013) 3–18. http://dx.doi.org/10.1016/j.diin.2013.02.003.

[27] D. Quick, K.-K.R. Choo, Digital droplets: Microsoft SkyDrive forensic data remnants, Futur. Gener. Comput. Syst. 29 (6) (2013) 1378–1394. http://dx.doi.org/10.1016/j.future.2013.02.001.

[28] D. Quick, K.-K.R. Choo, Forensic collection of cloud storage data: does the act of collection result in changes to the data or its metadata? Digit. Investig. 10 (3) (2013) 266–277. http://dx.doi.org/10.1016/j.diin.2013.07.001.

[29] M. Shariati, A. Dehghantanha, B. Martini, K.-K.R. Choo, Ubuntu one investigation: detecting evidences on client machines, in: K.-K.R. Choo, R. Ko (Eds.), Cloud Security Ecosystem, Syngress, Cambridge, MA, 2015, pp. 429–446.

[30] B. Blakeley, C. Cooney, A. Dehghantanha, R. Aspin, Cloud storage forensic: hubiC as a case-study, in: 2015 IEEE 7th International Conference on Cloud Computing Technology and Science (CloudCom), 2015, pp. 536–541. http://dx.doi.org/10.1109/CloudCom.2015.24.

[31] M. Shariati, A. Dehghantanha, K.-K.R. Choo, SugarSync forensic analysis, Aust. J. Forensic Sci. 48 (1) (2016) 95–117. http://dx.doi.org/10.1080/00450618.2015.1021379.

[32] F. Daryabar, A. Dehghantanha, K.-K.R. Choo, Cloud storage forensics: MEGA as a case study. Aust. J. Forensic Sci. (2016) http://dx.doi.org/10.1080/00450618.2016.1153714.

[33] F. Daryabar, A. Dehghantanha, B. Eterovic-Soric, K.-K.R. Choo, Forensic investigation of OneDrive, Box, GoogleDrive and Dropbox applications on Android and iOS devices. Aust. J. Forensic Sci. (2016) 1–28, http://dx.doi.org/10.1080/00450618.2015.1110620.

[34] C. Cho, S. Chin, K.S. Chung, Cyber forensic for Hadoop based cloud system, Int. J. Sec. Appl. 6 (3) (2012) 83–90.

[35] J. Dykstra, A.T. Sherman, Acquiring forensic evidence from infrastructure-as-a-service cloud computing: exploring and evaluating tools, trust, and techniques, Digit. Investig. 9 (2012) S90–S98. http://dx.doi.org/10.1016/j.diin.2012.05.001.

[36] B. Martini, K.-K.R. Choo, Remote programmatic vCloud forensics: a six-step collection process and a proof of concept, in: 2014 IEEE 13th International Conference on Trust, Security and Privacy in Computing and Communications, 2014, pp. 935–942. http://dx.doi.org/10.1109/TrustCom.2014.124.

[37] B. Martini, K.-K.R. Choo, Distributed filesystem forensics: XtreemFS as a case study, Digit. Investig. 11 (4) (2014) 295–313. http://dx.doi.org/10.1016/j.diin.2014.08.002.

[38] Z. Zafarullah, F. Anwar, Z. Anwar, Digital forensics for Eucalyptus, in: Proceedings of the 2011 Frontiers of Information Technology (FIT 11), 2011, pp. 110–116.

[39] K.-K.R. Choo, Organized crime groups in cyberspace: a typology, Trends Organ. Crime 11 (3) (2008) 270–295.

[40] K.-K.R. Choo, R.G. Smith, Criminal exploitation of online systems by organized crime groups, Trends Organ. Crime 11 (3) (2008) 270–295.

[41] Net Applications, Mobile/tablet operating system market share, 2014. Available online at: https://www.net-marketshare.com/operating-system-market-share.aspx?qprid=8&qpcustomd=1 (accessed 30 June 16).

[42] Desktop operating system market share, 2014. Available online at: https://www.netmarketshare.com/operating-system-market-share.aspx?qprid=10&qpcustomd=0 (accessed 30 June 16).

[43] J. Williams, ACPO good practice guide for digital evidence, Association of Chief Police Officers, 2012.

[44] B. Martini, K.-K.R. Choo, An integrated conceptual digital forensic framework for cloud computing, Digit. Investig. 9 (2) (2012) 71–80. http://dx.doi.org/10.1016/j.diin.2012.07.001.

[45] N. Thethi, A. Keane, Digital forensics investigations in the cloud, in: Proceedings of the International Advanced Computing Conference (IACC 14), 2014, pp. 1475–1480.

[46] K. Kent, S. Chevalier, T. Grance, H. Dang, Guide to integrating forensic techniques into incident response, in: Technical Report, NIST, Gaithersburg, MD, 2006.

[47] VMware Inc., VMware Workstation 5.5. What files make up a virtual machine? VMware Inc. Available online at: https://www.vmware.com/support/ws55/doc/ws_learning_files_in_a_vm.html, 2016 (accessed 30 June 16).

[48] B. Carrier, Digital forensics tool testing image (#8), 2004. Available online at: http://dftt.sourceforge.net/test8/index.html (accessed 30 July 16).

[49] B. Malmström, P. Teveldal, Forensic Analysis of the ESE Database in Internet Explorer 10, Halmstad University, Halmstad, 2013.

[50] C. Wilson, DCode Date, Free Digital Forensic Tools, Available online: http://www.digital-detective.net/digital-forensic-software/free-tools/, 2016 (accessed 30 July 16).

Residual Cloud Forensics: CloudMe and 360Yunpan as Case Studies

A. Dehghantanha*, T. Dargahi†

*University of Salford, Salford, United Kingdom †Islamic Azad University, Tehran, Iran

1 INTRODUCTION

The use of cloud computing in the information and communications technologies (ICT) sector has become a main trend in recent years. Cloud services come in three models, software as a service (SaaS), platform as a service (PaaS), and infrastructure as a service (IaaS) [1, 2]: SaaS is often presented as a subscription-based model and has a multitenant environment, where various clients (such as web browser, desktop clients, mobile devices) can access its applications through the Internet. PaaS is provided as a platform that allows users to develop and deploy customized applications. IaaS is a self-service model where clients are allowed to set up an infrastructure and run any software they prefer [3].

The ever increasing interest in using cloud storage services raises several security and privacy issues [4–8]. Therefore there is an exponential growth in demand for a forensic investigative study of the existing cloud platforms [9] in order to discover data remnants of forensic value on client devices [10–15]. However, since processing of digital data in cloud computing systems varies from one provider to another, the acquisition and analysis of digital evidence is different within different platforms and cloud storage providers [14]. As mentioned by Taylor et al. [3], the dynamic nature of data processed in the cloud raises the issue of having a proper method for data seizure in order to conduct an accurate investigation.

Most of the cloud forensics relevant academic publications focus on the issues and challenges faced by digital forensics practitioners and the digital forensic framework for conducting forensic investigations in the cloud environment, with only a few publications that emphasize the technical side of cloud forensics. Cloud forensic academic literature that studies the technical perspective often focuses on the forensic analysis on the server-side. The reason for the lack of technical-focused papers might be the highly restrictive access permissions to conduct server analysis in the datacenters of cloud service providers. It is only during recent years that more papers are beginning to adopt cloud forensics framework, which was used to conduct a forensic identification, preservation, and extraction of data in various cloud services on the client-side. Among them are ownCloud [16, 17], Microsoft SkyDrive [8, 18, 19], Google Drive [8, 18, 20–23], Dropbox [8, 17, 18, 20, 23–25], SugarSync [24, 26], to name a few. In Table 1, we present a summary of the investigated cloud platforms in the literature, categorized by the type of cloud services, ie, SaaS, and IaaS, that are forensically investigated.

In this research study we carry out a forensic investigation on two cloud storage platforms, ie, *CloudMe* [27], and *360Yunpan* [28], considering several file operations, such as upload, access, and download. CloudMe [27] is a European cloud service, which is owned by *CloudMe AB* company, founded in 2012. It offers secured cloud storage, file synchronization, and client software for managing cloud data across various client devices, including GoogleTV and Samsung Smart TV.

360Yunpan [28] is a China-based cloud service. A distinguishing feature of 360Yunpan is its huge storage capacity, ie, 36 TB free of charge space for its users. The free huge storage space of the cloud could be a good motivation for performing criminal activities.

1.1 Contribution

Considering CloudMe and 360Yunpan as case studies, we answer the following research questions:

1. What kind of data could be recovered after using CloudMe and 360Yunpan on Windows 8.1, Android KitKat 4.4.2, and Apple iOS 8.0?
2. What kind of data could be recovered after accessing CloudMe and 360Yunpan through web-browsers: Internet Explorer (IE), Google Chrome (GC), and Mozilla Firefox (MF)?
3. What forensic artifacts could be recovered after analyzing the network traffic and capturing the live memory?
4. What data remains on Windows 8.1, Android KitKat 4.4.2, and Apple iOS 8.0 after using inbuilt apps?
5. Are the MD5 of the files downloaded during the acquisition process identical to original files? If no, what are the changes?
6. Is the timestamp information remaining the same during the process of upload, storage, and download from cloud storage?

We believe that our experimental results will help the forensic investigators to better understand the potential artifacts that could be found on the client side of the aforementioned two cloud services.

2 RESEARCH METHODOLOGY

In order to conduct our experiments, we adopted the cloud forensics framework proposed by Martini and Choo [40] (Fig. 1), which is based on NIST [41] and McKemmish [42] frameworks. In this section we explain the adoption of the framework in this research: the steps of the framework, as well as the process used to conduct the research.

The first step of the framework is *Commence (scope)*, in which we outline the scope of the experiments. The focus of this study is to identify the data remnants that are locatable after performing the following actions: *upload*, *access*, *download*, and *delete* by using the cloud service through *web browser* or the *client software*. We carried out our experiments using three different web browsers: *Microsoft Internet Explorer*, *Google Chrome*, and *Mozilla Firefox*. Moreover, we targeted the following data remnants: username, password, file names, date and time, or the presence of client software, as well as the indication of cloud services. Furthermore, we captured and analyzed memory as an important source of evidence, as well as network traffic.

The second step of the framework is *Prepare*, in which we set up the virtual environments to answer the research questions, which are explained in Section 1.1. We took advantage of virtual environments due to the lack of physical hardware devices. Besides, in terms of memory capturing, adopting virtual environment is easier, as we can perform memory capture by copying the files in "VMEM" format when the VM is running. Moreover, in terms of network traffic capturing, the use of a virtual environment is more convenient, as it can be done by running "Wireshark" on the host machine to monitor and capture the network traffic on the virtual machine.

The third step of the framework is *Identify and Collect*, in which we recognize the files that contain the required information to conduct the analysis. We consider the following files: virtual hard drives (VMDK) of each VM folder, the memory instances (VMEM files), and network capture file (PCAP) as well.

The fourth step is *Preserve (forensic copy)*. In digital forensic acquisition and analysis, the potential digital evidences should be obtained in a forensically sound manner. Therefore a forensic copy of each of the required files should be acquired using a forensically sound tool, such as "HashCalc" to calculate the hash values in MD5 to ensure the integrity of the data.

The next step of the framework is *Analyze*, in which the analysis of the obtained data is carried out. We performed this step utilizing a set of forensic analysis tools, including (but not limited to) "Process Monitor 3.05," "Regshot 1.9.0," "Nirsoft Web Browser PassView 1.4.3," and "Hex Workshop 6.8" (detailed information about the adopted tools are explained in Section 2.1).

The sixth step is *Present*, in which we have to present the evidential data. Generally, the reporting should consist of the information on all processes carried out, the tools and applications used in the investigation and restrictions, if any, to avoid false conclusions.

In the next step, ie, *Feedback*, the important information discovered in the experiments should be shared with the IT community to allow the forensics practitioners to locate the required information and to find out the security issues. Besides, it is also important to report the issues and improvements faced during the examinations, in order to provide a guideline for future examinations.

Finally, the last step of the framework is *Complete*, which concludes the investigation results.

2.1 Experimental Setup

We carried out our experiments considering four settings on different operating systems (OS): (a) Windows browser-based, (b) Windows app-based, (c) Android app-based, and (d) iOS app-based. Table 2 provides detailed information of the considered cloud services and operating systems.

We carried out our experiments using the Enron Email Dataset[1] (the August 21, 2009 Version, which we downloaded on the 17th November 2014) and performed four operations

---

[1] https://www.cs.cmu.edu/~./enron/

TABLE 1 A Brief Overview of the Existing Cloud Storage Forensics Research Studies

Cloud Services	SaaS											IaaS										Amazon
	Google				Amazon	Amazon Cloud	Amazon															
References	Dropbox	Drive	SkyDrive	Box	S3	Drive	AWS	OneDrive	ownCloud	Flicker	PicasaWeb	iCloud	UbuntuOne	hubiC	Mega	Evernote	SugarSync	Hadoop	vCloud	XtreemFS	Eucalyptus	EC2
Daryabar et al. [23]	✓	✓	–	✓	–	–	–	✓	–	–	–	–	–	–	–	–	–	–	–	–	–	–
Shariati et al. [26]	–	–	–	–	–	–	–	–	–	–	–	–	–	–	✓	–	✓	–	–	–	–	–
Daryabar et al. [29]	–	–	–	–	–	–	–	–	–	–	–	–	–	–	–	–	–	–	–	–	–	–
Quick et al. [19]	–	–	✓	–	–	–	–	–	–	–	–	–	–	–	–	–	–	–	–	–	–	–
Chung et al. [20]	✓	✓	–	–	✓	–	–	–	–	–	–	–	–	–	–	✓	–	–	–	–	–	–
Federici et al. [18]	✓	✓	✓	–	–	–	–	–	–	–	–	–	–	–	–	–	–	–	–	–	–	–
Grispos et al. [24]	✓	–	–	✓	–	–	–	–	–	–	–	–	–	–	–	–	✓	–	–	–	–	–
Martini et al. [17]	✓	✓	–	–	–	–	–	✓	✓	–	–	–	–	–	–	–	✓	–	–	–	–	–
Marturana et al. [21]	–	–	–	–	–	–	–	–	–	✓	✓	–	–	–	–	–	✓	–	–	–	–	–
Quick et al. [25]	✓	–	–	–	–	–	–	–	–	–	–	–	–	–	–	–	–	–	–	–	–	–
Quick et al. [8]	✓	✓	✓	–	–	–	–	–	–	–	–	–	–	–	–	–	–	–	–	–	–	–
Quick et al. [22]	–	✓	–	–	–	–	–	–	–	–	–	–	–	–	–	–	–	–	–	–	–	–
Hale et al. [30]	–	–	–	–	–	✓	–	–	–	–	–	–	–	–	–	–	–	–	–	–	–	–
Oestreicher [31]	–	–	–	–	–	–	–	–	–	–	–	✓	–	–	–	–	–	–	–	–	–	–
Martini et al. [32]	–	–	–	–	–	–	–	–	–	–	–	–	–	–	–	–	–	–	✓	–	–	–
Martini et al. [33]	–	–	–	–	–	–	–	–	–	–	–	–	–	–	–	–	–	–	–	✓	–	–
Marty [34]	–	–	–	–	–	–	✓	–	–	–	–	–	–	–	–	–	–	–	–	–	–	–
Dykstra et al.[35]	–	–	–	–	–	–	–	–	–	–	–	–	–	–	–	–	–	–	–	–	–	✓
Cho et al.[36]	–	–	–	–	–	–	–	–	–	–	–	–	–	–	–	–	–	✓	–	–	–	–
Blakeley et al.[37]	–	–	–	–	–	–	–	–	–	–	–	–	–	✓	–	–	–	–	–	–	–	–
Anwar et al.[38]	–	–	–	–	–	–	–	–	–	–	–	–	–	–	–	–	–	–	–	–	✓	–
Shariati et al.[39]	–	–	–	–	–	–	–	–	–	–	–	–	✓	–	–	–	–	–	–	–	✓	–

(✓), analyzed; (–) not analyzed.

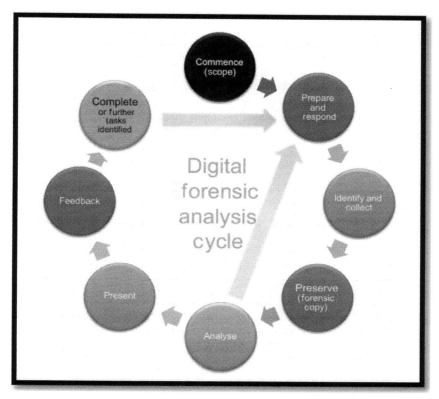

FIG. 1 Adopted cloud forensics framework [40].

TABLE 2 List of Considered Cloud Services and Operating Systems

Cloud Service	Operating System	Version
CloudMe (3 GB)	Windows 8.1	1.8.8
	Android KitKat 4.4.2	1.7.2
	Apple iOS 8.0	1.8.4
YunPan (36 TB)	Windows 8.1	6.0.1.1090
	Android KitKat 4.4.2	6.0.11
	Apple iOS 8.0	4.1.0

on each of the platforms: upload, download, open, and delete. We carried out the operations using the following files:

- `arora_savedmail.rar`,
- `arora_savedmail.docx`,
- `arora_savedmail.txt`,

– `arora_savedmail.rtf`,
– `arora_savedmail.jpg`.

We applied MD5 algorithm on the files of the dataset, using "Hash Calc version 2.02" in order to track down the originality of the files before and after the operations. Moreover, we used VMware Workstation 10.0, in order to build the virtual machines (VMs) needed for the experiments. We created a VMs for Windows 8.1 64 bit, which we used in both Windows-based experiments, having the following specification: one CPU, 1-GB RAM, and 20-GB virtual hard disk. Table 3 depicts the software configuration for Windows-based experiments.

TABLE 3 Initial Environment Configuration for Windows-Based Experiments

Setting	Tools	Version
Windows browser-based	Nirsoft web browser PassView	1.4.3
	Nirsoft IE cache viewer	1.5.3
	Nirsoft Mozilla cache viewer	1.66
	Nirsoft Chrome cache viewer	1.61
	Internet Explorer	11
	Mozilla Firefox	33.0
	Google Chrome	39.0.2171.65
Windows app-based	Regshot	1.9.0
	Process Monitor	3.05

In order to conduct the experiments on Android, we installed a ported version of Android KitKat 4.4.2 ISO image on VMware Workstation 10 with the following configuration: one CPU, 1-GB internal memory, and 15-GB internal storage.

For the experiments of iOS platform, we utilized an iPad Mini 2 version 8.0. The adopted tools are: "iPhone Backup Browser version 1.2.0.6", and "Hex Workshop version 6.8". The credentials set up for the experiments are listed in Table 4.

TABLE 4 Credentials Used During the Experiments

Credentials	Descriptions
Virtual Machine	Full name: AliceName AliceFamily
	User name: Alice
	Password: A@12345
Cloud Service	
CloudMe	User name: Bob25775
	Password: B@12345
360YunPan	User name: Bob25775@gmail.com
	Password: B@12345

2.1.1 Windows 8.1 Client Application Based

We installed Windows 8.1 in a VMware workstation, without any extra applications. We carried out three operations on the could services: upload, download, and delete. We did not perform open operation, because the dataset is available offline for the user. Besides, we performed installation and uninstallation of the client app. The set up for the experiments are as shown in Fig. 2.

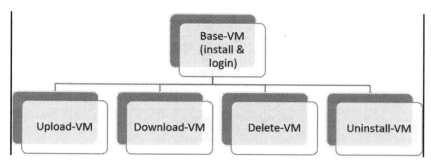

FIG. 2   Set up for Windows client application based experiments.

2.2 Windows 8.1 Browser Based

We installed the three most popular web browsers, ie, Microsoft Internet Explorer (IE), Google Chrome (GC), and Mozilla Firefox (MF) on the VMs. The operations carried out in the VMs for browser-based cloud usage are upload, open, download, and delete as shown in Fig. 3.

The browser remnant files are considered as one of the sources of evidence that could be identified easily when a user is accessing the cloud services via online interface. Therefore, we investigated the browser cache. The tools that can be utilized for extracting the browser caches are "Nirsoft Cache Viewer" for IE, GC, and MF. Besides that, in order to recover the username and password used for the cloud services, we used "Nirsoft Web Browser Passview" [43].

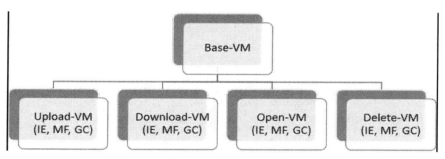

FIG. 3   Set up for Windows browser based experiments.

2.3 Android KitKat 4.4.2 Client Application Based

We adopted a virtual machine VMware Workstation 10 with an Android KitKat 4.4.2 operating system installed, to conduct our experiments on Android. The ported Android operating system is rooted by default; therefore we could directly conduct the experiments. The main focus of the evidence source was the internal memory and network traffic, as it was not possible for us to use the VMDK file for analysis. The experiments stages are shown in Fig. 4.

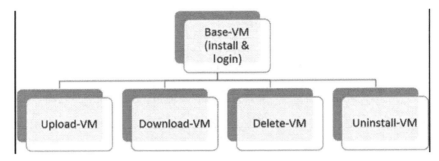

FIG. 4   Set up for Android application based experiments.

2.4 Apple iOS 8.0 Client Application Based

We used an iPad Mini 2 running iOS 8.0, to conduct the iOS experiments. We downloaded the cloud services app used in the experiments from Apple Store: "CloudMe", and "360 YunPan HD" apps. We carried out upload, open, download, and delete operations as shown in Fig. 5. During the experiments, we also installed and uninstalled the applications to identify if there is any additional sources of evidential data. In order to identify the sources of evidence in iOS, we used iTunes to back up the device. We used a forensically sound tool for iOS forensic, named "iPhone Backup Browser," to investigate the backup files. Moreover, iOS does not support uploading files, other than photos, directly using the device. Therefore, the upload operation for CloudMe is done with the help of Dropbox, while the upload for 360Yunpan is done using the web browser, as there is no upload option available.

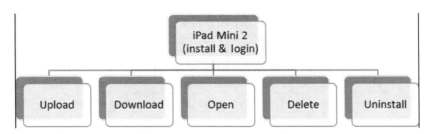

FIG. 5   Set up for iOS client application based experiments.

3 RESULTS AND DISCUSSION

This section presents the evidence identification and preservation methods used in the experiments. Moreover, we provide the findings of the experiment, which are the residual forensic artifacts that were generated and left in the client devices during the installation and uninstallation of client-side application. We performed three file operations (upload, download, delete) in four different settings (Windows 8.1 client application-based, Windows 8.1 browser-based, Android KitKat 4.4.2, and Apple iOS 8.0). The collected findings will then be followed with an analysis and a presentation of the summary of findings.

3.1 Evidence Source Identification and Preservation

Before utilizing the datasets in the experiment, we applied hash algorithm using "HashCalc 2.02" on all the five dataset files. This is to ensure that the integrity of the datasets can later be verified after the experiment and to check if the original content of the datasets were altered during the file operations.

We analyzed the evidences separately for each experiment setup using a range of forensic tools. For Windows 8.1 client application- and browser-based experiments, we took snapshots of the virtual machine. We could analyze the .vmem (virtual live memory) and .vmdk (virtual hard disk) files using "AccessData FTK Imager 5.5" and "Hex Workshop 6.8.0.5419", respectively. The analysis of the live memory is conducted in "Hex Workshop" by using search keywords, such as the cloud storage provider name (CloudMe, or 360Yunpan), user credentials (Bob25775, B@12345), and dataset filenames (arora_savedmail). This also applies to the experiments running on Android KitKat 4.4.2 virtual machine.

During the installation, uninstallation, and file operations, we captured the network traffic using "Wireshark 1.12.1" running on the host machine. We analyzed the captured .pcap files, using "Wireshark" adopting custom filters and keyword searches.

Other forensic tools that we used are: "Process Monitor version 3.1" for monitoring registry changes in the Windows 8.1 client-application experiment; "SQLite DB Browser 3.4.0" for viewing .db files; "RegRipper 2.8" for analyzing registry files extracted from the Windows 8.1 .vmdk files; "PList Explorer version 1.0" for viewing and analyzing Apple iOS 8.0 backup files. We recorded the timestamps of each of the datasets before proceeding with the upload to the cloud storage, which will later be verified with the timestamps recorded after sync and download. It should be noted that the modified time usually remains the same before upload, after upload, and after download unless there is a difference in the device's local time. The MAC timestamps for the datasets used in the file operations of each cloud service running on different platforms recorded and presented in Section 3.3.

3.2 Evidence Collection

Evidence collections for research experiments that are running on virtual machine such as Windows 8.1 app-based, Windows 8.1 browser-based, and Android KitKat 4.4.2 app-based have similar evidence collection methods. For every operation conducted on the virtual machine, the running virtual machine is taken as a snapshot in VMware Workstation 10 to preserve the data in virtual live memory and the virtual hard disk. At the same time, the network traffic is captured using "Wireshark 1.12.1" for analysis. All the collected evidences then hashed using "HashCalc 2.02" to generate their MD5 file hashes as a precaution to verify if there were alterations made on the evidence after analysis. These evidences are analyzed in the host machine using the forensic tools that are mentioned in Section 3.1.

For the Apple iOS 8.0 app-based research experiment, there was a limitation in the collection of evidence. Due to the newness of the operating system (at the time of experiments), there were no jailbreaking solution for it. Therefore it was impossible for us to achieve root and gather more evidence. The alternative solution was to utilize the in-built backup feature that comes with Apple devices. Using iTunes as backup solution, we were able to create something similar to a snapshot, which can be accessed online and analyzed later.

3.3 Examination and Analysis

In this section we present the findings of our analysis on CloudMe, and 360Yunpan running on Windows 8.1 (client application-based and web browser-based), Android KitKat 4.4.2, and Apple iOS 8.0.

3.3.1 Cloud Service: CloudMe

In this section we report our findings on CloudMe in several sections based on the underlying platforms.

WINDOWS 8.1—CLIENT APPLICATION BASED

CloudMe 1.8.8 is a SaaS cloud storage service, for which the client application could be located on the user's hard disk. Users are given the option to selectively sync files instead of CloudMe synching all the files in the local folder. Therefore the experiments for CloudMe includes an extra operation for sync. The installation of CloudMe 1.8.8 client application for Windows creates directories in several locations:

- `\ProgramFiles (x86)\CloudMe\CloudMe` which is executable file for starting CloudMe
- `\% USERPROFILE % \Documents\Cloudme` which is the local CloudMe folder
- `\% LOCALAPPDATA % \CloudMe` which stores user-specific sync and file management metadata

CloudMe stores user-specific sync and file management data such as sync logs, cache database, and other user details and configurations. Analysis on the CloudMe folder in local app data found a text log `2014-11-23.txt` containing login information of the user as shown in Fig. 6.

```
2014-11-23 12:04:30: LOGIN->SSLSUPP: true  host:  "https://os.cloudme.com/v1/"
2014-11-23 12:04:33: Logged in as: "bob25775"
2014-11-23 12:04:33: 1.8.3 or older, clean document table.
```

FIG. 6 Login information of the user in the `2014-11-23.txt` file.

Other files such as `cache.db` contains more forensically valuable data as it includes the multiple SQL tables including "user_ table" that stores user details as shown in Fig. 7, as well as "syncfolder_ document_ table" that indexes files synched and stored in the users CloudMe storage. The "user_ table" stores the unique userID, username, and device name including the time of creation of the CloudMe client application.

Examination of the Windows 8.1 live memory shows CloudMe leaves traces of user information such as user ID, username, user first name and last name, and last login time as

	user_id	username	devicename	schedule_daily	:hedule_time_ind:	chedule_day_inde	use_scheduler	created	speed_limit_type
	Filter	Filter	Filter	Filter	Filter	Filter	Filter	Filter	Filter
1	12886014603	bob25775	win8-testdownl...	0	0	0	true	2014-11-30 02:3...	MAX

FIG. 7 "user_ table" stores CloudMe user details.

shown in Fig. 8. Other useful forensic artifacts include traces of file synchronization, which is found during the upload of sample dataset into CloudMe cloud storage. CloudMe also leaves traces in the live memory during download operation when users log into their CloudMe account on a new client device. The files from the CloudMe account are synched into the local CloudMe folder as shown in Fig. 9.

```
02A266E5  6D 6C 6E 73 3A 78 63 72 3D 22 74 74 70 3A 2F 2F 78 63 65 72 69 6F   mlns:xcr="http://xcerio
02A266FC  6E 2E 63 6F 6D 2F 78 63 52 65 70 6F 73 69 74 6F 72 79 2E 78 73 64 22   n.com/xcRepository.xsd"
02A26713  3E 0A 3C 75     65        69       3E  32        38     30     34   30 73 3C   >.<userid>12886014603</
02A2672A        73     72     64 4                       61 60 65       62        35   userid><username>bob25
02A26741        35 3C 2F 4E 73                  61 65          3C 66 69 72 73 74 6E 61 6D 65   75</username><firstname
02A26758  3E 42 6F 62 4E 61 6D 65 3C 2F 66 69 72 73 74 6E 61 6D 65 3E 3C 6C 61   >BobName</firstname><la
02A2676F  73 74 6E 61 6D 65 3E 42 6F 62 46 61 6D 69 6C 79 3C 2F 6C 61 73 74 6E   stname>BobFamily</lastn
02A26786  61 6D 65 3E 3C 6C 6F 63 61 6C 65 3E 65 6E 5F 55 53 3C 2F 6C 6F 63 61   ame><locale>en_US</loca
02A2679D  6C 65 3C 2F 6C 61 73 74 6C 6F 67 69 6E 3E 32 30 31 34 2D 31 31 2D 31   le><lastlogin>2014-11-1
02A267B4  32 54 30 31 3A 33 31 3A 32 32 5A 3C 2F 6C 61 73 74 6C 6F 67 69 6E 3E   2T01:31:22Z</lastlogin>
```

FIG. 8 CloudMe user details found in live memory.

```
16BAFC68  78 74 22 20 20 0A 73 65 6E 64 52 65 71 75 65 73 74 3A 20 72 65 71 75   xt" .sendRequest: requ
16BAFC7F  65 73 74 2D 6E 61 6D 65 3A 20 20 22 61 72 6F 72 61 5F 73 61 76 65 64   est-name: "arora_saved
16BAFC96  6D 61 69 6C 2E 74 78 74 22 20 20 7C 20 72 65 71 75 65 73 74 2D 74 79   mail.txt" | request-ty
16BAFCAD  70 65 3A 20 20 22 31 22 20 20 0A 61 64 64 46 69 6C 65 45 6E 74 72 79   pe: "1" .addFileEntry
16BAFCC4  54 6F 50 61 72 65 6E 74 3A 20 20 22               61 65       35   ToParent: "arora_saved
16BAFCDB        61 69 6C 2E 74 78 74 20 20 0A          6C     75     4D     52 71   mail.txt" .CloudMeRequ
16BAFCF2        73     3A 20 20 64 6F 77 6E 6C          20 20 3A 20 48 6F 73   est: "download" : Hos
16BAFD09  74 2D 3E 20 22 68 74 74 70 73 3A 2F 2F 38 33 2E 31 34 30 2E 32 34 31   t-> "https://83.140.241
16BAFD20  2E 31 30 2F 76 31 2F 22 20 20 0A 53 74 61 72 74 20 64 6F 77 6E 6C 6F   .10/v1/" .Start downlo
16BAFD37  61 64 3A 20 20 22 43 3A 2F 55 73 65 72 73 2F 41 6C 69 63 65 2F 44 6F   ad: "C:/Users/Alice/Do
16BAFD4E  63 75 6D 65 6E 74 73 2F 43 6C 6F 75 64 4D 65 2F 61 72 6F 72 61 5F 73   cuments/CloudMe/arora_s
16BAFD65  61 76 65 64 6D 61 69 6C 2E 74 78 74 22 20 20 0A 44 6F 77 6E 6C 6F 61   avedmail.txt" .Downloa
```

FIG. 9 Data remnants showing files downloaded during sync to local CloudMe folder.

The network traffic between the local client application and CloudMe cloud storage was also captured when the file operations were conducted in CloudMe. CloudMe uses TLSv1.2 [Transport Level Security version 2] to encrypt the connection between the client-app and remote cloud service. Hence, we were not able to read the data from the network streams. However, we could find out the SSL certificate used by CloudMe; which is StartCom Class 3 issued by StartCom Ltd as shown in Fig. 10. Uninstallation of the client application removes the local root folder, but leaves the configuration files containing sync log which has no valuable data, and cache.db which only contains user CloudMe account details.

Table 5 shows the timestamps for DOCX and JPG captured before uploading (first row) and upon downloading (second row), and sync (third row). The MAC timestamps for upload and sync matches, whereas the timestamps for download varies for some of the file types. We suspect that CloudMe may be sensitive to file types during the file operations.

WINDOWS 8.1—WEB BROWSER BASED

In what follows we demonstrate our findings separated by the performed actions.

```
StartCom Ltd.1+0)..U..."Secure Digital Certificate Signing1806..U.../StartCom Class 3
Primary Intermediate Server CA0..
140506121946Z.
170506184817Z0..1.0...U.
..kXxfOo3K1579JXr81.0....SE1.0...U...
Ostergotlands1.0...U....Link.ping1.0...U.

CloudMe AB1.0...U...
*.cloudme.com1.0...*.H..
.....da@xcerion.com0.."0
..*.H...
..........0..
..........0.6..wy..................!.......k...J?....k..u...(2..d)P.......k..,./.Y9.........
[........-..|..F.~..)...Uz"%........-...v~.i!..-.........H.j........"...|...j...
9..?.O;........).'.T".@vb0lU......,....;.........ul.....Cv..4,.......-......=.J......
a...........0...0...U....0.0...U..........0...U.%..0...+..........
+........0...U........Q..............s.).0...U.#..0.....B..b...2.+A>{.\..K0%..U...0..
*.cloudme.com..cloudme.com0..V..U. ...M0..I0...g.....0..;..+......7...0..*0..
+........"http://www.startssl.com/policy.pdf0....+.......0..0'.StartCom Certification
Authority0.......This certificate was issued according to the Class 3 validation
requirements of the StartCom CA policy, reliance only for the intended purpose in
compliance of the relying party obligations.05..U...0,0*.(.&.$http://crl.startssl.com/
crt3-crl.crl0....+.......0..09..+......0..-http://ocsp.startssl.com/sub/class3/server/
ca08..+.....0..6http://aia.startssl.com/certs/
sub.class3.server.ca.crt0#..U....0...http://www.startssl.com/0
                                 *.H
```

FIG. 10   Network stream showing certifcate used by CloudMe.

UPLOAD—LIVE MEMORY/BROWSER CACHE   We could discover the action of uploading files ("syncUpload") in the memory as shown in Fig. 11. The only critical information found in the browsers caches is the URL address of "www.cloudme.com" located with "bob25775," which we believe to be the username of the cloud service (Fig. 12).

OPEN/VIEW—LIVE MEMORY   We could recover the filename along with the cloud service URL address identified from the memory of the machine. We found "exportwriter.zoho.com" in the memory, which we believe has been used to preview the document.

DOWNLOAD—LIVE MEMORY/BROWSER CACHE   We were not able to find out any obvious evidence showing the download action for CloudMe. However, there were records of the filename discovered as part of the URL address in the memory as shown in Fig. 13. Analyzing the browsers' cache, we discovered files along with the file size, the last accessed time, as well as the URL address showing the cloud service CloudMe as part of it (Fig. 14).

DELETE—LIVE MEMORY   The deletion of files in CloudMe cloud service is identified by the action "action=\removeEntry\" followed by the filename as displayed in Fig. 15.

ANDROID KITKAT 4.4.2—CLIENT APPLICATION BASED

We downloaded CloudMe 1.7.2 for Android from Google Play. The installation of CloudMe creates a directory to store user configuration files: /storage/emulated/0/Android/data.com.xcerion.android. CloudMe leaves traces of user credentials of both client device and cloud service account on the client device internal memory as shown in Fig. 16.

TABLE 5 Timestamp and MD5 of Original, Sync, and Downloaded Files

	MD5	Created	Modified	Accessed
docx	4d16f5b7e1d5f8ea195bd87a600c6815	11/30/2014 (01:44:45)	11/17/2014 (14:15:45)	11/30/2014 (01:44:45)
	4d16f5b7e1d5f8ea195bd87a600c6815	11/30/2014 (01:44:45)	11/17/2014 (14:15:44)	11/30/2014 (01:44:45)
	4d16f5b7e1d5f8ea195bd87a600c6815	11/30/2014 (01:35:32)	11/30/2014 (01:35:32)	11/30/2014 (02:31:04)
jpg	7f5ce91bb949b29c8d2deefaeb999d0f	11/30/2014 (01:44:48)	11/17/2014 (00:24:40)	11/30/2014 (01:44:48)
	7f5ce91bb949b29c8d2deefaeb999d0f	11/30/2014 (01:44:48)	11/17/2014 (00:24:40)	11/30/2014 (01:44:48)
	7f5ce91bb949b29c8d2deefaeb999d0f	11/30/2014 (01:36:41)	11/30/2014 (01:36:43)	11/30/2014 (02:32:52)
rar	f90f08cb35307de7b5b44e1c3ffd1445	11/30/2014 (01:44:50)	11/17/2014 (14:33:20)	11/30/2014 (01:44:50)
	f90f08cb35307de7b5b44e1c3ffd1445	11/30/2014 (01:44:50)	11/17/2014 (14:33:20)	11/30/2014 (01:44:50)
	f90f08cb35307de7b5b44e1c3ffd1445	11/30/2014 (01:41:44)	11/30/2014 (01:41:44)	11/30/2014 (02:32:58)
rtf	7f5ce91bb949b29c8d2deefaeb999d0f	11/30/2014 (01:44:50)	11/17/2014 (14:19:54)	11/30/2014 (01:44:50)
	7f5ce91bb949b29c8d2deefaeb999d0f	11/30/2014 (01:44:48)	11/17/2014 (00:24:40)	11/30/2014 (01:44:48)
	7f5ce91bb949b29c8d2deefaeb999d0f	11/30/2014 (01:59:49)	11/30/2014 (01:59:49)	11/30/2014 (02:33:07)
txt	83d78201914c892021290de6185f375c	11/30/2014 (01:44:51)	11/17/2014 (14:12:42)	11/30/2014 (01:44:51)
	83d78201914c892021290de6185f375c	11/30/2014 (01:44:51)	11/17/2014 (14:12:42)	11/30/2014 (01:44:51)
	83d78201914c892021290de6185f375c	11/30/2014 (01:44:51)	11/30/2014 (02:12:42)	11/30/2014 (02:33:09)

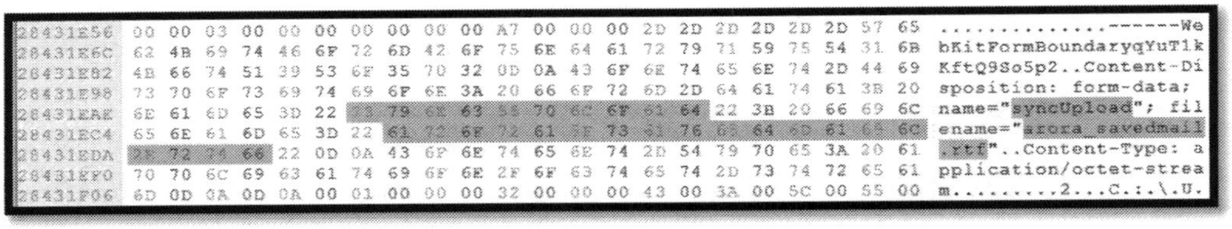

```
28431E56  00 00 03 00 00 00 00 00 00 00 A7 00 00 00 2D 2D 2D 2D 2D 2D 57 65  ..............------We
28431E6C  62 4B 69 74 46 6F 72 6D 42 6F 75 6E 64 61 72 79 71 59 75 54 31 6B  bKitFormBoundaryqYuT1k
28431E82  4B 66 74 51 39 53 6F 35 70 32 0D 0A 43 6F 6E 74 65 6E 74 2D 44 69  KftQ9So5p2..Content-Di
28431E98  73 70 6F 73 69 74 69 6F 6E 3A 20 66 6F 72 6D 2D 64 61 74 61 3B 20  sposition: form-data;
28431EAE  6E 61 6D 65 3D 22 73 79 6E 63 55 70 6C 6F 61 64 22 3B 20 66 69 6C  name="syncUpload"; fil
28431EC4  65 6E 61 6D 65 3D 22 61 72 6F 72 61 5F 73 61 76 65 64 6D 61 69 6C  ename="arora_savedmail
28431EDA  2E 72 74 66 22 0D 0A 43 6F 6E 74 65 6E 74 2D 54 79 70 65 3A 20 61  .rtf"..Content-Type: a
28431EF0  70 70 6C 69 63 61 74 69 6F 6E 2F 6F 63 74 65 74 2D 73 74 72 65 61  pplication/octet-strea
28431F06  6D 0D 0A 0D 0A 00 01 00 00 00 32 00 00 00 43 00 3A 00 5C 00 55 00  m.........2...C.:.\.U.
```

FIG. 11 The result of "filename" keyword searched.

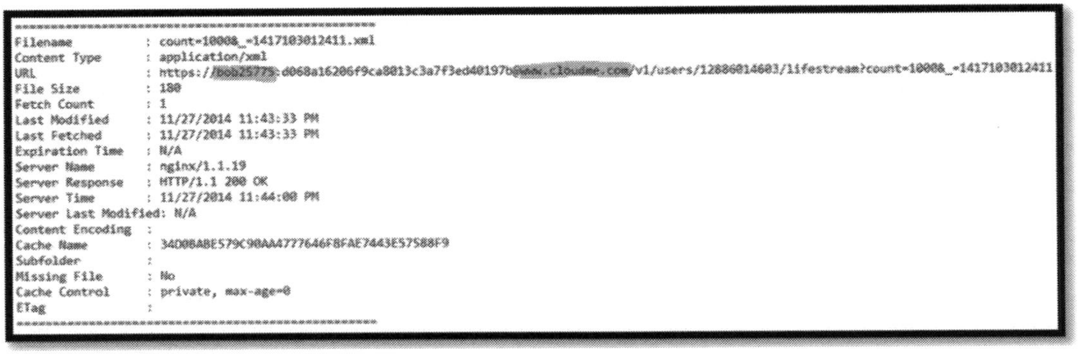

```
==================================================
Filename          : count=1000&_=1417103012411.xml
Content Type      : application/xml
URL               : https://bob25779:d068a16206f9ca8013c3a7f3ed40197b@www.cloudme.com/v1/users/12886014603/lifestream?count=1000&_=1417103012411
File Size         : 180
Fetch Count       : 1
Last Modified     : 11/27/2014 11:43:33 PM
Last Fetched      : 11/27/2014 11:43:33 PM
Expiration Time   : N/A
Server Name       : nginx/1.1.19
Server Response   : HTTP/1.1 200 OK
Server Time       : 11/27/2014 11:44:00 PM
Server Last Modified: N/A
Content Encoding  :
Cache Name        : 34D08ABE579C90AA4777646F8FAE7443E57588F9
Subfolder         :
Missing File      : No
Cache Control     : private, max-age=0
ETag              :
==================================================
```

FIG. 12 Browser cache showing cloud service provider as well as username.

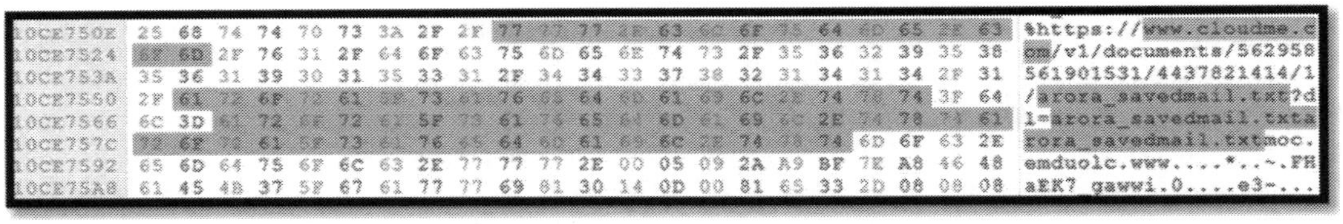

```
10CE750E  25 68 74 74 70 73 3A 2F 2F 77 77 77 2E 63 6C 6F 75 64 6D 65 2E 63  %https://www.cloudme.c
10CE7524  6F 6D 2F 76 31 2F 64 6F 63 75 6D 65 6E 74 73 2F 35 36 32 39 35 38  om/v1/documents/562958
10CE753A  35 36 31 39 30 31 35 33 31 2F 34 34 33 37 38 32 31 34 31 34 2F 31  561901531/4437821414/1
10CE7550  2F 61 72 6F 72 61 5F 73 61 76 65 64 6D 61 69 6C 2E 74 78 74 3F 64  /arora_savedmail.txt?d
10CE7566  6C 3D 61 72 6F 72 61 5F 73 61 76 65 64 6D 61 69 6C 2E 74 78 74 61  l=arora_savedmail.txta
10CE757C  72 6F 72 61 5F 73 61 76 65 64 6D 61 69 6C 2E 74 78 74 6D 6F 63 2E  rora_savedmail.txtmoc.
10CE7592  65 6D 64 75 6F 6C 63 2E 77 77 77 2E 00 05 09 2A A9 BF 7E A8 46 48  emduolc.www....*..~.FH
10CE75A8  61 45 4B 37 5F 67 61 77 77 69 81 30 14 0D 00 81 65 33 2D 08 08 08  aEK7_gawwi.0....e3-...
```

FIG. 13 Filename discovered within the memory along with cloud service provider.

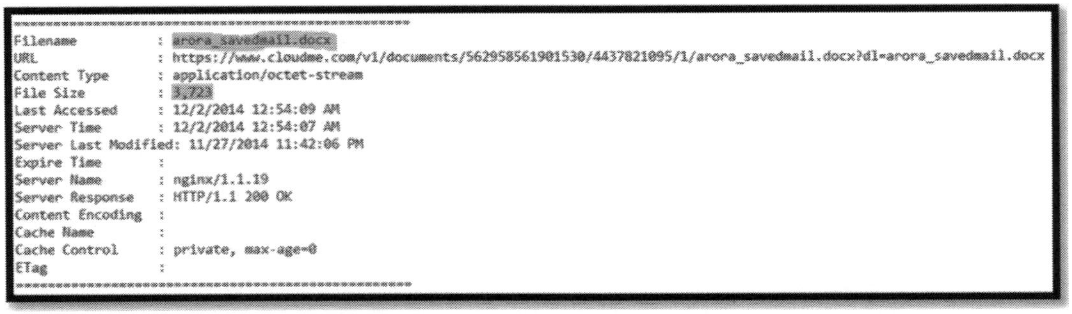

```
==================================================
Filename          : arora_savedmail.docx
URL               : https://www.cloudme.com/v1/documents/562958561901530/4437821095/1/arora_savedmail.docx?dl=arora_savedmail.docx
Content Type      : application/octet-stream
File Size         : 3,723
Last Accessed     : 12/2/2014 12:54:09 AM
Server Time       : 12/2/2014 12:54:07 AM
Server Last Modified: 11/27/2014 11:42:06 PM
Expire Time       :
Server Name       : nginx/1.1.19
Server Response   : HTTP/1.1 200 OK
Content Encoding  :
Cache Name        :
Cache Control     : private, max-age=0
ETag              :
==================================================
```

FIG. 14 Result of browser cache showing filename and other information.

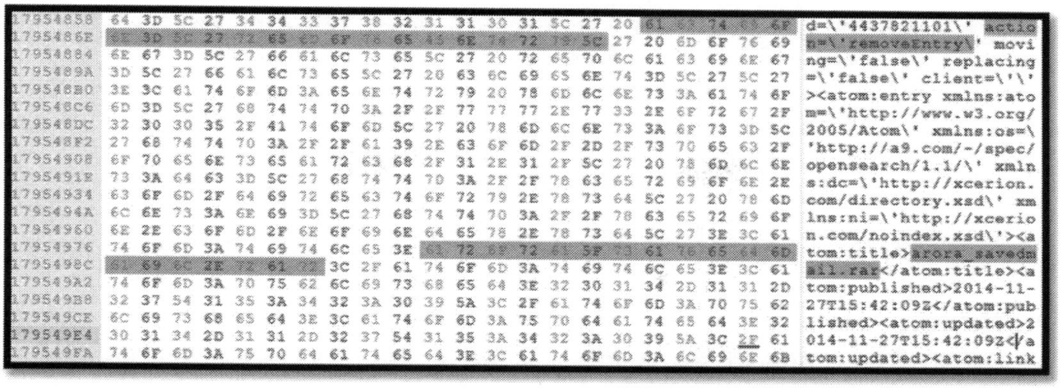

FIG. 15   Result of memory showing deletion of file.

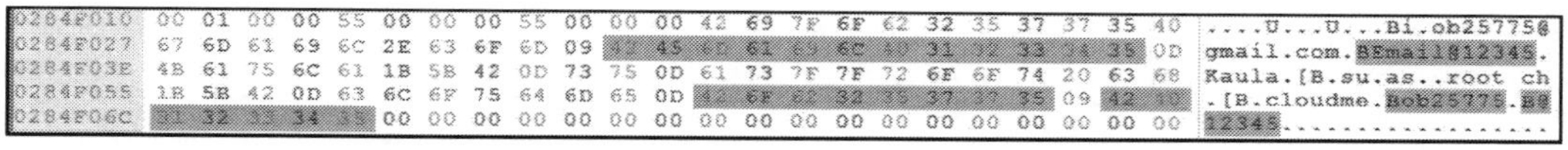

FIG. 16   User credentials for client device and CloudMe account are found in internal memory.

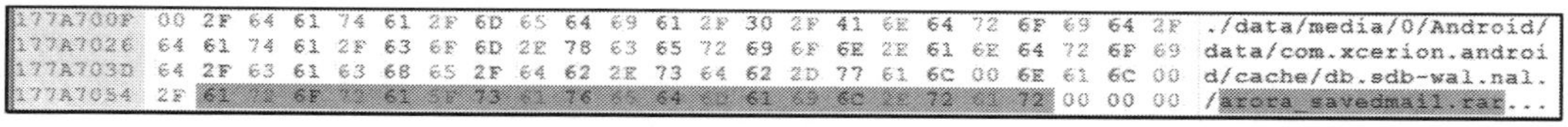

FIG. 17   Filename found in local CloudMe cache.

Searching the internal memory by dataset filenames shows that the internal memory contains traces of upload, download, and delete activity in CloudMe. Fig. 17 shows the files that are stored in the local CloudMe cache folder on the client device. We could not find evidence of the actual download activity in the internal memory. However, the downloaded files are found in the default Android download folder. As for file deletion activity, the keyword search "delete" shows a chunk of data in the internal memory that indicates the presence of file being deleted as shown in Fig. 18.

During the experiments, we captured the network traffic using "Wireshark 1.12.1" during the file operations. Analysis of pcap files show that CloudMe uses the same SSL encryption as the PC-app version for Android mobile version, which is StartCom. Further analysis using keyword search only returned results with traces of CloudMe account username and device type but no other user account data (Fig. 19).

The downloading of dataset files from CloudMe storage into the client device did not leave any traces of activity as no filename or metadata are found. However, some of the file contents are recoverable from the network streams such as the RTF and TXT files (Fig. 20). Uninstallation of CloudMe mobile client application did not leave traces in the internal memory and network.

```
20692077 32 33 36 34 20 34 30 39 36 0A 2F 73 74 6F 72 61 67 65 2F 65 6D 75 6C  2364 4096./storage/emul
2069208E 61 74 65 64 2F 30 2F 44 6F 77 6E 6C 6F 61 64 2F 61 72 6F 72 61 5F 73  ated/0/Download/arora_s
206920A5 61 76 65 64 6D 61 69 6C 2E 6A 70 67 2E 6A 70 67 20 33 34 38 33 35 32  avedmail.jpg.jpg 348352
206920BC 20 36 38 38 20 38 31 62 30 20 30 20 31 30 32 38 20 31 34 20 33 30 39   688 81b0 0 1028 14 309
206920D3 31 30 33 39 36 31 36 20 31 20 30 20 30 20 31 34 31 38 30 31 32 33 37  1039616 1 0 0 141801237
206920EA 32 20 31 34 31 38 30 31 32 33 37 31 20 31 34 31 38 30 31 32 33 37 31  2 1418012371 1418012371
20692101 20 34 30 39 36 0A 2F 73 74 6F 72 61 67 65 2F 65 6D 75 6C 61 74 65 64   4096./storage/emulated
20692118 2F 30 2F 44 6F 77 6E 6C 6F 61 64 2F 61 72 6F 72 61 5F 73 61 76 65 64  /0/Download/arora_saved
2069212F 6D 61 69 6C 2E 72 61 72 20 33 31 37 32 32 33 20 36 32 34 20 38 31 62  mail.rar 317223 624 81b
20692146 30 20 30 20 31 30 32 38 20 31 34 20 33 30 39 31 30 33 39 39 32 30 20  0 0 1028 14 3091039920
2069215D 31 20 30 20 30 20 31 34 31 38 30 31 32 33 39 32 20 31 34 31 38 30 31  1 0 0 1418012392 141801
20692174 32 33 39 38 20 31 34 31 38 30 31 32 33 39 38 20 34 30 39 36 0A 2F 73  2398 1418012398 4096./s
2069218B 74 6F 72 61 67 65 2F 65 6D 75 6C 61 74 65 64 2F 30 2F 44 6F 77 6E 6C  torage/emulated/0/Downl
206921A2 6F 61 64 2F 61 72 6F 72 61 5F 73 61 76 65 64 6D 61 69 6C 2E 72 74 66  oad/arora_savedmail.rtf
206921B9 20 35 39 32 31 20 31 36 20 38 31 62 30 20 30 20 31 30 32 38 20 31 34   5921 16 81b0 0 1028 14
206921D0 20 33 30 39 31 30 34 30 30 33 32 20 31 20 30 20 30 20 31 34 31 38 30   3091040032 1 0 0 14180
206921E7 31 32 34 30 31 20 31 34 31 38 30 31 32 34 30 31 20 31 34 31 38 30 31  12401 1418012401 141801
206921FE 32 34 30 31 20 34 30 39 36 0A 2F 73 74 6F 72 61 67 65 2F 65 6D 75 6C  2401 4096./storage/emul
20692215 61 74 65 64 2F 30 2F 44 6F 77 6E 6C 6F 61 64 2F 61 72 6F 72 61 5F 73  ated/0/Download/arora_s
2069222C 61 76 65 64 6D 61 69 6C 2E 74 78 74 20 31 34 32 33 20 38 20 38 31 62  avedmail.txt 1423 8 81b
```

FIG. 18 Dataset files residing in Download folder.

```
GET /v1/documents/562958562113864/4438344026/1 HTTP/1.1
Host: os.cloudme.com:80
Connection: Keep-Alive
User-Agent: CloudMe 1.7.2 (VMware Virtual Platform; Android 4.4.2; en_US)
Authorization: Digest username="bob25775", realm="os@xcerion.com",
nonce="EV7MSLAhnUnxH5MsIxELF4jjrfE=", uri="/v1/
documents/562958562113864/4438344026/1", response="249cfd8fa9e0a89e6ed4395d26f75282",
qop=auth, nc=00000001, cnonce="7e94327fdebd45dab95953a8c14e8d66", algorithm="MD5"
```

FIG. 19 Network stream extracted.

```
Message-ID: <5661256.1075859175761.JavaMail.evans@thyme>
Date: Mon, 23 Apr 2001 06:52:01 -0700 (PDT)
From: paul.schiavone@enron.com
To: harry.arora@enron.com, steve.wang@enron.com, robert.stalford@enron.com,
.hai.chen@enron.com
Subject: Homer City Info.
Mime-Version: 1.0
Content-Type: text/plain; charset=us-ascii
Content-Transfer-Encoding: 7bit
X-From: Schiavone, Paul </O=ENRON/OU=NA/CN=RECIPIENTS/CN=PSCHIAVO>
X-To: Arora, Harry </O=ENRON/OU=NA/CN=RECIPIENTS/CN=Harora>, Wang, Steve </O=ENRON/
OU=NA/CN=RECIPIENTS/CN=Swang3>, Stalford, Robert </O=ENRON/OU=NA/CN=RECIPIENTS/
CN=Notesaddr/cn=4411df41-44f2b565-8625690a-7419e9>, Chen, Hai </O=ENRON/OU=NA/
CN=RECIPIENTS/CN=Notesaddr/cn=e57648ec-75e3c6ec-86256965-5469d0>
X-cc:
X-bcc:
X-Folder: \Harry_Arora_Jan2002\Arora, Harry\Inbox\Saved Mail
X-Origin: Arora-H
X-FileName: harora (Non-Privileged).pst

WHAT WE KNOW:

1. Purchased by Edison Mission Energy in March 1999 for 1.8 billion from GPU and NGE
Generation.
.
2. Total generation capacity = 1,884 MW (3 coal fired turbines)
.
3. One of the largest and lowest cost sources of power in the Mid-Atlantic
.
4. Only major coal-fired facility in region with direct high voltage access to both
NYPP and PJM
```

FIG. 20 Contents of .txt file of the dataset.

APPLE IOS 8.0—CLIENT APPLICATION BASED

We could identify the appdata of CloudMe as "com.xcerion.icloud.iphone" in the backup files. The evidences for the installation activity of the application are discoverable from the files, namely "Manifest.mdbd", "Manifest.plist", and "Info.plist" (Fig. 21). Whereas we found the login activity evidence from "xcerion.icloud.iphone.plist" (Fig. 22), where the username and first login name are revealed to be "bob25775".

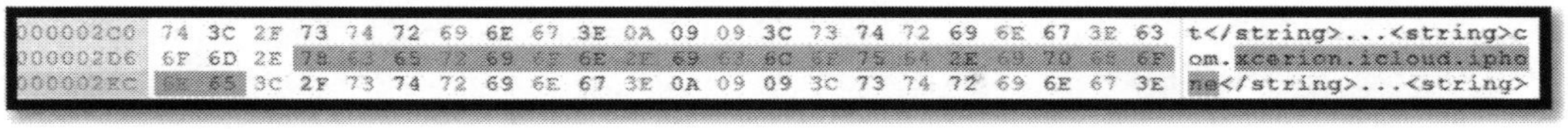

FIG. 21   Result showing installed application in the file of Info.plist.

The upload option in CloudMe of iOS version only allowed the upload of photo. Thus we uploaded the dataset with JPG format. The datasets with file formats RTF and DOCX were the only supported files that could be uploaded to CloudMe by accessing the files using Dropbox and "open with" CloudMe.

We performed the open operation on three of the files. The files that we could discover in the backup being downloaded are: "arora_ savedmail.rtf" and "arora_ savedmail.docx". However, there is no record of the downloaded file with JPG format. The directory of the downloaded files is "Documents/Inbox/[filename]". As for download and delete operations, there is not such options available for CloudMe in iOS platform. We could not discover any appdata for CloudMe after the uninstallation of the application.

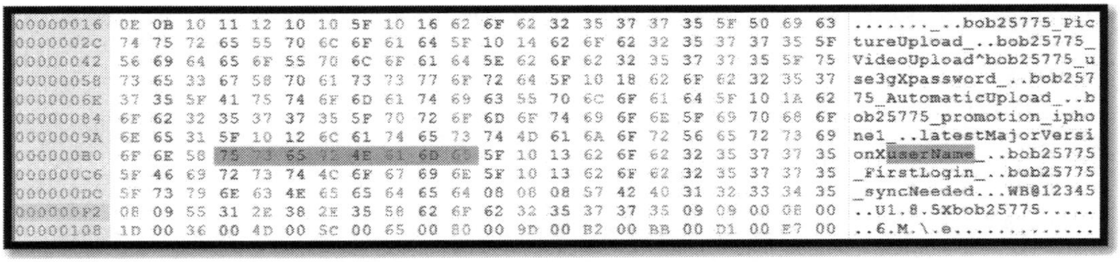

FIG. 22   Result of keyword "username" search within the file of xcerion.icloud.iphone.plist.

Table 6 shows the timestamp of the DOCX and RTF files, as well as JPG file format, which are being uploaded and downloaded during the experiments. When the files are uploaded,

TABLE 6   Timestamps of Original and Downloaded Files

	Created	Modified	Accessed
docx	11/16/2014 (12:05:35)	11/17/2014 (14:15:43)	11/16/2014 (12:05:35)
	11/16/2014 (17:37:49)	11/16/2014 (17:37:49)	
rtf	11/16/2014 (12:05:35)	11/17/2014 (14:19:52)	11/16/2014 (12:05:35)
	11/16/2014 (17:38:13)	11/16/2014 (17:38:13)	
jpg	11/16/2014 (12:05:35)	11/17/2014 (14:24:40)	11/16/2014 (12:05:35)
	11/16/2014 (17:58:47)	11/16/2014 (17:58:47)	

the date modified changed to the date and time being uploaded. Meanwhile, both date created and date modified changed to the downloaded date when the files are being downloaded.

3.3.2 Cloud Service: 360Yunpan

In this section we report our findings on 360Yunpan in several sections, based on the underlying platforms.

WINDOWS 8.1—CLIENT APPLICATION BASED

360Yunpan client application provides users with 36 TB of online storage and it synchronizes all the folders on the user client application without the need to store the files on the users local machine. The installation of 360Yunpan 6.0.1.1090 client application creates a virtual drive on the computer, which allows users to see all their folders and directly manage their content stored on the cloud from any device. However, the virtual drive can only be opened and accessed when the application is running and the user is logged in. The installation of the app also creates a folder named 360CloudUI and 360Login which stores log files, application specific configuration files, and other related files for Yunpan client application. The list of files created during the installation is as follows:

- `\ProgramFiles(x86)\360\360WangPan\360WangPan.exe`
- `\% USERPROFILE% \AppData\Roaming\360CloudUI`
- `\% SERPROFILE% \AppData\Roaming\360Login`

Yunpan client sync metadata information is stored in "`% appdata% \360CloudUI`" directory, which stores a number of files containing sync information in the "log" file format, as well as user and application specific data in the files with "ini" file format. The configuration file shows traces of user specific data. The "LastAccount" directive shows the unique user ID generated by Yunpan during sign up and "CacheRootPath" shows the current directory of configuration files as shown in Fig. 23. In Fig. 24,"http" shows the IP address of the service provider of Yunpan; "cip" is the ip address of local machine; "pwd" directive only shows the encrypted password of the user cloud service credentials when the checkbox is ticked for the client to remember the password during sign in.

```
[setting]
ShowSuspension=0
SuspensionPos_x=1234
SuspensionPos_y=396
CacheRootPath=C:\Users\Alice\AppData\Roaming\360CloudUI
LockHotKeyVCode=220
LockHotKeyFlag=6
loginpage=1
LastAccount=1337960040
LastUserName=Bob25775@gmail.com
LastAvatarImgPath=C:\Users\Alice\AppData\Roaming\360Login\1337960040\bhead.jpg
LastAccountType=1
LastNickName=
LastCookie=
```

FIG. 23   `uiconfig.ini` containing account ID and username.

```
[user]
last_sync_ok=0
name=1337960040
type=0
pwd=
syncpath=C:\Users\Alice\AppData\Roaming\360CloudUI\Cache\1337960040
total_size=11382200205312
used_size=3031215
LastLottery=0
apitime=1417198345
apiindex=0
http=106.38.184.116
apiname=tel
cip=175.136.20.20
```

FIG. 24 `uiconfig.ini` file containing userID, syncpath, and pwd fields.

360Yunpan also generates sync and file metadata during file operations and stores them in the 360CloudUI folder under different configuration files. The sync.log file contains history of the file operations that users have carried out including login as shown in Fig. 25, uploading, and delete (Fig. 26) operations. The logs for downloading were not recorded.

```
[2014-11-20 14:02:09.965] status 0(wait_login) -> 1(logining)

[2014-11-20 14:02:09.965] [req] login

[2014-11-20 14:02:13.715] [stat] command User.login, 3734ms

[2014-11-20 14:02:13.715] [resp] login ok. qid:1337960040, token:2944931753.61.f589fe76.1337960040.1416463334

[2014-11-20 14:02:13.715] status 1(logining) -> 2(login_ok)
```

FIG. 25 `sync.log` showing login activity.

```
[2014-11-29 02:24:17.424] [db] Transaction Begin

[2014-11-29 02:24:17.752] [req] delete \win8 uploads\arora_savedmail.docx

[2014-11-29 02:24:18.443] [resp] success, type:3(del) \win8 uploads\arora_savedmail.docx

[2014-11-29 02:24:18.494] status 5(monitor) -> 6(ok)
```

FIG. 26 `sync.log` showing delete activity.

Analysis on the live memory shows traces of username, userID, and a possible password as shown in Fig. 27. The password string is then analyzed using "Hash Identifier v1.1" to identify the type of hash being used on the password, but the results shows that the hash is unidentifiable. Regardless, there is still potential for further investigation.

The installation of 360Yunpan also made changes to the registry in Windows 8.1. Based on the registry data extracted, 360Yunpan starts up when the system boots and creates traces when user runs the program as shown in Fig. 28.

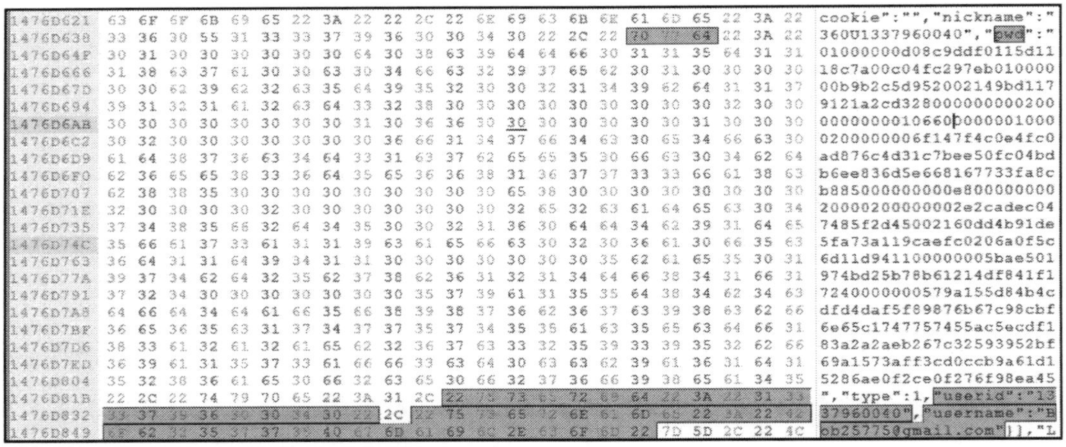

FIG. 27   UserID, username and possible password found in live memory.

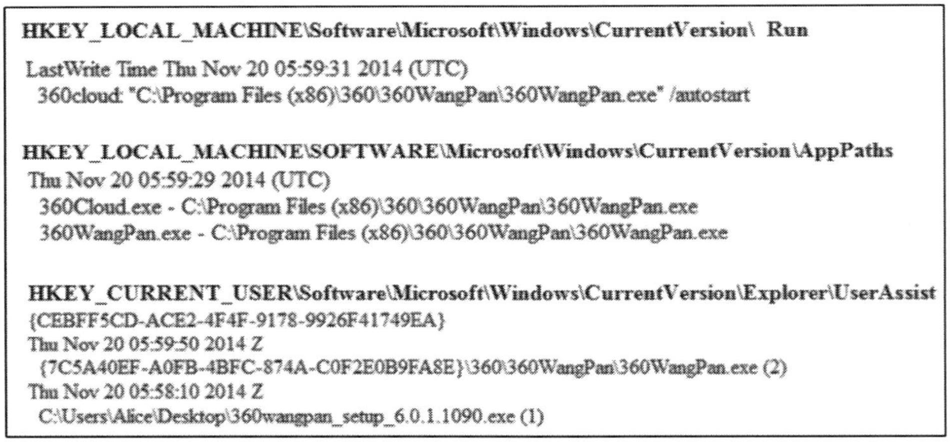

FIG. 28   Changes in registry keys during installation and use of 360Yunpan.

Analysis of the network traffic while performing operations on the files shows that 360Yunpan does not use any secure encryption or issued any certificate from any certificate authority for interactions between the client application and 360Yunpan cloud storage. The only information that could be found about the server-side is that 360Yunpan uses its own server—360server. As such, there were more data remnants gathered during the network traffic capture. Since the connection is not encrypted, using keyword searches, such as userid, username, and dataset filename, returns positive results for sync activity (as shown in Fig. 29). Similar results are obtained for upload, delete, and uninstallation. The upload activity that was captured in the network shows file metadata such as the filename, file size, MD5 hash, creation time, and modification time.

The timestamps for each of the datasets are recorded before uploading and upon downloading in 360Yunpan. The timestamps for each of the dataset before upload and download

```
GET /intf.php?
method=User.getUserDetail&qid=1337960040&devtype=UI&v=6.0.1.1090&devid=f68b775e2be50a44
a3a7ab3adc6782fb&devname=&rtick=7206529375672217 6&sign=068f7b9e1578dafd95f7dc763ea42486
&ofmt=xml&pid=home& HTTP/1.1
Accept: */*
User-Agent: UI/6.0.1.1090
Host: api61.yunpan.360.cn
X-QIHOO-HOST: api61.yunpan.360.cn
Cookie: token=3535409544.61.a25c16bb.1337960040.1416319950;
Accept-Encoding: gzip
Connection: Keep-Alive
Cache-Control: no-cache
```

FIG. 29   TCP stream showing user sync activity after logging in.

are the same. This is due to the virtual nature of the 360Yunpan hard drive, which does not store the files on the local machine and instead directly uploads them into the cloud as shown in Table 7.

WINDOWS 8.1—WEB BROWSER BASED

We adopted "Web Browser PassView" during the analysis of Yunpan cloud service. However, we could only identify the username for Internet Explorer (Fig. 30). In what follows we demonstrate our findings while performing several operations, ie, upload, open/ view, download, delete.

UPLOAD—LIVE MEMORY/BROWSER CACHE   We could find the LoginName in the memory as shown in Fig. 31. We used the keyword "name="files[]"; filename=" to identify the files uploaded. As it can be seen in Fig. 32, we could discover the *filename* along with the method name "upload," meaning that a file with the *filename* has been uploaded to the cloud service. Moreover, we found out that the files with names as highlighted in Fig. 33 have been uploaded to yunpan.360.cn using Chrome version 39.0.2171.65. We found the same evidence for the action of uploading files using Firefox version 33.0 under user "bob25775%2540gmail.com."

Investigating the browsers cache, we could locate the username and encrypted password for Yunpan for all the three browsers in the URL part of the cached address as showed in Fig. 34.

UPLOAD—NETWORK TRAFFIC   Analyzing the network traffic we could identify that the user with login name "bob25775%40gmail.com" has uploaded a file named "arora_savedmail.docx" to yunpan.360.com at 27 Nov 2014 10:27:19 GMT (refer to Fig. 35). Moreover, we could recover the content of the uploaded file in TXT format using Chrome by analyzing the network traffic (as shown in Fig. 36), as well as RTF format. The rest of the file formats, such as DOCX (Fig. 37), and JPG were encrypted, while we could discover several files names in the file of RAR format (Fig. 38), and we believe that they are the archived files. We found same evidences using the browser Firefox.

OPEN/VIEW—LIVE MEMORY/BROWSER CACHE   We could discover the preview of the files in Yunpan easily from the method "method=preview" followed by the filename as shown in Fig. 39. Moreover, the version of web browsers that are used to access yunpan.360.cn to preview the file using "docviewer" is recoverable. Similar to the evidence discovered in memory, the cache of the three of the browsers has captured the URL address with "method=preview" and filename.

TABLE 7 Timestamps and MD5 of Original Files and Downloaded Files

	MD5	Created	Modified	Accessed
docx	4d16f5b7e1d5f8ea195bd87a600c6815	11/17/2014 (14:35:25)	11/17/2014 (14:15:45)	11/17/2014 (14:35:25)
	4d16f5b7e1d5f8ea195bd87a600c6815	11/17/2014 (14:35:25)	11/17/2014 (14:15:45)	11/17/2014 (14:35:25)
jpg	7f5ce91bb949b29c8d2deefaeb999d0f	11/17/2014 (14:35:25)	11/17/2014 (12:24:40)	11/17/2014 (14:35:25)
	7f5ce91bb949b29c8d2deefaeb999d0f	11/17/2014 (14:35:25)	11/17/2014 (12:24:40)	11/17/2014 (14:35:25)
rar	f90f08cb35307de7b5b44e1c3ffd1445	11/17/2014 (14:35:25)	11/17/2014 (14:33:20)	11/17/2014 (14:35:25)
	f90f08cb35307de7b5b44e1c3ffd1445	11/17/2014 (14:35:25)	11/17/2014 (14:33:20)	11/17/2014 (14:35:25)
rtf	97ae2ca81f0a88bb78eacceb22e2964b	11/17/2014 (14:35:25)	11/17/2014 (14:19:54)	11/17/2014 (14:35:25)
	97ae2ca81f0a88bb78eacceb22e2964b	11/17/2014 (14:35:25)	11/17/2014 (14:19:54)	11/17/2014 (14:35:25)
txt	83d78201914c892021290de6185f375c	11/17/2014 (14:35:25)	11/17/2014 (14:12:42)	11/17/2014 (14:35:25)
	83d78201914c892021290de6185f375c	11/17/2014 (14:35:25)	11/17/2014 (14:12:42)	11/17/2014 (14:35:25)

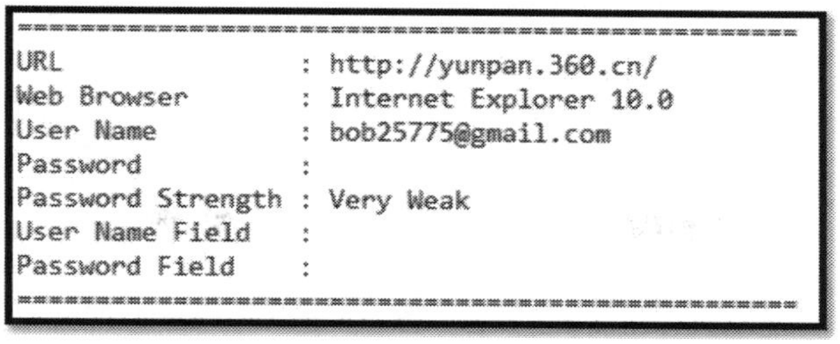

FIG. 30   The result of Web Broswer PassView.

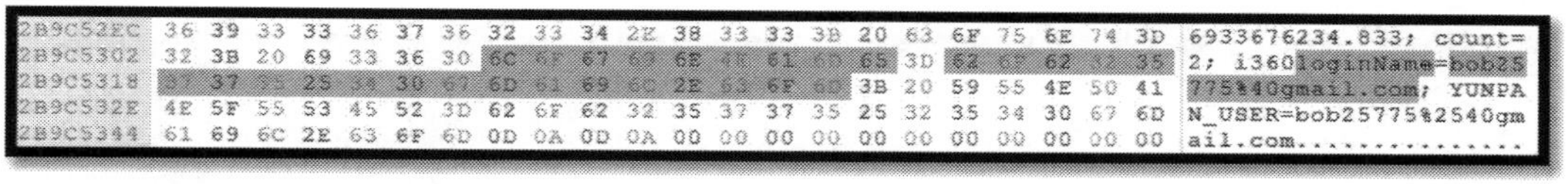

FIG. 31   The result of keyword loginname searched.

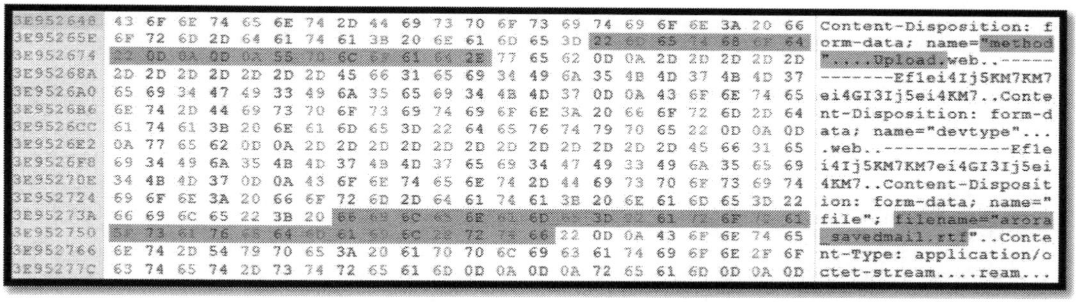

FIG. 32   The result of searching keyword filename=.

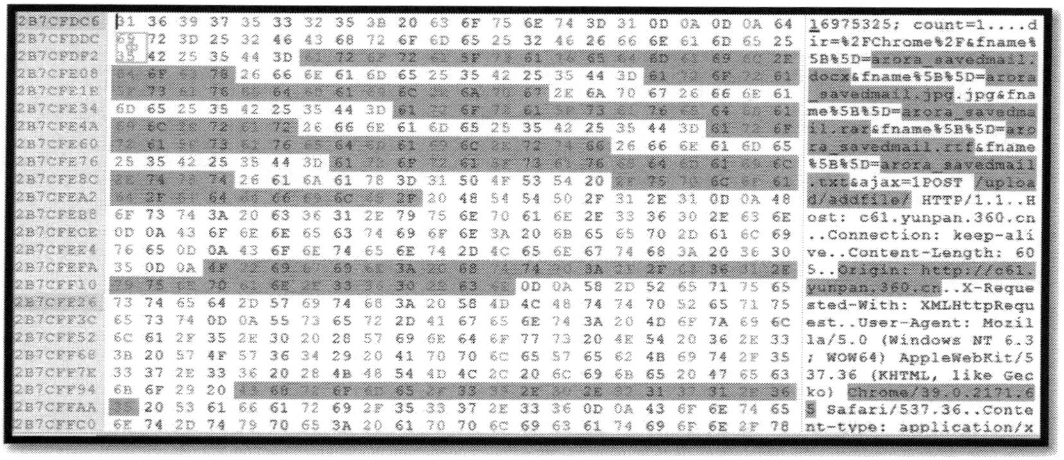

FIG. 33   Files that has been uploaded to yunpn.360.cn using Chrome/39.0.2171.65.

```
==================================================
Filename         : YELQRYG9.json
Content Type     : application/json
URL              : https://login.360.cn/?o=sso&m=login&requestScema=http&from=pcw_cloud&rtype=data
                   &func=QHPass.loginUtils.loginCallback&userName=bob25775%40gmail.com&pwdmethod=1
                   &isKeepAlive=0&token=7b1b7b3f5995e4bb&captFlag=1&captId=i360&captCode=&lm=0&validatelm=0
                   &password=c7175a2cefaaba16ebe150bf00cc9af3&r=1417083969956&callback=QiUserJsonP1417083961035
Last Accessed    : 11/27/2014 6:26:11 PM
Last Modified    : N/A
Expiration Time  : N/A
Last Checked     : N/A
Hits             : 1
File Size        : 880
Subfolder Name   : HJSR8UMK
Full Path        : C:\Users\Alice\AppData\Local\Packages\windows_ie_ac_001\AC\INetCache\HJSR8UMK\YELQRYG9.json
Missing File     : No
==================================================
```

FIG. 34 Yunpan Cached Address.

```
POST /file/detectFileExists HTTP/1.1
Accept: */*
Content-Type: application/x-www-form-urlencoded UTF-8
X-Requested-With: XMLHttpRequest
Referer: http://c61.yunpan.360.cn/my/index/#%2FIE%20upload%2F
Accept-Language: en-US
Accept-Encoding: gzip, deflate
User-Agent: Mozilla/5.0 (Windows NT 6.3; WOW64; Trident/7.0; Touch; rv:11.0) like Gecko
Host: [illegible]
Content-Length: 61
Connection: Keep-Alive
Cache-Control: no-cache
Cookie: count=4; i360[illegible] YUNPAN_USER=bob25775%2540gmail.com; token=1986353458.61.63cd4742.1337960040.1417083998;
__guid=3537848.3881362115386492000.1416978550984.7986; Q=u%3D360H1337960040%26n%3D%261e%3DLz9vZwH3AmHyAQoaoJScoP5wo2O%3D%26m%3D%26qid%3D1337960040%261m%
3D_t00df551a583a87f4e9%26src%3Dpcw_cloud%26t%3D1; T=s%3D59419775 32c12a800300cbfe0ac2b15e%26t%3D1417083997%261m%3D%261f%3D1%26sk%3D39cd1bf2faaac411efe8d842e873e5fa%
26mt%3D1417083997%26rc%3D%26v%3D2.0%26a%3D0; count=5

dir=%2FIE%2[illegible]%2F[illegible]%5D[illegible]&ajax=1HTTP/1.1 200 OK
Server: 360Server
Date: Thu, [illegible]
Content-Type: application/x-javascript;charset=utf-8
Transfer-Encoding: chunked
Connection: keep-alive
Vary: Accept-Encoding
X-Powered-By: PHP/5.2.5
Expires: Mon, 26 Jul 1997 05:00:00 GMT
Cache-control: private
Content-Encoding: gzip

54
..........V3-*..W.2...r.....bJ.L.Sb3M.L..l#C..RS#.4%.....D%.j......b%....Z..!.uD...
0
```

FIG. 35 Result of network traffic analysis with loginname and filename discovered.

```
[illegible]
------WebKitFormBoundaryjuznAOxKjAAfGYKK
Content-Disposition: form-data; name="file"; [illegible]
Content-Type: text/plain

Message-ID: <5661236.1075859173761.JavaMail.evans@thyme>
Date: Mon, 23 Apr 2001 06:52:01 -0700 (PDT)
From: paul.schiavone@enron.com
To: harry.arora@enron.com, steve.wang@enron.com, robert.stalford@enron.com,
 hai.chen@enron.com
Subject: Homer City Info.
Mime-Version: 1.0
Content-Type: text/plain; charset=us-ascii
Content-Transfer-Encoding: 7bit
X-From: Schiavone, Paul </O=ENRON/OU=NA/CN=RECIPIENTS/CN=PSCHIAVO>
X-To: Arora, Harry </O=ENRON/OU=NA/CN=RECIPIENTS/CN=Harora>, Wang, Steve </O=ENRON/OU=NA/CN=RECIPIENTS/CN=Swang3>, Stalford, Robert </O=ENRON/OU=NA/CN=RECIPIENTS/
CN=Notesaddr/cn=4411df41-44f2b565-8625690a-7419e9>, Chen, Hai </O=ENRON/OU=NA/CN=RECIPIENTS/CN=Notesaddr/cn=e57848ec-75e3c6ec-86256965-5469d0>
X-cc:
X-bcc:
X-Folder: \Harry_Arora_Jan2002\Arora, Harry\Inbox\Saved Mail
X-Origin: Arora-H
X-FileName: harora (Non-Privileged).pst

WHAT WE KNOW:

1. Purchased by Edison Mission Energy in March 1999 for 1.8 billion from GPU and NGE Generation.

2. Total generation capacity = 1,884 MW (3 coal fired turbines)

3. One of the largest and lowest cost sources of power in the Mid-Atlantic

4. Only major coal-fired facility in region with direct high voltage access to both NYPP and PJM

5. Company has stated plans to invest 200 million to upgrade plants, pollution controls, and life extension

6. Issued approximately 1.1 billion in bonds in August 2000.  (8.50% 2016, 8.3% 2009)
------WebKitFormBoundaryjuznAOxKjAAfGYKK--
```

FIG. 36 Content of uploaded file in TXT format.

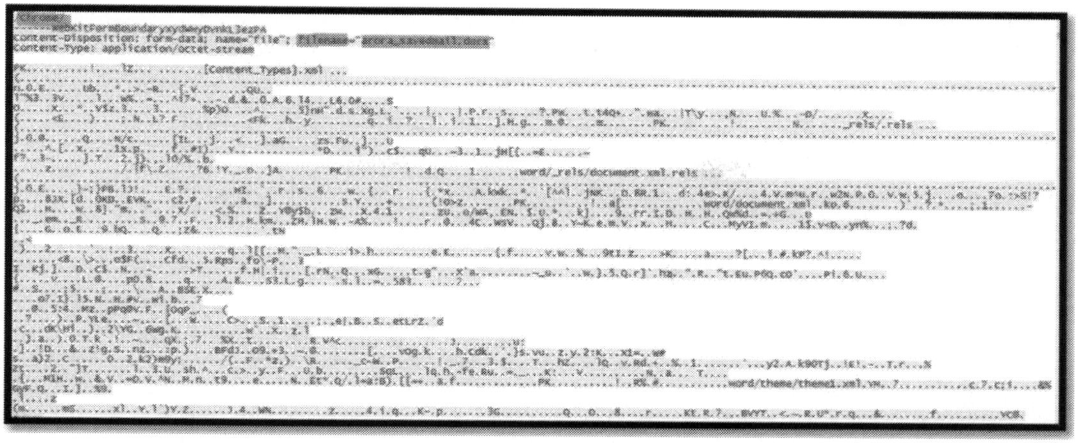

FIG. 37 File in DOCX format.

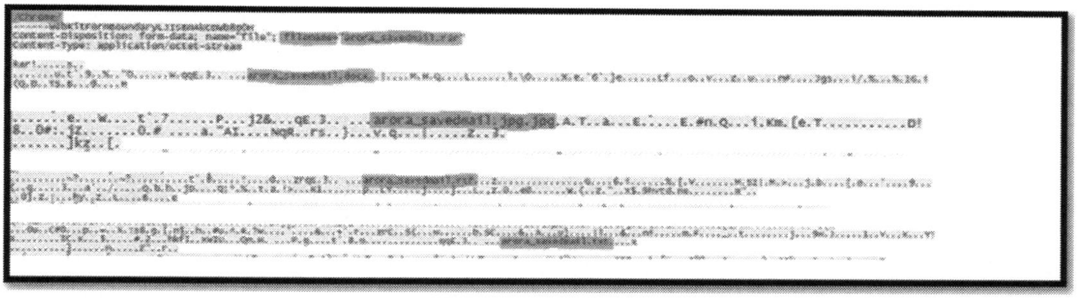

FIG. 38 File in JPG format.

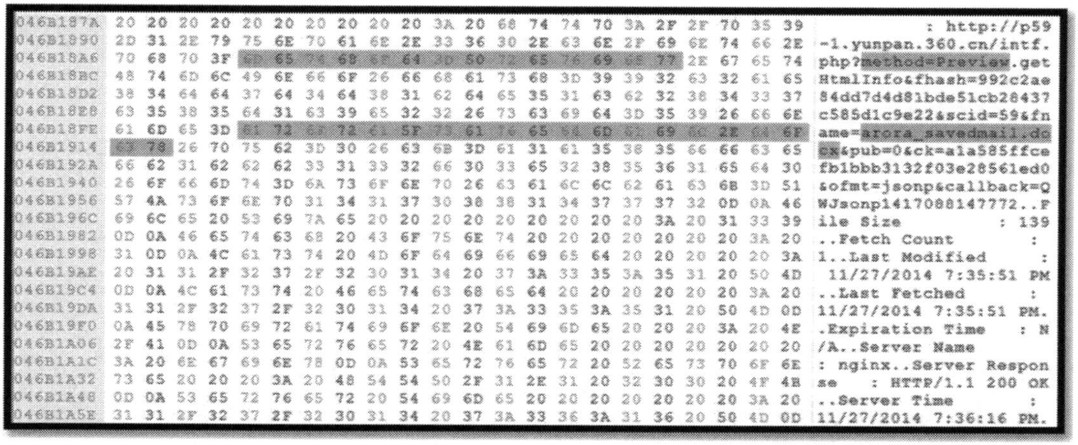

FIG. 39 Result of "method=previed" discovered.

OPEN/VIEW—NETWORK TRAFFIC   Analyzing the network traffic, we could capture the same data as memory and cache analysis: "method=preview" is identified as well as the cloud service Yunpan.360.cn and the filename being previewed (Fig. 40). Moreover, the filename in TXT format and the content of the file is recoverable.

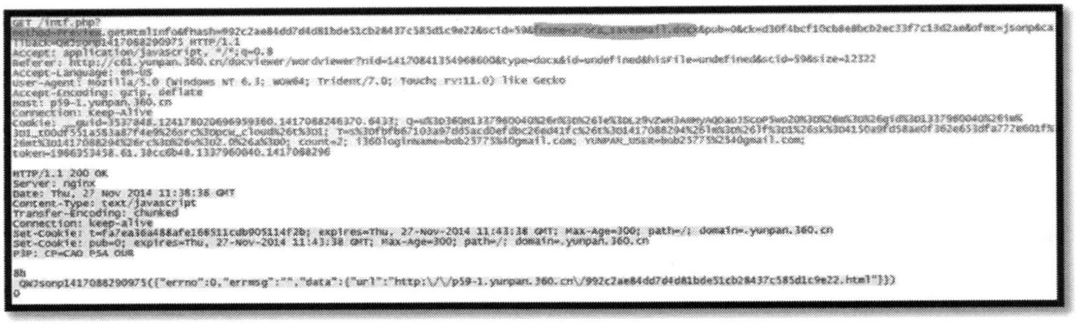

FIG. 40   Result of network traffic with "method=preview" and filename.

DOWNLOAD—LIVE MEMORY   During the analysis of the live memory, we discovered that there were files being downloaded from Yunpan using Internet Explorer, Chrome, and Mozilla Firefox. Fig. 41 shows a part of the memory where the file, "arora_ savedmail.jpg. jpg", has been downloaded ("method=download") using Chrome 29.0.2171.65. The memory also captured the content of the file named "arora_ savedmail.txt" which was not encrypted.

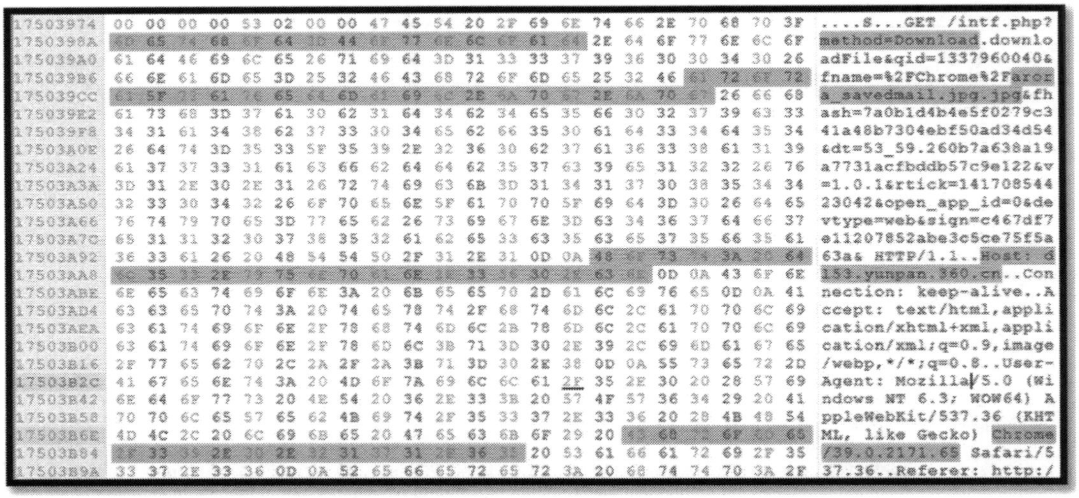

FIG. 41   Result showing the action of file downloaded from yunpan.360.cn.

DOWNLOAD—NETWORK TRAFFIC The network traffic captured the action of files downloading from YunPan. As shown in Fig. 42, the user with "loginName=bob25775% 40gmail. com" has used the "method=download" to download the files from yunpan.360.cn. There were also same evidences for different files format, being downloaded using three browsers, Internet Explore, Chrome, and Mozilla Firefox.

```
GET /intf.php?method=Download:downloadFile&qid=1337960040&fname=%2FIE+Upload%
2Farora_savedmail.docx&fhash=992c2ae84dd7d4d81bde51cb28437c585d1c9e22&dt=53_59.9e3131b3
4297bd9bc77b2c4683198ff1&v=1.0.1&rtick=14170874087093&open_app_id=0&devtype=web&sign=ea
d39a67c5e7e5f0803439dd70e88e9f& HTTP/1.1
Accept: text/html, application/xhtml+xml, */*
Referer: http://c61.yunpan.360.cn/my/index/
Accept-Language: en-US
User-Agent: Mozilla/5.0 (Windows NT 6.3; WOW64; Trident/7.0; Touch; rv:11.0) like Gecko
Accept-Encoding: gzip, deflate
Host: d153.yunpan.360.cn
Connection: Keep-Alive
Cookie: __guid=3537848.634815987327261800.1417087288775.2846; Q=u%3D360H1337960040%26n%
3D%261e%3DLZ9ZWH3AmHyAQOaoJScoP5wo20%3D%26m%3D%26qid%3D1337960040%26im%
3D1_t00df551a583a87f4e9%26src%3Dpcw_cloud%26t%3D1; T=s%
3D017b781f360eff88447c1dc1d56a7bf1%26t%3D1417087349%261m%3D%261f%3D1%26sk%
3Ddf24e2ab8572da424de408af80035caf%26mt%3D1417087349%26rc%3D%26v%3D2.0%26a%3D0;
count=2; i360loginName=bob25775%40gmail.com; YUNPAN_USER=bob25775%2540gmail.com;
token=1986353458.61.ef22d2a9.1337960040.1417087350

HTTP/1.1 200 OK
Server: 360Server
Date: Thu, 27 Nov 2014 11:23:30 GMT
Content-Type: application/octet-stream
Connection: keep-alive
Accept-Ranges: bytes
Content-Transfer-Encoding: binary
Content-Length: 12322
Content-Disposition: attachment; filename="arora_savedmail.docx"
```

FIG. 42 The result of network traffic showing the file downloaded from yunpan.360.cn.

DELETE—LIVE MEMORY There is no obvious evidences showing the deletion of files in Yunpan, however we have discovered the "buttonid= delete" has been selected as shown in Fig. 43.

DELETE—NETWORK TRAFFIC From the network traffic, we were able to identify the deletion of file from "POST /file/recycle" followed by the filename and date highlighted in the Fig. 44. There were also similar evidences discovered for all the three considered browsers, along with different file types.

As for the timestamp of the dataset, we discovered that when the files are being uploaded, the date modified will be altered to be the date and time when the files are uploaded. However, when the files are downloaded, the date modified will changed to the date and time of the downloading.

ANDROID KITKAT 4.4.2—CLIENT APPLICATION BASED

360Yunpan for Android platforms was not available in Google Playstore (at the time of experiments). The .apk file had to be downloaded from its official website. Upon installation, 360Yunpan creates a directory for storing user configuration files in "data/data/com.qihoo.yunpan" as shown in Fig. 45.

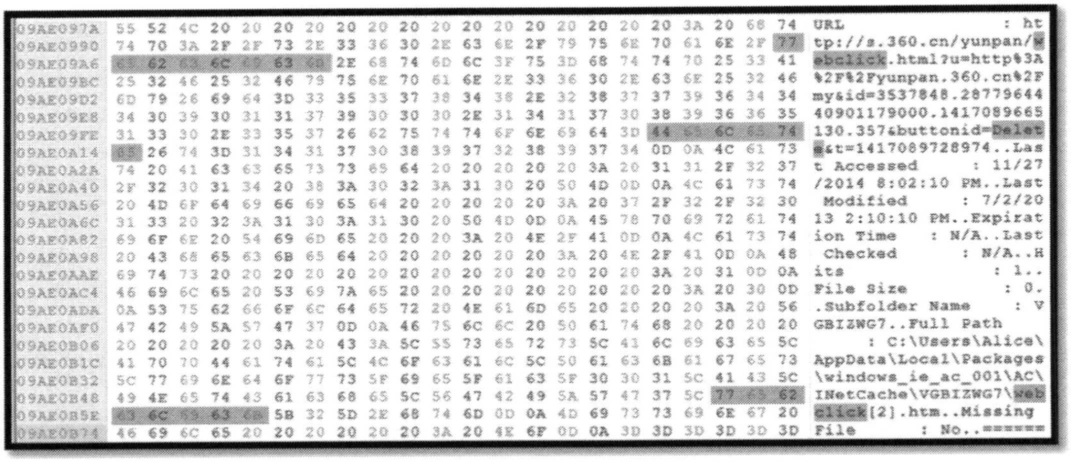

FIG. 43   The action of file being deleted.

FIG. 44   The deletion of file identified.

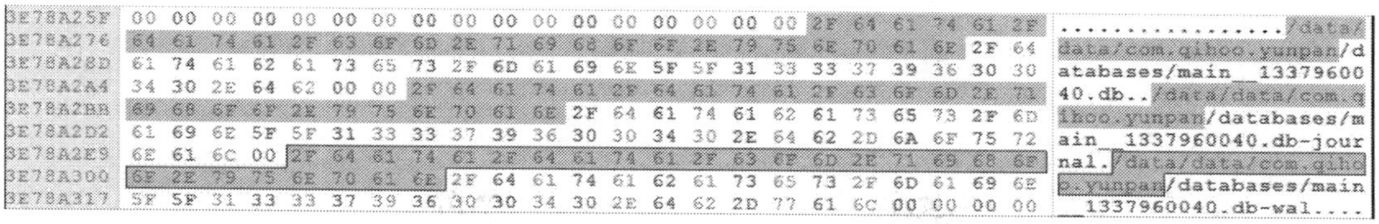

FIG. 45 Directory containing user account conifguration for 360Yunpan.

Analysis on the internal memory of Android 4.4.2 captured during the installation of 360Yunpan application shows traces of navigation to the 360Yunpan official website, and the downloaded `apk` file in the memory as shown in Fig. 46. 360Yunpan leaves traces of user account data such as user email and 360Yunpan unique user ID in the internal memory as shown in Fig. 47, as well as username and password of the mobile client application (Fig. 48).

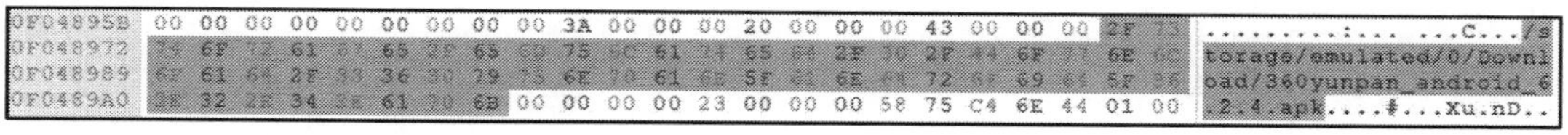

FIG. 46 Downloaded apk file residing in the default Android download folder.

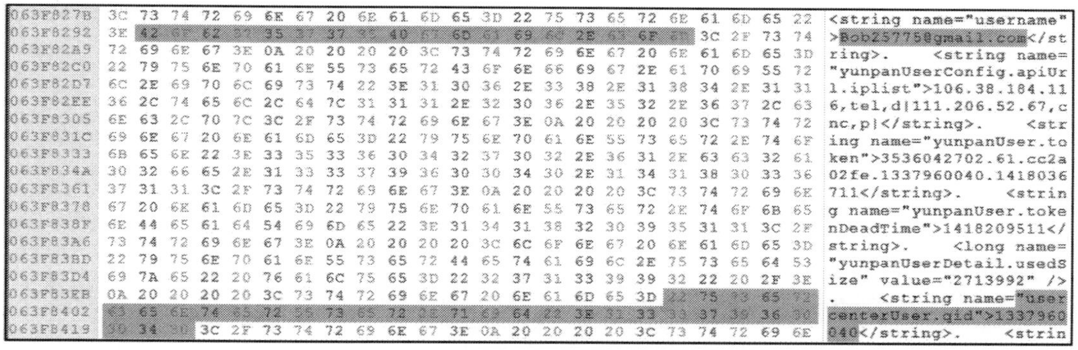

FIG. 47 Downloaded `apk` file residing in the default Android download folder.

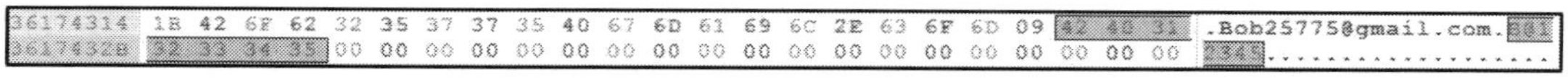

FIG. 48 User credentials for 360Yunpan such as username and password are found

Further analysis of the internal phone memory found that 360Yunpan leaves traces of file activity in the client device such as file download. However, we could not find any data remnants for file upload, delete and uninstallation. We captured the downloading of files into a new client device after logging into the test user account. Fig. 49 shows the files synching onto the client device from the cloud storage after logging in, including filename, date, and time.

During the file operations, we captured the network traffic using Wireshark 1.12.1 on the host machine. Analysis of `pcap` files shows that 360Yunpan uses SSL encryption for mobile

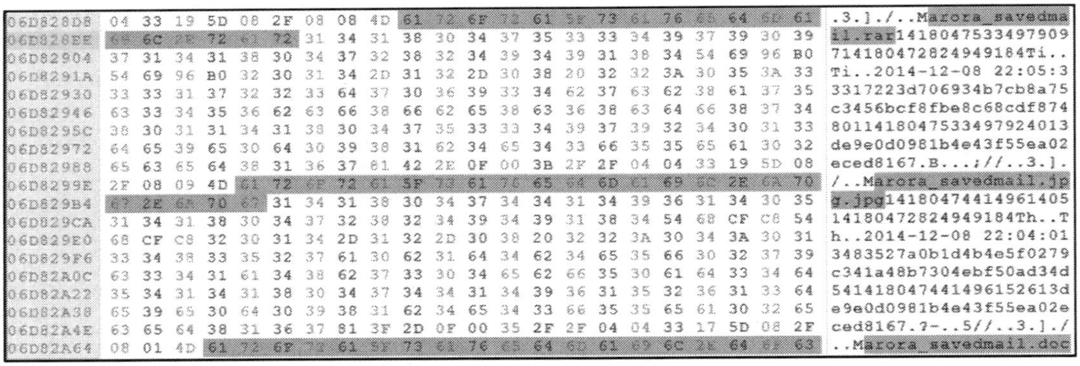

```
06D828D8  04 33 19 5D 08 2F 08 08 4D 61 72 6F 72 61 5F 73 61 76 65 64 6D 61   .3.]./..Marora_savedma
06D828EE  69 6C 2E 72 61 72 31 34 31 38 30 34 37 35 33 33 34 39 37 39 30 39   il.rar1418047533497909
06D82904  37 31 34 31 38 30 34 37 32 38 32 34 39 34 39 31 38 34 54 69 96 B0   714180472824949184Ti..
06D8291A  54 69 96 B0 32 30 31 34 2D 31 32 2D 30 38 20 32 32 3A 30 35 3A 33   Ti..2014-12-08 22:05:3
06D82930  33 33 31 37 32 32 33 64 37 30 36 39 33 34 62 37 63 62 38 61 37 35   3317223d706934b7cb8a75
06D82946  63 33 34 35 36 62 63 66 38 66 62 65 38 63 36 38 63 64 66 38 37 34   c3456bcf8fbe8c68cdf874
06D8295C  38 30 31 31 34 31 38 30 34 37 35 33 33 34 39 37 39 32 34 30 31 33   8011418047533497924013
06D82972  64 65 39 65 30 64 30 39 38 31 62 34 65 34 33 66 35 35 65 61 30 32   de9e0d0981b4e43f55ea02
06D82988  65 63 65 64 38 31 36 37 81 42 2E 0F 00 3B 2F 2F 04 04 33 19 5D 08   eced8167.B...;//..3.].
06D8299E  2F 08 09 4D 61 72 6F 72 61 5F 73 61 76 65 64 6D 61 69 6C 2E 6A 70   /..Marora_savedmail.jp
06D829B4  67 2E 6A 70 67 31 34 31 38 30 34 37 34 34 31 34 39 36 31 34 30 35   g.jpg1418047441496140 5
06D829CA  31 34 31 38 30 34 37 32 38 32 34 39 34 39 31 38 34 54 68 CF C8 54   14180472824949184Th..T
06D829E0  68 CF C8 32 30 31 34 2D 31 32 2D 30 38 20 32 32 3A 30 34 3A 30 31   h..2014-12-08 22:04:01
06D829F6  33 34 38 33 35 32 37 61 30 62 31 64 34 62 34 65 35 66 30 32 37 39   3483527a0b1d4b4e5f0279
06D82A0C  63 33 34 31 61 34 38 62 37 33 30 34 65 62 66 35 30 61 64 33 34 64   c341a48b7304ebf50ad34d
06D82A22  35 34 31 34 31 38 30 34 37 34 34 31 34 39 36 31 35 32 36 31 33 64   5414180474414961526 13d
06D82A38  65 39 65 30 64 30 39 38 31 62 34 65 34 33 66 35 35 65 61 30 32 65   e9e0d0981b4e43f55ea02e
06D82A4E  63 65 64 38 31 36 37 81 3F 2D 0F 00 35 2F 2F 04 04 33 17 5D 08 2F   ced8167.?-..5//..3.]./
06D82A64  08 01 4D 61 72 6F 72 61 5F 73 61 76 65 64 6D 61 69 6C 2E 64 6F 63   ..Marora_savedmail.doc
```

FIG. 49   Contents of the dataset synch includes filename, date and time of synch.

version of the client application, which is issued by WoSign (Fig. 50). However, it is still possible to recover some data remnants showing file activities conducted between the mobile client application and 360Yunpan cloud storage. The activities found are login, upload, and download. Other information includes the device type and 360Yunpan user ID. Fig. 51 shows the network activity of uploading the datasets, where the filename and metadata are recognizable.

FIG. 50   SSL certificate used by 360Yunpan mobile client.

During the downloading of dataset files into the client device no filename or metadata are found. However, some of the file contents can be seen in the network streams such as the .rtf and .txt files (Fig. 52). Uninstallation of 360Yunpan mobile client application did not leave traces in the internal memory and network.

The results of analyzing timestamps for each of the datasets before uploading and upon downloading in 360Yunpan is similar to what we found for the Windows 8.1 client-based experiment. The timestamps for each of dataset before upload and download are the same. This may be due to the virtual nature of the 360Yunpan hard drive, which does not store the files on the local machine and instead direct uploads them into the cloud.

```
GET /intf.php?
method=Sync.getAddrV4&qid=1337960040&devtype=android&v=6.2.4&devid=&devname=VMware
+Virtual
+Platform&rtick=72164248662342144&sign=514c9e84cae925212ff92d02246edb75&ofmt=json&pid=h
ome& HTTP/1.1
Accept-Encoding: gzip
Cookie: fname=%2Fandroid+kitkat%
2Farora_savedmail.docx;fsize=12322;fctime=1416204944;fmtime=1416204944;fattr=0;fhash=99
2c2ae84dd7d4d81bde51cb28437c585d1c9e22;fsum=e2ebc277476a0f44e68d926c9d689e90;is_created
ir=1;token=3536042702.61.cc2a02fe.1337960040.1418036711;
X-QIHOO-HOST: api61.yunpan.360.cn
Host: api61.yunpan.360.cn
User-Agent: Mozilla/4.0 (compatible; MSIE 7.0; Windows NT 5.1)
Connection: Keep-Alive
```

FIG. 51 Upload activity is captured and found.

```
Message-ID: <5661256.1075859175761.JavaMail.evans@thyme>\u13\'0d}
\par \pard\plain \s20\sb0\sa0\dbch\af7\dbch\af5\afs20\loch\f5\fs20{\rtlch \ltrch\loch
Date: Mon, 23 Apr 2001 06:52:01 -0700 (PDT)\u13\'0d}
\par \pard\plain \s20\sb0\sa0\dbch\af7\dbch\af5\afs20\loch\f5\fs20{\rtlch \ltrch\loch
From: paul.schiavone@enron.com\u13\'0d}
\par \pard\plain \s20\sb0\sa0\dbch\af7\dbch\af5\afs20\loch\f5\fs20{\rtlch \ltrch\loch
To: harry.arora@enron.com, steve.wang@enron.com, robert.stalford@enron.com, \u13\'0d}
\par \pard\plain \s20\sb0\sa0\dbch\af7\dbch\af5\afs20\loch\f5\fs20{\rtlch \ltrch\loch
\tab hai.chen@enron.com\u13\'0d}
\par \pard\plain \s20\sb0\sa0\dbch\af7\dbch\af5\afs20\loch\f5\fs20{\rtlch \ltrch\loch
Subject: Homer City Info.\u13\'0d}
\par \pard\plain \s20\sb0\sa0\dbch\af7\dbch\af5\afs20\loch\f5\fs20{\rtlch \ltrch\loch
Mime-Version: 1.0\u13\'0d}
\par \pard\plain \s20\sb0\sa0\dbch\af7\dbch\af5\afs20\loch\f5\fs20{\rtlch \ltrch\loch
Content-Type: text/plain; charset=us-ascii\u13\'0d}
\par \pard\plain \s20\sb0\sa0\dbch\af7\dbch\af5\afs20\loch\f5\fs20{\rtlch \ltrch\loch
Content-Transfer-Encoding: 7bit\u13\'0d}
\par \pard\plain \s20\sb0\sa0\dbch\af7\dbch\af5\afs20\loch\f5\fs20{\rtlch \ltrch\loch
X-From: Schiavone, Paul </O=ENRON/OU=NA/CN=RECIPIENTS/CN=PSCHIAVO>\u13\'0d}
\par \pard\plain \s20\sb0\sa0\dbch\af7\dbch\af5\afs20\loch\f5\fs20{\rtlch \ltrch\loch
X-To: Arora, Harry </O=ENRON/OU=NA/CN=RECIPIENTS/CN=Harora>, Wang, Steve </O=ENRON/
OU=NA/CN=RECIPIENTS/CN=Swang3>, Stalford, Robert </O=ENRON/OU=NA/CN=RECIPIENTS/
```

FIG. 52 Contents of .rtf file of the dataset.

APPLE IOS 8.0—CLIENT APPLICATION BASED

The application of Yunpan for iPad device is known as "360 YunPan HD" in Apple Store. The appdata for this cloud service in iOS platform is identified as "com.360.yunpanhd". We could discover traces of installing the application from "info.plist", "manifest.mdbd", and "Manifest.plist" (Fig. 53). However, we could not find any login information.

```
00000134  6D 2E 61 70 70 6C 65 2E 4D 61 70 73 5F 10 11 63 6F 6D 2E 61 70 70  m.apple.Maps_..com.app
0000014A  6C 65 2E 77 65 62 61 70 70 31 5F 10 10 63 6F 6D 2E 33 36 30 2E 79  le.webapp1_..com.360.y
00000160  75 6E 70 61 6E 68 64 5F 10 10 63 6F 6D 2E 61 70 70 6C 65 2E 77 65  unpanhd_..com.apple.we
00000176  62 61 70 70 5E 63 6F 6D 2E 61 70 70 6C 65 2E 74 69 70 73 5F 10 14  bapp^com.apple.tips_..
```

FIG. 53 The result showing application name in the file of Manifest.plist.

There is no upload option available for iOS version of Yunpan thus the datasets have been uploaded to the cloud service via web browser in order to carry out the experiments. We were able to load all the five file types, however preview was only available for files with format JPG, DOCX, and TXT. After loading the files, they were downloaded and saved the directory `Documents/c3eb49937bff58e03d20886e174d2f12/yunpan/ios/[filename]`. We were able to discover the file names from the memory analysis (Fig. 54).

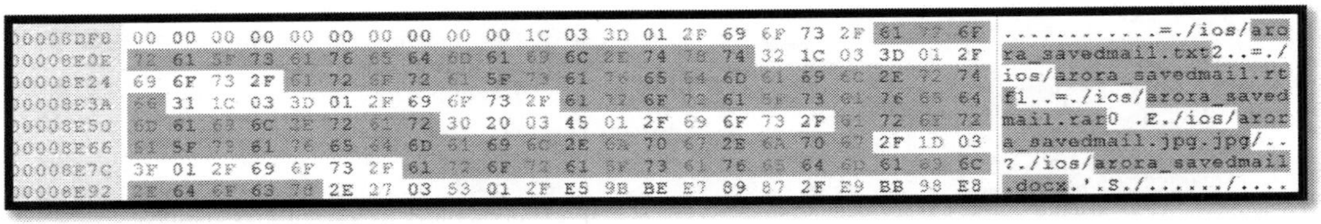

FIG. 54   Filename discovered in the memory.

We performed the download operation by saving JPG file to gallery, downloading of RAR file, and there is no download option for files format with DOCX, RTF, and TXT. However the files have been downloaded by themselves when loaded for preview. The filename of the five datasets have been discovered from the file directory `Documents/c3eb49937bff58e03d20886e174d2f12.db`. After the deletion of the files, we could not find any traces of filename. Moreover, there was no traces on the appdata, after uninstallation of the application.

4 REPORTING AND PRESENTATION

In this section we report our findings on each of the cloud platforms in Tables 8 to 13. The presented tables are subjected to change depending on applicability. (Y) shows the experimented section, while (N) depicts not-experimented section, and (NF) means there is no finding in a particular source of evidence.

4.1 Cloud Service: CloudMe

In this section we provide reports of our findings while investigating CloudMe on Windows 8.1 web browser-based application in Table 8, Android 4.4.2 mobile client application in Table 9, and Apple iOS 8.0 mobile client application in Table 10.

4.2 Cloud Service: 360Yunpan

In this section we provide reports of our investigative study on 360Yunpan, considering Windows 8.1 client application (Table 11), Android 4.4.2 mobile client application (Table 12), and Apple iOS 8.0 mobile client application (Table 13).

5 CONCLUSION

In this chapter we conducted a forensics investigative study on two cloud storage services, ie, CloudMe, and 360Yunpan. In conclusion, we could find valuable forensic evidence related to CloudMe and 360Yunpan cloud storage accounts from various platforms. Data remnants such as user credentials, device names, filenames, and proof of activity can be found through various sources of evidences such as hard drives, live memory, internal phone memory and backup files, network traffic, and more. The gathered data further

TABLE 8 CloudMe Investigation—Windows 8.1 Client Browser Application

Installation of client software (ie, what can be found in the stored files (ie, within Program Files, AppData, etc.), registry, and network traffic?). Other than setup and configuration data, we are particularly interested in looking for user-specific cloud service and authentication data (password file and the encryption method)		Y		
	Upload	**Download**	**Delete**	**Sync**
Accessing web-based cloud app (What data remnants can be found in browser history, cache, cookies, etc. after a user has accessed web-based cloud app?)	Y	Y	Y	Y
Prefetch files	N	N	N	N
Link files	N	N	N	N
Pagefile.sys (can be extracted from FTK, similar to RAM analysis)	N	N	N	N
Thumbcache files	N	N	N	N
Event log files (event viewer)	N	N	N	N
Registry files	NF	NF	NF	NF
Unallocated space (can be extracted from FTK, similar to RAM analysis)	NF	NF	NF	NF
& recycle bin (FTK)	NF	NF	Y	NF
Network analysis (ie, server ip addresses/range, timestamps (do they correlate with the time you started up cloud service?), certificate used, keywords that could be used to filter only traffic of relevance)	Y	Y	Y	N
System volume information	N	N	N	N
RAM	Y			
Compare the MD5 and creation, last added, last accessed, last modified times of files before and after file transfers (uploaded/downloaded/synced)	Y	Y	Y	Y
Uninstallation of client software (ie, what data remnants left in the stored files, registry, network traffic?)		Y		

TABLE 9 CloudMe Investigation—Android 4.4.2 Mobile Client Application

	Upload	**Download**	**Delete**	**Sync**
Cloud app (if any) related artifacts (installation directory, credentials, timestamps of relevance from the plist (ios)/sqlite files)	N	N	N	N
Internal Memory	Y	Y	Y	Y
Compare the MD5 and creation, last added, last accessed, last modified times of files before and after file transfers (uploaded/downloaded/synced)	Y	Y	Y	Y
Network analysis	Y	Y	Y	Y
Uninstallation		Y		

TABLE 10 CloudMe Investigation—Apple iOS 8.0 Mobile Client Application

	Upload	Access/ Open	Download	Delete	Sync
Web-based cloud app artifacts (ie, what can be found in browser history, cache, cookies, etc. after a user has accessed web-based cloud app using a browser?)	N	N	N	N	N
Cloud app (if any) related artifacts (installation directory, credentials, timestamps of relevance from the plist (ios)/ sqlite files)	Y	Y	N	N	N
Optional: RAM	N	N	N	N	N
Optional: Compare the MD5 and creation, last added, last accessed, last modified times of files before and after file transfers (uploaded/downloaded/synced)	N	N	N	N	N
Optional: Network analysis	N	N	N	N	N
Uninstallation	No evidence discovered.				

TABLE 11 360Yunpan Investigation—Windows 8.1 Client Application

Installation of client software (ie, what can be found in the stored files (ie, within Program Files, AppData, etc.), registry, and network traffic?). Other than setup and configuration data, we are particularly interested in looking for user-specific cloud service and authentication data (password file and the encryption method)	Y		
	Upload	**Download**	**Delete**
Accessing web-based cloud app (what data remnants can be found in browser history, cache, cookies, etc. after a user has accessed web-based cloud app?)	Y	Y	Y
Directory listings: determining the sync/file management metadata, and files/ folders added/removed during each cloud usage circumstance, ie, folders containing sync metadata information	Y	Y	Y
Prefetch files	N	N	N
Link files	N	N	N
Pagefile.sys (can be extracted from FTK, similar to RAM analysis)	N	N	N
Thumbcache files	N	N	N
Event log files (event viewer)	N	N	N
Registry files	Y	Y	Y
Unallocated space (can be extracted from FTK, similar to RAM analysis)	NF	NF	NF
& Recycle bin (FTK)	NF	NF	Y
Network analysis: server ip addresses/range, timestamps (do they correlate with the time that cloud service started up?), used certificate, keywords that could be used to filter only traffic of relevance	Y	Y	Y
System volume information	N	N	N
RAM	Y	Y	Y
Compare the MD5 and creation, last added, last accessed, last modified times of files before and after file transfers (uploaded/downloaded/synced)	Y	Y	Y
Uninstallation of client software: what data remnants left in the stored files, registry, network traffic?	Y		

TABLE 12 360Yunpan Investigation—Android 4.4.2 Mobile Client Application

	Upload	Download	Delete
Cloud app (if any) related artifacts: installation directory, credentials, timestamps of relevance from the plist/ sqlite files)	N	N	N
Internal Memory	Y	Y	Y
Compare the MD5, creation, last added, last accessed, last modified times of files before and after file transfers (uploaded/ downloaded/ synced)	Y	Y	Y
Network analysis	Y	Y	Y
Uninstallation		Y	

TABLE 13 360Yunpan Investigation—Apple iOS 8.0 Mobile Client Application

	Upload	Access/ Open	Download	Delete	Sync
Web-based cloud app artifacts: what can be found in browser history, cache, cookies, etc. after a user has accessed web-based cloud app using a browser?	N	N	N	N	N
Cloud app (if any) related artifacts: installation directory, credentials, timestamps of relevance from the plist (ios)/ sqlite files	Y	Y	Y	Y	N
Optional: RAM	N	N	N	N	N
Optional: Compare the MD5, creation, last added, last accessed, last modified times of files before and after file transfers (uploaded/ downloaded/ synced)	N	N	N	N	N
Optional: Network analysis	N	N	N	N	N
Uninstallation			No evidence discovered.		

proves that each of the two cloud services leave digital footprints when file operations are carried out, as well as installation and uninstallation of the client application. This will help forensic investigators in rearranging and timelining the sequence of events for presentation as forensic evidence.

Some of the things to be highlighted are the implementation of encryption for each of the cloud storage services and the registry footprints. Although 360Yunpan offers the largest storage capacity free of charge, the security of the files during the transfer is weak compared to CloudMe. Due to the transparency of the data during file transfer, it was easy to sniff the traffic and gather much needed forensic evidence. In contrast, CloudMe leaves less digital footprints compared to 360Yunpan. The uninstallation of CloudMe, although leaves configuration files, it does not change any registry keys in addition to the use of encryption during the transfer of files. Therefore CloudMe is much more privacy preserving. As explained throughout the paper, it is easy to recover user credentials from the internal memory on Android platforms. Therefore there is a need for forensic investigators to reach a better understanding of the challenges in this regard.

References

[1] P. Mell, T. Grance, The NIST Definition of Cloud Computing, NIST Special Publication 800-145, NIST, Gaithersburg, MD, 2011.

[2] K.-K.R. Choo, Cloud computing: challenges and future directions, Trends and Issues in Crime and Criminal Justice 400 (2010) 381–400, http://aic.gov.au/media_library/publications/tandi_pdf/tandi400.pdf.

[3] M. Taylor, J. Haggerty, D. Gresty, R. Hegarty, Digital evidence in cloud computing systems, Comput. Law Security Rev. 26 (3) (2010) 304–308.

[4] D. Chen, H. Zhao, Data security and privacy protection issues in cloud computing, in: Proceedings of the International Conference on Computer Science and Electronics Engineering, ICCSEE'12, 1, IEEE, 2012, pp. 647–651.

[5] C.A. Ardagna, M. Conti, M. Leone, J. Stefa, An anonymous end-to-end communication protocol for mobile cloud environments, IEEE Trans. Services Comput. 7 (3) (2014) 373–386.

[6] S. Hosseinzadeh, S. Hyrynsalmi, M. Conti, V. Lepp, Security and privacy in cloud computing via obfuscation and diversification: a survey, in: Proceedings of the 7th International Conference on Cloud Computing Technology and Science, CloudCom'15, IEEE, 2015, pp. 529–535.

[7] D. Quick, B. Martini, R. Choo, Cloud storage forensics, Syngress, Cambridge, MA, USA, 2013.

[8] D. Quick, K.-K.R. Choo, Forensic collection of cloud storage data: does the act of collection result in changes to the data or its metadata? Digit. Invest. 10 (3) (2013) 266–277.

[9] A. Aminnezhad, A. Dehghantanha, M.T. Abdullah, A survey on privacy issues in digital forensics, Int. J. Cyber-Security Digit. Foren. 1 (4) (2012) 311–323.

[10] A. Dehghantanha, K. Franke, Privacy-respecting digital investigation, in: Proceedings of the 12th Annual International Conference on Privacy, Security and Trust, PST'14, IEEE, 2014, pp. 129–138.

[11] F.N. Dezfoli, A. Dehghantanha, R. Mahmoud, N.F.B. Mohd Sani, F. Daryabar, Digital forensic trends and future, Int. J. Cyber-Security Digit. Foren. 2 (2) (2013) 48–76.

[12] F. Daryabar, A. Dehghantanha, N.I. Udzir, N.F.b.M.o.h.d. Sani, S. Bin Shamsuddin, A survey about impacts of cloud computing on digital forensics, Int. J. Cyber-Security Digit. Foren. 2 (2) (2013) 77–94.

[13] F. Daryabar, A. Dehghantanha, A review on impacts of cloud computing and digital forensics, Int. J. Cyber-Security Digit. Foren. 3 (4) (2014) 183–199.

[14] M. Damshenas, A. Dehghantanha, R. Mahmoud, S. bin Shamsuddin, Cloud computing and conflicts with digital forensic investigation, Int. J. Digital Content Tech. Appl. 7 (9) (2013) 543.

[15] A. Aminnezhad, A. Dehghantanha, M.T. Abdullah, M. Damshenas, Cloud forensics issues and opportunities, Int. J. Inform. Process. Manag. 4 (4) (2013) 76–85.

[16] B. Martini, K.-K.R. Choo, Cloud storage forensics: ownCloud as a case study, Digit. Invest. 10 (4) (2013) 287–299.

[17] B. Martini, Q. Do, K.-K.R. Choo, Mobile cloud forensics: an analysis of seven popular Android apps, in: R. Ko, K.-K.R. Choo (Eds.), Cloud Secur. Ecosyst., Syngress, Cambridge, MA, 2015, pp. 309–345. http://dx.doi.org/10.1016/B978-0-12-801595-7.00015-X.

[18] C. Federici, Cloud data imager: a unified answer to remote acquisition of cloud storage areas, Digit. Invest. 11 (1) (2014) 30–42.

[19] D. Quick, K.-K.R. Choo, Digital droplets: Microsoft SkyDrive forensic data remnants, Future Generat. Comput. Syst. 29 (6) (2013) 1378–1394.

[20] H. Chung, J. Park, S. Lee, C. Kang, Digital forensic investigation of cloud storage services, Digit. Invest. 9 (2) (2012) 81–95.

[21] F. Marturana, G. Me, S. Tacconi, A case study on digital forensics in the cloud, in: Proceedings of the International Conference on Cyber-Enabled Distributed Computing and Knowledge Discovery, CyberC'12, IEEE, 2012, pp. 111–116.

[22] D. Quick, K.-K.R. Choo, Google drive: forensic analysis of data remnants, J. Netw. Comput. Appl. 40 (2014) 179–193.

[23] F. Daryabar, A. Dehghantanha, B. Eterovic-Soric, K.-K.R. Choo, Forensic investigation of OneDrive, Box, GoogleDrive and Dropbox applications on Android and iOS devices, Aust. J. Foren. Sci. (2016) 1–28. http://dx.doi.org/10.1080/00450618.2015.1110620.

[24] G. Grispos, W.B. Glisson, T. Storer, Using smartphones as a proxy for forensic evidence contained in cloud storage services, in: Proceedings of the 46th Hawaii International Conference on System Sciences, HICSS, IEEE, 2013, pp. 4910–4919.

[25] D. Quick, K.-K.R. Choo, Dropbox analysis: data remnants on user machines, Digit. Invest. 10 (1) (2013) 3–18.

[26] M. Shariati, A. Dehghantanha, K.-K.R. Choo, SugarSync forensic analysis, Aust. J. Foren. Sci. 48 (1) (2016) 95–117.

[27] CloudMe, https://www.cloudme.com/en.

[28] 360Yunpan, http://yunpan.360.cn/.

[29] F. Daryabar, A. Dehghantanha, K.-K.R. Choo, Cloud storage forensics: MEGA as a case study, Aust. J. Foren. Sci. (2016), http://dx.doi.org/10.1080/00450618.2016.1153714.

[30] J.S. Hale, Amazon cloud drive forensic analysis, Digit. Invest. 10 (3) (2013) 259–265.

[31] K. Oestreicher, A forensically robust method for acquisition of iCloud data, Digit. Invest. 11 (2014) S106–S113.

[32] B. Martini, K.-K.R. Choo, Remote programmatic vCloud forensics: a six-step collection process and a proof of concept, in: Proceedings of the 13th International Conference on Trust, Security and Privacy in Computing and Communications, TrustCom'14, IEEE, 2014, pp. 935–942.

[33] B. Martini, K.-K.R. Choo, Distributed file system forensics: XtreemFS as a case study, Digit. Invest. 11 (4) (2014) 295–313.

[34] R. Marty, Cloud application logging for forensics, in: Proceedings of the ACM Symposium on Applied Computing, ACM, 2011, pp. 178–184.

[35] J. Dykstra, A.T. Sherman, Acquiring forensic evidence from infrastructure-as-a-service cloud computing: exploring and evaluating tools, trust, and techniques, Digit. Invest. 9 (2012) S90–S98.

[36] C. Cho, S. Chin, K.S. Chung, Cyber forensic for hadoop based cloud system, Int. J. Security Appl. 6 (3) (2012) 83–90.

[37] B. Blakeley, C. Cooney, A. Dehghantanha, R. Aspin, Cloud storage forensic: hubiC as a case-study, in: Proceedings of the 7th International Conference on Cloud Computing Technology and Science, CloudCom'15, IEEE, 2015, pp. 536–541.

[38] F. Anwar, Z. Anwar, Digital forensics for eucalyptus, in: Proceedings of the Frontiers of Information Technology, FIT'11, IEEE, 2011, pp. 110–116.

[39] M. Shariati, A. Dehghantanha, B. Martini, K. Choo, Ubuntu One investigation: detecting evidences on client machines, in: R. Ko, K.-K.R. Choo (Eds.), Cloud Security Ecosystem, Syngress, Cambridge, MA, USA, 2015, pp. 429–446.

[40] B. Martini, K.-K.R. Choo, An integrated conceptual digital forensic framework for cloud computing, Digit. Invest. 9 (2) (2012) 71–80.

[41] K. Kent, S. Chevalier, T. Grance, H. Dang, Guide to integrating forensic techniques into incident response, NIST Special Publication, NIST, Gaithersburg, MD, 2006.

[42] S. McKemmish, G. Acland, B. Reed, Towards a framework for standardising recordkeeping metadata: the Australian recordkeeping metadata schema, Records Manag. J. 9 (3) (1999) 173–198.

[43] Nirsoft, WebBrowserPassView v1.58, 2015. http://www.nirsoft.net/utils/web_browser_password.html (Accessed 20 January 2015).

15

An Android Cloud Storage Apps Forensic Taxonomy

M. Amine Chelihi, A. Elutilo, I. Ahmed, C. Papadopoulos, A. Dehghantanha

University of Salford, Salford, United Kingdom

1 INTRODUCTION

Mobile applications have increasingly adopted the Android operating system as a standard, with backing from market share figures, 82.8% of smartphones have incorporated the Android operating system [1]. These statistics and features highlight the importance and relevance of the Android OS for smartphone manufacturers worldwide [2]. Android operating system has amassed over 1.4 billion users worldwide as of 2016 according to the Google CEO [3] this is due to its wide acceptability and increased usage among the world's mobile phone populace [4]. Cloud computing is an umbrella under which the majority of Internet related services are classified. Many cloud applications are increasingly developed for Android platform and many Android applications are now running through cloud services [5]. Therefore more attacks are directed against Android platforms through cloud services or cloud applications vulnerabilities [6]. As the use of technology has afforded substantial breakthroughs in investigative cases, it is now required that the forensic investigators be able to acquire and analyze persistent data, volatile data, and other sensitive information from different platforms [7]. Many investigation tools were developed to assist acquisition, collation, and analysis of data in ways that maintain the chain of evidence [8]. Mobile forensic investigators are required to integrate technology and law in the investigation of many traditional crimes such as drug dealing and copyright infringement, which are facilitated by mobile and cloud technologies [9,10]. Audio files, images, videos, messages, notes, and emails are just a few possible remnants that can be extracted during mobile investigations from social networking, instant messaging, and cloud and mobile platforms [11–15]. As the cyber world becomes heavily reliant on mobile and cloud storage technologies, it is only palpable that these two mediums would experience the most cyberattacks and intrusion attempts as they hold vital information of the concerned organizations or individuals [16,17].

Methods, techniques, and strategies must be implemented to not only defend or protect these mediums but also to ensure their forensics readiness [9]. The fast pace of change in mobile and cloud technologies mandates utilizing many different tools and techniques for investigation of these platforms [16,17]. Previous researchers [18–20] have carried out experiment on applications to determine what user information or activity the average applications collects with a view to improving the forensic understanding of the tested applications by creating taxonomies from their studies.

The taxonomy created in this paper would aid in investigation of cloud based storage applications and reflect residual artifacts of 31 different cloud apps on an android mobile device which aids in correlation of evidences between user's activities and remnants of cloud applications resided on the device.

The remainder of this paper is structured as follows, firstly the experiment set-up that details the cloud storage applications, environment, devices, and operating systems used is described. Secondly results and discussion that illustrates our findings and end results of this experiment. Finally the paper is concluded and several future researches are suggested.

2 EXPERIMENT SETUP

In order to select cloud storage application that would cover a majority of users, two major criteria were considered, targeting free applications and also the user ratings for the cloud storage applications. This gives a basis for strong and efficient cloud storage application taxonomy to be developed. Free applications were selected as majority of users would rather download the free cloud storage application as they do not require commercial services. In return of search query "cloud storage applications" 240 free cloud storage applications were shortlisted and only 31 were selected from these based on their user ratings and download numbers [21]. Thirty-one applications that best fit the selection criterial were chosen. Thirty-one cloud storage applications are deemed adequate in accordance with previous works [15] in the forensic investigation of cloud storage services.

The selected applications can be found in Appendix 1. In this paper Android cloud storage applications were examined using the popular forensics tool MicroSystemation XRY (version 6.16.0) from MSAB on a Windows operating system (Win 10 Pro). Cloud storage applications were sourced from Google Play Store. Applications selected are all available and free to download. The applications were picked out from a pool of over 240 cloud applications (the total number of cloud applications on google play as at Mar. 10, 2016), however, the scope of this project only focuses on cloud-storage based applications.

A sheer number of users utilize those popular apps daily, analyzing those apps would cover a high percentage of possible cases that may require forensics investigation, and there might be a good chance to examine vulnerabilities that could be exploited by cyber criminals under any circumstances. When investigating mobile devices that are likely to contain data which could be decisive in criminal investigations or which can be presented as forensic evidence, it is expected that files and applications that have been executed or transferred on the mobile devices can still be accessed if the need arises. Files and data on devices can still be retrieved from mobile device even after they have been deleted. The data extraction tool has the capability to pull out data that has been removed on various applications depending on the security and technological level of the application.

XRY (version 6.16.0) is installed on the machine in order to carry out the forensic extraction and analysis legally. The Asus Nexus 7 Google tablet was used for the running and analysis of the selected android cloud storage applications. The analysis was conducted on Android operating system version KitKat (4.4.4) due to the difficulty the XRY tool encountered trying to capture after upgrading Asus Nexus 7 Google tablet to the latest Android version Marshmallow (6.0.1). A version downgrade was required in order to resolve this issue, the downgrade was done using Nexus Root Toolkit (2.4.1) [22].

Factory reset was carried out after examining each cloud storage application, this was done to ensure that no interferences or mix up from previously examined applications was recorded as part of the result for the subsequent application examined. This technique also eliminated the possibility of any dataset remnants from the previous examined application will not be carried over to subsequent data extractions thereby guaranteeing a more accurate investigation.

The Nexus Root Toolkit (2.4.1) was used for the rooting of the Asus Nexus 7 Google tablet, this toolkit is widely used for rooting Nexus devices and furthermore as XRY was unable to automatically root the device [23]. Operating system vendors have restriction on the privileges, access and rights that normal users do not have the authentication to access so in order to gain maximum privileges and full control of the Android operating system (Android 4.4.4 (KitKat)). This would allow access with root privileges, applications on the device can now run with privileged commands hereby giving access to control the CPU and Kernel of the device [24].

In order to sniff only network traffic generated by the examined applications and not by other services and programs running in the background, a separated hotspot was created in order to avoid interference from devices or applications on the same network. Similar to authors of previous works [25] in creating a hotspot in order to meet this very important pre requisite, the Asus Nexus 7 Google tablet was placed on a separate network established using Connectify (2016.0.3.36821 Pro), which allowed having a hotspot with specific IP addresses and this separated the Asus Nexus 7 Google tablet's IP address from the local network. It must be exclusively network traffic between the applications and their communications between the Asus Nexus 7 Google tablet, and the server on an isolated network.

As done in previous studies [26,27] Connectify was used to set up a hotspot connection, which connects the tablet to the laptop and separates it from the main local network, the laptop then works as a server or a gateway for the Asus Nexus 7 Google tablet and hence making it easier to monitor the traffic sent from the Asus Nexus 7 Google tablet to the server. Wireshark (2.0.2) was used to monitor and capture the traffic of the Asus Nexus 7 Google tablet on that specific connection. The IP address of the Asus Nexus 7 Google tablet is fixed (192.168.121.103) as used for this project. This IP address would serve as the source while the IP address of the server is (192.168.121.1) as it works as a gateway for the Asus Nexus 7 Google tablet. Wireshark (2.0.2) has also been used by [26] for sniffing network traffic in similar forensic work.

For appraisal of data extracted by the XRY tool for this experiment, a forensic dataset was chosen and files were selected based on certain criteria and utilized for the purpose of the experiment. The chosen files were adopted as exhibits that would be uploaded for every cloud storage application. This gives a fair and accurate ground that the files and documents used are of optimal integrity and were compromised to alter results. We chose the EDRM dataset which provides industry standard reference dataset of electronically stored information (ESI) used for forensic and other e-discovery works [28]. Specifically 11 files of different formats and extension, the files chosen were based on the need to cover the most common file extensions and types which cater to different media and document contents. In line with works by authors [12] who made use of the EDRM dataset in their forensic research on similar cloud storage applications. The dataset is exhibited in Appendix 2 of this paper.

3 DISCUSSION

Extracted data from each application were examined and the datasets were identified, presented and documented. These traces, effects and remnants of the files together with other activities or action by the cloud storage application on the Asus Nexus 7 Google tablet were tabulated.

The reason behind choosing the corresponding multimedia files for this experiment is that forensics investigators usually tend to capture multimedia remnants from the suspect's device; this will most probably be used as a proof of evidence in the court, files like images and audio files contain a lot of sensitive data, one image could simply open or close the case. Documents are of a high importance too, in the real world, many leaked documents contained a sheer amount of sensitive data, and that is due to lack of proper security for these documents. Having put documents of certain information in this experiment, helped us track that information while searching for the documents' remnants among the extracted data. Often when the documents are deleted, they leave behind some remnants which sometimes can be in a readable format, even though the data may not be complete, it sometimes gives an indication on what the full information was. Supposedly, in a real-life forensics investigation process, a suspect's device is used to store a couple of documents on the cloud, any retrieved information from the document file may hold a high amount of valuable information that could be presented as a proof of evidence.

Internal storage contains installed applications and their data are stored on mobile devices and sometimes they leave some remnants, this information can be potentially sensitive or incriminating therefore they play a pivotal role in the forensics investigation of suspected mobile devices in cases of law prosecution and forensic investigations of such devices.

Internal memory, though volatile in nature, is much faster to write to and read from in comparison with other forms of storage such as hard disk drives. Data in the internal memory normally remains intact while the device is powered on but loses it when the power goes off [29]. This previously hindered forensic investigation of such part of the memory but with the advent of tools such as XRY it is now possible to recover some of this data through acquisition. This is also shown in Appendix 3 in the remnants column (those remnants were found in the internal storage as cache files).

Network analysis is important to monitor, capture, and analyze network traffic packets that hold network information. The network analysis provides investigators with relevant IP addresses, ports, protocols, and URL's assessed by the cloud storage applications as well as attempted connections [30]. This can prove to be vital information in tracing criminal activities. Appendix 4 depicts some of the network traffic observed when these applications were sharing files on the Internet.

The protocols used by these applications were identified and listed with check marks denoting which application makes use of which protocols; these can be crucial for forensic investigating and ethical hacking of devices and networks. The User Datagram Protocol (UDP) stream from the Domain Name Service (DNS) and multicast Domain Name System (MDNS) show paths taken by some application when users upload content unto the cloud via their application, these paths can be used varying and specifically based on the motive for investigation, analysis or monitoring network traffic. The streams give a little insight into the kinds of information that these applications generate as they peruse the networks and store user content on the cloud platforms. As shown in Appendix 4 some of the applications display the paths they take during installation, registration, and running of services. Few applications leave traces in plain text of their origin website, which is likely to be the provider which hosts these cloud services.

4 RESULTS

The applications examined share a similar criteria, each application stores data on the cloud so it could be accessible by the user either from the phone (device) or using a website (in most cases). Some applications selected use a third party cloud service in order to store data on the cloud, which may come in handy especially when the app offers other services like managing files or exploring the phone's storage.

Typically, each application requires a sign up in order to use its cloud service, and for most applications, we were able to upload data on the cloud from their home website.

For better results, we ensured that the dataset was uploaded to the cloud service using a different device other than the tablet, to avoid having remnants from the internal storage interfering with the data retrieved from the application itself, even though XRY lists out the data found and the path of where the data was found particularly. Remnants found on */mnt/ sdcard/* are discarded, for some applications the dataset sample was transferred directly to the tablet, and then uploaded to the cloud application, which is why some remnants could be recovered from that particular path and not from the app itself.

4.1 Database

When extracting the data, we noticed that some applications generated *db* files and stored them in a particular path within the internal storage, among the experimented applications, 15 apps generated *db* files in the internal memory, and the following is a list of the apps along with the paths where the *db* files were stored:

- *File Expert*: */data/data/xcxin.fehd/databases/*
- *GCloud*: */data/data/com.genie9.gcloudbackup/databases/*
- *Mail.Ru*: */data/data/ru.mail.cloud/databases/*
- *Cloud Magic*: */data/data/com.cloudmagic.mail/databases/*
- *Degoo*: */data/data/com.degoo.android/databases/*
- *Pcloud*: */data/data/com.pcloud.pcloud/databases/*
- *XXL Box*: */data/data/com.xxlcloud.xxlbox/databases/*

- *ZeroPC: /data/data/com.zeropc.tablet/databases/*
- *File Manager: /data/data/fm.clean/databases/*
- *4Sync Cloud: /data/data/com.forsync/databases/*
- *Asus Web: /data/data/com.ecareme.asuswebstorage/databases/*
- *FileBay.co: /data/data/com.sflcnetwork.filebayco/databases/*
- *Folder Sync: /data/data/dk.tacit.android.foldersync.lite/databases/*
- *MyCloud: /data/data/com.wdc.wd2go/databases/*
- *Pogoplug: /data/data/com.wdc.wd2go/databases/*

The applications intended here are under both Groups 2 and 3, as applications from Group 1 did not generate any db files.

Notice that the path for this particular file, always shows same directory names: *"data/ data/generated_file_name/databases/"* these kind of paths are inaccessible to the user. Check Appendix 3 for more information on the applications and their db files.

4.2 Storage

The artifacts retrieved from the dataset are usually found on the internal storage folder which is accessible by the user, such as the pictures folder, the music folder and so on. A good observation would be that some images were not retrieved and yet their thumbnails were, and from a simple thumbnail a lot of information may be obtained during the forensics investigation process, it may not show all the details as the number of pixels in thumbnails is obviously much lower than the those of an original image, however, using some image processing tools, a lot of evidence could be extracted from a simple thumbnail.

The following lists the findings of the extracted data within the internal storage, which includes *Pictures, Documents, Audio files*, and *Web files*.

4.2.1 Pictures

We were able to retrieve images from some applications, as mentioned before, those retrieved images may not have the same size, resolution, and file details as the original ones, however, those images were viewable, and are enough to be shown as evidence for forensics investigation purposes. The following applications showed recovered artifacts (i.e., original pictures, thumbnails, cache images):

- *Box*
- *GCloud*
- *Mail.Ru*
- *Cloud Magic*
- *Just Cloud*
- *XXL Box Secure*
- *Zero PC*
- *File Manager*
- *ZipCloud*
- *Folder Sync Lite*
- *MyCloud*

See Appendix 3 for the full list of applications and their respective findings.

4.2.2 Documents

For some applications, the following documents were retrieved from the internal storage and were in a readable format too: *.doc, .pot, and .pdf*. Most apps did not show any retrieved document files during the extraction, except for a minority of apps, those are as follow:

- *Cloud Magic*
- *XXL Box Secure*
- *File Manager*
- *DropSend Android Cloud*
- *Folder Sync Lite*
- *MyCloud*

4.2.3 Web Files

A variety of applications stored web files from the correspondent dataset used in the experiment (*.xml and .html*) in the internal storage and hence it was retrievable and readable too. The apps are as follow:

- *XXL Box Secure*
- *File Manager*
- *Zip Cloud*
- *DropSend Android*
- *Folder Sync Lite*
- *MyCloud*

4.2.4 Audio

The audio file from the selected dataset was recovered from a minority of applications only and was playable, those applications are:

- *Just Cloud*
- *XXL Box Secure*
- *File Manager*
- *Folder Sync Lite*
- *My Cloud*

Upon analyzing the extracted data, the path of the retrieved audio file showed the following: "*mnt/sdcard*" that is an evidence of the existence of data or artifact on the internal storage of the device, and is accessible by the user. While the path "*/data/data/*" may not be accessible by a regular user, but that is not the case for any forensic investigator examining the device for evidence. Appendix 3 illustrates these results and clarifies the retrieved files for each of the 31 applications.

As a conclusion to these results, we can state that based on the amount of files retrieved from each app in this experiment we could categorize them into three groups according to how much data (artifact) was recovered, the first group of applications showed no recovered data on XRY, which we will classify in this paper as (Group 1), while some applications generated database files in the internal storage only while the files from the dataset were not recovered, we call this group (Group 2), and finally (Group 3) showed database files as well as most of the data stored in the cloud was retrieved. As shown in Table 1, cloud applications used in this experiment can be categorized into three groups.

TABLE 1   Classification of Apps Based on This Study

Applications Classification		
Group 1	**Group 2**	**Group 3**
Box	File Expert	Mail.Ru
DropBox	Degoo	GCloud
Google Drive	PCloud	Cloud Magic
Adobe Creative Cloud	4Sync Cloud	Just Cloud
One Drive	Asus Web Storage Cloud	XXL Box Secure
Yandex	FileBay.co	ZeroPC
Tesorit	PogoPlug Cloud	File Manager
Egnyte		Zip Cloud
Bitcasa		Drop Send Android Cloud
IDrive Cloud		Folder Sync Lite
JohoSpace		My Cloud (WD)
Mega Cloud		

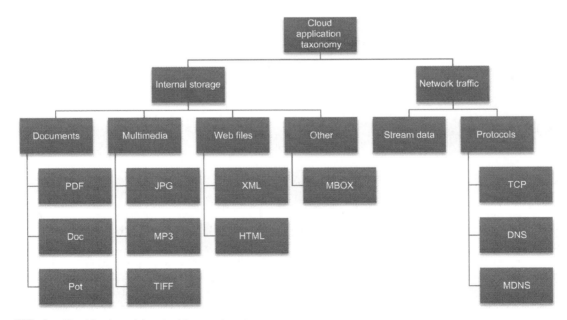

FIG. 1   Classification of data in this experiment.

The diagram in Fig. 1 illustrates the classification of data recovered during this taxonomy forensics experiment, some applications showed a lot of recovered data, while others showed no trace of those files, this diagram facilitates an understanding on how to categorize and tabulate the data recovered. This taxonomy was coined from the intricate analyzing of the recovered remnant from the extraction processes. It is a comprehensive and relevant taxonomy in the field of cyber cloud forensics. This is depicted in the detailed results and discussions sections of this paper.

5 CONCLUSION AND FUTURE WORKS

Mobile forensics, and specifically Android forensics, continues to be a growing field of research. As the Android platform and its architectures continue to evolve, the current research will facilitate forensic investigators in recovering sources of evidence [31–36].

The main purpose of this paper is to contribute to the forensics field and particularly the Android mobile forensics. With a taxonomy experiment on Android cloud applications, we deem its necessity in this particular area of research as the taxonomy for cloud applications is minimal. Using the taxonomy and forensics model, we conducted a fundamental analysis on 31 popular cloud applications; the findings are tabulated and presented appropriately in appendix section.

Finally, as part of our future work, we intend to examine other cloud applications on other platforms (i.e., IOS) and devices, and push the investigation by performing physical data acquisition on those apps in order to capture dumps from the device's memory which may lead to even more promising findings. However, more research is still needed in order to provide better directions on addressing different challenges of mobile forensics, and prompt further discussion on the development of different forensic taxonomies in variety of contexts.

APPENDIX 1 LIST OF APPLICATION VERSIONS

App ID	App Name	App Version
1	*Box*	3.7.5
2	*File Expert*	7.1.8
3	*GCloud*	5.4.95
4	*Mail.Ru*	4.4.0.15562
5	*MEO Cloud*	2.1.0
6	*Cloud Magic*	8.1.32
7	*Drop Box*	5.2.6
8	*Degoo*	1.9.7
9	*One Drive*	3.9.1
10	*Just Cloud*	1.2.4

Continued

App ID	App Name	App Version
11	PCloud	1.12.05
12	XXL Box Secure	1.0.2
13	ZeroPC	2.5.5
14	File Manager	4.0.4.9
15	ZipCloud	1.2.4
16	4Sync Cloud	3.27.0
17	Adobe Creative Cloud	2.3.460
18	Asus Web Storage Cloud	3.1.8.0408
19	Bitcasa Drive	4.25.5
20	DropSend Android Cloud	1.0.0-rc6
21	Egnyte	6.8.5
22	FileBay.co Secure Storage	1
23	Foldersync Lite	2.8.5.90
24	IDrive Cloud Online Backup	3.6.32
25	JohoSpace Backup – Restore & Migrate	3.6.3
26	Mega Cloud	3.0.6.official
27	MyCLoud (WD)	4.4.3
28	Pogoplug Cloud	5.11.0.19
29	Tesorit Cloud	2.1.386.443
30	Yandex Disk	2.65
31	Google Drive	2.4.141.16.34

APPENDIX 2 DATASET LIST (EDRM)

Dataset ID	File Name and Extension	File Type
1	Student-Documentation.pdf	PDF document
2	Malaventura_-_12_The_Queen.mp3	Media file audio
3	IMG_3084.jpg	JPEG image
4	IMG_3085.jpg	JPEG image
5	EDRM.html	HTML document
6	Disposing-of-Digital-Debris-Information-Governance-Practice-and-Strategy_Page_02.tif	TIFF image

Continued

Dataset ID	File Name and Extension	File Type
7	*Disposing-of-Digital-Debris-Information-Governance-Practice-and-Strategy_Page_05.tif*	TIFF image
8	*Disposing of Digital Debris Sample 1.pot*	Microsoft powerpoint document
9	*Disposing of Digital Debris – 97.doc*	Microsoft word document
10	*DERM Statistical Data Sample 1 Unicode.xml*	XML document
11	*Cindyloh3333@gmail.com.mbox*	MBOX e-mail file

APPENDIX 3 RETRIEVED ARTIFACTS

App ID	App Name	DB Files	Path	JPEG	TIF	DOC	POT	PDF	XML	HTML	Mp3	MBOX
1	Box	N/A	N/A	✓	✗	✗	✗	✗	✗	✗	✗	✗
2	File Expert	FileExpert.db	/data/data/xcxin.fehd/databases/	✗	✗	✗	✗	✗	✗	✗	✗	✗
3	GCloud	GCloudDB, db_music, db_video, syncdata.db	/data/data/com.genie9.gcloudbackup/databases/	✓	✗	✗	✗	✗	✗	✗	✗	✗
4	Mail.Ru	adman.db, isp. taxonomy@mail.ru, google_analytics_v4.db	/data/data/ru.mail.cloud/databases/	✓	✓	✗	✗	✗	✗	✗	✗	✗
5	MEO Cloud	N/A	N/A	✗	✗	✗	✗	✗	✗	✗	✗	✗
6	Cloud Magic	google_analytics_v2.db	/data/data/com.cloudmagic.mail/databases/	✓	✓	✓	✓	✓	✗	✗	✗	✗
7	Drop Box	N/A	N/A	✗	✗	✗	✗	✗	✗	✗	✗	✗
8	Degoo	google_analytics_v4.db	/data/data/com.degoo.android/databases/	✗	✗	✗	✗	✗	✗	✗	✗	✗
9	One Drive	N/A	N/A	✗	✗	✗	✗	✗	✗	✗	✗	✗
10	Just Cloud	N/A	N/A	✓	✗	✗	✗	✗	✗	✗	✓	✗
11	PCloud	PCloudDB, PCloudDB_wal, PCloudDB_shm, google_analytics_v4.db	/data/data/com.pcloud.pcloud/databases/	✗	✗	✗	✗	✗	✗	✗	✗	✗
12	XXL Box Secure	Monitor.db, data.db, account.db	/data/data/com.xxlcloud.xxlbox/databases/	✓	✓	✓	✓	✓	✓	✓	✓	✓
13	ZeroPC	com.zeropc.tablet.queue.db, com.zeropc.tablet.cache.db	/data/data/com.zeropc.tablet/databases/	✓	✓	✓	✗	✗	✗	✗	✗	✗
14	File Manager	clanfilemanager.db, google_tagmanager.db, google_analytics_v4.db	/data/data/fm.clean/databases/	✓	✓	✓	✓	✓	✓	✓	✓	✓
15	ZipCloud	N/A	N/A	✓	✗	✗	✗	✗	✗	✗	✗	✓

#	App	Files	Path										
16	4Sync Cloud	Cloud.db, sdk4.uploads.db, sdk4.uploads.db-shm, sdk4.uploads.db-wal, google_analytics_v4.db	/data/data/com.forsync/databases/	✗	✗	✗	✗	✗	✗	✗	✗	✗	✗
17	Adobe Creative Cloud	N/A	N/A	✗	✗	✗	✗	✗	✗	✗	✗	✗	✗
18	Asus Web Storage Cloud	AWS.db, awsbackup	/data/data/com.ecareme.asuswebstorage/databases/	✗	✗	✗	✗	✗	✗	✗	✗	✗	✗
19	Bitcasa Drive	N/A	N/A	✗	✗	✗	✗	✗	✗	✗	✗	✗	✗
20	DropSend Android Cloud	N/A	N/A	✗	✓	✓	✓	✓	✓	✓	✓	✗	✗
21	Egnyte	N/A	N/A	✗	✗	✗	✗	✗	✗	✗	✗	✗	✗
22	FileBay.co Secure Storage	google_analytics_v4.db	/data/data/com.sflcnetwork.filebayco/databases/	✗	✗	✗	✗	✗	✗	✗	✗	✗	✗
23	Foldersync Lite	foldersync.db	/data/data/dk.tacit.android.foldersync.lite/databases/	✓	✓	✓	✓	✓	✓	✓	✓	✓	✗
24	IDrive Cloud Online Backup	N/A	N/A	✗	✗	✗	✗	✗	✗	✗	✗	✗	✗
25	JohoSpace Backup- Restore & Migrate	N/A	N/A	✗	✗	✗	✗	✗	✗	✗	✗	✗	✗
26	Mega Cloud	N/A	N/A	✗	✗	✗	✗	✗	✗	✗	✗	✗	✗
27	MyCLoud (WD)	wd-files-demo-cache.db, wd-files-cache.db	/data/data/com.wdc.wd2go/databases/	✓	✓	✓	✓	✓	✓	✓	✓	✓	✓
28	Pogoplug Cloud	VISUALS, POGOPLUG	/data/data/com.pogoplug.android/databases/	✗	✗	✗	✗	✗	✗	✗	✗	✗	✗
29	Tesorit CLoud	N/A	N/A	✗	✗	✗	✗	✗	✗	✗	✗	✗	✗
30	Yandex Disk	N/A	N/A	✗	✗	✗	✗	✗	✗	✗	✗	✗	✗
31	Google Drive	N/A	N/A	✗	✗	✗	✗	✗	✗	✗	✗	✗	✗

APPENDIX 4 NETWORK TRAFFIC

App ID	App Name	Protocols Used			MDNS	Relevant Stream Data DNS
		TCP	MDNS	DNS		

1.	Box	✓	✓	✓	`._googlecast._tcp.`
					`local................._googlecast._`
					`tcp.local..`
					
					`M-SEARCH * HTTP/1.1`
					`Host:239.255.255.250:1900`
					`ST:urn:schemas-upnp-`
					`org:device:MediaRenderer:1`
					`Man:"ssdp:discover"`
					
					`MX:3`
						`NOTIFY * HTTP/1.1`
						`LOCATION:http://192.168.201.1:0/`
						`HOST: 239.255.255.250:1900`
						`SERVER: WINDOWS, UPnP/1.0,`
						`MicroStack/1.0.4103`
						`NTS: ssdp:alive`
						`USN: uuid:a343c163-d6a5-4e47-9ae6-`
						`1ed85ce82f5d`
						`CACHE-CONTROL: max-age=1800`
						
						`NT: uuid:a343c163-d6a5-4e47-9ae6-`
						`1ed85ce82f5d`

2.	File Expert	✓	✓		`M-SEARCH * HTTP/1.1`
					`Host:[FF02::C]:1900`
					`ST:urn:schemas-upnp-`
					`org:device:MediaRenderer:1`
					`Man:"ssdp:discover"`
					
					`MX:3`
						`NOTIFY * HTTP/1.1`
						`LOCATION:http://192.168.201.1:0/`
						`HOST: 239.255.255.250:1900`
						`SERVER: WINDOWS, UPnP/1.0,`
						`MicroStack/1.0.4103`
						`NTS: ssdp:alive`
						`USN: uuid:a343c163-d6a5-4e47-9ae6-`
						`1ed85ce82f5d`
						`CACHE-CONTROL: max-age=1800`
						
						`NT: uuid:a343c163-d6a5-4e47-9ae6-`
						`1ed85ce82f5d`

3.	GCloud	✓	✗	✓	`M-SEARCH * HTTP/1.1`
					`Host:239.255.255.250:1900`
					`ST:urn:schemas-upnp-`
					`org:device:MediaRenderer:1`
					`Man:"ssdp:discover"`
					
					`MX:3`
						`NOTIFY * HTTP/1.1`
						`LOCATION:http://192.168.201.1:0/`
						`HOST: 239.255.255.250:1900`
						`SERVER: WINDOWS, UPnP/1.0,`
						`MicroStack/1.0.4103`
						`NTS: ssdp:alive`
						`USN: uuid:a343c163-d6a5-4e47-9ae6-1ed85`
						`ce82f5d::upnp:rootdevice`
						`CACHE-CONTROL: max-age=1800`
						
						`NT: upnp:rootdevice`

#	Service			Network traffic
4.	Mail.Ru	✓	✗	(UDP stream): .....cloclo12.datacloudmail.ru.......
5.	MEO Cloud	✓	✗	
6.	Cloud Magic	✓	✗	
7.	Drop Box	✓	✓	
8.	Degoo	✓	✗	
9.	One Drive	✓	✓	(UDP stream): _805741C9._sub._googlecast._tcp. local.......... (UDP stream): c.........cid-59DAFF70AD928598.users. storage.live.com......
10.	Just Cloud	✓	✗	
11.	PCloud	✓	✗	(UDP stream): .3........binapi.pcloud.com..... And......p-par17.pcloud.com.....
12.	XXL Box Secure	✓	✗	-
13.	ZeroPC	✓	✗	(UDP stream): m<........v1.zeropc.com.....
14.	File Manager	✓	✗	
15.	ZipCloud	✓	✗	(UDP stream): sq.......thumbnails backupgrid.net.....
16.	4Sync Cloud	✓	✓	...............1h5.ggpht.com......
17.	Adobe Creative Cloud	✓	✗	NOTIFY * HTTP/1.1 LOCATION: http://192.168.201.1:0/ HOST: 239.255.255.250:1900 SERVER: WINDOWS, UPnP/1.0, MicroStack/1.0.4103 NTS: ssdp:alive USN: uuid:a343c163-d6a5-4e47-9ae6- 1ed85ce82f5d::urn:schemas-upnp- org:device:InternetGatewayDevice:1 CACHE-CONTROL: max-age=1800 NT: urn:schemas-upnp- org:device:InternetGatewayDevice:1	.............cc-api-storage.adobe. io...... #..........android.clients.google. com......

Continued

App ID	Applications		Protocols Used			Relevant Stream Data	
	App Name		TCP	MDNS	DNS	MDNS	DNS

18.	Asus Web Storage Cloud		✓	✓	✓	`.u...........android.clients.google. com......`	`M-SEARCH * HTTP/1.1`
							`Host:[FF02::CJ]:1900`
							`ST:urn:schemas-upnp-`
							`org:device:MediaServer:1`
							`Man:"ssdp:discover"`
							
							`MX:3`

19.	Bitcasa Drive		✓	✓		`...........bitcasa.cloudfs.io.....`	`.............._googlecast._tcp.`
							`local............................_googlecast._`
							`tcp.local........................—`
							`googlecast._tcp.`
							`local.......................__googlecast._`
							`tcp.local........................—`
							`googlecast._tcp.local......`

20.	DropSend Android Cloud		✓	✗	✓	`M-SEARCH * HTTP/1.1`
						`Host:239.255.255.250:1900`
						`ST:urn:schemas-upnp-`
						`org:device:MediaServer:1`
						`Man:"ssdp:discover"`
						`MX:3`
							`NOTIFY * HTTP/1.1`
							`LOCATION:http://192.168.201.1:49860/`
							`HOST: 239.255.255.250:1900`
							`SERVER: WINDOWS, UPnP/1.0,`
							`MicroStack/1.0.4103`
							`NTS: ssdp:alive`
							`USN: uuid:a343c163-d6a5-4e47-9ae6-`
							`1ed85ce82f5d::urn:schemas-upnp-org:`
							`service:Layer3Forwarding:1`
							`CACHE-CONTROL: max-age=1800`
							`NT: urn:schemas-upnp-`
							`org:service:Layer3Forwarding:1`

21.	Egnyte		✓	✗	✓	`.>...........decide.mixpanel.com.....`
						`...........api.mixpanel.com.....`
							`NOTIFY * HTTP/1.1`
							`LOCATION:http://192.168.201.1:0/`
							`HOST: 239.255.255.250:1900`
							`SERVER: WINDOWS, UPnP/1.0,`
							`MicroStack/1.0.4103`
							`NTS: ssdp:alive`
							`USN: uuid:a343c163-d6a5-4e47-9ae6-`
							`1ed85ce82f5d::upnp:rootdevice`
							`CACHE-CONTROL: max-age=1800`
							`NT: upnp:rootdevice`

Continued

#	App				Network traffic

22.	FileBay.co Secure Storage	✓	✗	✓	`6............www.facebook.com......`
					`M-SEARCH * HTTP/1.1`
					`Host:239.255.255.250:1900`
					`ST:urn:schemas-upnp-`
					`org:device:MediaRenderer:1`
					`Man:"ssdp:discover"`
					`MX:3`
					
					`.q............android.clients.google.`
					`com......`
					`` `H..........r2--sn-aig16n76.gvt1. ``
					`com......`
					`T.......cdn.ywxi.net.....`
					`NOTIFY * HTTP/1.1`
					`LOCATION:http://192.168.201.1:49860/`
					`HOST: 239.255.255.250:1900`
					`SERVER: WINDOWS, UPnP/1.0,`
					`MicroStack/1.0.4103`
					`NTS: ssdp:alive`
					`USN: uuid:a343c163-d6a5-4e47-9ae6-`
					`1ed85ce82f5d_1`
					`CACHE-CONTROL: max-age=1800`
					`NT: uuid:a343c163-d6a5-4e47-9ae6-`
					`1ed85ce82f5d_1`

23.	Foldersync Lite	✓			`..._googlecast._tcp.`
					`local..............._googlecast._`
					`tcp.local.`
					`...........ssl.google-analytics.`
					`com......`
					`M-SEARCH * HTTP/1.1`
					`HOST: 239.255.255.250:1900`
					`MAN: "ssdp:discover"`
					`MX: 1`
					`ST: urn:dial-multiscreen-`
					`org:service:dial:1`
					
					`NOTIFY * HTTP/1.1`
					`LOCATION:http://192.168.201.1:0/`
					`HOST: 239.255.255.250:1900`
					`SERVER: WINDOWS, UPnP/1.0,`
					`MicroStack/1.0.4103`
					`NTS: ssdp:alive`
					`USN: uuid:a343c163-d6a5-4e47-9ae6-`
					`1ed85ce82f5d_1`
					`CACHE-CONTROL: max-age=1800`
					`NT: uuid:a343c163-d6a5-4e47-9ae6-`
					`1ed85ce82f5d_1`

24.	IDrive Cloud Online Backup	✓	✗		`6..........evsweb16`
					`idrivesync.com......`
					`.I..........evs`
					`idrivesync.com......`
					
					`NOTIFY * HTTP/1.1`
					`LOCATION:http://192.168.201.1:0/`
					`HOST: 239.255.255.250:1900`
					`SERVER: WINDOWS, UPnP/1.0,`
					`MicroStack/1.0.4103`
					`NTS: ssdp:alive`
					`USN: uuid:a343c163-d6a5-4e47-9ae6-`
					`1ed85ce82f5d_1`
					`CACHE-CONTROL: max-age=1800`
					`NT: uuid:a343c163-d6a5-4e47-9ae6-`
					`1ed85ce82f5d_1`

| Applications | | Protocols Used | | | Relevant Stream Data | |
App ID	App Name	TCP	MDNS	DNS	MDNS	DNS

25.	JohoSpace Backup – Restore & Migrate	✓	✗	✓	`.P..........www.manage.jsbackup.net......`
					
					`M-SEARCH * HTTP/1.1`
					`Host:[FF02::C]:1900`
					`ST:urn:schemas-upnp-org:device:MediaRenderer:1`
					`Man:"ssdp:discover"`
					`MX:3`
						`NOTIFY * HTTP/1.1`
						`LOCATION:http://192.168.201.1:0/`
						`HOST: 239.255.255.250:1900`
						`SERVER: WINDOWS, UPnP/1.0.`
						`MicroStack/1.0.4103`
						`NTS: ssdp:alive`
						`USN: uuid:a343c163-d6a5-4e47-9ae6-1ed85ce82f5d`
						`CACHE-CONTROL: max-age=1800`
						`NT: uuid:a343c163-d6a5-4e47-9ae6-1ed85ce82f5d`

26.	Mega Cloud	✓	✗		`M-SEARCH * HTTP/1.1`
					`Host:[FF02::C]:1900`
					`ST:urn:schemas-upnp-org:device:MediaRenderer:1`
					`Man:"ssdp:discover"`
					`MX:3`
						`NOTIFY * HTTP/1.1`
						`LOCATION:http://192.168.201.1:0/`
						`HOST: 239.255.255.250:1900`
						`SERVER: WINDOWS, UPnP/1.0.`
						`MicroStack/1.0.4103`
						`NTS: ssdp:alive`
						`USN: uuid:a343c163-d6a5-4e47-9ae6-1ed85ce82f5d_1`
						`CACHE-CONTROL: max-age=1800`
						`NT: uuid:a343c163-d6a5-4e47-9ae6-1ed85ce82f5d_1`

27.	MyCLoud (WD)	✓	✓		`M-SEARCH * HTTP/1.1`
					`HOST: 239.255.255.250:1900`
					`MAN: "ssdp:discover"`
					`MX: 4`
					`ST: ssdp:all`
						`NOTIFY * HTTP/1.1`
						`LOCATION:http://192.168.201.1:0/`
						`HOST: 239.255.255.250:1900`
						`SERVER: WINDOWS, UPnP/1.0.`
						`MicroStack/1.0.4103`
						`NTS: ssdp:alive`
						`USN: uuid:a343c163-d6a5-4e47-9ae6-1ed85ce82f5d_1`
						`CACHE-CONTROL: max-age=1800`
						`NT: uuid:a343c163-d6a5-4e47-9ae6-1ed85ce82f5d_1`

#	Service			

28.	Pogoplug Cloud	✓	✓	`_DC295335._sub._googlecast._tcp.`
				`local.......`
					`NOTIFY * HTTP/1.1`
					`LOCATION:http://192.168.201.1:0/`
					`HOST: 239.255.255.250:1900`
					`SERVER: WINDOWS, UPnP/1.0,`
					`MicroStack/1.0.4103`
					`NTS: ssdp:alive`
					`USN: uuid:a343c163-d6a5-4e47-9ae6-`
					`1ed85ce82f5d`
					`CACHE-CONTROL: max-age=1800`
					`NT: uuid:a343c163-d6a5-4e47-9ae6-`
					`1ed85ce82f5d`

29.	Tesorit CLoud	✓	✗	`.#..........1h3.ggpht.com`
				`connectify......`
				`.q..........r14--sn-aigln6k.gvt1.`
				`com....`
				`M-SEARCH * HTTP/1.1`
				`Host:[FF02::CJ]:1900`
				`ST:urn:schemas-upnp-`
				`org:device:MediaRenderer:1`
				`Man:"ssdp:discover"`
				`MX:3`
					`NOTIFY * HTTP/1.1`
					`LOCATION:http://192.168.201.1:0/`
					`HOST: 239.255.255.250:1900`
					`SERVER: WINDOWS, UPnP/1.0,`
					`MicroStack/1.0.4103`
					`NTS: ssdp:alive`
					`USN: uuid:a343c163-d6a5-4e47-9ae6-`
					`1ed85ce82f5d_1`
					`CACHE-CONTROL: max-age=1800`
					`NT: uuid:a343c163-d6a5-4e47-9ae6-`
					`1ed85ce82f5d_1`

30.	Yandex Disk	✓	✗	`M-SEARCH * HTTP/1.1`
				`Host:[FF02::CJ]:1900`
				`ST:urn:schemas-upnp-`
				`org:device:MediaRenderer:1`
				`Man:"ssdp:discover"`
				`MX:3`
					`[&..........`
					`uploader7h.disk.yandex.net......`
					`NOTIFY * HTTP/1.1`
					`LOCATION:http://192.168.201.1:0/`
					`HOST: 239.255.255.250:1900`
					`SERVER: WINDOWS, UPnP/1.0,`
					`MicroStack/1.0.4103`
					`NTS: ssdp:alive`
					`USN: uuid:a343c163-d6a5-4e47-9ae6-`
					`1ed85ce82f5d`
					`CACHE-CONTROL: max-age=1800`
					`NT: uuid:a343c163-d6a5-4e47-9ae6-`
					`1ed85ce82f5d`

31.	Google Drive	✓	✓	✓	

References

[1] T. Hornyak, Android grabs record 85 percent smartphone share, Retrieved from: http://www.pcworld.com/article/2460020/android-grabs-record-85-percent-smartphone-share.html, 2014 (18.02.16).

[2] A. Kumar, B. Xie, Handbook of Mobile Systems Applications and Services, CRC Press, Boca Raton, FL, 2012. Retrieved from: https://books.google.co.uk/books?hl=en&lr=&id=VCWMCgAAQBAJ&oi=fnd&pg=PP1&dq=2.%09Kumar,+A.+%26+Xie,+B.+(2012).+Handbook+of+mobile+systems+applications+and+services.+Boca+Raton:+CRC+Press&ots=iM7-3IZaHM&sig=wv6RShQVPBywH_wtUzJbtg9D8BI.

[3] J. Vincent, Android is now used by 1.4 billion people, Retrieved from: http://www.theverge.com/2015/9/29/9409071/google-android-stats-users-downloads-sales, 2015.

[4] A. Stevenson, Top 10 Android benefits over Apple iPhone, Retrieved from: http://www.v3.co.uk/v3-uk/news/2336474/top-10-android-benefits-over-apple-iphone/page/3?mt=143&mv2=370&mv=969, 2014.

[5] J. Tee, Top five ways cloud computing impacts mobile application development teams, TheServerSide.com. Retrieved from: http://www.theserverside.com/feature/Top-five-ways-cloud-computing-impacts-mobile-application-development-teams, 2012.

[6] M. Ganji, A. Dehghantanha, N. IzuraUdzir, Cyber warfare trends and future, Adv. Inf. Sci. Serv. Sci. 5 (2013) 1–10. Retrieved from: http://search.proquest.com/openview/cdd017512e93963c0f2ac8f2e88d3c5f/1?pq-origsite=gscholar.

[7] M. Damshenas, A. Dehghantanha, A survey on digital forensics trends, Int. J. Cyber-Secur. Digit. Forensic 3 (4) (2014) 235. Retrieved from: http://go.galegroup.com/ps/i.do?id=GALE%7CA387349458&sid=googleScholar&v=2.1&it=r&linkaccess=fulltext&issn=23050012&p=AONE&sw=w.

[8] D. Mohsen, D. Ali, M. Ramlan, A survey on digital forensics trends, Int. J. Cyber-Secur. Digit. Forensic 3 (4) (2014) 209–235.

[9] M. Damshenas, A. Dehghantanha, R. Mahmoud, S. bin Shamsuddin, Cloud computing and conflicts with digital forensic investigation, Int. J. Digit. Content Technol. Appl. 7 (9) (2013) 543. Retrieved from: http://search.proquest.com/openview/43636b97fc3d6f8d5332b32bb9c1637e/1?pq-origsite=gscholar.

[10] M. Yusoff, R. Mahmod, M. Abdullah, Mobile forensic data acquisition in Firefox OS, Cyber Secur. Cyber Warf. Digit. Forensic 3 (4) (2014) 209–235. Retrieved from: http://ieeexplore.ieee.org/xpls/abs_all.jsp?arnumber=6913967.

[11] A. Aminnezhad, A. Dehghantanha, Cloud forensics issues and opportunities, Int. J. Inf. Process. Manag. 4 (4) (2013) 76. Retrieved from: https://www.researchgate.net/profile/Mohd_Taufik_Abdullah2/publication/276010807_Cloud_Forensics_Issues_and_Opportunities/links/5556f1cb08ae980ca60c9daf.pdf.

[12] F. Daryabar, A. Dehghantanha, B. Eterovic-Soric, K.-K.R. Choo, Forensic investigation of OneDrive, Box, GoogleDrive and Dropbox applications on Android and iOS devices, Aust. J. Forensic Sci. 48 (2016) 1–28, http://dx.doi.org/10.1080/00450618.2015.1110620.

[13] S. Mohtasebi, A. Dehghantanha, Defusing the hazards of social network services, Int. J. Digit. Inf. Wirel. Commun. 1 (2) (2011) 504–516. Retrieved from: http://sdiwc.net/digital-library/defusing-the-hazards-of-social-network-services.html.

[14] S. Mohtasebi, Smartphone forensics: a case study with Nokia E5-00 mobile phone, J. Digit. Forensic Secur. Law 1 (3) (2011) 651–655. Retrieved from: http://sdiwc.net/digital-library/smartphone-forensics-a-case-study-with-nokia-e500-mobile-phone.

[15] T.Y. Yang, A. Dehghantanha, K.-K.R. Choo, Z. Muda, Windows instant messaging app forensics: Facebook and Skype as case studies, PLoS ONE 11 (3) (2016), http://dx.doi.org/10.1371/journal.pone.0150300.

[16] F. Daryabar, A. Dehghantanha, N.I. Udzir, N.F.b.M. Sani, S. bin Shamsuddin, A review on impacts of cloud computing on digital forensics, Int. J. Cyber-Secur. Digit. Forensic 2 (2) (2013) 77–94.

[17] F. Daryabar, A. Dehghantanha, N.I. Udzir, N.F.b.M. Sani, S. bin Shamsuddin, A survey about impacts of cloud computing on digital forensics, Int. J. Cyber-Secur. Digit. Forensic 2 (2) (2013) 77–94. Retrieved from: http://sdiwc.net/security-journal/Browse-Archive.php?ptid=1&ptsid=66&vnum=2&inum=2.

[18] A. Azfar, K.-K.R. Choo, L. Liu, An android social app forensics adversary model, in: 2016 49th Hawaii International Conference on System Sciences (HICSS), Koloa, HI, 2016, pp. 5597–5606, http://dx.doi.org/10.1109/HICSS.2016.693.

[19] A. Azfar, K.R. Choo, L. Liu, Forensic taxonomy of popular android mHealth apps, in: Proceedings of the 21st Americas Conference on Information Systems (AMCIS 2015), 2015. Retrieved from: http://aisel.aisnet.org/cgi/viewcontent.cgi?article=1217&context=amcis2015.

[20] A. Azfar, K.-K.R. Choo, L. Liu, An android communication app forensic taxonomy. J. Forensic Sci. (2016), http://dx.doi.org/10.1111/1556-4029.13164.

[21] S. Falk, A. Shyshka, The Cloud Marketplace: a capability-based framework for cloud ecosystem governance, Retrieved from: http://www.diva-portal.org/smash/get/diva2:721103/FULLTEXT01.pdf, 2014.

[22] S. Nammi, How to revert back from Android L to KitKat, Retrieved from: http://nexusandme.com/revert-back-from-android-l-to-kitkat/, 2014.

[23] R.A. Mushcab, P. Gladyshev, The significance of different backup applications in retrieving social networking forensic artifacts from android-based mobile devices, in: Second International Conference on Information Security and Cyber Forensics, 2015, pp. 66–71. Retrieved from: http://ieeexplore.ieee.org/xpls/abs_all.jsp?arnumber=7435508.

[24] F. Daryabar, A. Dehghantanha, B. Eterovic-Soric, K.-K.R. Choo, Forensic investigation of OneDrive, Box, GoogleDrive and Dropbox applications on Android and iOS devices. Aust. J. Forensic Sci. (2016), http://dx.doi.org/10.1080/00450618.2015.1110620.

[25] M.W. Park, Y.H. Choi, J.H. Eom, T.M. Chung, Dangerous Wi-Fi access point: attacks to benign smartphone applications, Pers. Ubiquit. Comput. 18 (6) (2014) 1373–1386, http://dx.doi.org/10.1007/s00779-013-0739-y.

[26] R.A. Ashraf, Performance Analysis of Video Call Application on Tablet Using 3G Network, Retrieved from: UTeM, Melaka, 2013. http://eprints.utem.edu.my/13869/.

[27] D.C.T. Lo, K. Qian, W. Chen, T. Rogers, A low cost, portable platform for information assurance and security education, in: Proceedings—IEEE 15th International Conference on Advanced Learning Technologies: Advanced Technologies for Supporting Open Access to Formal and Informal Learning, ICALT 2015, 2015, pp. 111–113, http://dx.doi.org/10.1109/ICALT.2015.132.

[28] EDRM, New EDRM resource provides emerging data types for e-discovery testing new EDRM Enron email data set, Retrieved from: http://www.edrm.net/resources/data-sets/edrm-enron-email-data-set, 2010.

[29] Microsoft, Volatile and nonvolatile storage devices, Retrieved from: https://msdn.microsoft.com/en-us/library/ms940147(v=winembedded.5).aspx, 2006.

[30] R. Shimonski, The Wireshark Field Guide: Analyzing and Troubleshooting Network Traffic, Newnes, 2013. Retrieved from: http://www.sciencedirect.com/science/article/pii/B9780124104136000012.

[31] B. Martini, Q. Do, K.-K.R. Choo, Mobile cloud forensics: an analysis of seven popular Android apps. in: R. Ko, R. Choo (Eds.), The Cloud Security Ecosystem, Syngress, Cambridge, MA, 2015, pp. 309–345, http://dx.doi.org/10.1016/B978-0-12-801595-7.00015-X (Chapter 15).

[32] B. Martini, Q. Do, K.-K.R. Choo, Conceptual evidence collection and analysis methodology for Android devices. in: R. Ko, R. Choo (Eds.), The Cloud Security Ecosystem, Syngress, Cambridge, MA, 2015, pp. 285–307, http://dx.doi.org/10.1016/B978-0-12-801595-7.00014-8.

[33] M. Shariati, A. Dehghantanha, B. Martini, K.-K.R. Choo, Ubuntu one investigation: detecting evidences on client machines. in: R. Ko, R. Choo (Eds.), The Cloud Security Ecosystem, Syngress, Cambridge, MA, 2015, pp. 429–446, http://dx.doi.org/10.1016/B978-0-12-801595-7.00019-7 (Chapter 19).

[34] F. Daryabar, A. Dehghantanha, K.-K.R. Choo, Cloud storage forensics: MEGA as a case study, Aust. J. Forensic Sci, http://dx.doi.org/10.1080/00450618.2016.1153714.

[35] S.H. Mohtasebi, A. Dehghantanha, Towards a unified forensic investigation framework of smartphones, Int. J. Comput. Theory Eng 5 (2) (2013) 351–355.

[36] D. Mohsen, D. Ali, K.-K.R. Choo, R. Mahmud, M0Droid: an android behavioural-based malware detection model, J. Inf. Privacy Secur. 11 (3) (2015) 141–157, http://dx.doi.org/10.1080/15536548.2015.1073510.

Index

Note: Page numbers followed by *f* indicates figures and *t* indicates tables.

A

AccessData FTK, 95
AIM forensics
  .BLT format, 26–27
  buddy icons, 33
  buddy List, 26–27, 30
  conversations, 30–32
  Happening messages, 33–34
  IM logs, 32–33
  installation, 27–28
  netscan function, 29
  network information, 29*t*
  OFT3 file transfer header, 32, 32*f*
  RAM in plaint text, 30–31*f*
  registry key, 27, 27*f*
  transferred files, 30–32
  unicode string format, 31
  uninstallation, 34
Android emulator 1.0.5, 190–191
Android KitKat 4.4.2
  CloudMe, 253–254, 254*f*
    downloaded files, 261, 262*f*
    installation, 258
    internal memory, 258, 261*f*
    local CloudMe cache, 261
    network traffic, 261, 262*f*
    reporting and presentation, 278, 279*t*
    RTF and TXT files, 261, 262*f*
    Wireshark 1.12.1, 261
  360Yunpan
    apk file, 275, 275*f*
    dataset synch, 275, 276*f*
    reporting and presentation, 278, 281*t*
    .rtf and .txt files, 276, 277*f*
    SSL encryption, 275–276, 276*f*
    timestamps, 276
    upload activity, 275–276, 277*f*
    user configuration files, 273, 275*f*
    username and password, 275, 275*f*
Antiforensic techniques
  analog cameras, 148
  development of, 148–151, 149–150*f*
  DVR, 148, 151, 151*t*
  monitor, 148
  open source tools, 151, 152*t*
  prototype tool, 160–161, 161*f*
  test-device-DVR1, 152–155, 152*t*, 153–154*f*, 154*t*
  test-device-DVR2, 155–157, 156–157*t*
  test-device-iPhone, 157–159, 158*t*, 160*f*
  video evidence, 147
Apple iOS 8.0
  CloudMe, 254, 254*f*, 263–264, 263*t*, 263*f*, 278, 280*t*
  360Yunpan, 277–278, 277–278*f*, 281*t*
Artifacts
  potential evidentiary, 16*t*
  Skype, 14–15
  Viber, 14
  WhatsApp, 15–16
Association of Chief Police Officers (ACPO), 208
AVTECH's EagleEyes application, 151, 157

B

Backtrack dd Imager, 95–96
BitTorrent, 186

C

Cellebrite, 166, 168
Cloud computing, 1–2
  CSSP, 205, 208*t*
  experiment setup
    on iOS, 212–213
    on windows, 209–212
  forensic investigation
    collection and preservation, 209
    evidence source, 209
    examination and analysis, 209
  Iaas, 205, 207*t*
  JustCloud
    account creation, 221
    APPLICATION.log, 225
    BACKUP.log, 225
    Cache.db-wal, 226*f*
    client application files, 225
    DOWNLOADER.log, 225
    downloads, 231
    email address and passwords, 233*f*
    FX, recovered artifacts, 223*t*, 227*t*, 232*t*
    GC, recovered artifacts, 223*t*, 228*t*, 233*t*
    IM, recovered artifacts, 222*t*, 226*t*, 232*t*
    on iOS, 234

Cloud computing (Continued)
  LICENCE.log, 225
  link files, 228
  memory, 224
  mpcb_backup_conf.db, 225
  mpcb_settings.db, 225
  network traffics, 224
  NTFS log, 226
  ONLINE_FOLDER.log, 226
  prefetch folder, 226
  recovered artifacts, 222t
  RoomKey and shared message, 224f
  thumbcache files, 228
  uninstallation, 229–231
  user and device name, 224f
  window events, 228
Paas, 205
pCloud
  account creation, 234–237
  account registration, 243f
  client application files, 234–236, 238
  downloads, 239
  email address and password, 236f
  FX, recovered artifacts, 235t, 241t
  GC, recovered artifacts, 236t, 242t
  IE, recovered artifacts, 235t, 240t
  on iOS, 239–244
  json file, 242f
  link files, 237
  memory, 234
  network traffics, 234
  prefetch folder, 239
  registry, 236
  thumbcache files, 237
  uninstallation, 237–239
  window events, 236, 238–239
Saas, 205, 207t
SpiderOak
  account creation, 213
  client application files, 213–217, 220
  downloads, 221
  email address, 216f
  FX, recovered artifacts, 215t
  GC, recovered artifacts, 215t
  ID and name, 216f
  IE, recovered artifacts, 215t
  on iOS, 221
  keyword search, 214t
  link files, 218, 221
  memory, 213
  MFT, 217
  network traffics, 213
  NTFS log, 220
  observation, 218

  paging file, 218
  prefetch folder, 218, 220
  recovered password, 216f
  registry, 217, 220
  thumbcache, 218
  unallocated space, 218, 221
  uninstall wizard, 219–221
  windows events, 218, 220
Cloud forensic framework(s), 2
CloudMe
  Android KitKat 4.4.2, 253–254, 254f
    downloaded files, 261, 262f
    installation, 258
    internal memory, 258, 261f
    local CloudMe cache, 261
    network traffic, 261, 262f
    reporting and presentation, 278, 279t
    RTF and TXT files, 261, 262f
    Wireshark 1.12.1, 261
  Apple iOS 8.0 client application, 254, 254f, 263–264,
      263t, 263f, 278, 280t
  definition, 248
  evidence collections, 255–256
  evidence source identification and preservation, 255
  iOS platform, 252, 252t
  Windows-based experiments, 252, 252t
  Windows 8.1 Browser, 253, 253f
    deletion, 258, 261f
    downloading, 258, 260f
    open/view, 258
    reporting and presentation, 278, 279t
    uploading, 258, 260f
  Windows 8.1 client application, 253, 253f
    installation, 256
    live memory, 256–257, 257f
    local CloudMe folder, 256–257, 257f
    network traffic, 257, 258f
    timestamps, 257, 259t
    2014-11-23.txt file, 256, 256f
    user_ table, 256, 257f
Cloud of Things (CoT), 137
Cloud services, 249, 250t
Cloud storage service provider (CSSP), 205, 208t
Cognitive reflection test (CRT), 82–83, 84f
Computer Forensics Tools Testing (CFTT), 92
Conceptual EASY training model
  acceptable behavior, 123–125
  awareness, 120, 120f
  cybersecurity courses, 120
  education, 120, 120f
  engaging stakeholders, 115f, 116t, 117–120f, 122,
      123–124f
  routine activity theory, 120–121, 121t
  simple teaching method, 125–127, 126–127f

training, 120, 120f
yardstick, 127
Cybercrime, 1
Cybersecurity, 131–132
Cyberspace, 141

D

Digital closed-circuit television (CCTV) systems
analog cameras, 148
development of, 148–151, 149–150f
DVR, 148, 151, 151t
monitor, 148
open source tools, 151, 152t
prototype tool, 160–161, 161f
test-device-DVR1, 152–155, 152t, 153–154f, 154t
test-device-DVR2, 155–157, 156–157t
test-device-iPhone, 157–159, 158t, 160f
video evidence, 147
Digital forensic framework (DDF), 8–9
adopted forensic tools, 11t
examination and analysis, 10–11
identification and analysis, 13–14
logical acquisition, 12–13
mVoIP applications, 11, 12t
reporting and presentation, 10–11
setup phase, 11–12
Digital forensic research workshop challenge 2013
dataset (DFRWS), 189–191
Digital forensics, 1
Digital video recorder (DVR)
test-device-DVR1, 151–152t, 152–155,
153–154f, 154t
test-device-DVR2, 151t, 155–157, 156–157t
test-device-iPhone, 151t, 157–159, 158t, 160f
Dionaea, 114f
captured malware, 117, 117f
IP address, breakdown of attacks, 114–116, 116t
malware download, 116, 116t
Raspberry Pi, 112, 113t
SMB, 113
SQLite, 113
targeted ports, breakdown of, 114, 115f
time of day, breakdown of attacks, 114, 115f
DiskDigger tool, 103–106, 104–105f

E

Electronically Erasable Programmable Read Only
Memory (EEPROM), 9
Emerging technologies, 132–133, 141
Employee information security awareness and
education training. See Honeypots
EnCase, 167
Encase Evidence (E01) format, 24
Explore, Investigate, and Correlate (EIP), 171–172

F

Facebook, 64
Firefox operating systems (FxOS)
applications, 76–77
capturing network activities, 67–69, 69f
conducting network analysis, 69, 70f
design, 65
Dropbox cloud storage, 63–64
executing activities, 67, 68t
Facebook, 64, 70–72, 72t
FxOS simulator, 65, 70
Google Drive cloud storage, 63–64
hubiC, 64
MEGA cloud client application, 64
memory image (.ffm), 44
Microsoft SkyDrive, 63–64
network traffic analysis methodology, 66, 66f
ownCloud, 63–64
phone image (.ffp), 44
Skype Windows Store application, 64
social media and instant messaging services, 43
SugarSync cloud storage, 64
TCP port 80 and 443, 63–64
Telegram, network analysis on, 74–75, 76t
Twitter, network analysis on, 72–73, 74t
virtual environment network adapter, 64, 64t
virtual machines preparation, 66–67, 66t, 67f
Foremost tool, 100–101, 100f, 102–103f
Forensics data recovery tools
AccessData FTK, 95
analysis, 97, 98f
architecture, 92–93
Backtrack dd Imager, 95–96
botnets system, 92
CFTT, 92
challenging areas, 94
dd image, 97, 99t, 99f, 106, 107f
DiskDigger, 103–106, 104–105f
Foremost, 100–101, 100f, 102–103f, 103
FTK image, 97, 98t, 99f, 106, 107f
image acquisition process, 94–96, 95f
memory acquisition, 93
Nexus 4 phone, 92–93
Phone Image carver, 97, 97t
Recover My Files, 101, 101–103f, 103
Recovery Mode variables, 93
Samsung Galaxy S2 i9100, 94
Samsung Star 3G phone, 92–93
SCADA system, 92
validation and integrity check ID number, 95–96, 96t
zip folder, 96
Forensic Toolkit (FTK), 167
Viber, 14
WhatsApp, 15

Forensic visualization
  analysis, 165
  challenges, 168–169
  computer hard-drive, 171
  data statistics, 169
  digital forensics, 164
  e-Discovery software, 164, 170, 172–174, 173–174t
  EIP, 171–172
  identification, 164
  information visualization, 169
  large data sets, 169–170
  portable devices
    Australian Communications and Media
      Authority, 163
    blue Nokia mobile telephone, 165
    Cellebrite, 166
    forensically sound software, 165
    forensic software and tools, 167
    illegal narcotics, 166
    mobile forensic data, 166
    narcotics, 166
    phone text message folder, 166
    prevalence of, 163
    seized red Nokia mobile telephone, 165
    XRY, 165–166
  presentation, 165
  preservation, 164
  selection criteria, 176, 177t
    cone trees, 180
    DocuBurst, 180
    errors, 176
    experience, 176
    glyphs, 180
    meaning, 175
    parallel coordinates, 179
    rules, 175
    scatter plots, 179
    ThemeRiver, 179
    transparency, 176
    tree-maps, 179
  text-based application, 170–171
  time-based visualization methods, 171
  visualizing security and privacy data, 170

G
Google Drive cloud storage, 63–64

H
Hash Calc version 2.02, 252
Honeypots
  conceptual EASY training model
    acceptable behavior, 123–125
    awareness, 120, 120f
    cybersecurity courses, 120
    education, 120, 120f

    engaging stakeholders, 115f, 116t, 117–120f, 122,
      123–124f
    routine activity theory, 120–121, 121t
    simple teaching method, 125–127, 126–127f
    training, 120, 120f
    yardstick, 127
  Dionaea, 114f
    captured malware, 117, 117f
    IP address, breakdown of attacks, 114–116, 116t
    malware download, 116, 116t
    Raspberry Pi, 112, 113t
    SMB, 113
    SQLite, 113
    targeted ports, breakdown of, 114, 115f
    time of day, breakdown of attacks, 114, 115f
  Kippo, 114f
    command line, 118–119, 124f
    files downloaded, 119, 119f
    IP connections, 118
    Mysql, 113
    passwords, 117–118, 118f
    Raspberry Pi, 112, 113t
  operational level, 128
  strategic level, 127
hubiC, 64
Hyper Text Markup Language (HTML), 22

I
iCloud, 187
Information and communication technologies (ICT),
  133, 138
Infrastructure as a service (IaaS), 205, 207t, 247
Instant messaging (IM)
  AIM forensics
    .BLT format, 26–27
    buddy icons, 33
    buddy List, 26–27, 30
    conversations, 30–32
    Happening messages, 33–34
    IM logs, 32–33
    installation, 27–28
    netscan function, 29
    network information, 29t
    OFT3 file transfer header, 32, 32f
    RAM in plaint text, 30–31f
    registry key, 27, 27f
    transferred files, 30–32
    unicode string format, 31
    uninstallation, 34
  AIM protocol, 23
  data security, 21–22
  description, 21
  research methodology
    AIM experiments, 25f
    NAT, 24

user details, 23*t*
VM Snapshots, 24*t*
on Windows 8.1, 26*t*
Instant messaging mobile applications, 2
Intrusion detection system (IDS), 139
Investigation analysis
  instant message
    account registration, 57, 58*f*
    image findings, 58–59, 59*t*
    OpenWapp communication string, 58*f*, 59
    telegram keywords, 56, 56*f*
    URL keywords, 57, 57*f*
  social media
    application keyword, 51, 52*f*
    profile name, 51, 53*f*
    search process, 53, 54*f*
    URL keyword, 51, 52*f*
    username, 52, 53*f*
iTunes, 191

J
JustCloud
  account creation, 221
  APPLICATION.log, 225
  BACKUP.log, 225
  Cache.db-wal, 226*f*
  client application files, 225
  DOWNLOADER.log, 225
  downloads, 231
  email address and passwords, 233*f*
  FX, recovered artifacts, 223*t*, 227*t*, 232*t*
  GC, recovered artifacts, 223*t*, 228*t*, 233*t*
  IM, recovered artifacts, 222*t*, 226*t*, 232*t*
  on iOS, 234
  LICENCE.log, 225
  link files, 228
  memory, 224
  mpcb_backup_conf.db, 225
  mpcb_settings.db, 225
  network traffics, 224
  NTFS log, 226
  ONLINE_FOLDER.log, 226
  prefetch folder, 226
  recovered artifacts, 222*t*
  RoomKey and shared message, 224*f*
  thumbcache files, 228
  uninstallation, 229–231
  user and device name, 224*f*
  window events, 228

K
Kippo, 114*f*
  command line, 118–119, 124*f*
  files downloaded, 119, 119*f*
  IP connections, 118

Mysql, 113
passwords, 117–118, 118*f*
Raspberry Pi, 112, 113*t*

M
Malicious code, 136
MD5 algorithm, 252
MD5 hash values, 44, 50, 50*t*
MEGA cloud client application, 64
Microsoft SkyDrive, 63–64
Mobile dating Apps, 10
Mobile device management (MDM), 139
Mobile device security, 1–2
  forensics investigation guideline, 84–86, 85*f*
  iOS platform, 82
  issues, 79–80
  malware, 80–81
  QR code
    average scores, 83, 83*t*
    behavioral response, 83
    cognitive impulsivity, 82–85
    limitations, 86–87
    malicious application, 81
    online web-based questionnaire, 82
    participants, 82
    smartphones security, familiarity with, 82, 84, 84*t*
    social engineering tool, 81
    scenario-based role-play experiment, 80

N
NAND and RAM flash memories, 10
Network address translation (NAT), 24
Network analysis. *See* Firefox operating systems (FxOS)
NirSoft IEPassView 1.32, 192
Nuix, 167

O
OpenWapp communication string, 58*f*, 59
ownCloud, 63–64, 186–187

P
pCloud
  account creation, 234–237
  account registration, 243*f*
  Amazon Cloud Drive, 187
  Android app-based experiments
    install and login, 195, 196*f*
    uninstall, 195–197, 197*f*
    upload, 195, 196*f*
  BTSync client app, 186
  client application files, 234–236, 238
  client-side encryption, 186
  cloud storage services, 187, 187*t*
  definition, 186
  downloads, 239

pCloud *(Continued)*
    Dropbox, 186–187
    email address and password, 236*f*
    FX, recovered artifacts, 235*t*, 241*t*
    GC, recovered artifacts, 236*t*, 242*t*
    Google Drive, 186–187
    iCloud, 187
    IE, recovered artifacts, 235*t*, 240*t*
    Information Security Management Systems, 186
    on iOS, 239–244
    json file, 242*f*
    link files, 237
    memory, 234
    Microsoft SkyDrive, 186–187
    network traffic, 200, 234
    ownCloud, 186–187
    prefetch folder, 239
    quality management system, 186
    registry, 236
    research methodology
        Android, 190–191
        browsers, 189
        Hex Workshop 6.7, 189
        iOS, 191, 197–198, 197–199*f*
        iphonebackupbrowser-r38, 189
        OS, 189
        stages, 188, 188*f*
        test, 189
        Ubuntu, 191, 198, 199–200*f*
        Windows, 189–190, 190*f*
        Wireshark 1.12.3, 189
    thumbcache files, 237
    uninstallation, 237–239
    Window Browser-based experiments
        install and login, 192, 192*f*
        upload, 192, 192*f*
    window events, 236, 238–239
    Windows app-based experiments
        delete, 194, 194*f*
        install and login, 193–194, 194*f*
        uninstallation process, 194–195, 194*f*
Phone Image carver, 97, 97*t*
Platform as a service (PaaS), 205, 247
Predictive Analytics Software (PASW), 82
Process Monitor version 3.1, 255

Q
Qualitative methods, 135

R
Recover My Files, 101, 101–103*f*, 103
Root Browser 2.2.3, 190–191
Routine activity theory (RAT), 134
    conceptual EASY training model, 112, 120–121, 121*t*

criminal opportunity, 133
Cyberspace, 141
cyber threat landscape
    guardianship, 138–142, 139–140*t*
    motivation, 136–137, 136*f*, 141
    opportunities, 137–138
digital forensic strategies, 142
forensic awareness and capability, 142
ICT, 133
incident handling, 142
juvenile population, 134
legal and regulatory challenges, 142
methodology
    data analysis, 135
    data collection, 134, 135*t*, 135*f*
society's prosperity, 133
SPE, 133
systematic security strategies, 142–143
uses, 133

S
Samsung Star 3G phone, 92–93
Server Message Block (SMB), 113
Skype Windows Store application, 64
Social media and instant messaging services
    analysis
        instant message investigation, 56–60
        social media investigation, 51–56
    cybercrime, 41
    experiments
        host machine preparation, 45–46
        installation, 46–47
        MD5 hash value images, 50, 50*t*
        phone image and memory image, 46
        steps and activities, 47–48
    FxOS, 43
    IPAQ Pocket PC, 42
    malicious activities, 41
    methodology
        forensic evidences, 45, 45*f*
        Geeksphone, 43
        MD5 hash values, 44
    mobile platforms, 43*t*
Software as a service (SaaS), 205, 207*t*, 247
Sony Pictures Entertainment (SPE), 133
SpiderOak
    account creation, 213
    client application files, 213–217, 220
    downloads, 221
    email address, 216*f*
    FX, recovered artifacts, 215*t*
    GC, recovered artifacts, 215*t*
    ID and name, 216*f*
    IE, recovered artifacts, 215*t*

on iOS, 221
keyword search, 214*t*
link files, 218, 221
memory, 213
MFT, 217
network traffics, 213
NTFS log, 220
observation, 218
paging file, 218
prefetch folder, 218, 220
recovered password, 216*f*
registry, 217, 220
thumbcache, 218
unallocated space, 218, 221
uninstall wizard, 219–221
windows events, 218, 220
SugarSync cloud storage, 64

T
Telegram, 74–75, 76*t*
360Yunpan
Android KitKat 4.4.2
apk file, 275, 275*f*
dataset synch, 275, 276*f*
reporting and presentation, 278, 281*t*
.rtf and .txt files, 276, 277*f*
SSL encryption, 275–276, 276*f*
timestamps, 276
upload activity, 275–276, 277*f*
user configuration files, 273, 275*f*
username and password, 275, 275*f*
Apple iOS 8.0 client application, 277–278, 277–278*f*, 281*t*
definition, 248

WINDOWS 8.1-client application
configuration files, 264, 264–265*f*
installation, 264–265, 266*f*
live memory, 265, 266*f*
network traffic, 266, 267*f*
reporting and presentation, 278, 280*t*
sync.log file, 265, 265*f*
timestamps, 266–267, 268*t*
WINDOWS 8.1-web browser
deletion, 273, 274*f*
downloading, 272–273, 272–273*f*
Internet Explorer, 267, 269*f*
open/view, 267, 271–272*f*, 272
uploading, 267, 269–271*f*
Twitter, 72–73, 74*t*

V
Virtual machines (VMs), 189
Visual Analytics, 167
VMware Workstation 10.0, 252
VMware Workstations (VMs), 23
Voice over Internet Protocol (VoIP) application, 7
features, 8*t*
Skype, 7–8, 8*t*
Viber, 7–8, 8*t*
WhatsApp, 7–8, 8*t*

W
Windows Mobile smartphone, 9
Wireshark 1.12.3, 189, 191

X
XRY, 165–166

Made in the USA
Coppell, TX
28 March 2020